Western Maryland
CATHOLICS

1819 - 1851

Compiled by
Richard T. Koch
Phyllis I. Davidson

CLEARFIELD

Printed for
Clearfield Company, Inc., by
Genealogical Publishing Co., Inc.
Baltimore, Maryland
1998, 2000, 2012

ISBN 978-0-8063-4830-8

Made in the United States of America

Table of Contents

ACKNOWLEDGMENT

We are grateful to our friend Thomas E. Lancaster of Cumberland, Maryland, for the loan of one of the microfilms from which much of this material was obtained.

ABBREVIATIONS

The abbreviations used are those familiar to genealogists, but bear listing:

abt.	- about
b	- born
bapt.	- baptized
c/o	- child of (sex unknown)
d	- died
d/o	- daughter of
FC	- First Communion
p#	- page number
prob.	- probable
Sps	- sponsor(s)
s/o	- son of
w/o	- wife of
wid/o	- widow of
_____	- indistinguishable or blank
name	- questionable rendition
<	- before
>	- after

Name abbreviations using the superscript notation were as recorded. These were replaced in the Every Name Index with an apostrophe for legibility; e.g. Robt became Rob't. Surname spellings are as presented in the records, unless otherwise noted.

INTRODUCTION

Our quest for knowledge of our own ancestors leads us to many sources and requires us to include their extended families, friends, and neighbors. The latter, if not related in earlier generations, may become so in later ones. This likelihood is especially true for those of the Roman Catholic faith, whose doctrines encumber interfaith marriages. Our purpose for publishing this material is to make it readily available to those genealogical researchers seeking to learn more about their ancestors.

This book, entitled *Western Maryland Catholics 1819-1851,* is an outgrowth of an earlier manuscript "St. Ignatius and St. Mary" (1995) by the same authors. *Western Maryland Catholics* includes all of the former manuscript, but it is enhanced with additional data found in other ledgers from the same time period (1819-1844) and extending through 1851. The overall result is a six-fold increase in material. Unexplained gaps in chronological material still exist. It is unknown if some records were lost, or if they were included in another church's records. Indeed, these four ledgers are sometimes misidentified as being those of St. Patrick of Cumberland. St. Ignatius at Mt. Savage, Maryland, and St. Mary's of Cumberland were the first Catholic Churches in Allegany County. They were served jointly by early priests. For this reason we have identified the priest performing the rite for each marriage or baptism. The book *A Century of Growth* by Rev. Thomas J. Stanton (1900) contains histories of the various Catholic Churches of western Maryland and identifies the priests associated with each.

Prior to this time, itinerant priests from such places as Conewago, Pennsylvania; Westminster, Maryland; Taneytown, Maryland; and Hagerstown, Maryland, performed the rites of marriage and baptisms, placed the names in their pocket ledgers (or on scraps of paper) and transferred them into their own church records. Records from the forenamed areas do contain names of Catholics known to have lived in or near Allegany County, Maryland, and should be consulted by researchers for information prior to 1819.

WESTERN MARYLAND CATHOLICS 1819-1851

The faith of these people played a significant role in their lives as they left the local church, moved westward, and built new churches in their frontier communities. One of these churches was St. Luke in Danville, Knox County, Ohio. This book also includes some of the parents and children of those whose names can be found in another manuscript, *St. Luke* (1995), which covers the years 1829 through 1900.

When possible, the names of the priests performing the rites are indicated by their initials, as listed below. Page numbers that follow these initials in parentheses are not identified as to a specific ledger because they were not so specified on the microfilm.

BLO-	B. Leonard Obermeyer
BSP-	Bertrand S. Piot
FXM-	Francis Xavier Marshall
HM-	Henry Myers
JR-	James Redmond
JBB-	John B. Byrne
NDY-	Nicholas D. Young [O.J.D.]
TR-	Timothy Ryan

The first section of the book gives a brief history of Catholicism in western Maryland. The following section contains surviving lists of names obtained from various church activities. The third section includes the marriages recorded from 2 May 1819, followed by the Register of Baptisms, which presents the baptismal dates, and (if recorded) birthdates from 1 May 1819. Names of sponsors are also included in these records. Available death or burial records are presented in the fifth section, these being the least complete of the surviving records. Finally, an Every Name Index is supplied. Corrections and additions made by the authors are included in brackets [ ]. Underlined names indicate questionable interpretation.

ADDITIONS

The following names were regretfully omitted, in the final compilation, of the index for the book *Western Maryland Catholics 1819–1851*, compiled by Richard T. Koch and Phyllis I. Davidson, Clearfield Publishing Company, 1998.

A BRIEF HISTORY OF WESTERN MARYLAND CATHOLICS

We must start with some background on the Roman Catholic Church at Mt. Savage, Maryland. A book by Rev. Thomas J. Stanton, *A Century of Growth Vol I*[1] was published in 1900 and serves this purpose well. This book is a somewhat accurate account of the Roman Catholic Church in western Maryland. We have included some exerpts from this work. Because St. Mary's Church in Cumberland was served jointly with St. Ignatius in Mt. Savage, we cannot separate the history of the two churches.

"St. Mary's Church of Cumberland may truthfully be called the mother of all the Churches of Allegany County. It is historically certain that Catholicity had an existence in Cumberland, although very shadowy at the beginning, as far back as the French and Indian War.....As far back as 1770, ~~Joseph~~ [Josiah][2] Frost must be added to the pioneer Catholics; and ten years later, the Arnolds, the Porters and the ~~Logistons~~ [Logsdons] were dwelling at what became Arnold's Settlement [later called Mt. Savage]. The first Catholic death recorded is that of John Arnold, April 26, 1791. His last will and testament is the third filed for record in the Orphans' Court of Allegany County.....The first priest, of whose visits to Cumberland we have any authentic records to view, was an Irish priest named Dennis Cahill. [He was instrumental in building, (about 1792), the old log church (St. Mary's) in Cumberland]....From 1795 to 1799, the only priest that visited Cumberland....was the illustrious missionary, Rev. Prince [Demetrius Augustine] Galitizin. .... According to the records of Allegany County Courthouse, the following marriage licenses were issued to Catholics:

> October 31, 1795, Ralph Logsdon and Margaret Arnold
> September 11, 1796, John Mattingly and Onea [Honora] Arnold
> May 10, 1797, Gabriel Porter and Rebecca Frost
> November 11, 1799, John Logsdon and Patience Arnold

All of whom were married by D. A. Galitzin, Catholic priest....He first exercised his ministry at Conewago, [Pennsylvania], and made missionary

---

[1] Volume I of this book is currently (1996) available in the Frostburg branch of the Allegany Co., Maryland, library system, although the book is in poor condition. The Family History Center (LDS) in Salt Lake City has a copy of both volumes.

[2] Strikethroughs indicate erroneous text; corrections and added comments are given in brackets [ ].

1

excursions to Upper Maryland and Virginia." [This comment could explain how some of the rites of known local residents were recorded among the Conewago records.] Rev. Felix Brosius, who came to America as a travelling companion of Prince Galitzin, occasionally visited the Cumberland area. Father Brosius was stationed at Taneytown, Maryland.

It was not until 1819 that the first resident pastor, Rev. James Redmond, was appointed to Cumberland. He served until June 1821. Rev. Michael D. Young, a Dominican priest, from St. Joseph in Ohio, appears in the records for three months thereafter. Rev. Timothy Ryan[3] had charge of St. Mary's for eight years, followed by an ex-Jesuit, Rev. Francis Xavier Marshall, who remained for five years. Rev. Henry Myers was appointed pastor in 1836 and began building a brick church.

"The old parish of Mt. Savage was first known by the name of 'Arnold's Settlement,' after Archibald Arnold, the proprietor of a hotel located on the old road called 'Turkey Foot Road.' .... The first Mass celebrated at Arnold's Settlement was said at the home of Archibald Arnold, by Rev. Stephen Theodore Badin, in the year 1793.....About the year 1810, the Rev. Nicholas Zocchi, an Italian priest, began to visit the Settlement. He came from Taneytown, [Maryland]. During 1812 the Settlement was visited occasionally by Rev. Matthew Ryan of Hagerstown.....In 1819 Father Timothy Ryan began to attend the mission, three or four times a year, for five years. During the visits of the Fathers Ryan the first church was built at 'the Settlement'. It was very small, and connected with the Arnold Hotel. On the side opposite the Altar was an old time regulation fireplace.....About 1824 Rev. Francis Roloff began visiting this mission.... In 1829 Father Francis X. Marshall began to attend the Settlement jointly with St. Mary's in Cumberland. During the six years of his pastorate he built a new brick church, dedicated as St. Ignatius. The lot on which the church stood was donated by Archibald Arnold, and is still part of St. Patrick's cemetery. Francis Marshall left near the end of 1835. For the next five years the church was served by Rev. Henry Myers and Rev. Bertrand S. Piot. It was looked on as a mission of Cumberland, although in reality, the Mt. Savage congregation far outnumbered that of Cumberland.... Father Leonard Obermeyer of Cumberland attended the parish occasionaly. He was assisted

---

[3] Rev. Timothy Ryan commenced his service here on 3 Sep 1821.

A BRIEF HISTORY

by Rev. Charles C. Brennan, who became the first resident pastor at Mt. Savage, with Eckhart, [Frostburg], Barrelville, and Wellersburg as outlying missions."

To expand this background further, we next quote from a hand-written short history contained in the microfilmed records:

Cumberland Mission

"In 1836 the Rev. Henry Meyers was stationed in Cumberland, he being the first resident priest of that place, [see above]. At that time the mission embraced nearly all of Allegany County and some of the adjacent parts of Virginia and Pennsylvania. The Cumberland Church then was the old log one built towards the close of the 18th Century. In 1838 the old part of the present^(1848) brick church was built. In 1841 Rev. L. Obermeyer was appointed Pastor of the mission, who in 1843 added 40 feet to the front of the church & in 1845 had the altar & steeple erected. In 1846 the bell & organ were purchased. Near the close of 1845 the mission was divided, the Rev. W. Brennan taking the upper portion of it. In 1849 the German Church was opened in Cumberland. In 1850 the New Church of St. Patrick was begun and was dedicated 23 Nov 1851." [See Summary of Catholic Ceremonies Table on page 4.]

The microfilm copies[4] of church records identified as St. Patrick of Cumberland contain records from St. Mary's and St. Ignatius, as confirmed by the records of the priests performing the rites of baptisms and marriages. Material has been abstracted from these microfilms but does not constitute a complete copy of what is included thereon. Reference to the additional material can be made at the Maryland State Archives, Annapolis MD.[5]

---

[4] Maryland Archives, M-3461.
[5] See further reference on page 216

Summary of Catholic Ceremonies 1841-1854 (p2)

Year	Bapt	First Comm	Conf	Easter duties	Mgrs	Dths
1841	167	3	-	-	35	36
1842	175	11	-	532	30	22
1843	205	24	-	617	30	51
1844	218	18	46	618	34	39
1845	219	35	-	825	46	62
1846	147	22	-	738	32	83
1847	104	33	-	654	22	50
1848	125	36	129	635	21	39
1849	95	37	-	609	50	91
1850	121	39	-	505	54	68
1851	109					
1852	66					
1853	67		120			
1854	61	16				

LISTS OF NAMES

Lists of parishioners have survived for some specific events, and are presented in this section. The first of these is for Easter Confessions and Communions for 1820. The First Communions portion of this list is dated 23 Apr 1820, thus this list follows by one year the first marriage and first baptism.

EASTER CONFESSIONS [2 Apr] 1820 (p112, 113)

Archibald Arnold		Jacob Blubaugh	
Honor Mattingly		Maria Arnold	
Lucy Mattingly		Samuel McKenzie	
Mary Mattingly		Baptist Mattingly	
Rachel Blubaugh	-5	Mrs. Nancy McKenzie	-30
Ann Magers		Stephen Blubaugh	
Susan Durbin		John Mattingly	
Cecelia Mattingly		Augustus Green [Bk]	
Mrs. Ann Arnold		Henry Mattingly	
Mary Logsdon	-10	Stephen Wine [Bk]	-35
Honor Mattingly		Moses McKenzie	
Hanna Mattingly		William Arnold	
Ambrose Magers		Mary Logsdon	
George Mattingly		Ellen McKenzie	
Mary Magers	-15	Jamy Worth	-40
Nancy Magers		Reaf [Raphael] Logsdon	
William Logsdon		Aaron McKenzie	
Charles Mattingly		Mrs. James Logsdon	
Honor Mattingly		Mrs. Jane Magers	
Joseph Mattingly	-20	Ann Jememiah Blubaugh	-45
Margaret Durbin		Patience Logsdon	
James Mattingly		Joseph Logsdon	
Nancy Timmonds		Mrs. Ann McKenzie	
Fanny Logsdon		Daniel McKenzie	
Johnzee Arnold	-25	Susanna Mattingly	-50

5

EASTER CONFESSIONS [2 Apr] 1820 cont. (p112, 113)

David Logsdon		John Durbin	
Mrs. Nancy Timmonds		John Logsdon	
Mrs. Elizabeth Arnold		Anastasia McKenzie	
Eligah Durbin		Honor Blubaugh	
Peggy Logsdon	-55	John McKenzie	-80
Honor Durbin		Sarah Payne	
Nancy Logsdon		Gabriel McKenzie	
Margaret Logsdon		Ann Clister	
Margaret Logsdon		Josua McKenzie	
Francis Dean	-60	Daniel O'Brien	-85
Edward Logsdon		John Mattingly	
Samuel Mattingly		Nathan Magers	
Edward Logsdon		Milly Mahawney [Bk]	
Mary Arnold		Gabriel McKenzie	
Antony Arnold	-65	James McKenzie	-90
Liddy Porter		Catherine Hixonbaugh	
Nathan McKenzie		Joseph Logsdon	
Mary Logue		Catherine McKenzie	
Elijah Durbin		William Magers	
Ellen Mattingly	-70	Mrs. John Porter	-95
Henry Mattingly		Mary McKenzie	
Honor Blubaugh		John Hoctor	
Jonathan Arnold		Sarah Carter	
Thomas Porter		Catherine Frost	
Mary McKenzie	-75	Margaret Logsdon	-100
		Ellen McKenzie	

[Order Preserved]

FIRST COMMUNIONS

First Communions were usually administer at about age 11, when the youth had received Catechism instructions and been accepted into the Church. The lack of a resident priest until 1819 probably delayed the age at which many of the following took their first communion. Note that the numbering continues from the previous list, although dated three weeks later.

LISTS OF NAMES

FIRST COMMUNIONS 23 Apr 1820 (p113)

Anthony Durbin		Michael Porter	-120
Maria Krigbaum		Moses McKenzie	
Jesse Mattingly		Sarah Durbin	
Betsy McKenzie	-105	John Durbin	
Samuel McKenzie		Widow Lucy McVicker	
George Durbin		Margaret McKenzie	-125
Nancy Porter		Samuel McKenzie	
John Logsdon		Honor Durbin	
Fanny Arnold	-110	Caleb McKenzie	
Baptist Durbin		Mary Blubaugh	
Mary Arnold		Benjamin Durbin	-130
Aaron Hixonbaugh		Samuel Durbin	
Margaret Mattingly		Maria Krigbaum	
Mary Durbin	-115	Honor Blubaugh	
Elizabeth Magers		Andrew McKay	
Honor Mattingly		Margaret Logsdon	-135
Margaret Arnold		Laurence Logsdon	
Catherine Durbin			

EASTER 31 May 1821 (p113-115)

Ann Magers		Honor Mattingly	
Mary Magers		Fanny Arnold	
Cecelia Mattingly		Gabriel McKenzie	
Elizabeth Arnold		Eligah Durbin	
Mary Logsdon	-5	Hanna Mattingly	-20
Margaret Arnold		Honor Mattingly	
James Mattingly		Anastasia McKenzie	
Ann Clister		Catherine Hixonbaugh	
Archibald Arnold		Nathan Magers	
Joseph Mattingly	-10	Nancy Mattingly	-25
William Arnold		Susan Mattingly	
Henry Mattingly		Fanny Logsdon	
Peggy Logsdon		Polly Logsdon	
Anthony Durbin		Benjamin Blubaugh	
Elizabeth Magers	-15	Margaret Mattingly	

7

EASTER 31 May 1821 [cont.] (p113-115)

Margaret Logsdon		Sarah Pane [Payne]	-70
John Logsdon		Catharine McKenzie	
Margaret Logsdon		Nancy Porter	
Catherine Durbin		Catherine Porter	
Amb[rose] Magers	-35	Michael Porter	
Honor Mattingly		Old Mrs. Durbin	
Polly Arnold		Mrs. McKenzie	
John Mattingly		William Morgan	
Margaret Logsdon		Daniel McKenzie	
Geo Durbin		Baptist Mattingly	
Mary Durbin		Catharine Frost	-80
Maria Arnold		Nathan McKenzie	
Mrs. Polly Arnold		Nancy Timmons	
Nancy Logsdon		Eligah Durbin	
Charles Mattingly		Hanna McKenzie (conv)	
Jesse Mattingly		William Logsdon	
John Durbin		Mary Hixenbaugh	
Samuel McKenzie		Samuel McKenzie	
John Mattingly		Stephen Blubaugh	
Samuel Mattingly	-50	Susanna Durbin	
Ellen Mattingly		Moses McKenzie	-90
Mary Logue		Rachel Blubaugh	
Edward Logsdon Sr.		Patience Logsdon	
Ann Arnold		James McKenzie	
Jane Logsdon		Ann McKenzie	
Ellen McKenzie		Aaron Hixenbaugh	
Jacob Blubaugh		Stephen Blubaugh	
Honor Blubaugh		Benjamin Durbin	
Geo Mattingly		Mary Blubaugh	
Polly Mattingly	-60	Mariann Durbin	
Raphael Blubaugh		Raphael Logsdon	-100
Margaret Logsdon		Milly Mahawney (Bk)	
Henry Mattingly		John Zee Arnold	
Mary McKenzie		John McKenzie	
John Logsdon		Gabriel M'K Porter (FC)	
Margaret Durbin		Margaret Porter (FC)	
Eleanor Mattingly		Stephen Wines (Bk)	
Francis Dean		Mrs. Nancy Timmonds	
Ann Jemmah Blubaugh		Josua McKenzie	

LISTS OF NAMES

EASTER 31 May 1821 [cont.] (p113-115)

Alley Arnold
Elizabeth Krigbaum -110
David Logsdon
Maria Krigbaum
Aaron McKenzie
Elizabeth Squires
Edward Logsdon Jr.
Jenny Worth
Joseph Logsdon

Honor Durbin
John Durbin
Honor Blubaugh -120
Baptist Durbin
Liddy Porter
William Magers
Jane Magers
Samuel McKenzie -125

EASTER CONFESSIONS of 1824 (p16,17)

Elisa Clister*
Samuel McKenzie*
Mr. John Durbin*
Daniel McKenzie*
Catherine Clister*
Joseph Mattingly
Mrs. Trullinger
Mary McKenzie*
Aaron McKenzie*
Rebecca Porter
Eligah Durbin*
Jane Worth [B]
James Mattingly
Mary Mattingly
Aaron Hixonbaugh*
Augustus McKenzie*
George Durbin*
Mrs. Hixonbaugh*
James McKenzie*
Mrs. Murphy
James Murphy
Margaret Mattingly
Mary Sophia [B]
John Durbin*
Mary Eliza Porter
* Spelling modified

Baptist Mattingly
Elisa Mattingly
John Mattingly
Mrs. Porter
Nathan McKenzie*
Rebecca Porter
Joseph Arnold
Mrs. Preston
Susan Krigbaum*
Anna Krigbaum*
James Mattingly
Mrs. Moses Porter
John McKenzie*
Mrs. John McKenzie
George Mattingly
John Arnold
Eligah Durbin*
Mrs. Aaron McKenzie*
Stephen Blubaugh
Eleanor McKenzie*
Mary Logsdon*
Paul Arnold
Mary Arnold
Edward Logsdon*
Henry Mattingly
[total 118]

EASTER CONFESSIONS of 1824 [cont.] (p16,17)

Fanny Logsdon*
John Durbin*
Elisa Preston
William Arnold
Mrs. Edward Logsdon*
Mrs. Eligah Durbin*
Francis Mattingly
Mary Durbin*
Antony Arnold
Elisa Magers*
Michael Mattingly
Ambrose Magers*
James Mattingly
Samuel McKenzie*
Sarah Payne*
John Mattingly
Lucy Mattingly
Nathan Arnold
Margaret Arnold
Benjamin Blubaugh
Mrs. John Mattingly
Antony Durbin*
Mrs. Henry Porter
Susan Mattingly
George Blubaugh
Milly Mahawney* [B]
Gabriel McKenzie*
Mr. Samuel McKenzie*
Moses McKenzie*
Cecelia Mattingly
Mrs. Elisa Arnold
Francis Dean
Johnzee Arnold*
Mary Magers*
* Spelling modified

Jacob Blubaugh
"Old" Mrs. Logue
Mrs. Samuel Mattingly
Mrs. Nathan Magers*
Nathan Magers*
Mrs. Johnzee Arnold*
William Logsdon*
Mrs. Jacob Blubaugh
Honora Mattingly
Susanna Durbin*
Jesse Mattingly
Mrs. Ben Blubaugh
John Logsdon*
Jane McKenzie*
Charles Mattingly
"Old" Mrs. Logsdon*
Mrs. Antony Arnold
David Logsdon*
Margaret Logsdon*
Mrs. Eligah Durbin*
John Logsdon*
Fanny Arnold
Jerimy Arnold
Catherine McKenzie*
"Old" Mrs. Blubaugh
Edward Connelly
Catherine Durbin*
Honora Durbin*
Mrs. John Logsdon*
Mrs. Stephen Blubaugh
Mary Blubaugh
Rachel Payne*
Mary Arnold
Rebecca Mattingly
[total 118]

"Easter Confessions [in] 1826 were in number 140, which were kept in another book. - T. Ryan." [This record was not found.]

LISTS OF NAMES

EASTER CONFESSIONS 30 May 1827 Tim'y Ryan (p115)

Old Mr. Arnold (prob. Archibald)
Miss Rebecca Mattingly
Miss Susanna Mattingly
Old Mr. McKensey
Mrs. Ralph Logsdon
Miss Rebecca Porter
Miss Mary Mattingly
Jessy McKenzie
Ralph Logsdon
Miss Catherine Durbin
Old Mrs. Logue
Old Mrs. Betsy Arnold
Miss Honora Hixenbaugh
Miss Mary Majors
Mrs. Sam'l Mattingly
Old Ellen McKensey

Mrs. _____ Majors
Miss Elisa Mattingly
Old Mrs. McKenzie
Mrs. Hixenbaugh
Mr. Moses McKenzie
Mrs. Moses McKenzie
Mr. John McKenzie
Mr. Michael Mattingly
Mr. Ambrose Magers
Miss Jane Mattingly
Miss Lucy Mattingly
Mr. Anthony Arnold
Mrs. Daniel McKinsey
Miss Delila Prestin
Mrs. Lucy McKusker

CONFESSIONS 03 Jun 1827 (p116)

Miss Mary Durbin
Mrs. John McKenzie
Janet Worth (colored)
Mr. Elija Durbin
Old Mr. McKenzie, Aaron
Miss Anastasia McKenzie
Mrs. Jane Gaiety
Mr. Aaron Hixenbaugh
Mrs. Angima J Blubaugh
Mrs. _____ Preston
George Pane
Mr. Baptist Mattingly
Mrs. Samuel Durbin
Mrs. Fanny Logston

Mr. John Mattingly Jr.
Mr. John Mattingly
Miss Sicila Mattingly
Mrs. John Durbin
Mrs. John McKenzie
Miss Rebecca McKensey
Mrs. Henry Porter
Miss Margaret Arnold
Miss Honora Mattingly
Mrs. William Logston
Mr. James McKenzie
Mr. Charles Mattingly
Mr. Edward Logston Jr.
Mrs. Edward Logston

11

CONFESSIONS 03 Jun 1827 [cont.] (p116)

Milley A Mahawny (colored)
Mrs. Jane Moore
Mr. William Logston
Mr. John Durbin
Mr. George Durbin
Mr. John Mattingly
Miss Elisa Frost
Mrs. Honora Durbin
Mrs. Joe Logston
Old Mary Logston
Old Mary McKenzie
Mrs. John Porter
Mr. James Mattingly
Francis Mattingly
Mr. Jacob Blubaugh
Mrs. Francis Dean
Mr. Henry Mattingly
Mr. John Logston
Mrs. Eliga Durbin Sr.
Miss Catherine McKenzie
Mr. John[n] Arnold [Jonathan]

Miss Rachel Pane
Mr. Samuel McKensey
Mrs. Eli Ridgeley
Mr. George Mattingly
Mr. Ralph Logston
Mr. Henry Porter
Mrs. George Mattingly
Mrs. Elisa Trimble
Miss Fanny Arnold
Mr. Antony Durbin
Mrs. Conrad Krigbaum
Mrs. Maria Smith
Mrs. Maria Combs
Mrs. Betsey Smith
Stephen Wine (colored)
Mr. Jessy Mattingly
Mr. John (?) McKensey
Mr. John Carter
Miss Susanna Krigbaum
Miss Elisa Krigbaum

CONFESSIONS 7 & 8 Jun 1827 at Selbyport-T Ryan (p117)

Mr. Leo Smith
Mrs. Leo Smith
James Roddy
Elleonora Roddy
Wm Roddy
John Cole
Mrs. John Cole
Mrs. Hill
Peter McCleary
Sam'l Jamison
Mrs. Jamison
Priscilla Jamison
Richard Jamison

Jeremiah Jamison
Mr. Sam'l Mattingly
Mr. Sam'l Durbin
Sarah Anna [colored]
Clay Perry [colored]
Mrs. John Winter
Mrs. Mary Blubaugh
Mr. Wilm Carter
Mrs. Jonsey Arnold
Mr. Eliga Durbin Jr.
Old Edward Logsdon
Mr. Frances Dean
Old Mrs. Logston

LISTS OF NAMES

CONFESSIONS 7 & 8 Jun 1827 at Selbyport-[cont.]

Miss Catherine Moore
Mrs. Elias Porter
Mr. __ Tobin
Bill, Peter, Lucy, Catherine,
Suzy, Polly, Maria, Elisa,
Charles, Vead {colored}

Gabriel McKenzie
Mrs. Vandy Porter

CONFESSIONS 12 Jan 1828 (p118)

Mrs. Francis Dean
Mary Majors
Mrs. C. Garlick
Rebecca Porter
Mrs. Majors
Mrs. S. Mattingly
Old S. McKensey

Mary Logston
Henry Mattingly
Old Eliga Durbin
Old Mrs. Eliga Durbin
Mary Blubaugh
Rachel Pane

EASTER CONFESSIONS 24 Apr 1828 (p118)

Old Mr. Arnold {*prob Archibald*}
Old Mrs. Logston
Cecilia Mattingly
Old Sam'l Mattingly
Mrs. Majors
Mary Majors
Mary McKensey

Mrs. Sam'l Mattingly
Mrs. Francis Dean
Old Ellen McKensey-   [10]
Cloey Green (cd)
Jane Mattingly
James Mattingly
Henry Mattingly

The next list , dated the following day, [Good Friday], continues with the number count from [Maundy] Thursday Confessions

13

EASTER CONFESSIONS 25 Apr 1828 (p118)

Michael Mattingly
Mrs. James Mattingly
Mrs. Gabriel McKensey
Mrs. Henry Mattingly
Fanny Logsdon
Elisa Mattingly [20]
Mrs. Ralph Logston
Sally Green (cd)
John McKenzey
Ambrose Majors
George Mattingly
Jeremy McKensey
Mrs. George Mattingly
Mrs. Peter Bear
Jacob Blubaugh
Milly (cd) [30]
Mrs. John McKensey
Wilm Ha[y]den
Anastatia McKensey
Eliga Durbin Sr.
George Durbin
James McKensey
Jane Worth (cd)
John Durbin
Mary Mattingly
John McKensey [40]
Old Elisa Arnold
Old Mrs. Logue
Mrs. John Durbin
Lucy Mattingly
Raphael Pane
Susanna Arnold
Henrietta Arnold
Mary Blubaugh
Mary Durbin
Ben Blubaugh [50]

Mrs. Stephen Blubaugh
Rachel Pane
Old Edward Logston
Nathan Arnold
Mrs. Susa[h] Lowry
Old Mary Logston
Jonathan Arnold
Honora Mattingly
Francis Mattingly
Wil[m] Arnold [60]
Mrs. Joseph Logston
Jonsey Arnold
Rebecca Porter
Mrs. Eliga Durbin
Catherine McKinsey
Stephen Blubaugh
Mrs. Moses McKensey
Catherine Durbin
Mrs. John Logston
Francis Dean [70]
John Logston Jr.
Old Mrs. McKensey
George Durbin
John Mattingly Sr.
Mrs. Hixenbox
John Logston Sr.
Honora Durben
Old Mrs. Blubaugh
Mrs. Jacob Blubaugh
Eliga Durben [80]
Ralph Blubaugh
Antony Durben
Gabriel McKensey
Mrs. Wil[m] Logston
Sam[l] Durben
Margaret Arnold

EASTER CONFESSIONS 25 Apr 1828 [cont.] (p118)

Moses McKensey
Mrs. John McKensey
Nancy Carter
Wil[m] Logston   [90]
Mrs. Eliga Durbin Jr.
Henry Porter
Charles Mattingly
Mrs. Henry Porter
Susanna Krigbaum
David Logston
Mrs. Isaac Smith
Stephen Wines (col)
Baptist Mattingly
Aaron Hixenbox   [100]
Anna Krigbaum
Mrs. John Porter
Mrs. Henry Krigbaum
Nancy Porter
Mrs. James Gariety
Mrs. Ben Blubaugh
John Tobin
Henry Krigbaum

Honora Elisa Hixenbox
Aaron McKensey Jr.   [110]
Rebecca Mattingly
Mrs. McQuicker
Anastatia Hixenbox
Antony Arnold
Rebecca McKensey
Jessie Mattingly
Mrs. Edward Logston
Mrs. Sam[l] Durbin
Mrs. Thomas Porter
Sam[l] Mattingly   [120]
Ralph Logston Sr.
Fanny Logston
John Logston
Ralph Logston Jr. [05 May 1828]
Samuel McKenzie Jr.
Wil[m] Carther [*Carter*]
George Pane
Edward Logston
John Carther [*Carter*]
Mary Mattingly   [130]

CONFESSIONS 03 Aug 1828 (p120)

Mrs. John Winter
Rachel Colman
Mrs. Mes[k] Frost
Mrs. Sam[l] McKenzie

Sam[l] McKensey
Elisabeth Kreigbaum
Peter Preston
Joseph Logston

The following two lists are very helpful to genealogists using these records, in that they give us ages of those partaking of their First Communion. We can therefore determine birth years that predate the surviving records in most cases.

FIRST COMMUNION: The names of those admitted 01 Nov 1829
(p120)

Mary Arnold age 19
Susannah Mattingly w/o Henry age 23
Henrietta Arnold age 15
Honora Elisa Hixenbaugh age 15 (or)18
Anna Logsdon age 13
Susanna Arnold age 18
Rachel Paine age 19
Clotilda Green coloured girl age 20
Sarah Green coloured girl age 18

Jacob Pain age 16
Henry Crickbaum age 23
Jeremiah Arnold age 20
David Durbin age 13
Benedict Logsdon age 12
Mary Mattingly age 15
Hannah Mattingly w/o Jas age 21
David Logsdon age 21
George Blubaugh age 30

[total 18]

FIRST COMMUNION: The names of those admitted 06 Jun 1830, this Octave Day of Pentacost. (p122)

Nancy Carter age 21
Honora Durbin age 12
Nancy Arnold age 14
Matilda McVigger age 10
John Logsdon age 21
Elizabeth Carter age 14
Rachel More age 15
Sarah More age 16
Robert (?) age 18
Ellen Mattingly age 41

Anastasia Hixenhaugh age 20
James Getty age 22
Jeremiah McKenzie age 18
Leo McKenzie age 15
Elizabeth McKenzie age 16
Sylvester Mattingly age 12
Margaret Durbin age 12
Francis Logsdon age 10
Mary Durbin age 9

total 19

EASTER CONFESSIONS April 1830

Ellen Ridgeley
Sam[l] McKinsey Sr.
Stephen Wines (coloured man)
Elizabeth Hixenbaugh
Aaron Hixenbaugh
Lucy McVigger
Sarah Durbin
Jane More (coloured woman)

Anna McKinzie
Sam[l] F. McKenzie Jr.
George Durbin
Catherine McKinzee
James Mattingly
Jonathan Arnold
Silvester Mattingly
Jeremiah Arnold

LISTS OF NAMES

<u>EASTER CONFESSIONS</u> April 1830 [cont.]

Jacob Pain
Esther Winters
Mary Arnold
Rachel Pain
Elias Mattingly
Mary Mattingly
Mary Magers
Anna Magers
John Mattingly
Stephen Blubaugh
Sarah   (bk)
Patience Logsdon
Henry Durbin
Margaret Durbin
Hillen Mattingly
Elija Durbin
Grandmother Logue, age 98 years
Archibald Arnold
Jesse Mattingly
Polly Mattingly
John Logsdon
Francis Mattingly
Michael Mattingly
Margaret Logsdon
Jane Mattingly
Cecilia Mattingly
Raphael Logsdon
Fanny Logsdon
Henrietta Arnold
Rachel McKenzee
Ann Arnold
Betsey Carter
Margaret Durbin
Mrs. Kreighbaum
Sarah McKinzee
Jane More

Ann Timmonds
Fanny Lain
Baptist Mattingly
Sarah <u>Brieves</u>
Wil^m Logsdon
O. Filia Timmonds
Honora Durbin of Sarah
Sarah More
Elisa Garietty
Matilda McVigger
Jerome Timmonds
Ann Mattingly
Hannah Mattingly
Wm Arnold
Susan Arnold
Ann Blubaugh
Johnzee Arnold
Mary McKinzee
Ambrose Magers
Jacob C. _____
Margaret Mattingly
Antony Durbin
Lucy Mattingly
Catherine McKinzee
Catherine Hixenbaugh
Anastatia Hixenbaugh
James McKinzie
George Blubaugh
Elizabeth Krigbaum
Fanny Krigbaum
Ann Logston
David Durbin
Nancy Carter
Jeremiah McKinzee
Joseph Logsdon
Charles Mattingly

EASTER CONFESSIONS April 1830 [cont.]

Nancy Porter
Ann Krigbaum
Margaret McKinzee
Susan Durbin
Henry Krigbaum
Honora Durbin
Honora Blubaugh
Margaret Durbin
John Durbin
Elisabeth Logsdon
Margaret Durbin
Mrs. Logsdon
Sam[l] Mattingly
Ben. Logsdon
Margaret Logsdon
Rebecca Mattingly
Honora Mattingly
Lydia Porter
Ellen Mattingly
Wm Arnold
John Logston
Ralph Logsden
Elisabeth Smith
Susanna Mattingly
Sarah McKinzee
Henry Mattingly
Margaret McKenzie

James Getty
Rebecca Garlitz
Jane Getty
Joanna _____
Susan Krigbaum
Catherine Frost
Maria Smith
Hellen McKinzee
Mary Ann Mattingly
George Mattingly
Milly (colored woman)
Polly Bare
Polly Dean
Susan Lowery
Maud McKinzee
David Logsdon
Clotila Jones (black woman)
Margaret Durbin
Elizabeth Carter
Joseph Arnold
Cecilia Arnold
Wm Arnold
Nathan Arnold
Jacob Blubaugh
Anna Durbin
Francis Dean
Priscilla Krigbaum

EASTER CONFESSIONS & COMMUNION 1831 (p122, 123)

Old Mrs. S. McKinzee
Sarah   (black woman)
Anas[a] Hixenbaugh
Mary Krigbaum
Matila McViger
Honora Blubaugh

Ann Logsdon
David Durbin
Mary Mattingly
Lucy Mattingly   [10]
Harriet Millison
Mary McKenzie

18

EASTER CONFESSIONS & COMMUNION 1831 [cont.] (p122, 123)

Maria Porter (FC)		Antony Durbin	
Polly Bare		Margaret McKenzie[50]	
Francis Mattingly		Cicilia Durbin	
Jonathan Arnold		Jesse Mattingly	
Nancy Arnold of Johnzee		Baptist Mattingly	
Betsey Carter		_____ Moore	
Bendic[t] Logsdon		Lucy McVigger	
Mich[l] Mattingly	[20]	Sarah Durbin	
Patience Logsdon		Elizabeth Krigbaum	
Ellen Mattingly		Ellen Winter	
Jane Mattingly		Mary Mattingly	
Ellen Mattingly		Rebecca Mattingly	[60]
Silvester Mattingly		George Durbin	
Milly *of Mattingly*		Rebecca Garlitz	
Cat[h] McKinzee		James Getty	
Stephen Blubaugh		Jane Getty	
Elisa Mattingly		Elizabeth Logsdon	
Robert (blackman)	[30]	Rachel McKenzee	
Jane (colored woman)		Elis'bet Carter	
John Zee Arnold		Rebecca M_____	
Nancy Durbin		Susan Durbin	
Catherine Hixenbaugh		Lydia Mattingly	[70]
Margaret Durbin		Henry Mattingly	
Elijah Durbin		Margaret McKenzee	
John Mattingly		Mary McKenzee	
Moses McKenzee		Mary Magers	
Ralph Logsdon		John Logsdon	
Nancy Mattingly	[40]	John More	
Fanny Lain		Liddy _____	
Sally More		Agnes Arnold	
Sophia Hixenbaugh		Sam[l] Durbin	
Ellen McKinzey		Antony Arnold	[80]
George Blubaugh		David Logsdon	
Peter Rerhig		Charles Mattingly	
Margaret Logsdon		Ambrose Magers	
Samuel McKenzee		Henry Hixenbaugh	

EASTER CONFESSIONS & COMMUNION 1831 [cont.] (p122, 123)

Raphael Blubaugh
Mary Ann Mattingly
Jeremiah Arnold
Catherine McKensie
Maria Carter
Sam[l] McKinzee Jr. [90]
Margaret Durbin
Henrietta Arnold
Nancy Carter
Mary Arnold
Lydia Arnold
Honora Durbin
Margaret Durbin
Raphael Logsdon
George Mattingly
John Durbin [100]
Nancy McKinzee
Margaret Logsdon
Jas McKinzee
Jeremiah McKinzee
Rachel Coper
Elijah Durbin
James Mattingly
John Logsdon
Wm Logsdon
Leo McKinzee [110]
Rachel Pain
John Pain
Wm Logsdon

Pat McKenzie
Joseph McKenzie
Mr. R. Logsdon
Grandmother Logue
Mother Blubaugh
Sarah Garlitz [120]
Polly Bare
Ann Jamison
Elisa McKinzee
Christian Garlitz
Honora Hixenbaugh
Margaret Durbin
Wm Arnold of Antony
Celilia Mattingly
Grandfather Arnold [Archibald]
Mrs. J. Porter [130]
Wm Porter
Mrs. Frost
Francis Logsdon
Susan Lowery
Fanny Arnold
Elisabeth Porter
Betsey Carter (FC)
James Porter
Wm Porter
Henry Porter [140]
Wm Dicisand
Margaret McKenzie
Rachel Crow (FC), July 2[d] 1831

LISTS OF NAMES

CHOIR FUND 07 Aug 1831 (p124)

We the undersigned promise to pay the sums annexed to our names to be paid onto Patrick Mathias for the purpose of teaching and forming a choir of singing for this R. Catholic Church. [*Sums omitted because they are marked up as payments received; therefore difficult to read. Manyare possibly actual signatures for those who could write are included.*]

Francis X. Marshall
Jon^{a} Arnold
Archibald Arnold
Anthony Arnold
Elijah Durbin
Saml Mattingly
John Logsdon
David Logsdon
George Durbin
Anton Durbin
Raphael Logsdon
Saml Durbin
Jess Mattingly
Peter Krigbaum
Henry Krigbaum
Francis Dean
Joseph Twigg
Thomas M. Porter
C. Krigbaum
Charles Mattingly
John Durbin
Geo Mattingly
Joseph Logsdon
Raphael Logsdon
John Mattingly
Mrs. Krigbaum
Wm Logsdon
Moses McKenzie of Dan'l
John Porter
Mrs. Logsdon

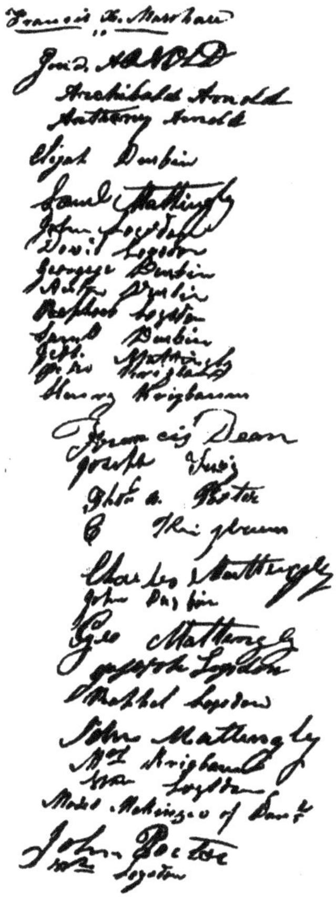

CHOIR FUND 07 Aug 1831 [cont.] (p125)

This Choir fund continues on the second of two pages microfilmed upside down. It is unknown if the lists were upside down within the actual record. The writing on this page appears to be that of one person.

Susan Durbin
Margaret Durbin
Nancy Durbin
Honora Durbin
Rebecca Logsdon
Ann Logsdon
Cicilia Mattingly
Jane Mattingly
Mary Ann Mattingly
David Logsdon*
George Durbin*
Anthony Durbin*
George Mattingly
Bessie Logsdon
Francis Logsdon
David Durbin
Honora Durbin
Silvester Mattingly
Sally Norse
Tobacca Norse
Peter Krigbaum
Jermy Arnold
Harriet Arnold
Ann Twig
* [on previous page also]

LISTS OF NAMES

Our next list is for subscriptions made by members of the congregation for the purpose of erecting the Brick Church. Unfortunately it is undated. A second list entitled "A Copy of ____ ____ ____", found on page 109, is also undated and contains essentially the same information, with amount of subscription paid and evaluation of individual work done added to fulfill their pledges. Because of the additional information and what appears to be ink smears on the original list, the Copy, ibid., is presented on the following page. Differences with the original list are noted.

The second name is that of Rev. Francis X. Marshall. His name first appears in the baptism of Helen E. McKenzie on 27 Sep 1829 and last appears in the baptism of William C. Krigbaum on 20 Jun 1835. Archibald Arnold, a strong supporter of the Church, wrote his will 13 May 1832, and Francis X. Marshall was one of witnesses. The fact that Archibald's name does not appear on either list suggests we can date it between Archibald's will date and Rev. Marshall's departure "near the end of 1835". The Copy, ibid, would have to be dated nearer the completion of the brick church, which was built during Rev. Marshall's tenure.

Records are difficult to read

Subscriptions for a New Brick Church
[c1835 at Mt. Savage] (p109, 110)

Rt. Rev. Dr. Whitfield	Sub[d] $50 and paid	$ 50
Rev[d] Francis X. Marshall	" 50 and paid	650
Jonathan Arnold[1]	" 50 pd 50 and worked to	147.12½
Francis Dean	" 50 pd 50 and worked to	109.62½
John Mattingly	" 50 pd early $19 and work to[2]	37.57½
Samuel Mattingly	" 25 pd 20 and worked to	60.50
George Mattingly	" 25 pd 25 and worked to	44.37½
Henry Mattingly	" 25 pd 25	25.00
Anthony Arnold	" 20 and worked to	38.37½
Henry Krigbaum	" 15 pd 15	15.00
Baptist Mattingly	" 10 pd 10	10.00
Samuel Durbin	" 10 pd 10	10.00
Joseph Twigg	" 5 pd 5	5.00
Elijah Durbin Sr.	" 5 pd 5	5.00
Ambrose Magers	" 20 pd 20 and worked to	36.87½
John Durbin	" 5 pd 5	5.00
John McKenzie	" 6.25 pd 6.25	6.25
Elijah Durbin Jr.	" 2 pd 2	2.00
Samuel F. McKenzie	" 5 pd 5	5.00
Christian Garlitz	" 5 pd 5	5.00
Sam[l] McKenzie of Sam[l]	" 10 pd 10	10.00
Peter Baer	" 2 pd 2	2.00
Wiliam (sic) Ridgely	" 5[3]	
Andrew Bruce	" 5	

"The Boarding of the work people was given by the members of the Congregation in general as they were able: Except John Mattingly and Raphael Logsdon who gave nothing at all."

---

[1] Original list has notation following Jonathan Arnold's name "[value?] of the lot on which the church stands $147.12½". Also two additional rows: "Strangers   Sub[d] $83.12 and Small sums paid by many $142." The total subscribed is shown as $1516.82½. It also has a notation "The above is a true account of the <u>Cash</u> of the above named brick Church and by who paid. Given from my hand. Francis X. Marshall Pastor."

[2] Original list has noted at bottom of the page "N. B. The above Named John Mattingly Sr. Subscribed fifty Dollars towards the above named Church, and paid but nineteen in Cash, the remainder of his above stated sum was work. Francis X. Marshall Pastor."

[3] William Ridgely & Andrew Bruce appear to be the only two who did apply anything towards their pledge.

24

LISTS OF NAMES

"Also in Suporting (sic) and giving a living to the priest John Mattingly in four and _____ Francis X. Marshall Pastor"

Support of Catholic Clergyman 08 Nov 1836 (p1, 2)

We the undersigned members of the Holy Roman Catholic Church in Cumberland, Allegany County, promise to pay the annual Sum annexed to our names, in quarterly payments, to any Clergyman approved of, by our Most Rev[d] Bishop of the Diocess of Baltimore. Yearly subscriptions to commence as soon as any Rev[d] Gentleman takes charge of the Congregation. [Payments included since it may indicate family conditions, deaths, or moves.]

Names [St. Mary]	Pledged $ .cts	Nov $ .cts	Feb $ .cts	May $ .cts	Aug $ .cts
B. Mattingly	10	2.50	2.50	2.50	2.50
John Black	10	2.50	2.50	2.50	2.50
E. Mullen	5	1.25			
M. Sherry	5	1.25	1.25	1.25	1.25
T. McGin	2	.50	.50	.50	.50
P. Scott	2	.50	.50	left	left
J. Fealy	5	left	left	left	left
N. Sweeney	2.50	left	left	left	left
J. Downy	2.50	left	left	left	left
J. Null	5	1.25	1.25	1.25	1.25
P. McDonald	5	1.25	1.25	1.25	1.25
P. Martin	1	2.50	2.50	2.50	2.50
H. Corrigan	5	1.25			
T. Timmons	2	.50	.50	.50	.50
T. Fealy	20	5.00	5.00	left	left
B. O'Roarke	5	1.25	1.25	1.25	1.25
Th Healy MD	10	2.50	2.50	2.50	2.50
P. Smith	10	2.50	2.50	2.50	
D. Brosnahan	2	.50	.50	left	left

Support of Catholic Clergyman [cont.] 08 Nov 1836 (p1, 2)

Names [St. Mary]	Pledged $ .cts	Nov $ .cts	Feb $ .cts	May $ .cts	Aug $ .cts
P. O'Neill	10	2.50	2.50	2.50	2.50
J[S] Fitzpatrick	10	2.50	2.50	2.50	2.50
H. Mattingly	6	1.50	1.50	1.50	1.50[4]
B. Turner	4	left	left	left	left
L. Moore	5	1.25	1.25		
W. O'Brien	2	left	left	left	left
H. Messman	2	.50	.50		
P. Reifs	2				
J[S] Mattingly	5	1.25	1.25	1.25	1.25
J[S] Brady	5	1.25	1.25	1.25	1.25
S. M. Semmes	10	3.00	2.00	2.00	3.00
J[O] Brenan	5	left	left	left	left
O. Reynolds	5	left	left	left	left
J[S] Reilly	2	left	left	left	left
H. Wonstreet	4	1.00	1.00	1.00	1.00
P. Murphy	2	.50	dead	----	----
P. Donclan	2.50	.62½	dead	----	----
J[O] Clancy	5	1.25	1.25	1.50	
J[O] McGettigin	10	2.50	2.50	2.50	
E. McDonald	5	1.25	1.25	1.25	1.25
J. Mullan	5		1.25		
Cap. W. Welsh	5				
F[k] Schrider	3	1.00	1.00	.50	0.50
P. Purcell	1				
W. Mathews	10	2.50	2.50	2.50	2.50
P. Rereick	3	.75	.75	.75	.75
Vaily	1	.25	.25	.25	
B. Brown	10	2.50	2.50		
H. Mulholand	2	.50	.50	.50	.50
H. Dressman	2	.50	.50		
H. Harmon	3				
P. Conoy	5				
Mrs. Creighbaum	3	.75	.75	.75	.75 [5]

[4] H. Mattingly credited with $2.98 paid on next year.
[5] Mrs. Creighbaum credited with $3.00 paid on next year.

LISTS OF NAMES

Support of Catholic Clergyman 22 Nov 1836 (p71, 72)

We the undersigned, promise to contribute, in quarterly payments, in advance, the sums annexed to our several names, for the support of the Catholic Clergyman who may be sent to attend us. [Payments included since it may indicate family conditions, deaths or moves.]

Names [St. Ignatius]	Pledged $ .cts	Nov $ .cts	Feb $ .cts	May $ .cts	Aug $ .cts
Jonathan Arnold	10	2.50	2.50	2.50	2.50
Francis Dean	10	2.50	2.50	2.50	2.50
John Mattingly	10	2.50	2.50	2.50	2.50
Raphael Logsdon	6	1.50	1.50		
Anthony Logsdon	5	1.25	1.00	1.25	
George Mattingly	6	1.50	1.50	1.50	1.50
William Logsdon	5	1.50	1.00	1.00	1.50
Samuel Mattingly	6	1.50	1.50	1.50	1.50
Ambrose Magers	6	1.50	1.50	1.00	2.00
Joseph Logsdon	4	1.00			
Eligah Durbin	4	1.00	1.00	1.00	
Samuel Durbin	3	.75	.75	.75	.75
John Durbin	2.50	.50	0.00	1.00	1.00
Catherine Frost	10	2.50	2.50		
George Durbin	1	.25	.25	.25	.25
Gabriel McKenzie	1	.25	.25		
C. Garlits	2	.50	.50	.50	.50
Samuel B. McKenzie	1	.25	.25	.25	.25
Leo McKenzie	1	.25	.25	.25	.25
Jeremiah McKinzie	1	.25	.25	.25	.25
Charles Mattingly	2	.50	.50	.50	.50
Joseph Twigg	2	.50	.50	.50	.50
Patience Logsdon	3	.75	.75	.75	.75
Anthony Durbin	1.50	.50	.50	--	.50
George Blubaugh	1	.25	.25	.25	.25
Raphael Blubaugh	2	.50	.50	.50	.50
John Blubaugh	.50	.12½	.12½	.12½	.12½
David Durbin	.50	.12½	.12½	.12½	.12½
Joseph McKenzie	.50	.12½	.12½	.12½	.12½
Francis Logsdon	.50	.12½	.12½	.12½	.12½

Support of Catholic Clergyman 22 Nov 1836 [cont.] (p71, 72)

Names [St. Ignatius]	Pledged $ .cts	Nov $ .cts	Feb $ .cts	May $ .cts	Aug $ .cts
Henry Krigbaum	5	2.50	--	1.50	1.00
John McKenzie	1	.25	.25	.25	.25
H. Porter of M.	3		1.00		
Lucy McVicor	.50		.50		
Francis Zury	1.50				
H. Hogmire	.25				
Sam McKenzie of Sam	2.00	.50	.50		

[Another column indicating "paid", where appropriate, was omitted.]

Subscriptions for a Chalice-18 Mar 1837 (p93)

Rev. H. Myers
Mrs. Arnold
Ambrose Magers
Mrs. Dean
Francis Porter
B. Mattingly
Nathan Arnold
Archibald Arnold [?]
Sam Durbin
George Blubaugh
Anthony Logsdon
Mary Baer
Eliz. Carter
Sam Mattingly
W. Logsdon of R.
Ben'd Logsdon
Leo McKenzie
James Mattingly
Gabl McKenzie
H. Porter
Sam McKenzie
Sam McKenzie of S.

Jon Arnold
Jerime Arnold
Joh. Blubaugh
Ann Magers
Jacob Wines
Mrs. Krigbaum
Margaret Arnold
Anthony Arnold Jr.
Honora Durbin
Patience Logsdon
Elias Logsdon
Liddia Porter
Henrietta Arnold
H. Krigbaum
J. Twigg
D. Durbin
Jos McKenzie
Michael Mattingly
H. Porter
W. Porter
Rap Logsdon
George Mattingly

W. Logsdon
W. Arnold
Francis Dean
Mary Magers
H. Mattingly
George Logsdon
W. Arnold of Anthony
Anthony Arnold Sr.
Sarah Durbin
W. Logsdon of J.
Teresa Logsdon
Eliz. Logsdon
John Mattingly
C. Mattingly
Rap Logsdon of R.
Jer. McKenzie
Francis Logsdon
Joh. Garlitz
JS Porter
Jos McKenzie
Pat McKenzie
Francis Zury

LISTS OF NAMES

On the same page, in a different handwriting (undated) is a list of those donating for **Flowers to decorate the Altar**. This will add some of the non-breadwinners to our lists of parishioners. (p94)

Honora Durbin	Hanna Durbin	Ann Arnold
Anastasia Logsdon	Ann Magers	Mary Magers
Teresa Logsdon	George Logsdon	Elias Logsdon
W. Logsdon	Mich Mattingly	Mary Mattingly
Mary A. Mattingly	H. Long	D. Durbin
Margaret Durbin	Matilda Logsdon	Mary Baer
Rachel Mattingly	Rebecca Logsdon	Susan Arnold
Ann Durbin	Benedict Logsdon	Margaret Durbin
George Durbin	Susan Krigbaum.	

Collected by Miss Hon. Durbin daughter of Elizabeth

Our next list is another Easter list, which may be incomplete, but is for the year 1837.

Easter Communions & Confessions 1837 (p130)

Old Sam McKenzie	Jonathan Arnold	Jeremiah Arnold
William Arnold	Frances Logsdon	John Mattingly Sr.
Michael Mattingly	Silvester Mattingly	Francis Mattingly
Nelly Mattingly	Cecilia Mattingly	Elijah Durbin
Margaret Durbin Sr.	Peggy Durbin	Honora Durbin
Nancy Durbin	George Durbin	Anthony Durbin
David Durbin	George Mattingly	Harriet Long
Mary Ann Mattingly	Polly Mattingly	Milley (colored)
Raphael Logsdon Sr.	Benedict Logsdon	Francis Logsdon
Raphael Logsdon Jr.	Sam Mattingly	Charles Mattingly
Mrs. [Chas] Mattingly	Rebecca Mattingly	Francis Dean
Polly Dean	Mary Baer	Catherine McKenzie
Polly McKenzie	Ambrose Magers	Nancy Magers
Mary Magers	Old Mrs. Porter	Nancy Porter
Sam Durbin	Sarah Durbin	Honora Durbin
George Blubaugh	Nancy McKenzie	Polly Logsdon
Patience Logsdon	Anastasia Logsdon	Jos Twigg
Mrs. Twigg	Janney Creighbaum	H. Creighbaum
Mrs. Creighbaum	Susan Creighbaum	Prisc. Creighbaum

Easter Communions & Confessions 1837 [cont.] (p130)

John Arnold of Anthony	H. Mattingly	Js Mattingly
Mrs. Mattingly	W. Logsdon	Mrs. Logsdon
John Durbin	Mrs. Durbin	Old Mrs. Logsdon
Mary Rereigh	Peter Rereigh	Mrs. Rereigh
Eliz Carter	Mrs. Carter	Stephen (colored)
Old Mrs. Smith	Matilda McVicer	[Mr.] Suing & Mrs. Suing

[The following material is noted separately, but obviously belongs here chronologically.]

20 Nov 1837	Rec'd from Mr. Geo Mattingly the sum of $ 2.50.
23 Jan 1838	Received from C. Mattingly the sum of $ 13.00
20 Feb 1838	Received from J. Mattingly the sum of $ 6.75
(undated)	Received from Mrs. Myers the sum of $ 20.00

Subscriptions for Support of the Clergyman from 20 May 1838 (p73, 74)
[List includes quarterly payments for two years, not included herein.]

John Mattingly Sr.	Jonathan Arnold	F(rancis) Dean
Raphael Logsdon Sr.	William Logsdon	Henry Krigbaum
Catherine Frost	Patience Logsdon	Mrs. Magers
Samuel Durbin	Joseph Logsdon	Anthony Arnold
Charles Mattingly	Ralph Logsdon Jr.	Joseph Twigg
John Durbin	Henry Porter	Ch Beale
Peter Baer	John Porter	Francis Logsdon
Michael Mattingly	Francis Mattingly	Francis Porter
B[enedict] Logsdon	George Logsdon	Josiah Frost
Mary A. Mattingly	Henry Porter of Mich.	Henry Mattingly Sr.
George Blubaugh	Archibald Arnold ?	John Mattingly Jr.
William Mattingly	John Blubaugh	John Porter of H.
John G. Smith	Mrs. Porter (Cy's wife)	Thomas Porter
John Richart	William Arnold	Henry Scherman ?
John McKenzie	John L. Arnold	(illegible) Jr.
George Durbin	William Logsdon of Penn[a]	

LISTS OF NAMES

04 Jun 1838 thru 24 Nov 1839 Received from Mich[l] Mattingly
[21 separate listings of various sums]. B. S. Piot.

FIRST COMMUNION 1838 (p9)

Catherine Brown	John More	Mary Vonstreet
Marcellus Brown	Mary Ann McKensie	Mary Carter
Sarah McKenzie		

CONFIRMATIONS 1839 (p8)

John Bapt Mulcahey	Mary Ann Carter	Teresa Keble
Mary Goulden	Mary Dillon	Peter Dillon
Amanda Masters	Judith Ann Brian	Sophia Rooney
John Cain	Mary Coffey	Mary Ann Eliz Blubaugh
Patrick Martin	Mary Ann Martin	Henry Mattingly Jr.
Simon Blubaugh	Catherine Luddy	Catherine Coners
Thomas Leo	Sarah Leo	Mary Ryan
Elizabeth Murphy	Margaret McCortey	Mary Duffy
Henry Denman	Magdalena Turner	Bridget McGonigle
George Hankin	Magdalina Lipold	Eugena McCana
Henry B. Martin	Thomas Landragan	Gerad Souleen
Catherine Cross	Jane Ann Riley	Henry Vigor
Mary Barry	Catherine Ann King	Regina Kraus
James Quigly	Patrick Coner	Jane Emilia Donaghoe
Rebecca Ellen Donaghoe		

FIRST COMMUNIONS 19 Apr 1840 (p10)

Petronella Brown	Mary Martha Mattingly	Catharine Turner
Elizabeth Cross	Lucy McCormick	Mary McCormick
Mary Jane Mattingly	Mary O'Brian	Anna Brown
Mary Ann McGirr	Martha Ann Pury (Col)	John Vonstreet
Tobias Truly (Conv[t] Col)	Mary Ann Schifferdecker	John Ryan
Matilda May [Arnold]*		

* a convert married to Joseph Arnold

31

FIRST COMMUNIONS 07 Jun 1840 Penticost (p10)

Frances Ann Ryan	Martha Ann Masters	Mary Ann Smith
Margaret Row	Ellen McCorkery	Mary Kennedy
Mary Catharine Hays	Henry Vicor	

27 of Jul 1849 (p10) Ann Maria June Spicer made her first Communion, Hampshire County, Virginia

01 Aug 1840 (p10) Sarah Dougherty, wife of James Daugherty made her first Communion (a convert)

10 Apr 1841 (p10) Maria Anna & Maria Josephine Hornbaugh made their first Communion in Cumberland

__ __ 1841 (p11) Ger Girk from Old Town

FIRST COMMUNIONS 1842 (p11)

21 Mar 1842 Francis Smithin

03 Apr 1842 Low Sunday
Margaret Kebel, Sarah Brown, Martha Kraig (col),
Michael Murry, Pat McCormack, John Mattingly
William Mattingly, Christopher Mattingly, Patrick Donlen

soon after Joseph Byrne (adult)

17 Sep 1842 Mary Garlitz (adult & convert)

FIRST COMMUNIONS 1843 (p11)

13 Apr 1843 Holy Thursday Cumberland
Jane Wallace, Sarah Ryan, Mary Mullen,
Bridget McCormac, Christ Rourke, Joseph Hodel,
Cha[s] Heffner, John A. Mealy, Pat[k] Kennedy
Demet Kreighbaum

LISTS OF NAMES

FIRST COMMUNIONS 1843 [cont.] (p11)

08 Oct 1843 Mt. Savage Church

David Logsdon, Jos Logsdon of Jos, Henry Garlitz, Jos Getty, John Murry, Pat[k] Scott, Hannah Arnold, Cecilia Logsdon, Elizabeth Dean, Ellen M. Lowery, Mary Logsdon, Mary Murry, Helena McKenzie, Eliza Ryan

FIRST COMMUNIONS 1844 (p11)

02 Jun 1844 Trinity Sunday Cumberland

Mary Burnett (adult, conv)

16 Jun 1844

Harriett Hayden (adult & convert), Catherine O'Brien, Ellen O'Brien, Catherine Masters, Alice McGir, Cecilia Mattingly, Susan Mattingly, Arthur McGir, Frances Mattingly, Sam[l] Mattingly, Henry Wonstreet Ambrose Scnibely, Jos Scnibely, Thomas McClery

13 Oct 1844 (p11) [Mt. Savage] Sara Holtzman, Maria Keon (convert)

13 Oct 1844 Cumberland (p9)

Demet Kreighbaum, John Mealy, Cha[s] Heffner, Jos Schnibly, Benj Brown Jr., Arth McGir, Pat[k] Kennedy, Jno Ryan, W[m] Mattingly, Sam[l] Mattingly, Jno Mattingly Jr., Christ. Mattingly, Fran[s] Mattingly Ber[d] Kohlman, Amb Magers, Cath Weisling, Cecilia Mattingly, Ellen Lowrey, Martha Mattingly Sarah Holtzman, Martha Kraig (cld), Cath O'Brien, Alice McGir, Mary Burnet, Ellen O'Brien, Cath Masters, Mary J. Mattingly, Sarah Brown, Mary Mullen, Mary Hershbereger, Mary A. McGir, Ann Brown, Martha Masters, Petronella Byrne, Polly Bacon Martha Perry (cld), Jane Wallace, Bridget Murtaugh, Ann Smith, Margrt McCofrey, Emily Denner, Sarah Ryan, Elizb'h Berkman, Maria Kain, Susan Mattingly, Marg't Cahel

Dec 1844 (Mt. Savage) Mrs. Reynolds (convert)

FIRST COMMUNIONS 1845 (p11)

Jan 1845 (Mt. Savage) Thos Sheriden

30 Mar 1845 Low Sunday Cumb^d (p12)
Edward Silk, James Darkey, Thomas Hopkins,
Thomas Donelly, John Cooney, Ann Redmon,
Marg^t Redmon, Elizb^t Noonan, Mary Kennedy,
Christina Wonstret, Teresa Healey, Ellen Murry,
Mary A. Murry, Mary Laughlin, Roseann Murphy,
Mary Brown, Bridgt Degnon, Susan McMahan,
Sabrina Kennedy, Mary Melia, Fanny Burton (convert)

01 Nov 1845 (p12)
John Mathews, Jona Kreigbaum, Humphy Holland
Wm Arkins, Cath Ryan, Margt Reily, Mary Hodel,
Mary Logsdon, Matilda Wright, Margt Gormon
Rose Ellen Mattingly, Ann M. Kreighbaum,
Anastasia Mattingly

FIRST COMMUNIONS 1846 (p12)

02 Mar 1846 Mr. Wheeler (convert), Mr. Garrahan (convert & adult)

12 Jul 1846 Susan Sigerson

19 Jul 1846 Mary Jane Donelly (adult), Harriet Smith (adult)

09 Aug 1846 Geo McKenzie (adult)

15 Aug 1846 Margt McCoy(adult)

13 Sep 1846 Cath McLaughlin, Susan C. Tippett, Barbary A. Brown,
Sarah Burke, Mary Adelsberger, Mary Leitiger,
Rose Ann Melia, Ann Danner, Ellen Stapleton,
Mary McCarty, Jno Meyers, Franc^s Brosnahan,
Jno Muller, Jno Brien, Simeon Mattingly,
Darby Monahan (adult)

LISTS OF NAMES

FIRST COMMUNIONS 1847 (p12)

04 Apr 1847   Sarah Mullen

11 May 1847   Matilda Hein (adult & convert)

06 Jun 1847   Pat^k Murphy (adult)

27 Jun 1847 (p12, 13)

> Lasres Hamilton (adult), Garret Barry, Francis Masters,
> Jno Cavanaugh, Ed Oldlam, Geo Byrne, Ellen Downey
> Mary Gormon, Mary Mclaughlin, Mary Shea,
> Mary Holland, Bridget Byrne, Nancy Donovan,
> Mary Buckley, Mary Dowling, Mary Ryan, Ellen Dolan,
> Margt Myers, Margt O'Brien, Mary Ann Twigg,
> Ann Adelsberger, Cath McAuley, Sarah Conlon,
> Ellen Colvin, Mary A. Dolan, Elizb^t McAuley, Leo Cahill

10 Oct 1847 (p13) Eliz^t C Doonen (adult & convert)

07 Nov 1847 (p13) Ann Messmen, Sarah Doyle

FIRST COMMUNIONS 1848 (p13)

25 Mar 1848   Rebecca Ridgeley

27 Mar 1848   Thos Murry

07 May 1848

> Henry Gerdeman, Jos Ackers, Mich^l Miller,
> Herman Brown, Wm Mahony, Danl Donavon,
> Thos Wonstret, Pat^k Gainer, Henry Shriver,
> Jon Wilbrick, Ja^s Noonan, Geo Tippetts,
> Martha Adelsberger, Danl Brosnahan, Thomas Hodel,
> Mary Ann Shane, Ellen McAuley, Ann McAuley,
> Ann Gordon, Ann Brien, Alexona Garland,
> Maria Gainer, Elizabeth Melia, Bridget Melia,
> Ellen Donovan, Rose Cahill, Elisah Jerret (convert),
> Cath Cushman, Mary Kelley

CONFIRMATIONS 4 Jun 1848 (p9)

Thos Hodel
Wm Mahony
Gerret Barry
Fr Brosnahan
Jno Mattews
Saml Brosnahan
Math Adelsberger
Jas Noonan
Jno Miller
Michl Miller
J. P. Krighbaum
Lem Cross
Leo Cahill
Hen Shriver
Jno Gochey
Thos Hopkins
Jno Myers
Pat Kenny
K. Kervick
Wm Askins
Geo Tippett
Frank Masters
Jno Cavanagh
Ed Odlam
Jos Askins
Thos Wonstret
Herman Brown
Hump Holland
Hen Gerdernan
Pet Winbougher
Mrs. Wonstret
Tim Regan
Ed McDermott
Michl Bolend
Hen Wonstret
Geo McKenzie
Fr Sprag
Mrs. Winbougher
Thos Dolon
Mary Dowling

Con Helfrick
Jos Brokeman
Jno Willrich
Ed McCormick
Benj Ballaugh
Mary Brokeman
Cah McLaughlin
Marg Heldefer
Mary Hughes
Mary Melia
Sarah Brokeman
Mary Hornbaugh
Margt Yeager
Margt Flanigan
Mary Brown
Ann Danner
Ellen Colvin
Mary A. Dolan
Maria Gainer
Ellen McAuley
Margt Tuey
Mary Holean
M. A. Grenker
Ellen Dolon
Mary Kelley
Sabrina Kennedy
Rose A. Melia
Elis^h Melia
Brdg Melia
Maria Grace
Brd^t McDermot
Mary Bolen
Marg Rerig
Sarah Conlon
Margt Gouldon
Magt O'Brein
Mary A. Shane
Alexena Garlick
Ellen Downey
Keim Kervich (FC)

Brdt Lignon
Cath Wonstret
Hon McLaughlin
Margt Shane
Mary A. Twigg
Susan Tippett
Elisth Jerret
Ann Maguire
Mary Monahan
Cath Cushwa
Bridg Byrne
Rose Mattingly
Margt Myers
Rose Cahill
Mary Hodel
Ellen Stephson
Ellen Donavon
Sarah Doyle
Hart E. Smith
Ann Adelsberger
Jane Kelley
Ann Brien
Cath McAuley
Mary Buckley
Nancy Donavon
Ann McGavin
Mary Adelsberger
Ann Gouldon
Mary Coffey
Barbara Brown
Cath Viger
Ann Messman
Matilda Hein
Mary McLaughlin
Mary Ryan
Martha Finegan
Jane Donelly
Cath Faith
Ann McAuley
and 11 others [unnamed]

LISTS OF NAMES

FIRST COMMUNIONS 1848 [cont.] (p13)

07 May 1848 Ellen Downey, Margaret Rerig

04 Jun 1848 [See list on preceding page.]

30 Jul 1848 James Gaughe

06 Aug 1848 Adeline Myers (convert)

FIRST COMMUNIONS 1849 (p13, 14)

21 Mar 1849 Mrs. Saml McKenzie (convert)

22 Mar 1849 John Thompson (convert)

27 May 1849 Jos Ferley, Jno Henry Bersel, Henry Brokeman,
Saml Mattingly, Jno Adam Hipp, Anthony Gerdener,
Jno Henry Kulker, Jno Colvin, Michel Cavanaugh,
Patrick Jno Garner, James Howard, Thos Noonan,
Margt Muller, Mary Malone, Cath McGerry,
Eliz^t Shellhouse, Bridg^t Malone, Josephine Masters,
Cath Gramlick, Mary A. Campbell, Ellen O'Conner,
Bridg^t Fay, Marg Wa_____, Mary Larkin,
Bridg^t Gainer,   Mary Mc_____,
Cath Bergoin, Maria Healy

01 Jun 1849 Kevin White

27 Jul 1849 Leonadas Donelly

08 Aug 1849 Jno Reilly

21 Aug 1849 Jno Byrne

22 Aug 1849 Thos Crahan

02 Nov 1849 Pat^k Conelly

09 Dec 1849 Phebe Ann Kerfiel (convert)

37

FIRST COMMUNIONS 1850 (p14)

24 Feb 1850 Ortha Brady (convert)

03 Mar 1850 Mary Ann Wise

10 Mar 1850 Peter Wise (convert)

10 Apr 1850 Jane Lively (convert)

21 Apr 1850 John Brady, Jno Wise, Jos A. Cahill, Edward Dowling, Jno Hodel, Sebastian Gramlick, Jno O'Neill, Jno Howard, James Forester, Peter Mattingly, Baptist Mattingly, Stewart Hale, Bridget Ryan, Mary Brady, Rose Ann Quigly, Mary Weaver, Sarah Dowling, Cath Murphy, Virginia Ryan, Rosvia McNeve, Elisab^h Handel, Cath Lorella Smith, Johanna Regear, Emily Wise, Lickna Meyers, Mary Delany, Mary Elisa Null, Mary A. Purtell, Elisa Gainer, Margt Healy, Jane Green, Ann Mattingly, Cath Gainer, Ann Jane Reilly

01 May 1850 Joab Watts

FIRST COMMUNIONS 1851 (p15)

05 Feb 1851 Thos McLaughlin

08 Feb 1851 Mary McNair (convert)

11 Feb 1851 Thos Dolon

30 Mar 1851 Jos Mattingly, Mich^l Dowling, Wm Dowling, Peter Farrell, Mat^w Coffey, Nat^l Finegan, James Masters, John Shriver, Jas T. Mattingly, Pat^k Brady, Mary Ann Kean, Mary J. Quigly, Mary Brosnahan, Sarah Dougherty, Jane M. McLaughlin, Ann Gormon, Mary E. Carney, Mary Brodrick, Mary Brofey, Frances Byrnes, Christiana Ramus (convert), Rebecca Colvin, Melvina Benforce, Elizabeth Hanson, Charlotte Thompson

FIRST COMMUNIONS 1851[cont.] (p15)

05 Apr 1851   Elisabeth Cage (convert)

May 1851   (Undated; this placement is consistent with prior years.)
Mary Ann Kane, Mary Jane Quigly, Mary Brosnehan,
Sarah Dougherty, Jane McCaghan, Ann Gorman,
Mary Ellen Carney, Mary Brodrick, Mary Brofey,
~~Ann Whelen,~~ Frances Byrne, Christiana Ramus,
Rebecca Colvin, Cath Dolan, Melvina Benforce,
Elis^h Hanson, Elisabeth Cage, Charlot Thompson,
Joseph Mattingly, Mich^l Dowling, William Dowling,
Peter Farrell, Mat Coffey, ~~Jona Dicken,~~ Nat Finegan,
James Masters, John Shriver, James T. Mattingly,
~~Jno Brofey,~~ Pat^k Brady.
[Strike-throughs in original without explanation.]

24 Jun 1851   James McLaughlin

11 Jul 1851   Rebecca Hutson

This concludes the Lists of Names section.

MARRIAGES

The early Catholic marriage register(s) in Western Maryland are somewhat lacking in continuity due to ceremonies being performed by priests from outlying areas: Conewago, Pennsylvania; Frederick, Maryland; Hagerstown, Maryland; and sometimes by itinerant Jesuits. Certainly we would have expected marriages before late 1818. *Allegany County Maryland Marriages 1791-1847* by Margaret E. Myers (ACMM) were reconstructed from License Applications and those Court House records not destroyed by fire. Not all entries herein are found in ACMM. When we try to compare entries between these sources we find a great disparity between name spellings, even to the extent of identifying different people. Since the microfilm records are considered a Primary Source, they take precedence. Where the script was illegible, the ACMM was consulted. In the case of widows, where the ACMM differed in name, it was assumed it might be the maiden name and we entered it in brackets [ ] before the last name.

10 Nov 1818[1]	Married according to the laws of this State Samuel McKenzie & Hinny McKenzie after having obtained a dispensation from the Archbishop of Baltimore, the above persons being blood relations in the Second degree in the presence of several witnesses at the Church on Sunday afternoon. -JR (p157)
10 Nov 1818[2]	Married on the same day according to law John Durbin to Mary Winebrenner at the church in presence of many witnesses. -JR (p157)
02 May 1819	Married on the 2nd day of May 1819 by permission of the laws of the State of Maryland Stephen Blubaugh to Honor Logsdon all of Allegany County in presence of Jonathan Arnold. -JR (p157)
07 Nov 1819	Married agreeable to the laws of this State Thomas Porter to Mary Sapp; Witnesses: (blank). -JR (p157)
16 Jul 1820	Married agreeable to the laws of this State John Mattingly to Ann Magers with the mutual consent of their parents & friends, in the presence of several witnesses at the residence of John Mattingly his father. -JR (p157)

---

[1] Church records only have the year 1819, dates from ACMM.
[2] Ibid. above

03 Jun 1821	Married Joseph Logsdon to Mary Lowery by a license of the Court in presence of many witnesses at the house of Mr. Arnold. -JR (p158)
30 Jul 1821	Married Gabriel McKenzie to Rachel Blubaugh in the Catholic Church, many witnesses being present. -NDY [OJD] (p158)
18 Dec 1821	Married George Trullinger to Honora Durbin in the presence of many witnesses at her father's house. -TR (p158)
14 Apr 1822	Married Eliga (Elijah) Durbin to Margaret Logsdon in the Church in the presence of many witnesses. -TR (p158)
02 Dec 1822	Married John McKenzie to Margaret Logsdon in the Church in presence of many witnesses, who had a license from the Court. -TR (p158)
13 May 1823	Married Leonard Shircliff to Honora Mattingly in the Catholic Church, many witnesses being present. -TR (p158)
14 Oct 1823	Married William Shircliff to Anna Mattingly by a license of the Court in the presence of many witnesses in the Church. -TR (p159)
23 Nov 1823	Married James Murphy to Mary Hixonbaugh[3] in the presence of many witnesses in the Church; witnesses Benjamin Brown, Joseph Mattingly. -TR (p159)
28 Sep 1824	Married John Durbin to Margaret Logsdon in the presence of many witnesses in the Catholic Church; Witnesses: Joseph & James Mattingly, William Logsdon. -TR (p159)
09 Apr 1825	Married Baptist Mattingly to Miss Anna Timmonds by a license of the Court in the presence of many witnesses at her mother's house in Cumberland. -TR (p159)
31 Jul 1825	Married Evan John Porter to Elisabeth Clister by a license from the Court in the presence of many witnesses in the Catholic Church. -TR (p159)
27 Sep 1825	Married William Logsdon to Elizabeth Magers by a licence from the Court House in the presence of many Witnesses in the Catholic Church. -TR (p159)
23 Jul 1826	Married Henry Mattingly to Miss Susan Albright at her father's house in Pa. in the presence of many witnesses. -TR (p160)

---

[3] Last name illegible, taken from Allegany Co. marriage records.

11 Apr 1826   Married Peter McClary to widow [Ann] Hunter[4], by a license from the Court, in the presence of many witnesses at Mr. Wilm Correnton's house at the Brg Crossing. -TR (p160)

20 Jul 1826   Married James Kelly to Sarah Jacobs by a license from the Court in the presence of many witnesses at the house of Sarah Jacobs. -TR (p160)

03 Dec 1826   Married George Mattingly to Miss Mary Anna Koon after three publications in the presence of many witnesses in the Catholic Church on Sunday evening. -TR (p160)

06 Mar 1827   Married Edward Mullen to Miss Anna Blocker by a license of the Court in the presence of many witnesses at her father's house in Cumberland. -TR (p160)

08 Mar 1827   Married Francis Dean to Miss Mary Arnold by a license of the Court in the presence of many witnesses at her mother's house. -TR (p161)

11 Mar 1827   Married James Mattingly to Miss [Susanna][5] Albright at her father's house in Pennsylvania in the presence of many witnesses. -TR (p161)

01 Nov 1827   Married Anthony Arnold to Margaret Simpkins before many witnesses at the B[aptist] Mattingly's house in Cumberland. -TR (p161)

11 Jan 1828   Married Henry Krighbaum to Fanny Arnold in the Catholic Church in the presence of many witnesses. -TR (p161)

14 Jan 1828   Married Daniel Lowery to Susanna Mattingly by a license of the Court in the Catholic Church in the presence of many witnesses. -TR (p162)

11 Sep 1828   Married Samuel McKenzie to Catherine Durbin by a license from the Court in the Catholic Church in the presence of many witnesses. -TR (p162)

25 Jan 1829   Married by a license from the Court and a dispensation from the Archbishop, John Mattingly widower to Eleanor Winters, widow, at the house of the latter in the presence of many witnesses. -TR (p162)

__ May 1829   Married by a license from the Archbishop, Samuel McKenzie to Mary Blubaugh living in the state of Pa. at the house of Mrs. Blubaugh in the presence of many witnesses. -TR (p162)

---

[4] Last name illegible, taken from Allegany Co. marriage records.
[5] *The Descendants of Henry Mattingly 1750-1823*-1969 by Herman E. Mattingly shows her name as Susanna Albright and also gives an 1826 marriage of Henry Mattingly to Susan Albright.

__ May 1829 Married by a license from the Court, in the Catholic Church in the presence of many witnesses John Logsdon to Margaret Arnold. -TR (p162)

28 Sep 1829 Married David Logsdon to Rebecca Uhl in the house of his father in the presence of many witnesses. -FXM (p163)

07 Jan 1830 I married Jonathan Sapp from Knox County, Ohio, to Mary Durbin after three publications at her father's house in the presence of many witnesses. -FXM (p163)

07 Aug 1831 I married Jesse Tomlinson and Ann Hixonbaugh in the Catholic Church in the presence of many witnesses. -FXM (p163)

 [Data missing 07 Aug 1831 through 08 Jun 1834, although the following appear on page 163. See *Allegany County Maryland Marriages* for possible Catholic marriages during this period.]

08 Jun 1834 I married William Hannon [6] and Harriet Milborn. -FXM (p163)

23 Oct 1834 I married John Hammond and Ann Elisabeth Ridgely by license in her father's house in the presence of a great number of witnesses. -FXM (p163)

13 Nov 1834 I married Joseph Null[7] and Sarah Moore in her mother's house in Cumberland [MD] by a license of the Court in the presence of many witnesses. -FXM (p163)

27 Nov 1834 I married Philip Lahey and Catherine Carigan by license in one of the Shanties on the new road West of Cumberland 2 miles, in the presence of five or six witnesses. -FXM (p164)

 [Data missing between 27 Nov 1834 and 05 Feb 1837.]

05 Feb 1837 Raphael Logsdon was married to Rebecca Mattingly in the presence of many witnesses with a dispensation from the Archbishop. -HM (p164)

02 Apr 1837 Mr. Henry Karman was married to Elizabeth Hangerberger in Cumberland Church in presence of many witnesses. -HM (p111)

13 Apr 1837 Miss Matilda May was married to Joseph Arnold near the Mountain Church in the presence of many witnesses; Nancy Arnold bridesmaid, F. Mattingly bridegroom. -HM (p164)

---

[6] Allegany Co. Marriages lists him as William J. Henner.

[7] Allegany Co. Marriages lists him as Neill, I read the handwriting as Null.

44

MARRIAGES

16 Apr 1837	Miss Margaret Durbin was married to Charles Beale near the Mountain Church in the presence of many witnesses; Honora Durbin bridesmaid, Benedict Logsdon bridegroom. -HM (p164)
16 May 1837	Mr. James Timmonds was married to Mrs. E. Evinstine with License, in Cumberland in presence of many witnesses. -HM (p111)
24 Jul 1837	Mr. Henry Brown was married to Miss Elizabeth Vonstreet in Cumberland Church with license before many witnesses. -HM (p111)
03 Aug 1837	Mr. William Ryan was married to Miss Rebecca Bean at the McDaniel's residence near Old Town with license from the court from Hardy County VA (now WV). -HM (p111)
22 Sep 1837	Mr. W. Staunton was married to Miss Mary Ann Ridgely, at her father's residence, in presence of many. -HM (p111)
05 Nov 1837	F. [Fred'k] Truxell was married to Miss Laurcey Wessell in Cumberland before many witnesses. -HM (p111)
12 Nov 1837	Mr. F. [Frank] Fall was married to Miss Teresa Heyler born in Allegany County before many. -HM (p111)
16 Nov 1837	Mr. Jacob Workman was married to Miss Susan Arnold in presence of many. -HM (p111)
02 Feb 1838	Pat McGary was married to Margaret Murray before many. -HM (p112)
26 Feb 1838	Hugh McAlear was married to Mrs. Cat Fenegan at Old Town according to law. -HM (p112)
12 Mar 1838	Owen Hanford was married to Mrs. Mary Nealy in Cumberland before many. -HM (p112)
22 Mar 1838	John McClearey was married to Miss Maria Acktin near Shelbyport before many. -HM (p112)
28 Mar 1838	Owen Lynch was married to Miss Rosana McCuen in Cumberland. -HM (p112)
28 Mar 1838	Michael Livingham was married to Miss Mary Goulden near Cumberland before many. -HM (p112)
15 Apr 1838	Youck Poste was married to Elizabeth Rice at Samuel Durbin's house in Pennsylvania. -HM (p112)
15 Apr 1838	Laurence Will was married to Catolina Breaker at Samuel Durbin's house in Pennsylvania. -HM (p112)
15 Apr 1838	Phillip Will was married to Johanna Parker at Samuel Durbin's house in Pennsylvania. -HM (p112)

18 Apr 1838	Mr. John Rucker was married to Miss Annett Barcach, both of Allegany County, in Cumberland before many. -HM (p112)
23 Apr 1838	Mr. Pat O'Neil was married to Miss Elizabeth Edwards before several. -HM (p112)
28 May 1838	John Madden was married to Celia Dwyers, the first abt. 22 years old, the second abt. 16 years old, from the tunnel, Wit: Owen Burke, Michael Golden. -BSP (p112)
14 Jun 1838	Patrick Maher was married to Margareta Thay before many. -HM (p113)
14 Jun 1838	John Haney was married to Margarite Butler before several. -HM (p113)
14 Jun 1838	John Peters was married to Isabella Haupt before many. -HM (p113)
28 Jun 1838	Mr. John Trimble was married to Miss Elizabeth Hook before many witnesses. -HM (p113)
28 Jun 1838	Simon Fisher was married to Honora Ross (colored) with permission from their Masters. -HM (p113)
29 Jun 1838	Patrick Kenney was married to Catharine Hagan with license before many. -HM (p113)
30 Jun 1838	John Upperman was married to Mary Hoyle in presence of several. -HM (p113)
08 Jul 1838	Onder Finck was married to Elizabeth Hoyle before several. -HM (p113)
15 Jul 1838	Frederick Cropright was married to Mary Trestler in presence of Baptist Mattingly & (blank). -BSP (p113)
22 Jul 1838	Patrick Egan was married to Mary King in presence of Ch McDonald & many more. -HM (p114)
24 Jul 1838	Jacob Pitchert was married to Barbara Brown in presence of Milley, the cook of Dr. Healey. -HM (p114)
22 Aug 1838	Michael Millier was married to Caterine Haun in presence of Mr. Kelley & John Kearny. -HM (p114)
26 Aug 1838	Daniel Tierney was married to Ellen (blank) widow, at Blooming Rose, with dispensation of the impediment dispartis cultus, he not being baptized. -HM (p114)
02 Sep 1838	Patrick Carlos was married to Elizabeth Failar in presence of Gillen L. Ludig in Cumberland. -HM (p114)
08 Sep 1838	Caspar Brown was married to Elizabeth Newton in Cumberland, both of Allegany County. -HM (p114)

MARRIAGES

24 Sep 1838   John Flinn was married to Margaret Farrell in presence of many, in Cumberland. -HM (p114)

24 Oct 1838   Thomas Kevlaghan was married to Maria Ryan in presence of Mr. William Ryan, Mrs. Ryan & (blank), in Cumberland. -HM (p114)

04 Nov 1838   John Misal was married to Barbara Liver in presence of Miss Eliza Fitzgerald & several more. -HM (p115)

09 Nov 1838   Martin Haw was married to Johanna McCormick in presence of her brother and sister. -HM (p115)

10 Nov 1838   Mr. Richard Murphy was married to Miss Caroline Rowe in presence of four witnesses. -HM (p115)

11 Nov 1838   Joseph Bro_thin was married to Catharine Barneal in presence of several. -HM (p115)

22 Nov 1838   William Feirle was married to Elizabeth Bappert. -HM (p115)

06 Dec 1838   John Laney was married to Judath Noland in presence of Mr. Hopkins & Lady & several more. -HM (p115)

13 Dec 1838   Philip Cosgrove was married to Mary Duffy in presence of Mr. Peter Garahan's family & several more. -HM (p115)

14 Dec 1838   Adam Hammer was married to Elizabeth Crisland in presence of several. -HM (p115)

24 Jan 1839   Marcus Wanciler was married to Catharine Bart in presence of many. -HM (p115)

10 Feb 1839   John Reynolds was married to Honor Gaughour [Gaughan?] before Mr. Rush & Pety Havestry. -HM (p116)

12 Feb 1839   John Black was married to Lydia Ann Smith of Allegany County in presence of B. Mattingly & E. Mullan. -HM (p116)

14 Feb 1839   Nathan Arnold was married to Ellen Wade in presence of John Black, Mrs. Black & (blank). -HM (p116)

24 Mar 1839   Wallace and (blank), servants for Mr. Sam Coddington at Blooming Rose, was rehabititated (sic), by the usual promises, departus cultus, she not being baptized. -BSP (p116)

31 Mar 1839   Daniel Frotz was married to Mary Cashner in presence of Miss Esther Kearney & Miss C. Brown. -HM (p116)

05 Apr 1839   John Farrel was married to Mrs. Donlon in presence of Miss Garahan & (blank). -HM (p116)

25 Apr 1839   Adam Muth was married to Teresa Seporan before Mr. John Black & sister and many others. -HM (p116)

11 May 1839   Joseph Hempey was married to Catharine Schiefendecker in Cumberland in presence of Mr. J. Null & Mr. Kearney & others. -HM (p117)

17 Jun 1839   Andrew Brown was married to Barbara Lypold in Cumberland Church in presence of Mr. Brown's brother and several more. -HM (p117)

03 Jun 1839   Edward, servant of Mr. Jamison, was married to Ellen, servant of Mrs. Cassandra Robinett, with expressed permission; Wit: Francis Jamison, etc. -HM (p117)

28 Jun 1839   George Evans was married to Catharine Redmond near Old Town in presence of James Carr & Mrs. Egan and others. -HM (p117)

05 Jul 1839   Francis Polis was married to Anna Snowen in Cumberland in presence of Mr. Brown & his brother. -HM (p117)

24 Jul 1839   Patrick Fay was married to Ann McGarity in presence of Mrs. Coffey & (blank). -HM (p117)

18 Aug 1839   Greenbury Waters, a free cold man was married to Mary, servant of Mr. Huddleson of Flintstone in presence of several. -BSP (p118)

21 Aug 1839   Joseph Fisher was married to Catharine Leatner, both of Allegany County. -HM (p118)

21 Aug 1839   James Burke was married to Mary Fannon in presence of M. Prush & several more. -HM (p118)

08 Sep 1839   Henry Nios was married to Agnes Crevencamp, after three publications of the Banns of Marriage. -HM (p118)

12 Sep 1839   John Garlitz was married to Mary A. Garlitz, with dispensation of the 3rd degree of consanguinity in presence of Christy Garlitz, George Logsdon & others. -BSP (p118)

14 Sep 1839   Anthony Usters was married to Amelia Pagenhart in presence of M. Karney & several more. -HM (p118)

16 Sep 1839   Patrick Conway was married to Bridget Coley in presence of Wm Riley. -HM (p118)

12 Sep 1839   John Garlitz was married to Mary A. Garlitz with dispensation of the 3rd degree of consanguinity.-BSP (p119)

18 Sep 1839   Frantz Lampey was married to Anamelia Smitting in presence of John Smitting Jr. -HM (p119)

19 Sep 1839	Peter Hussey was married to Maria McDermot in presence of Mr. & Mrs. Rush. -HM (p119)
25 Sep 1839	John Holtzman was married in Cumberland to Mrs. Catharine Smith in presence of Mr. John Black & wife and Mr. G. Kelly & wife. -HM (p119)
26 Sep 1839	James Barrett was married to Maria Killbane in presence of Anthony Monaughan and the bride's brother. -BSP (p119)
03 Oct 1839	Lawrence Speelman was married to Mrs. Margaret Logsdon in the presence of Mr. Joseph Logsdon & wife and Miss Matilda McQuicker. -HM (p119)
05 Oct 1839	Thomas Larkin was married in Cumberland to Mary Silk in presence of John Black & wife and Peter Mulholland. -HM (p119)
12 Oct 1839	Patrick O'Farrel was married in Cumberland to the widow Bridget Mulreal in the presence of Mr. Riley & wife. -HM (p119)
20 Oct 1839	Charles Brown was married to Liehtia Marshall, with a dispensation of the impediment_____ _____, he not being baptised. -HM (p119)
24 Oct 1839	Daniel C. Bruce was married to Mary Ann Frost in the presence of Mrs. Frost, Mr. Simmes, etc. -BSP (p120)
26 Oct 1839	Daniel C. Bruce of Ohio was married to Mary Ann Frost in presence of Ab^r Sammes, Mrs. Krigbaum, etc. Service was made in person at Mrs. Frost and usual promise that the children could be raised Catholics by their mother. -BSP (p120)
30 Oct 1839	Hugh Maguire was married to Ann Love in presence of John O'Donal & William Riley. -HM (p120)
24 Nov 1839	Michael Mattingly was married to Honora Durbin, "cum dispensation super impedimentum consanguintatis in tertio gradum" in presence of John Mattingly Sr. & Jr., etc. -BSP (120)
06 Dec 1839	John Sullivan was married to Mary Smith in presence of Mrs. Whelan, in Cumberland. -HM (p120)
16 Dec 1839	John Sloan, a widower, was married to Miss Margaret Ward in Cumberland Church in presence of Mr. Conlon, Mrs. Fay & several others. -HM (p120)
16 Dec 1839	Peter and Nancy McCleary were remarried, she not having been baptized at their first marriage. -HM (p120)

24 Dec 1839   Mr. Francis Gramlick was married to Elizabeth Gramlick, with a dispensation from the Archbishop, they having been married out of the church, and he being her ~~stepbrother~~ [struck thru in record]. -HM (p120)

06 Jan 1840   John Hevrin was married to Margaret [Connelly?] Barret, widow of Patrick Barret, in presence of Mr. Coffey and many more -HM (p121) Note: [added later] "this marriage was invalid, they being related in the 2nd degree of consanguity."

07 Jan 1840   James Howe was married to Miss Mary Ann G. Gunter in presence of her father & mother's brother. -HM (p121)

12 Jan 1840   Aaron Hixonbaugh was married to Rachel Coleman in the Church before Francis Mattingly and Aaron's brother. -HM 121

23 Jan 1840   Francis A. Jamison was married to Eliza A. Robinette, near Flintstone, in presence of mother & brother and his brother and sisters. -HM (p121)

29 Jan 1840   William Herd was married to Hester Kearney in presence of her mother, sister & brothers. -HM (p121)

15 Feb 1840   Peter Rereick [Rahrig] was married to Margaret Shafrin after three publications in presence of Peter Rereick Jr. and M. Coffey. -HM (p121)

19 Feb 1840   Philip Garvin was married to Miss Catherine McCormick in presence of her father and brother. -HM (p121)

10 Mar 1840   Jonathan McAtee was married to Cassandra Twigg at Flintstone; wit: F. Jamison, Mr. Huddleson. -HM (p121)

17 Mar 1840   Thomas Salmon was married to widow Philbin in presence of Mr. & Mrs. Holtzman & many more. -HM (p122)

06 Apr 1840   Henry Viscamp was married to Sarah Dorsey, with dispensation of the impediment dispartates cultus, she not being baptized. -HM (p122)

19 Apr 1840   Joseph Zeller was married to Mary Glass in presence of John Black & wife. -HM (p122)

21 Apr 1840   Valentine Rerick [Rahrig] was married to Susan Creighbaum in presence of her father & mother. -HM (p122)

28 Apr 1840   Francis Mattingly was married to Jane Emilia Donahoe before her mother & Capt Welch. -HM (p122)

11 May 1840   John Shelhouse was married to Barbara Sneive in presence of her sister. -HM (p122)

MARRIAGES

28 May 1840	Francis Spetz was married to Catharine Haufman in presence of Mr. Francis Gramlick. -HM (p123)
28 May 1840	Henry Ferley was married to Catharine Cross in presence of Francis Gramlick. -HM (p123)
11 Jun 1840	Mr. Flannagan was married to Miss Ann House in presence of Mr. Arnold & Lady and his brothers. -HM (p123)
24 Jun 1840	Henry Dressman was married to Catherine Vonstreet in presence of Dr. S. Smith & Lady. -HM (p123)
15 Jul 1840	Harmon Jordan was married to Margaret Brown in presence of Mrs. Hurd. -HM (p123)
14 Aug 1840	John Langendorf was married to widow Teresa Hart in presence of Mr. Ferley.-HM (p123)
17 Aug 1840	Henry Fox was married to Mary Lavil (Laville?) in presence of Mr. J. Kearney & Mr. Coffey. -HM (p123)
17 Aug 1840	Patrick Cronin was married to Miss Nancy Arnold in presence of her sister, J. Arnold & Mr. Welch. -HM (p124)
26 Aug 1840	Andrew McMahon was married to Miss Mary Denney in presence of Mr. & Mrs. Gorman. -HM (p124)
26 Aug 1840	Edward Haney was married to Miss Jane Dougherty in presence of Mr. John Gorman & Francis McCormick. -HM (p124)
27 Sep 1840	John Street was married to Christina Fiechel in Old Town after the banns of matrimony had been thrice published, in presence of Mr. McAtee. -HM (p124)
22 Oct 1840	Thomas Foliet was married to Miss Rose Hussey in presence of her father & mother. -HM (p124)
01 Nov 1840	Harman Pulsing was married to Elizabeth ___ after (smeared) in presence of Mr. Michael Goulden. -HM (p124)
04 Nov 1840	Anthony Cain was married to Maria Wassen in presence of Mr. Heck & Mr. Harshbarger & Lady. -HM (p125)
06 Nov 1840	Thomas Gallagher was married to Miss Mary McCarvy in presence of Mr. Wm Hopkins & wife. -HM (p125)
12 Nov 1840	Redmond Morrison was married to Elizabeth Carter in presence of C. Carter & __ Anderson. -HM (p125)
17 Nov 1848	Matthew McCormick was married to Mary O'Brien in presence of her father & mother. -HM (p125)
02 Dec 1840	Harman Brogam was married to Elizabeth Tokenberger in presence of Mr. & Mrs. Vonstreet. -HM (p125)

26 Dec 1840   William Kerchburg was married to Mary Bramer in presence of her brother. -HM (p125)

12 Jan 1841   Joseph Lentz was married to Miss Catherine Morrison in presence of Mr. & Mrs. Kelly & Mrs. Null. -HM (p126)

22 Feb 1841   Thomas H. Scott was married to Miss Jane Kearney in presence of Mr. R. Byrne & her two sisters & mother. -HM (p126)

19 Mar 1841   James Campbell was married to Miss Mary McGovern in presence of Mr. Welch & Thomas McCauley. -HM (p126)

11 Apr 1841   Mr. Everet Henry Ludmotter was married to Miss Gertrude Lauames at Mr. S^l Durbin's house in Pensylvania in presence of John Mattingly. -HM (p126)

27 Apr 1841   Mr. Philip McCawley was married to Miss Catharine Manley in presence of Jno McNeff, Mary Kennedy, her father and several others in Cumberland Church. -BLO (p126)

28 Apr 1841   Thomas Donahoe was married to Miss Elizabeth Hendrixson with a dispensation of the impediment Cultus departedus, she not being baptized, in presence of her father & mother. -HM (p126)

11 May 1841   Christian Schaulde was married to Julia Tavelless in presence of Anthony Myers & Anna Cresser. They had been published from the Altar. -HM (p127)

18 May 1841   Peter Clarke was married to Miss Jane Langsdon in presence of Michael McDonald & Mary Cox. -BLO (p127)

20 May 1841   Martin Flatley was married to Rose Conly in presence of Thomas Turner, Nelly McDonald & others. -BLO (p127)

21 Mar 1841   Edward McDermit was married to Bridget Netnee in presence of Peter Netnee, Mary Kennedy & others. -BLO (p127)

28 May 1841   William Costello was married to Mary (Finey) Culcannon, widow, in presence of W. Duffy & Margaret Roe. -BLO (p127)

31 May 1841   John Fitzpatrick was married to Susan Smith in presence of Edward McQuade & Sophia Romney. -BLO (p127)

11 Jun 1841   Michael McLaughlin was married to Julia Loftus in presence of Anthony Loftus, Julia Sheridan & others. -BLO (p127)

12 Jun 1841   John McKelop was married to Elizabeth Reynolds at Mountain Church in presence of Mrs. McKelop & Mary Campbell.-BLO (p127)

MARRIAGES

01 Jul 1841   Joshua Lilly (Protestant) was married in Pennsylvania at the house of the widow Logsdon to Teresa Logsdon in presence of Bennet Logsdon, E. Mattingly & others. He previously promising to bring up his children in the Catholic Church. -BLO (p127)

01 Aug 1841   Francis Hyer was married to Hannah Greaser in presence of Herman Graeser & Elizabeth Ginter. -BLO (p128)

05 Aug 1841   Patrick Nugent was married to Ally I. McIntyre, widow, in presence of Hugh Griffin & Margaret Roe. -BLO (p128)

05 Aug 1841   Hugh Griffins was married to Ann McGraw in presence of Alex Atkinson & Roseann McCaffey. -BLO (p128)

20 Aug 1841   Michael Fitzmorris was married to Mary Hussey in presence of Michael Murray & Mary Kennedy. -BLO (p128)

31 Aug 1841   Stephen Thayer was married, at Peter McClery's, to Rebecca McClery in presence of her father and mother. They had been previously married out of the church. The Archbishop gave a dispensation (he not being baptized) to me to marry them. -BLO (p128)

08 Sep 1841   Henry Baslaggee was married to Eliza Ostings in presence of Fred Scholder and Alled Jender. -BLO (p128)

13 Sep 1841   Basil McKinzie was married to Elizabeth Durst in presence of Isreal Garlitz and Ellenora Robison. -BLO (p128)

13 Sep 1841   Thomas Moran was married to Frances Logsdon in presence of Michael McLaughlin and Susan Durbin. -BLO (p128)

18 Sep 1841   James McCabe was married to Margaret Roe in presence of Michael McGuire and Catherine Beatty. -BLO (p128)

07 Oct 1841   Alexander Atkinson was married to Rose Ann McCafferty in presence of Jno Trechler and Rose Ann Slater. Atkinson being a Protestant made previous the promise to bring up his children in the Catholic Church. -BLO (p128)

>10 Oct 1841   Widow Mary Maginnis was married to widower Patrick Horne in presence of Pat^K Correll and Ann Levina. -BLO (p129)

23 Oct 1841   Michael McGuire was married to Mary A. McMullin in presence of Jno Donlon & Cath Beatty. -BLO (p129)

03 Nov 1841   Henry Ott was married to Adelade Yeaden in presence of Fred^K Cramer & Elizabeth Dirk. -BLO (p129)

06 Nov 1841   John Reynolds was married to Bridget Kelly in presence of John Curneley & Mrs. Coffey, Mr. Coffey. -BLO (p129)

06 Nov 1841   Michael McAtee was married to Martha Ray in presence of Pat[K] Cole & Mary Martha Mattingly. -BLO (p129)

19 Nov 1841   Martin McGarey was married to Ann Scott in presence of Pat[K] McGarey & Mary Scott. -BLO (p129)

22 Nov 1841   Edward Dillan was married to Louise H. Howell in presence of Pat[K] Gorman, Pat[K] Nugent & Ann Nugent (added note: 25 Sep 1842 the parties were married validly after the baptism of the woman _____ marrying them in Nov. last, witnesses Mich[l] Kelly & Pat Coffee). -BLO (p129)

12 Dec 1841   John Hack was married to Elizabeth Schum in presence of John Schillhers & Henericy Messman by Rev. Mr. Rumbler of Baltimore. -BLO (p129)

15 Dec 1841   Anthony Arnold was married to Elizabeth Soyster in presence of Geo C. Perry & Mary A. Krinch. -BLO (p129)

28 Dec 1841   Balthason Rosenberger was married to Elizabeth Rhoad in presence of Mich[l] Weisel & Epha Weisel. -BLO (p129)

35 married within 1841

18 Jan 1842   Geo Steizer was married to Lenah Danner in presence of Margaret Danner & Mr. Kenney. -BLO (p129)

20 Jan 1842   James Dolan was married to Matilda Middleton in presence of Jno Barry & Mary Kenney. -BLO (p129)

07 Feb 1842   Patrick Rock was married to Catherine Byrne in presence of John Donlon & Mary Donlon. -BLO (p130)

08 Feb 1842   George Hart was married to Juliann Ann Rerig in presence of Vindelin Ferly, Peter Rerig, Pat[K] Cronin. -BLO (p130)

08 Feb 1842   Nicholas Berkart was married to Elizabeth Peirpet in presence of Geo Hart, Pat[K] Cronin and others. -BLO (p130)

01 Mar 1842   Leiloob Schneider was married to Eliz[h] Legland in presence of Mart Ruf & Jno Shafer by Rev. Mr. Rumpler. -BLO (p130)

08 Mar 1842   Barney Mibrick was married to Mary Wonstreet in presence of Geo Dressman & Ann Zeff. -BLO (p130)

10 Apr 1842   Thomas Cross, (unbapized) was married to Elizabeth Carter in presence of Benedict Logsdon & Mary A. Carter. The parties had been married by a squire in Pa. several months ago-dispensation of Abp [Archbishop]. -BLO (p130)

11 Apr 1842   Israel Garlitz was married to Ellen Robinson (prot) in presence of Leo McKenzie & Rosanna Finley. -BLO (p130)

12 Apr 1842   George Mattingly was married to Ann Kearney in presence of Andrew Gordon & Margaret Kearney. -BLO (p130)

MARRIAGES

05 May 1842   Miles Barret was married to Mary Allen in presence of Austin Tuey & Mary Tuey. -BLO (p130)

17 May 1842   Barney Riley was married to Catherine Gorman in presence of Mr. Jno Longstaff and Mrs. E. Coffey-BLO (p130)

19 Jun 1842   Thomas Hart was married to Biddy Fenagan in presence of Thos Larkin & Oney Hart. -BLO (p130)

20 Jun 1842   John Loftus was married to Mary McCormack in presence of Patrick Carlin & Mary Kennedy. -BLO (p131)

25 Jun 1842   Joseph Logsdon was married to Margaret White in presence of George Fear Jr. & Elizabeth White. -BLO (p131)

10 Jul 1842   Jesse Twigg was married to Mary Ann Kemp in presence of Jeremiah Arnold & Susan Durbin. -BLO (p131)

03 Aug 1842   Barney Rabet was married to Mary Lowery in presence of Caron Farrell & Margaret McNulty. -BLO (p131)

01 Sep 1842   Patrick Carroll was married to Rose Ann Slater in presence of James Qunnen & Mary Ann McGir. -BLO (p131)

10 Sep 1842   Richard McGann was married to Marcella Kain in presence of Patrick Keegan & Mrs. Beatty. -BLO (p131)

18 Sep 1842   Michael Mulholland was married to Louisa Teresa Jenkins in presence of Henry McKeon & Catherine Smith. -BLO (p131)

02 Oct 1842   Nail Farran was married to Mary Clarke in presence of John Clarke & Mary Mealy. -BLO (p131)

03 Oct 1842   Aneas McDonell was married to Martha Evans (Protestant) in presence of Matthew Coffy & Mrs. Coffy. -BLO (p131)

06 Oct 1842   Francis McCormack was married to Bridget Farrell in presence of Jno Buckley & Mary Cox. -BLO (p131)

09 Oct 1842   Francis Donelly was married to Mary Jane Smith in presence of William Logsdon & Susan Durbin. -BLO (p131)

24 Oct 1842   John Buckley, widower, was married to Mary Cox, widow, in presence of Thomas Kelly, Francis McCormack, and Mrs. O'Rourke. -BLO (p131)

06 Nov 1842   John Glass was married to Mary Ebell in presence of An[t] Hemstetter & Ja[S] Zeller. -BLO (p132)

07 Nov 1842   John Cusick was married to widow Mary Brady in presence of Mich[l] Degnon & Mary McKeun. -BLO (p132)

20 Nov 1842   Bernard Burns was married to Ann Cummerford in presence of James McKeun & Cath Conors. -BLO (p132)

02 Dec 1842   Frederick Cramer was married to Mary Krukin in presence of Ja[S] Cramer & Eliz[h] Deirger. -BLO (p132)

29 Dec 1842   Edward Gallaher was married to Betsy McAvoy in presence of Tho[S] Samon & Mary Kenedy. -BLO (p132)

30 marriages during 1842

14 Jan 1843   James McGuire was married to Mary Irons (protestant) in presence of Jno Donlon & Mary Condon. -BLO (p132)

27 Jan 1843   Peter Keenen was married to widow Bridget Brien in presence of Peter Reynolds & Hugh Donahoe. -BLO (p132)

31 Jan 1843   Michael Harrison was married to Mary Scott in presence of Tho[S] Rooney & Jane Clarke. -BLO (p132)

02 Feb 1843   Andrew Gondor was married to Miss Catherine Brown in presence of Pat[K] Carlin & Nancy Rutt. -BLO (p132)

13 Feb 1843   Leo McKinzie was married to (protestant) Johanna Garlitz in presence of Andrew Blocher & Lucy McKinzie. -BLO (p132)

05 Apr 1843   George Hildebrand contracted marriage with Catherine Schemmer (a protestant) the required (smeared) & Joseph Emmel. -BLO (p132)

20 Apr 1843   Miles Higgins was married to Margaret Smith in presence of Jno Sheriden & Mrs. Keenen. -BLO (p133)

30 Apr 1843   Christopher McDonald was married to Mary Hughes in presence of Pat[K] Farrell, Mrs. Dillon, Mat Coffey & her brother. -BLO (p133)

30 May 1843   Henry Ketter contracted marriage with Rebecca Helmet, a protestant after the ususal promises in presence of Valentine Shaeffer & Cath Deal. -BLO (p133)

30 May 1843   William Foley was married to Mary Rogers, widow, in presence of Ed King & Mary Burkley. -BLO (p133)

31 May 1843   John Timmons was married to widow Mary McGirk in presence of Pat[K] Smith & Mat Coffey. -BLO (p133)

04 Jun 1843   Henry Jackson, slave of (?) Jamison to Rosanna Gates, unbaptized, (being dispensed) in presence of negroes Frank Murphy & Sarah Long. -BLO (p133)

13 Jun 1843   William Mattingly contracted marriage with Eva Spall, unbaptized. The necessary dispensation being granted; Witnesses: his father Henry Mattingly and Sam F. McKenzie. They had previously gone before a squire in Pennsylvania to contract marriage. -BLO (p133)

MARRIAGES

13 Jun 1843	John G. Bevans contracted marriage with Ellen M. Ridgely (Acatholicus) in presence of John Cross & Elizabeth Bruce & many others. -BLO (p133)
21 Jun 1843	Henry I. Emmel contracted marriage with Brunigrunda Fisher (protestant) in presence of Mich[l] Weisel & Mary Sterkens. She previously made the requisite promises. -BLO (p133)
27 Jun 1843	Tho[s] Cunningham was married to Ann Farrell in presence of Mich[l] Hanlin & Mrs. McCormack, Pat Hopkins. -BLO (p133)
	[page 134 is blank]
29 Jun 1843	John Ennis was married to Widow Catherine Green in presence of Jesse Beatty & Mrs. Conlon. -BLO (p135)
20 Jul 1843	George Logsdon contracted marriage with Mary Lancaster, a baptized Protestant, after she made the required promise, at her mother's house Somerset Co., Pa. in the presence of Jno Lancaster & Christiana Wilhelm & others. -BLO (p135)
29 Jul 1843	Henry Garlitz married Lucy McKenzie, by dispensation of the Archbishop (first cousins) in presence of Charles Beal, Mrs. Geatty. They had some months since gone before a Squire in Pennsylvania -BLO (p135)
03 Aug 1843	William Gallaher was married to Mary Naun in presence of J. P.Duffy, Matilda Croft & others.-BLO (p135)
05 Aug 1843	Thomas Beatty was married to Sarah Brown in presence of Patrick Donahue & Mary Laughey. -BLO (p135)
19 Sep 1843	Lewis Rineberg, Protestant, was married to Hanna Gormon. Witnesses: John Garry & Hannah Mourel. -BLO (p135)
24 Sep 1843	John Havercomb was married to Catherine Ares in presence of Jno Brunner & several others. -BLO (p135)
24 Sep 1843	Patrick Finnegan was married to Mary Hussey in presence of Daniel Coin and Ann Maguire. -BLO (p135)
24 Sep 1843	William Harrison was married to Mary Riley (widow) in presence of Michael Ruddy & Mary Kinney. -BLO (p135)
17 Oct 1843	Christian [Myer] of Kingwood was married to Ann Mary Wiesling of Cumberland in presence of Geret Wiesling & Henry Lemon, after three publications. -BLO (p136)
17 Oct 1843	George Ruslein was married to Mary Cath Den[m]an in presence of Gar Weisling & Henry Lemon. -BLO (p136)

31 Oct 1843   Herman H. Stegmuller was married to Philomena Grottie in presence of Christ[n] Shuls & Eliz[n] Vercamp -BLO (p136)

09 Dec 1843   Anthony Hennagan was married to Mary Barret in presence of Jno McCormack & Mrs. Wheler. -BLO (p136)

28 Dec 1843   William Askins was married to widow Catherine Fitzpatrick in presence of Mr. Conlon, Peter Carney, & Mrs. O'Rourke. -BLO (p136)

30 marriages in 1843

21 Jan 1844   Thomas Henigen was married to Mary Evert in presence of Rich[d] Price & Marg[t] Mulehie & others. -BLO (p136)

[Even numbered pages are blank hereafter.]

11 Feb 1844   Andrew Arklie (or Asklie) was married to Dureraloh Lobeel (prot.) in Pennsylvania, near Wellersburg, she having previously made the requisite promises. Wit: John McCleery & Polly Carney. -BLO (p137)

13 Feb 1844   John R. Brook was married to Catherine M. Jamison in presence of Henry Adolphus Jamison, Catherine Smith, & others; the existing 3[d] degree of consangunity was prev. dispensed. -BLO (p137)

17 Feb 1844   Timothy Morathey was married to Julia [Murphy] Holland (widow) in presence of Maurice Murphy & Joanna Collins. -BLO (p137)

18 Feb 1844   Michael Larkin was married to Mary Conroy, both of Virginia, in presence of Jno Buckly, Mrs. Buckley, and several others. -BLO (p137)

21 Feb 1844   Henry Spicer was married to Hannah Hirons, unbaptized, in Virginia. The impediment departia Cultus being dispensed. Two years ago they went before a preacher to contract marriage. Wit: Sam[l] L. Topper, Ann Maria Spicer & others. -BLO (p137)

21 Apr 1844   Thomas Nolan was married to Mary O'Donnell in presence of Pat[k] Brady & Eliza Brown. -BLO (p137)

11 May 1844   Aaron, slave of Mr. Slicer, and Lucy, slave of Mrs. Byrne, engaged in marriage in presence of Mat Coffey & Jno B. Byrne. -BLO (p139)

16 May 1844   Martin Gramlick was married to Licetta Dernon in presence of Ant Helsen & Jno Wegman, she previously making the promises usually enacted of protestants. -BLO (p139)

15 Jun 1844   James Fitzgerald was married to Julia Cronin (widow) in presence of Mat Cavanaugh & Cath Regen. -BLO (p139)

MARRIAGES

18 Jun 1844   Joseph Lintz was married to Lucinda Mattingly in presence of Jno B. Byrne & Martha Mattingly. -BLO (p139)

03 Jul 1844   Anthony Rose was married to Matilda C. McCreay in presence of Erin Schafer & Mary A Stoeser. -BLO (p139)

09 Jul 1844   Bernard Reynolds was married to Mary Saunders (protestant) in presence of Mrs. M^CLaughlin & Mary A. Armstrong; the bride making the usual promises before the marriage. -BLO (p141)

11 Jul 1844   Thomas Lynch was married to Susan Tome, an unbaptized protestant, in presence of Jno Black & Teresa Healy. Previous to the marriage she made the usual promise to have the children baptized and brought up in the Cath. Church. Disparetas Cultus was dispensed. Both are from Moorefield, Virginia. -BLO (p141)

04 Aug 1844   Pat^k Keegan was married to Ann McDonald in presence of Mich^l Deheliss, Eliza Brown & others. -BLO (p141)

10 Aug 1844   Michael Madden was married to Bridgt Kelly in presence of Mich^l Naughton and Elizabeth Dean. -BLO (p141)

26 Aug 1844   James Barret was married to widow Mary Dixon in presence of Pat^k Carlin & Mary Sheridan. -BLO (p143)

01 Sep 1844   Charles Nolen was married to Catherine Bolden in presence of Jno Buckley, Mary Buckly & others. -BLO (p143)

10 Sep 1844   Casper Close was married to Ann Yeakel in presence of Wm Gessmer, Eliz^h Yeakel & others. -BLO (p143)

14 Sep 1844   Thomas Mullarkey was married to Mary McCuen in presence of Mich^l Degmon & Susan Ryan. -BLO (p143)

21 Sep 1844   John Nelson was married to Bridget McKellup in presence of Peter Clarke, Sarah Ryan & others. -BLO (p143)

26 Sep 1844   Darby Monahan was married to Mary Kennedy in presence of Mich^l Gorman, Ann McGuire & others. -BLO (p145)

28 Sep 1844   Michael Smith was married to Elizabeth Griffy (unbaptized) who had previously gone before a squire, contracted marriage in presence of Jno White, Mrs. Christy Garlitz, dispartus Cultus being dispensed. -BLO (p145)

01 Oct 1844   Henry Sanders was married to Ennis March in presence of Geo Hildebran & Ant Helsen. -BLO (p145)

05 Oct 1844   Robt Maloy was married to Sophia Rhooney in presence of Pat^k Farrell & Jane Wallace. -BLO (p145)

19 Oct 1844   Edward Barret was married to Ellen Lavelle in presence of And Monahan & Mary Murry. -BLO (p145)

23 Oct 1844   Peter Hein was married to Matilda Albright (protestant) in presence of Jno Hershberger, Mr. Weisel & Joseph Emmel She making the usual promises respecting the offspring. -BLO (p147)

31 Oct 1844   Patrick Mitchell was married to Anna Maguire in presence of Mich[l] Noughton and Teresa Healy. -BLO (p147)

03 Nov 1844   Thomas Leo, widower, was married to Catherine [Berry] Spollen, widow, in presence of John Hughes and Teresa Healy. -BLO (p147)

04 Nov 1844   Peter Freithof was married to Eva Brown after three publications. Witnesses: Geo Leifred and Emma Turner & others -BLO (p147)

12 Nov 1844   Jos Fate was married to Cath Hayes in presence of Peter Hein & Mrs. Knost. -BLO (p147)

28 Nov 1844   Daniel Flynn was married to Ellen McCan in presence of William McLaughlin and Mary McCan. -BLO (p149)

28 Nov 1844   Widower George Clop was married to widow Elizabeth Peter in presence of Hez White & Henry Meyers. -BLO (p149)

30 Dec 1844   Thomas Campbell was married to Catherine McGettigan in presence of Rich[d] O'Neill and John McCoffey. -BLO (p149)

34 Marriages during 1844

02 Jan 1845   Henry Foachtman was married to Mary Berkman in presence of Geo Berkman & Elizabeth Berkman. -BLO (p151)

02 Jan 1845   Stephen Laughlin was married to Ellen McCusker in presence of Owen Loftus and Catherine McCusker. -BLO (p151)

12 Jan 1845   Patrick Brady was married to Eliza Brown in presence of Michael Brady & Ann Johoe. -BLO (p151)

27 Jan 1845   Nicholas Hack was married to widow Catherine Rhinehard, both of Va., after three publications, in presence of Geo Hard and Henry Ferley. -BLO (p151)

28 Jan 1845   D. A. Daugherty married Rebecca E. Thistle, protestant, in presence of Richard Williams and Margaret Ann Thistle. The protestant party having made previously the usual promises. -BLO (p153)

02 Feb 1845   Widower Matthew Coffey married Margaret Mulcahey in presence of Peter Hein and widow Kelley. -BLO (p153)

60

MARRIAGES

04 Feb 1845   John Brunner was married to Mary Oaks in presence of Louis Lepold and Mrs. Tho[S] Gondor. -BLO (p153)

23 Mar 1845   Levi Moore married Lucinda Beall, after she (a protestant) promised that the offspring should be baptized & brought up in the Cath. Religion, in presence of Bern[d] Reynolds & Geo Durbin. -BLO (p153)

26 Mar 1845   Patrick Dunn was married to widow Margaret Brown in presence of Mat Coffey and widow Kelley. -BLO (p155)

29 Mar 1845   Henry Fraever was married to Catherine Trumpeter in presence of Mathias Bunker and Maria Trumpeter. -BLO (p155)

01 Apr 1845   Widower Pat[k] Lowry was married to Ellen Madden in presence of Jno Hanna and Teresa Healy. -BLO (p155)

17 Apr 1845   Widower John Kelley was married to widow Ann Daugherty in presence of Patrick Mulcahey and widow Mrs. Kelley. -BLO (p155)

30 Apr 1845   Pat[k] Lavelle was married to Catherine Karney in presence of Mich[l] Lavelle and Cath Kine. -BLO (p157)

03 May 1845   Mich[l] Berry of Va. was married to Catherine [Flinn] Mauray, widow, in presence of Mrs. Ryan and Ellen Hogan. -BLO (p157)

05 May 1845   Widower Peter Dillon was married to widow Sally Murry in presence of James Thompson and widow Kelly. -BLO (p157)

06 May 1845   James Kavanugh was married to Mary Quinn in presence of Michael Richards and Ann Quinn. -BLO (p157)

13 May 1845   Widower Patrick Kelley was married to widow Catherine Burke in presence of Patrick Maloy & widow Kelley. -BLO (p159)

21 May 1845   Michael Lannon was married to Screpta McBride, both of Virginia, in presence of Thomas Beatty & Bridgt Dagnon. Dispostas Cultus being dispenses previously, as she was not baptized. She made the usual promise regarding the baptism & religion of the offspring. -BLO (p159)

10 Jun 1845   John Kelley was married to Catherine Cane in presence of Pat[k] Daugherty and Mary Handly. -BLO (p159)

11 Jun 1845   John McKellup was married to Catherine Cummerford in presence of Hugh McKellup and Alice Cummerford. -BLO (p159)

26 Jun 1845   James Thompson was married to Mary Barret in presence of Thomas Beatty and Sarah Ryan. -BLO (p161)

29 Jun 1845   Jeremiah McKinzie was married to Catherine McKinzie (a dispensation for the 2nd degree of consanguity was previously granted by the Most Rev. Archbisop. Witness to the marriage [were] Pat^K Dorsey and Helen McKinzie. -BLO (p161)

03 Jul 1845   Patrick Conolly was married to Caroline Hartly, a protestant, in presence of John Kelley and Martha A. Bailsany, the bride having made the usual promises. -BLO (p161)

04 Jul 1845   James Tirnan was married to Elizabeth Kyle in presence of Tho^S Gilmartin & Cath Dunigan. -BLO (p161)

05 Jul 1845   William Cook, Catholic, and Catherine Sharp, unbaptized, in presence of Michael & Mary Conlon. The dispensation for departes cultus being previously granted to the bride who made the usual promises. -BLO (p163)

10 Jul 1845   Daniel McAully was married to Elizabeth Callahan in presence of Pat^K Gallaher and Mary A. Armstrong. -BLO (p163)

15 Jul 1845   Francis Carlin was married to Ann Campbell in presence of Richard O'Neill and Cath Carney. -BLO (p163)

19 Jul 1845   William McKillup was married to Alex Cummerfors in presence of James McKillup and Elizabeth Banter. -BLO (p163)

10 Aug 1845   William Hixenbaugh was married to Lydia Coleman (unbaptized) in presence of James Hixenbaugh and Elizabeth Murphy. The dispensation on account of dispantus cultus was previously granted & the bride made the usual promise to have the offspring baptized and educated in the Cath church. -BLO (p165)

18 Aug 1845   John David Stahl was married to widow Elizabeth Clair after three publications. He being a protestant made the usual promises previous to marriage. -BLO (p165)

20 Aug 1845   Michael Byrne was married to Catherine Farley in presence of Jno Kelley & Mary Crilley. -BLO (p165)

28 Aug 1845   Thomas Rooney was married to Mary Carbine in presence of Robt Catlin and Mary Brodrick. -BLO (p165)

14 Sep 1845   Herman Graser was married to Mary Oterman in presence of Hen Graser and Mary Rickelman. -BLO (p167)

MARRIAGES

28 Sep 1845	Henry, slave of Mr. Jamison, was married to Elizabeth, slave of Mr. Berry, in presence of negroes Aaron, Sarah & others. She, a protestant, made the required promises. -BLO (p167)
11 Oct 1845	Michael Collins was married to Jane Lively in presence of Henry Hughes and Ann Conlon. -BLO (p167)
19 Oct 1845	Casper H. Rohe was married to Elizabeth Tobe in presence of Ber^d Clerterman & Jon Wegman. -BLO (p167)
20 Oct 1845	Thomas Hagan was married to Cath Carney in presence of Peter & Jno Carney & others. -BLO (p167)
31 Oct 1845	Edward McManus to widow Ellen [Garrahan] Farley in presence of James Carey & Mary Carey. -BLO (p169)
13 Nov 1845	Henry Rollman was married to Jane Christina Starzler, a protestant, after the customary promises, in presence of Jno Fate & Cath Steimir. -BLO (p169)
16 Nov 1845	Henry Myers was married to Mary Felby by the German priest in presence of Fred^k Myer and Cath G. Eckelman. -BLO (p169)
25 Nov 1845	Thomas Beatty was married to Ann Barbary in presence of Jno Ennis & Mary Brown, she having previously made the usual promise exercised from protestants. -BLO (p169)
05 Dec 1845	Edward Dwyer widower was married to Margrt Mallon widow in presence of And. Conlon & Mary McMahan. -BLO (p169)
07 Dec 1845	Michael McDonnell was married to Mary Ann Lancaster, protestant, after the required promises, in presence of Owen Luddy & Elizabeth Lemar. -BLO (p171)
22 Dec 1845	John Donan was married to Elizabeth A. Pugh, unbaptized, in presence of James Durban & Mary Melia by auth. of Archbp, the necessary dispensation of Dispautus Cultus was granted and the usual promises were made by the protestant party. -BLO (p171)
28 Dec 1845	Albert Heager was married to Eva Goldsbaugh after three publications in presence of Peter Freithof & his wife. -BLO (p171)
29 Dec 1845	William Sigerson was married to Susan Kimmel, protestant, in presence of Margaret Mulcahey & Rose Ann McManus. The bride previously made the promise. -BLO (p171)

46 married in 1845

The marriages starting in 1846 are recorded on a separate microfilm (M3463).

06 Jan 1846	George Leipfreid was married to widow Teresa Muth in presence of Fr Gramlick and Hen Ferley. -BLO (p1)
15 Jan 1846	Martin Wolff was married to Elizabeth Firstenberg in presence of Cha^S Saturday & Hen Sanders. -BLO (p1)
20 Jan 1846	Henry Winkelman was married to Hannah E. McKinzie in presence of Ja^S Swanigan & Mary Brokeman. -BLO (p2)
20 Jan 1846	Joseph Leing was married to Mary Freiver in presence of Fred^k Leing & Mary Trumpter. -BLO (p2)
03 Feb 1846	Jno Goche was married to Mary Rickelman in presence of Fenis Byney & Mary E. Brokeman. -BLO (p4)
10 Feb 1846	Anthony Hoelsten was married to Elizabeth Piper in presence of Jno Wegman & Mary E. Brokeman -BLO (p4)
17 Feb 1846	Sylvester Mattingly was married to Ellen Hogan in presence of William Porter & Ellen Lowry. -BLO (p4)
05 Mar 1846	Jno Danch was married to Eva Steppe in presence of Jno Hershberger & Mich^l Keach. -BLO (p4)
23 Mar 1846	Michael Noughton was married to Ann E. Dean in presence of Tho^S Kelley & Marie Gainer. -BLO (p6)
28 Apr 1846	George Dressman was married to Mary Ann Trumpter in presence of Mathias Bringer & Elisb^h Berkman. -BLO (p6)
14 May 1846	John Kearney was married to Mary Martha Mattingly in presence of (blank) McHenry & Margaret Kearney. -BLO (p6)
15 May 1846	Thomas Carroll was married to widow Eliz^h Jackson in presence of Sim L. Gephard & Jno Folger. -BLO(p6)
18 May 1846	Pat^k Morris was married to Catherin Galvin in presence of Tho^S Whelan & Mary Morris.-BLO (p6)
25 May 1846	John Timms was married to Bridg^t Cregan in presence of Ja^S McDonel & M. A. McD_____. -BLO (p6)
16 Jun 1846	Geo Brinker was married to Louisa Landwies in presence of Casp Brinker & Eliz^t Berkman. -BLO (p8)
20 Jun 1846	Henry Messman was married to widow Eliza Sprayer in presence of Jno Wonstreet & Mary L. Landbeck. -BLO (p8)

04 Jul 1846   George M^{C}Kinzie was married to Susanna M^{C}Kinzie in presence of Jno B. Byrne & Margaret Coffey. They were married invalidly years ago by a preacher. Today in 3rd degree of consanganity____, was dispensed & the marriage made good. -BLO (p8)

13 Aug 1846   Thos Mahon was married to Catherine McKinney in presence of Jno Quinn & Ann Riley. -BLO (p8)

11 Sep 1846   Owen Kenedy was married to Eliza Ryan in presence of Tho^S Finney & Sarah Burke. -BLO (p8)

__ Sep 1846   Jno Pembroke was married to _____ Beall in presence of Eli Robison & Ellen Clegget (all negroes). -BLO (p8)

23 Sep 1846   Widower Wm Griffin was married to Catherin Downey in presence of Math^W Coffey & Mr. Davey. -BLO (p10)

24 Sep 1846   John Menner was married to Mary Botker in presence of And Burtken & Mary Brokeman. -BLO (p10)

04 Oct 1846   Geo Hammersmith was married to Maria C. Hamlin, after three publications, in presence of N____ Hart & Elisb^h Piper. -BLO (p10)

13 Oct 1846   Jno Heiltiffer was married to Catherin Prook in presence of Hen Brokeman & Jno Kneiss. -BLO (p10)

16 Oct 1846   Bartley Duneen was married to Maria Jones in presence of Oliver Duffey & Ellen Stapleton. -BLO (p10)

27 Oct 1846   Pat^k Kannaw was married to widow Cath Campbell in presence of Jno Beatty & Mary Brown. -BLO (p10)

30 Oct 1846   Peter Balthames was married to Cath Zilch, after three publications; she a protestant made the usual promises in regard to the rearing of the offspring in the Catholic Religion. Witnesses: widow Kelley & Mrs. Coffey. -BLO (p10)

05 Nov 1846   Mich^l Murry was married to Elisb^h Richmond, unbaptized, who was dispensed of departus cultus & she promised to have the offspring bapt. & brought up in the Cath. Church. Witness Jno Murry & Mary Calvins. -BLO (p12)

17 Nov 1846   Tho^S Richards was married to Ann Rhoney in presence of Jo^S Richards & Susan E. Tippett. -BLO (p12)

30 Nov 1846   Felix Tracy was married to Catherin Murphy in presence of Jno Moran & Ann Murphy. -BLO (p12)

10 Dec 1846   Henry M^{C}Laughlin was married to widow Harriet Heyden in presence of Isaac Starr & Matilda Fectig, he having previously made the promises always extracted of Protestants. -BLO (p12)

26 Dec 1846   John Fitzmorris was married to widow Mary Craley in presence of Matthew & Margaret Coffey. -BLO (p12)

18 Jan 1847   James Beatty was married to Mary McCarty in presence of Chas Kenna & Cath McLaughlin. -BLO (p14)

28 Jan 1847   Baptist Brooks, negro, was married to Charlotte, slave of Dr. O'Donnel in presence of Den^S Graham & Eliz Williams. -BLO (p14)

03 Feb 1847   Frank Laing was married to Johanna Schmeiger in presence of Jos Laing & Mary Schmeiger. -BLO (p14)

21 Mar 1847   Jno Mich^l Lehmeier was married to <u>Nottlunga</u> Ebel in presence of Geo Humel & M. A. Hammersmith. -BLO (p14)

05 Apr 1847   John Boyle was married to Ann Doyle in presence of Margaret Carroll & Levi Rice. -BLO (p14)

13 Apr 1847   James Nevens was married to Marietta Murphy in presence of Mich^l Hamilton & Cath Welsh. -BLO (p14)

15 Apr 1847   Jno Hoop, protestant, was married to Cath^n Heckert in presence of Con Hoop & Mary Landfist, he having promised to have offspring reared Catholic. -BLO (p14)

24 Apr 1847   Mark Mulligan was married to Ellen Kelley in presence of Jno Donlon & Maria Gainer. -BLO (p16)

01 May 1847   Fred^k Laing was married to Mary Laing, by dispensation of the 2nd degree of consanguinity granted by Most Rev. Archbishop, in presence of Jos Laing & Mathew Coffey. The parties had some months since [before] gone before a preacher to contract marriage. -BLO (p16)

05 May 1847   Thomas McGee was married to Elisabeth Noonan in presence of Tho^S Cox & Teresa Healy. -BLO (p16)

11 May 1847   Geo Dowden was married to Mary Logsdon in presence of Geo Hughes & Marg^t Dowden. He being a protestant made the usual promises that the offspring should be brought up Catholics. -BLO (p18)

13 May 1847   Barney Dropper was married to Elizabeth Starman in presence of Mich^l Ryan & Herman Flack. -BLO (p18)

11 Jun 1847   Widower Tho^S Larkin was married to widow Cath Lasalley in presence of <u>Coin^l</u> Raferty & Jane Heaney. -BLO (p18)

29 Jun 1847   Tho^S C. Coulehan was married to M. Amanda Masters in presence of Ja^S McHenry & Martha Masters -BLO (p18)

03 Jul 1847   Martin H. Severs was married to Mary A. Brokeman in presence of Jno H. Brokeman & Sophia <u>Koda.</u> -BLO (p18)

08 Jul 1847	Widower William Murphy was married to Nancy Lanigan in presence of Michael & Mary Tighe. -BLO (p18)
17 Aug 1847	John Morrison was married to Teresa Healy in presence of Hez White & Marg[t] Redmon.-BLO (p20)
30 Oct 1847	Michael Boland was married to Mary Connor in presence of Pat[k] M[c]Cauley & Maria Gainer. -BLO (p20)
31 Oct 1847	Francis Spray was married to Cath M. Shutmiller, after three publications, in presence of Casp Brinker & Cath Wonstreet. -BLO (p20)
14 Nov 1847	Mathew Coffey was married to Mary Vigor in presence of Peter Wombaugh & Cath Vigart. -BLO (p20)
21 Nov 1847	Joseph Hornhost was married to Dina Klosterman in presence of Caspar Rohe & Honor Gerdeman. -BLO (p20)
26 Nov 1847	Joseph Eberly was married to Catherin Herr in presence of Matilda Hein & Peter Poha. -BLO (p22)
22 Feb 1848	James J. M[c]Henry was married to Martha A. Masters in presence of Leo Knott & Catherin Masters. -BLO (p24)
26 Feb 1848	Patrick Mullen was married to Margaret Boyle in presence of Thomas Naughtin & Ann Caton. -BLO (p24)
29 Feb 1848	Robert Hunt was married to widow Margaret Cunningham in presence of Ed McLoorshock & Mrs. Coffey. -BLO (p24)
27 Apr 1848	William Allen was married to Cecilia Daugherty in presence of Peter Carney & Cath Slattery. -BLO (p24)
01 May 1848	Thomas Hogan was married to Ellen M. Lowery in presence of Sam[l] Mattingly & Cath Cushman. -BLO (p24)
07 May 1848	Joseph Wegman was married to Frances Ellott in presence of Dominick Wegman & Mary Brokeman. -BLO (p26)
29 Jun 1848	Dan[l] Gallahey, protestant, was married to Ann Tracy in presence of Tim Norton & Ellen Nolan, after the promises raising the children in the Catholic religion. -BLO (p26)
27 Jul 1848	Mich[l] Donally was married to Maria Lowery in presence of Pat[k] Monahan & Eliza Gainer. -BLO (p26)
13 Sep 1848	Geo McAleer was married to Mary Ann Colvin in presence of Jas Gallon & Ellen Colvin. -BLO (p26)
24 Sep 1848	Louis Lippola was married to Margaret Roth in presence of Peter & Matilda Hine. -BLO (p26)
29 Sep 1848	Bernard Coleman was married to Rosanna Henniger, after made sure the promises exacted of the protestant party, in presence of A. W. Bateler & Margaret Myers. -BLO (p28)

07 Oct 1848	Pat[k] Noland was married to Margaret Gardner in presence of Martin Noland & Mary Noland. -BLO (p28)
22 Oct 1848	Edw[d] Cassidy was married to widow Mary Forrester in presence of Jno M. Holme & Brdg[t] Farrell. -BLO (p28)
22 Oct 1848	Peter Carney was married to Mary Gerrety in presence of Jno Welsh & widow M[c]Laughlin. -BLO (p28)
30 Oct 1848	Jno Connor was married to Josephine Hornbaugh in presence of Jno Hanlen & Mary A. Hornbaugh. -BLO (p28)
20 Nov 1848	Edward M[c]Cormack was married to Mary Quinn in presence of Jno Henley & widow Sarah M[c]Laughlin. -BLO (p30)
21 Nov 1848	Henry Shafer was married to Teresa Deah in presence of George & Elizabeth Smith. -BLO (p30)
21 Nov 1848	John Wonstret was married to Mary Gray in presence of Francis Gray & Catherin Wonstret. -BLO (p30)
10 Dec 1848	John F. Cornecker was married to Elizabeth Messman by Rev. Mr. Krutch in presence of F. M. Gramlick & Ardoy Kebler. -BLO (p30)
17 Dec 1848	Cha[s] M[c]Dermot was married to Ann Plunkett in presence of Zach[a] Shayer & Margaret Kearney. -BLO (p30)
21 Dec 1848	Peter Fitzsimmons was married to widow Cath Slautery in presence of Tho[s] Duffey & Mary Gorrell. -BLO (p32)
01 Jan 1849	Peter Boyle was married to Mary Gorell in presence of James & Ann Carey. -BLO (p32)
03 Jan 1849	Jno Hurley was married to Janetta Cowan, protestant, she made the usual promises to have the offspring bapt. in the Church, in presence of Jno Hoglan & Mary M[c]Cormack. -BLO (p34)
07 Jan 1849	Ezekial White was married to Elenora Noisbaum in presence of Francis Henley & Mary Ann Plowman. -BLO (p34)
09 Jan 1849	Francis Fogman was married to Mary A. Busser in presence of Herman & Mary Berg____. -BLO (p34)
27 Jan 1849	James Noland was married to widow Brdg[t] Maguire in presence of Martin Noland & Cath Wickers. -BLO (p34)
29 Jan 1849	John Madden was married to Mary Larkin in presence of Thos Egan & Mary Ann Plowman. -BLO (p36)
30 Jan 1849	John Mullen was married to Barbara Rerig in presence of Peter Rerig & Gilligan Haictlin. -BLO (p36)

MARRIAGES

19 Feb 1849   Peter Fallon was married to Bridget Murry in presence of Henry McKeon & Mrs. Ja^s Cuningham. -BLO (p36)

19 Feb 1849   Edward Sherin was married to Nancy Gross (Cross?), protestant, who made the usual promises. Wits: Elijah Shambo & Rudolph Caricun. -BLO (p36)

20 Feb 1849   Andrew Rhinehardt was married to Estina Dunner in presence of Wm Gessner & Ann Dunner. -BLO (p36)

10 Mar 1849   Pat^k McKiltuk was married to Catherin O'Rourk in presence of Thos & Mary Ann McGirr. -BLO (p38)

17 Mar 1849   Jos Gegan was married to Catherin Hill in presence of Mrs. Murphy & Mary A. Boxley. -BLO (p38)

18 Mar 1849   James G. McNeir was married to Mary J. Brendt, she making the promises exacted of protestant in presence of J. N. McDay & Susan C. Tippet. -BLO (p38)

29 Mar 1849   Francis Gregory was married to Margaret Moran in presence of Jno Cuningham & Catherin Doyle. -BLO (p38)

10 Apr 1849   Pat^k Kelley was married to Cath O'Brien in presence of Mat^w Coffey & Cath Ryan. In virtue of the Facuties of the Most Archbishop, the dispensation of the 2nd & 3rd degree Mixt of consanguinity was granted. -BLO (p38)

17 Apr 1849   Casper Henry Brinker was married to Louisa M. Schultz in presence of Mathias Brinher & Cath Wicker. -BLO (p40)

22 Apr 1849   Wm P Wood was married to Harriet Smith in presence of Geo La___ & Mary Adelsberger, he having made the promises usually exacted of the protestant party. -BLO (p40)

24 Apr 1849   Jno Wagner was married to Mary Seifton in presence of Herman & Mary Gray. -BLO (p40)

01 May 1849   Fred^k Gerken was married to Rebecca M___bril, unbaptised, in presence of Henry Gerken & Cath Wicker; the impediment Disparitus Cultus was dispensed by the Most Rev. Archbishop. -BLO (p40)

12 May 1849   Hugh Maguire was married to Ann Fultess in presence of Michael Hanlon & Margaret Faulkner. -BLO (p40)

18 May 1849   Patrick Culohna was married to Bridg^t Dillon in presence of Mat Coffey & Sally Dillon. -BLO (p42)

24 May 1849   Robert Caton was married to Mariah Manly in presence of Mich^l Byrne & Cath McGilligan. -BLO (p42)

31 May 1849   Jno Gallaher was married to widow Elizabeth Foy in presence of Andrew Naughtin & Cath Vicker. -BLO (p42)

05 Jun 1849   Mich[l] Riley was married to Mary A. Weaver in presence of Ed Kane & Cath M[c]Laughlin; she made the usual promises of the prot. party. -BLO (p42)

05 Jun 1849   Richard Barret was married to Ellen Gaughen in presence of Cha[s] O'Donnel & Ann Reilly. -BLO (p42)

07 Jun 1849   John Welsh was married to widow Sarah M[c]Laughlin in presence of Jno Cassidy & Mary A. M[c]Aleer. -BLO (p44)

10 Jun 1849   Henry Borgman was married to Sibrina Kenedy in presence of Caspar Kasson & Mary Banley. -BLO (p44)

25 Jul 1849   Tho[s] Kelley was married to Margaret Kenney in presence of Mathew Kenney & Cath Cullen. -BLO (p44)

27 Jul 1849   Timothy Scolley was married to Mary Burke in presence of Michael Fallon & Mary Monahan. -BLO (p44)

19 Aug 1849   Pat[k] Lloyd was married to Mary Reilley in presence of Hugh Dunigan & Eliza Cuningham. -BLO (p44)

08 Sep 1849   Oliver Rhey (unbapt'd) was married to Ann Reilley by dispensation from the Most Rev.'d Archbishop. They had some months ago gone before a prot. preacher to contract marriage in Balt. He made the usual promises. Witnesses: P. J. Cahill & Johana (blank). -BLO (p46)

13 Sep 1849   Jno Callan was married to Ellen Hoffman (protestant) in presence of Leo Cahill & Johanna Melcher. His bride made the usual promises in regard to the baptism & rearing of the offspring in the Cath Religion. -BLO (p46)

25 Sep 1849   Jeremiah Browning was married to Mary Dick in presence of Jno Black & Susan I. Bernard. -BLO (p46)

29 Sep 1849   Pat[k] Gormon was married to Honor Caton in presence of Jno White & Mary A. Kelley. -BLO (p46)

04 Oct 1849   Michael Mulvay was married to Margaret Boland in presence of Martin Mulvay & Margaret _____. -BLO (p48)

14 Oct 1849   Tho[s] Cox was married to Mary Ann M[c]Gir in presence of Michael M[c]Donell & Cath M[c]Laughlin. -BLO (p48)

15 Oct 1849   Widower Mat[w] Coffey was married to Joanna Medler in presence of Jno Burke & Ann Glynn .-BLO (p48)

16 Oct 1849   Geo Griffith was married to Anna E. Cobb (protestant) in presence of Jeffries Maguire & Harriet Griffith. She made the usual promises of a protestant. -BLO (p48)

19 Oct 1849   Hugh Philips was married to Mary M[c]Cusker in presence of James Twigg & Cath M[c]Cusker. -BLO (p48)

MARRIAGES

27 Oct 1849	Martin Flemming was married to Brdg^t Connors in presence of Thomas Lynch & Elizabeth Galvin. -BLO (p50)
29 Oct 1849	Bernard Dolan was married to Margaret McGann in presence of James & Elizabeth Galvin. -BLO (p50)
01 Nov 1849	Widower Benj Barnet was married to widow Mary Brady in presence of Mat^W Coffey & Ann Fox. The protestant party made the usual promises. -BLO (p50)
09 Nov 1849	Michael Ruddy was married to Margaret Sheridan in presence of James Ennis & Cath Welsh. -BLO (p50)
15 Nov 1849	Mathew Kenny was married to Bridget Degnon in presence of Peter Kenny & Alice M^{C}Gir. -BLO (p50)
22 Nov 1849	James M^{C}Menamen was married to Bridget Cain in presence of Jno Cain & Ann Murphy. -BLO (p52)
24 Nov 1849	Zelman Browning was married to Elisabeth Ann Leo (Prot) in presence of B. Mattingly & Mary A. Carter, the bride making the usual promises. -BLO (p52)
08 Dec 1849	Tho^S Reiley was married to widow Mary White in presence of Martin Fartay & Ann Henry. -BLO (p52)
16 Dec 1849	Mich^l Tierney was married to Ellen Hughes in presence of Edw M^{C}Dermot & Ann Heyden. -BLO (p52)
16 Dec 1849	Timothy Reynolds was married to Brdg^t Hughes in presence of Marg^t Hughes & Mich^l Reynolds. -BLO (p52)
28 Dec 1849	William Fynan was married to Mary A. Kelly in presence of Owen Mulvany & Rebecca Sipe. -BLO (p54)
05 Jan 1850	Patrick Wynn was married to Frances Bartell in presence of Ben James & And Noonan. -BLO (p56)
06 Jan 1850	Martin Corcoran was married to widow Ann Dolan in presence of Mich^l Tierney & Mary Hannigan. -BLO (p56)
14 Jan 1850	Mathew Maguire was married to Bridget M^{C}Lain in presence of Pat^K Murphy & Susan G. Tippett. -BLO (p56)
17 Jan 1850	Pat^k Loghan was married to Brdg^t Dillon in presence of Thos M^{C}Neill & Sarah Leonard. -BLO (p56)
17 Jan 1850	Francis Farley was married to Betty Fallon in presence of Jno Fallon & Elisabeth Galvin. -BLO (p56)
17 Jan 1850	Tho^S Holland was married to Margaret Loghan in presence of Ann Kenny & Barley White. -BLO (p58)
26 Jan 1850	Michael Nalon was married to Mary A. Penny in presence of Devon Rhoney & Margaret Penny. -BLO (p58)

71

09 Feb 1850	Thomas Duffy was married to Rose Kelley in presence of Bernard Reynolds & Cath Colvins. -BLO (p58)
12 Feb 1850	Cornelius Sheridan was married to Rosanna Savage in presence of Pat^K Kelley & Mary Madden. -BLO (p58)
21 Feb 1850	William Kane was married to widow Margaret Gannon in presence of Tho^S Garret & Margaret Welsh. -BLO (p58)
15 Mar 1850	William Conklin was married to Bridget Duffy in presence of Pat^K ____ & Mary Carr. -BLO (p60)
18 Mar 1850	John Flanagan was married to Susan Whiteside in presence of John Roach & Ann Mahan.-BLO (p60)
31 Mar 1850	Tho^S O'Day was married to Marg^t Ward in presence of John Coen & Cath Sheridan. -BLO (p60)
11 Apr 1850	James Flynn was married to Ellen Timms in presence of Pat^K Braddock & Brdg^t Dougherty.-BLO (p60)
17 Apr 1850	Widower John Timms was married to Rose Carney in presence of John McDermot & Ellen Murray. -BLO (p60)
23 Apr 1850	Tho^S B. Allen was married to Julia Ann Doolen in presence of Henry Carter & widow Mary Coffey. -BLO (p62)
29 Apr 1850	Henry Brodburn was married to Ann Carnian in presence of William K__ive & Mary __sey. -BLO (p62)
30 Apr 1850	Geo Brown was married to Bridget Dougherty in presence of Pat^K ____ & ____ _aney. -BLO (p62)
19 May 1850	Michael McDonell was married to Catherin McAnarry in presence of Mich^l ____. -BLO (p62)
19 May 1850	Mich^l McAnarry was married to Cath Murray in presence of ____ ____& Mary ____. -BLO (p62)
20 May 1850	James Duncan was married to Ann Gallaher in presence of John Glenn & Cath Gar____. -BLO (p64)
08 Jun 1850	Geo Maloy was married to Cath Souders in presence of Andrew Clarke & Mary Clarke. -BLO (p64)
19 Jun 1850	Mich^l Lyons was married to widow Dolly Condry in presence of Jno Ruddy & Mary Kelley. -BLO (p64)
26 Jun 1850	Richd Horan was married to Cath Stanton in presence of Tho^S Mourey & Magd^a ____. -BLO (p64)
14 Jul 1850	John Hickey was married to Ellen Hickey in presence of Mat Coffey & Elisa ____. -BLO (p64)
17 Jul 1850	Widower And Malloy was married to widow Mary Lavella in presence of Jos ____ & Biddy Barrot. -BLO (p66)

MARRIAGES

17 Jul 1850	John Toole was married to Mary Toole in presence of Martin Auley & Sarah Welsh. -BLO (p66)
20 Jul 1850	Michael Barrot was married to widow Biddy Barrot in presence of Thos Carson & And Carson. -BLO (p66)
24 Jul 1850	Tho^S Reilly was married to Ann Garrity in presence of Ed Clarke & Mary Barrot. -BLO (p66)
15 Aug 1850	Tho^S Raferty was married to Mary Hanagan in presence of Ed M^{C}Dermot & Ann Hager. -BLO (p66)
21 Aug 1850	Edward Flynn was married to Mary Dumphry in presence of Ph Clark & Mary Morris. -BLO (p68)
31 Aug 1850	Patrick Gill was married to Ellen Martin in presence of Pat^k Shehan & Ellen Manning. -BLO (p68)
02 Sep 1850	Pat^k Kean was married to Mary Magadin in presence of Bart^W & Mary Kean. -BLO (p68)
15 Sep 1850	Pat^k Garrity was married to Cath Doyle in presence of Jno Cunningham & Cath Shehan. -BLO (p68)
29 Sep 1850	Widower Ezekiel White was married to Charlotte Herring, protestant, after she made the promises to agree to the offspring to be baptised & brought up in the Cath Church, in presence of Jno Robison & Ann M. Ainsworth .-BLO (p68)
01 Oct 1850	James White, non-catholic, was married to Mary Brown in presence of Jos Hadel & Mary Adelsberger, he having made the usual promises previously .-BLO (p70)
12 Oct 1850	James Carney was married to Cath Cushnagh in presence of Mich^l Carney & Cath Dudson. -BLO (p70)
12 Oct 1850	Henry Carter was married to Cath Clarke in presence of Randal M^{C}Donal & Marg^t Clarke. -BLO (p70)
13 Oct 1850	Mich^l Cannon was married to Ann Hines in presence of James Skally & Bridg^t Tulley. -BLO (p70)
26 Oct 1850	Jeremiah Shane was married to Mary Madden in presence of Pat^k Madden & Sarah Daily. -BLO (p70)
26 Oct 1850	Jno M^{C}Glenn was married to Mary M^{C}Tagua in presence of Ber^d Reynolds & Ann King. -BLO (p72)
01 Nov 1850	Widower Tho^S Gallise was married to Ann M^{C}Cue in presence of Ber^d M^{C}Cusker & Ann Garvey. -BLO (p72)
04 Nov 1850	Darby Carney was married to Ann Milvay in presence of And Ruth & Winifred Carney. -BLO (p72)

07 Nov 1850   Walter Clarke, protestant, was married to Ann Speed, after he made the usual promises, in presence of G .W. Dickerson & Julia Collins.-BLO (p72)

12 Nov 1850   Arthur Bulkee was married to Mary Jane Gallaher in presence of Ber[d] Bulkee & Jane Smith. -BLO (p72)

16 Nov 1850   James O'Neil was married to Margaret Ward in presence of Nich[s] & Catherin Curley. -BLO (p74)

24 Nov 1850   Peter Tierney was married to Cath Sheehin in presence of Peter Hall & Ann Hone. -BLO (p74)

25 Nov 1850   Mich[l] Loghan was married to Ann Noon in presence of Edward Murray & Elizabeth Murphy. -BLO (p74)

11 Dec 1850   Jno Kilgarland was married to Bridget Brennan in presence of Tho[s] Healey & Winfred Tierney. -BLO (p74)

15 Dec 1850   Hugh Lynch was married to Ann E. Wallace in presence of Mich[l] Carney & Ellen Colvin. -BLO (p74)

19 Dec 1850   Peter Bradly was married to Margaret M[c]Mahan in presence of Pet M[c]Mahan & Mary Curren. -BLO (p76)

20 Dec 1850   Mich[l] Nay was married to Mary Solon in presence of Peter Paden & Cath Fallon. -BLO (p76)

26 Dec 1850   Thos Lumbert was married to Mary Collins in presence of Dent Delay & Sarah J. Beal. -BLO (p76)

28 Dec 1850   Ant Moran was married to Ann Martin in presence of Pat Monahan & Ted M[c]Donogh. -BLO (p76)

01 Jan 1851   Claymore Frenke was married to Bernadine Welman in presence of Ant Luhrman & Cath Luhrman. Frenke, being a protestant, made the usual promises to have the offspring bapt & brought up in the Cath. Rel. -BLO (p78)

06 Jan 1851   Tho[s] Williams was married to Ann Glenn in presence of Hugh Manning & Mary M[c]Laughlin. -BLO (p78)

14 Jan 1851   Jno Reiley was married to Catherin Garahan in presence of Tho[s] Faulkner & Joh[a] Coffey. -BLO (p78)

13 Feb 1851   Wm Hussen was married to Bridget Tulley in presence of Pat[k] Moran & Elizabeth Farrell. -BLO (p78)

13 Feb 1851   Geo W Dickerson (protestant) was married to Mary A. Dougherty in presence of Lafayette Stodart & Jane Keaney, after he made the promise to have the offspring baptised & brought up Catholic. -BLO (p78)

15 Feb 1851   Widower M. Cordial was married to widow Marg[t] Gavan in presence of Mary Cusick & Mary Moody. -BLO (p82)

MARRIAGES

04 Mar 1851	Anthony Bohan was married to Mary Lynch in presence of Jno Samon & Cath McGilligan. -BLO (p80)
24 Mar 1851	Michael Mulcrone was married to Mary Havrin in presence of Miles McEnally & Mary Lavale. -BLO (p80)
27 Mar 1851	John Sammon was married to Margaret Donelly in presence of John Lock & Mary Sheridan. -BLO (p80)
04 Apr 1851	Teddy McDonogh was married to Margaret Coffin in presence of Pat Maden & Brdg^t Maden. -BLO (p80)
05 Apr 1851	Andrew Cage, protestant, was married to cogitionery Elizabeth Hutson, who was previously baptised and received into the church. He made the usual promises. Wits: Patrick Stanton & Elisabeth Sherwood. -BLO (p80)
08 Apr 1851	Michael Lyons was married to Mary Maguire in presence of Oliver Lyons & Brdg^t Mahan. -BLO (p82)
21 Apr 1851	John Newell was married to Mary O'Day in presence of Thos Kelley & Cath Lavin. -BLO (p82)
05 May 1851	Martin Meyers was married to Mary Elizabeth Cahill in presence of Peter & Matilda Hine. -BLO (p82)
16 May 1851	Henry Garrigen was married to widow Eleanor Ford in presence of Richd Conly & Mary Murphy. -BLO (p82)
31 May 1851	Martin Flanagan was married to Julia Connell in presence of Richd Barrot & Ellen Cahan. -BLO (p84)
09 Jun 1851	Marcus Doyle was married to Catherin Maher in presence of Thos Byrne & Mary McLaughlin. -BLO (p84)
18 Jun 1851	Thos Mulvay was married to Brdg^t Gilgin in presence of _____ & Mary ___tson. -BLO (p84)
19 Jun 1851	Pat^k Farrell was married to Mary E. Dowling in presence of Francis Murphy & Ann Farrell. -BLO (p84)
22 Jun 1851	William Moore was married to Bridget McQuillan in presence of Pat^k O'Connor & Marg^t Reynolds. (smeared), a protestant, previously made the usual promises exacted of the protestant party. -BLO (p84)
07 Jul 1851	Thos McTag was married to Margaret Lyons in presence of Jno Lyons & Marg^t Welsh. -BLO (p86)
09 Jul 1851	Patrick Kelley was married to Brdg^t Fogherty in presence of Pat^k Quinn & Brdg^t Burke. -BLO (p86)
19 Jul 1851	Dennis Sullivan was married to Ellen Connell in presence of John Madden & Jno Croly. -JBB (p86)

21 Jul 1851   John Malone was married to Julia White in presence of Ed Moran & Ellen Campbell. -JBB (p86)

23 Jul 1851   Pat^k Wetter was married to Cath Fox in presence of Martin Warren & Mary Coghlin. -JBB (p86)

24 Jul 1851   Francis Anakal was married to Christina Ramis in presence of _____. -BLO (p88)

26 Jul 1851   Hugh L. McManus was married to Eleanor Curran in presence of B. Daugherty & Clara Walker. -BLO (p88)

26 Jul 1851   John McManus was married to Clara Walker in presence of Bern^d Daugherty & Ellen McManus (Curran). -BLO (p88)

29 Jul 1851   Thomas E. Ogden, unbaptised, was married to Mary Ann Logsdon, by dispensation __ Disparitycultus from Very Rev. H. B. Coskey, Administrator of the Archbishop, he having previously promised that the offspring should be bapt^d & brought up Catholic; Wits: J. Coulehan & Wilemina Dern. -BLO (p88)

17 Aug 1851   Pat^k McCoffey (?) was married to Catherin McLaughlin in presence of Jno Cassidy & ___ McLaughlin. -BLO (p90)

21 Aug 1851   Mich^l Richards was married to Mary Coyle in presence of Pat^k Horan & Ann Ren__gham. -JBB (p90)

21 Aug 1851   Anthony Shelvin was married to Mary Garraty in presence of Mich^l Staunton & Brdg^t Cosgrove. -JBB (p90)

22 Aug 1851   John Wilson was married to Bridget Welsh in presence of Thos Leahy & Ellen Leahy. -JBB (p90)

26 Aug 1851   Thos Rowley was married to Honora McEnally in presence of J. Gibbons & M Mulhavin. -JBB (p90)

29 Aug 1851   Jas Lalley was married to Bridget Gibbons in presence of John ____ & Mary Malloy. -JBB (p92)

30 Aug 1851   Bern^d Maguire was married to Catherin Murphy in presence of Anty Mathias & Mary Kelly. -JBB (p92)

01 Sep 1851   John Rouard was married to Ellen Bohan in presence of Pat^k Murray & Marg^t McNamara. -JBB (p92)

05 Sep 1851   Michael Rowan was married to Bridget Lavelle in presence of Danl Higgins & Sophia Lavelle. -JBB (p92)

09 Sep 1851   Thos Cain was married to Mary Costello in presence of P. Fallon & Brid Fox .-JBB (p92)

11 Sep 1851   Pat^k Graney was married to Julia King in presence of Jno Rhoney & Mary Mulany. -BLO (p94)

MARRIAGES

| 13 Sep 1851 | And^W Clark was married to Cath Benson in presence of Bartley Joyce & Sarah Welsh. -BLO (p94) |

13 Sep 1851   And^W Clark was married to Cath Benson in presence of Bartley Joyce & Sarah Welsh. -BLO (p94)

13 Sep 1851   Widower F___ J. Darkey was married to Kesia Bird, protestant, after the usual promises, in presence of James Noonan & Susan Carson. -BLO (p94)

13 Sep 1851   Cha^S Murray was married to Fanny Nevins in presence of Jno Murray & Biddy Burke. -BLO (p94)

14 Sep 1851   Tho^S Conroy was married to Mary Graham in presence of Pat^k Winn & Cath Curley. -BLO (p94)

27 Sep 1851   Geo Ed Ways was married to Cath M^{C}Cahan in presence of John D. M^{C}Avoy & Sus Cath Libbit. -JBB (p96)

30 Sep 1851   Mich^l Cain was married to Mary M^{C}Donough in presence of Richd Gibbons & Marg^t M^{C}Anally. -JBB (p96)

01 Oct 1851   Dominick King was married to Mary Leahy in presence of Henry Barret & Mary Marg^t M^{C}Donald. -JBB (p96)

02 Oct 1851   James Brennan was married to Mary Ryan in presence of Thos Byrne & Cath Byrne. -JBB (p96)

03 Oct 1851   Thos Goramy was married to Bridget M^{C}Donald in presence of John McCarty & Ann Robinson. -JBB (p96)

14 Oct 1851   Danl M^{C}Namara was married to Marg^t Bannon in presence of Jas Noonan & Marg^t M^{C}Namara. -JBB (p98)

16 Oct 1851   Pat^k Regan was married to Sarah Coulan in presence of Frank M^{C}Caffrey & Mary Malony. -JBB (p98)

22 Oct 1851   Daniel M^{C}Ginnis was married to Susanna Carson in presence of Jas Noonan & Ann Garvey. -JBB (p98)

25 Oct 1851   Edward Manly was married to Sarah Jane Holmes in presence of Mich^l M^{C}Donough & Alice M^{C}Girr. Sarah Holmes, being protestant, made the usual promises. -JBB (p98)

27 Oct 1851   Thomas Dwyer was married to Marg^t Hevard in presence of Pat^K Daily & Sarah Daily. -JBB (p98)

16 Nov 1851   James M^{C}Donough was married to Sarah Welsh in presence of Pat^K Conolly & Sarah Welsh. -JBB (p100)

17 Nov 1851   John Roan was married to Brd^t M^{C}Mahan in presence of Thos Dugan & Brid^t Rohan. -JBB (p100)

17 Nov 1851   Barth^W Cain was married to Ellen Ryan in presence of Mich^l & Mary Cain. -JBB (p100)

18 Nov 1851   Danl Moran was married to Mary Morrison in presence of M. Morrison & Sarah Daily. -JBB (p100)

28 Nov 1851   Lawrence Leonard was married to Ell McDonald in presence of Pat^k Staunton & Brid^t Leonard. -JBB (p100)

28 Nov 1851   Thos McGraw was married to Brid^t Luhey in presence of Pat^k McHale & Ell Stapleton. -JBB (p102)

01 Dec 1851   James Mulligan was married to Marg^t Breene in presence of Wm Carter & Mary Mulligan. -JBB (p102)

03 Dec 1851   Martin Wall was married to Ell Conway in presence of Wm Downs & Sarah Daily. -JBB (p102)

09 Dec 1851   Pat^k McDunath was married to Mary Murphy in presence of H O'Brien & Brid Leonard. -JBB (p102)

23 Dec 1851   James Flynn was married to Margaret Gilmartin in presence of Thos Welsh & Cath Wynn. -JBB (p102)

27 Dec 1851   Thomas Welsh was married to Mary Monahan in presence of Mich^l Fanning & Seba Burke. -JBB (p104)

28 Dec 1851   John Hodel was married to Amy Twigg in presence of Gus Twigg & Sar Hodel. Amy Twigg, being a protestant, made the usual promises in presence of the witnesses to the marriage. -JBB (p104)

29 Dec 1851   Peter Brennen was married to Cath Wynn in presence of Hu^n O'Brien & Mary Carrol. -JBB (p104)

29 Dec 1851   John Rape was married to Bridgt Ferguson in presence of Pat^k Newbuey & Mary McHee. -JBB (p104)

This completes the marriages through the year 1851.

REGISTER OF BAPTISMS

This listing of baptisms combines material from four separate ledgers into one chronological (by baptismal date) listing in a single format. The actual records are presented in several formats, even tabular in one period, and sometimes misplaced chronologically. Birth dates are presented if they appeared.

01 May 1819	Samuel McKenzie b 11 Apr 1819 s/o John McKenzie & Hanna Tumbleson; Sps: Sam'l McKenzie & Hanna Redmond. -JR (p01)
01 May 1819	Joseph Trimble b about 4 yrs. ago s/o John Trimble and Elizabeth Arnold; Godfather Henry Porter & Godmother Catherine Porter. - JR (p01)
02 May 1819	Peter Clister b 02 Aug 1818 s/o Peter Clister & Anna Arnold; Sps: Samuel McKenzie & Jane McKenzie. - JR (p02)
02 May 1819	Basil McKenzie b 21 Jan 1819 s/o Moses McKenzie & Nancy Logue; Sps: Johnzy Arnold & Sarah Durbin. - JR (p02)
02 May 1819	John Thomas Garlitz b 04 Apr 1819 s/o Christopher Garlitz & Sarah McKenzie; Sps: James Bamber & Mary McKenzie. -JR (p02)
02 May 1819	Caleb McKenzie b 11 Jan 1819 s/o Caleb McKenzie & Margaret Magers; Sps: John McKenzie & Catherine McKenzie.-JR (p02)
02 May 1819	Dominic Blubaugh b 14 Nov 1818 s/o Jacob Blubaugh & Honora Logsdon; Sps: Samuel McKenzie & Annjaminia Blubaugh. -JR (p02)
02 May 1819	Elizabeth Flickinger b 14 Mar 1819 d/o George Flickinger & Esther Arnold; Sps: Moses McKenzie & Sarah McKenzie. -JR (p02)
03 May 1819	George Durbin b 07 Dec 1818 s/o Benjamin Durbin & Mary Waddle; Sps: Samuel Mattingly & Lucy Mattingly. -JR (p02)
03 May 1819	William Zachary Logsdon b 04 Oct 1818 s/o David Logsdon & Nancy Ann Mattingly; Sps: Joseph Logsdon & Hanna Mattingly. -JR (p03)
03 May 1819	John W. Hixonbaugh b 26 Mar 1819 s/o William Hixonbaugh & Catherine McKenzie; Sps: John McKenzie & Anastasia McKenzie. -JR (p03)

79

03 May 1819   Moses McKenzie b 03 Feb 1819 s/o Joshua McKenzie & Elizabeth Winter; Sps: Moses McKenzie & Ellen McKenzie. -JR (p03)

03 May 1819   Margaret Durbin b 01 Feb 1819 d/o Elijah Durbin & Margaret Arnold; Sps: Aaron McKenzie & Mary McKenzie. -JR (p03)

03 May 1819   John Mahawney b 16 Jan 1819 s/o Nathan Mahawney & Milly Pierce (Black people slave of Henry Mattingly); Sps: Stephen Wines & Jane Worth. -JR (p03)

01 Aug 1819   William McKenzie b 15 Feb 1818 s/o Samuel McKenzie & Rachel Durbin; Sps: Daniel McKenzie & Ann McKenzie "Supplied only the ceremonies he being privately baptised by a layman." -JR (p04)

01 Aug 1819   Mary Ann Ridgely b 31 Aug 1818 d/o Eli Ridgely & Eleanor Harding; Sps: Aaron McKenzie & Honora Mattingly. -JR (p04)

03 Nov 1819   Anthony Arnold b 14 Sep 1819 s/o Anthony Arnold & Mary Frost; Sps: Henry Mattingly & Maria Arnold. -JR (p04)

03 Nov 1819   Mary Elizabeth McKenzie b 21 Aug 1819 d/o Samuel McKenzie & Henrietta McKenzie; Sps: John McKenzie & Anastasia McKenzie. -JR (p04)

17 Apr 1820   Francis Logsdon b 11 Dec 1819 s/o Raphael Logsdon & Margaret Arnold; Sps: John Hocton & Frances Logsdon. -JR (p04)

17 Apr 1820   William Porter b 03 Feb 1820 s/o Henry Porter & Lydia Magers; Sps: John Durbin & Honora Mattingly. -JR (p04)

17 Apr 1820   Catherine Blubaugh b 14 Nov 1819 d/o Raphael Blubaugh & Catherine Clites; Sps: John Logsdon & Patience Arnold. -JR (p04)

17 Apr 1820   Rachel Blubaugh b 18 Feb 1820 d/o Stephen Blubaugh & Honora Logsdon; Sps: Joseph Logsdon & Rachel Blubaugh. -JR (p05)

17 Apr 1820   Mary Logsdon b 10 Dec 1819 d/o Edward Logsdon & Jane Mattingly; Sps: Henry Mattingly & Honora Mattingly. -JR (p05)

22 Apr 1820   Josiah Frost b 06 Oct 1819 s/o Meshack Frost & Catherine Magers; Bap. 25 Dec 1820 Sps: Francis Dean & Ann Magers "and supplied the ceremonies 22 Apr 1820". -JR (p05)

BAPTISMS

23 Apr 1820   Henrietta Smith b 29 Jan 1820 d/o Robert Smith & Rachel Johnson the child a slave of Mrs. Frances Bruce; Sps: Stephen Vine & Jenny Worth. -JR (p05)

23 Apr 1820   Ann Isabella Ridgely b 23 Nov 1819 d/o Eli Ridgely & Eleanor Harding; Sps: Jonathan Arnold & wife. -JR (p05)

15 Jul 1820   Mary Blubaugh b 05 May 1820 d/o Jacob Blubaugh & Honora McKenzie; Sps: Nathan Magers & Patience Logsdon. -JR (p05)

03 Dec 1820   Hezekiah Logsdon b 14 Apr 1820 s/o William Logsdon [of Lawrence] & Susanna Williams; Sps: John McKenzie & Maria Arnold. -JR (p05)

09 Dec 1820   Mary Carter b 16 Aug 1820 d/o Richard Carter & Sarah Logsdon; Sps: Raphael Blubaugh & Rachel Blubaugh. -JR (p06)

01 Jun 1821   Juliann Logsdon b 11 Dec 1820 d/o David Logsdon & Nancy Ann Mattingly; Sps: William Logsdon & Honora Mattingly. -JR (p06)

01 Jun 1821   Nathan Mattingly b 13 Apr 1821 s/o John Mattingly & Ann Magers; Sps: Henry Mattingly & Mary Magers. -JR (p06)

01 Jun 1821   Simon Arnold b 23 Jan 1821 s/o Johnzee Arnold & Ann Logsdon; Sps: Jacob Blubaugh & Honora Blubaugh. -JR (p06)

01 Jun 1821   Ann Durbin b 04 Apr 1821 d/o Elijah Durbin & Margaret Arnold; Sps: John Logsdon & Hanna Mattingly. -JR (p06)

01 Jun 1821   Ann Mary McKenzie b 01 Apr 1821 d/o [Joshua] McKenzie & Elizabeth Winter; Sps: John Durbin & Anastasia McKenzie.JR (p06)

02 Jun 1821   Harriet McKenzie b 10 Feb 1821 d/o John McKenzie & Hanna Tumbleson; Sps: Moses McKenzie & Catherine McKenzie. -JR (p06)

02 Jun 1821   Richard Wines, child of color, b 02 Jun 1821 s/o Richard Wines & Dianna Brisco; Sps: Molly Mahawney. -JR (p07)

02 Jun 1821   Jane Durbin b 27 Mar 1821 d/o Benjamin Durbin & Marian Waddle; Sps: John McKenzie & Rachel Blubaugh. -JR (p07)

03 Jun 1821   Joseph Preston b 29 Dec 1820 s/o Peter Preston & Elizabeth Durbin; Sps: [Jessie] McKenzie & Mary Mattingly. -JR (p07)

03 Sep 1821   Helen or Hillary McKenzie b 08 Jul 1821 d/o Moses & Nancy McKenzie; Sp: Honora Mattingly. Baptized by Father Timothy Ryan. (p07)

09 Sep 1821	Mary Sophia a convert 32 yrs of age. - TR (p07)
14 Sep 1821	Mary Jane Hile d/o [Rob Hile] & Margaret Hile; Sps: John Durbin & Margaret Pon -TR (p07)
22 Oct 1821	Mary Anjamina Blubaugh b 29 Aug 1821 d/o Ralph & Catherine Blubaugh; Sp: ?? Blubaugh. -TR (p07)
25 Oct 1821	Rebecca McClay b 25 Mar 1821 d/o Peter & Hanna McClay; Sps: John McKenzie & Mary Krigbaum. -TR (p08)
18 Nov 1821	Rebecca Blubaugh b 20 Oct 1821 d/o Jacob & Honora Blubaugh; Sps: William [Logsdon] & Mary Blubaugh. -TR (p08)
20 Jan 1822	Elinora Maria Ridgely b 01 Mar 1821 d/o Eli & Elinora Ridgely; Sps: Mrs. John Porter & Henry Porter. -TR (p08)
27 Jan 1822	George Sophia 10 yrs Jan 18th s/o Jane Sophia; Sps: Jane, Convert & Mother likewise. -TR (p08)
28 Jan 1822	Jane Porter a convert, woman of color - Michael Porter [maybe a slave of Michael Porter]. -TR (p08)
11 Feb 1822	Billy Hanna, here to for a heathen, 18 years old next May; Sps: Mary Logsdon. -TR (p08)
17 Mar 1822	Henrietta Hixonbaugh b 26 Feb 1822 d/o William & Cath Hixonbaugh; Sps: Anastasia & James McKenzie. -TR (p08)
17 Mar 1822	John Blubaugh b 12 Feb 1822 s/o Stephen & Honora Blubaugh; Sps: Margaret Logsdon. -TR (p08)
17 Mar 1822	Lucinda Porter b 02 Feb 1822 d/o Henry & Olivia [Lydia] Porter; Sps: Lucy Mattingly & Moses McKenzie. -TR (p08)
__ Mar 1822	Joseph, child of color b 26 Nov 1821 s/o ? & Fanny; Sps: Miss Nancy Porter. -TR (p09)
14 Apr 1822	Elizabeth Winter alias McKenzie, a convert -TR (p09)
01 May 1822	Catherine Blubaugh a convert.-TR (p09)
01 May 1822	Rebecca McClay b 25 Mar 1822 d/o Peter & Hanna McClay; Sps: John McKenzie. -TR (p09)
01 May 1822	Thomas Frost b 9 Feb 1822 s/o Mesech [Meshack]& Catherine Frost; Sps: John Mattingly & Mrs. Magers. -TR (p09)
18 May 1822	Elizabeth McKenzie b May 1822 d/o Gabriel & Rachel McKenzie; Sp: [?] Blubaugh. -TR (p09)

18 May 1822	Maurice Durbin b 08 Apr 1822 s/o John & Mary Durbin; Sp: Eli Durbin. -TR (p09)
19 May 1822	Elizabeth Garlitz b 20 Mar 1822 d/o Crosley [Christian] Garlitz & Sarah (McKenzie) Garlitz; Sps: [none listed]. -TR (p09)
28 May 1822	Samuel Basnet in 19th Year of Age, a convert. -TR (p10)
16 Jun 1822	Patrick Alexander Burns b 22 Nov 1821 s/o Father, "name I forget" [Andrew] & Margaret Burns; Sps: Alexander O'Brien & Ann O'Brien. -TR (p10)
20 Aug 1822	Margaret Porter, a convert. -TR (p10)
18 Aug 1822	William Logsdon b 08 Nov 1821 s/o Lawrence & Malinda Logsdon; Sps: William & Susanna Logsdon. -TR (p10)
22 Sep 1822	Honora Logsdon b 29 Jul 1822 d/o David & Nancy Ann Logsdon; Sps: Benjamin Durbin & Miss Mary Mattingly. -TR (p10)
10 Oct 1822	John McClay b 10 ?? s/o Peter & Anna McClay; Sps: T. ? & Mrs. McClay. -TR (p11)
22 Oct 1822	Jacob Lickner b 14 Mar 1815 s/o George & Ester Lickner; Sps: Nathan Majors & Mary McKenzie. -TR (p11)
22 Oct 1822	George Lickner b 16 Sep 1821 s/o George & Ester Lickner; Sps: Ralph Logsdon & Catherine McKenzie. -TR (p11)
17 Nov 1822	Mary Trullinger b 03 Oct 1822 d/o George & Honora Trullinger; Sps: Benjamin Durbin & Anastasia McKenzie. - TR (p11)
08 Dec 1822	Mary Blubaugh b 05 Nov 1822 d/o Benjamin & Honora Blubaugh; Sps: Margaret Logsdon. -TR (p11)
01 Dec 1822	Teresa Ann Logsdon b 07 Oct 1822 d/o John & Patience Logsdon; Sps: Mary Arnold. -TR (p12)
15 Jan 1823	Peoples Durbin b 12 Jan 1823 d/o Elijah & Margaret Durbin; Sps: Patience Logsdon. -TR (p12)
16 Mar 1823	Rachel Durbin b 12 Feb 1823 d/o Ben & Mary Durbin; Sps: Elijah Durbin & Lucy Mattingly. -TR (p12)
17 May 1823	Elinora McKenzie b 29 Mar 1823 d/o Jane McKenzie; Sps: Elinora McKenzie. -TR (p13)
18 May 1823	Mrs. Creamer a convert 24 years of age Sps: T. Ryan. -TR (p13)
18 May 1823	Richard Creamer b 23 Feb 1820 s/o Lucas & Elizabeth Creamer; Sps: [McKenzie]. -TR (p13)

15 Jun 1823	Rachel Porter, a convert, 37 years of age. -TR (p13)
15 Jun 1823	Samuel Smith b 12 Mar 1823 s/o Robert & Rachel Smith; Sps: Mrs. Margaret Logsdon. -TR (p13)
15 Jun 1823	[Felicita] Smith b Jan 1822 d/o Robert & Rachel Smith; Sps: Jane Worth. -TR (p13)
18 Jul 1823	Elinora Garlitz b 02 Jul 1823 d/o Christian & Sarah Garlitz; Sps: Elinora McKenzie. -TR (p13)
20 Jul 1823	John Preston b 04 May 1823 s/o Peter & Elizabeth Preston; Sps: John & wife Margaret McKenzie. -TR (p13)
08 Aug 1823	Dominic Carter b 08 Jul 1823 s/o Richard & Sarah Carter; Sps: Cecilia Mattingly. -TR (p13)
15 Aug 1823	Anna Krigbaum b 22 Jul 1822 d/o Conrad & Priscilla Krigbaum; Sps: Mrs. Krigbaum. -TR (p13)
19 Sep 1823	John McKenzie b 15 May 1823 s/o John & Hanna McKenzie; Sps: Helen McKenzie. -TR (p14)
19 Sep 1823	James Redmond McKenzie b 07 Sep 1823 s/o Gabriel & Rachel McKenzie; Sps: Catherine McKenzie. -TR (p14)
21 Sep 1823	Mary McKenzie b 08 Jan 1823 d/o Daniel & Elizabeth McKenzie; Sps: Mary Mattingly. -TR (p14)
21 Sep 1823	Leo Winters b 08 Oct 1823 s/o John & Easter Winters; Sps: John & Margaret McKenzie. -TR (p14)
21 Sep 1823	Simeon Logsdon b 02 Aug 1823 s/o Edward & Jane Logsdon; Sps: Anna McKenzie & T. Ryan. -TR (p14)
07 Nov 1823	Mary Elisa Mattingly b 05 Nov 1823 d/o John & Nancy Mattingly; Sps: Cecilia Mattingly. -TR (p14)
20 Nov 1823	Mary McKenzie b 14 Oct 1823 d/o John & Margaret McKenzie; Sps: Mary Arnold. -TR (p14)
21 Nov 1823	James Murphy in 23 year of his age, convert. -TR (p15)
22 Nov 1823	Mary Arnold b 28 Jul 1823 d/o Anthony & Mary Arnold; Sps: John & Fanny Logsdon. -TR (p15)
23 Nov 1823	William Logsdon b 23 Oct 1823 s/o Joseph & Mary Logsdon; Sps: Susanna Mattingly & T. Ryan. -TR (p15)
03 Mar 1824	Nancy Clister b 27 Oct 1823 d/o Peter & Nancy Clister; Sp: Margaret Logsdon. -TR (p15)
25 Apr 1824	Rebecca McKenzie b 04 Feb 1824 d/o Moses McKenzie & Marg't Porter; Sps: Mary Porter & Wm Logsdon. -TR (p15)
25 Apr 1824	James Trullinger b 29 Feb 1824 s/o George & Honora Trullinger; Sps: John Durbin & Fanny Logsdon. -TR (p15)

BAPTISMS

25 Apr 1824	Simeon Blubaugh b 24 Mar 1824 s/o Ralph & Catherine Blubaugh; Sps: Peggy Logsdon & Gabriel McKenzie. -TR (p16)
26 Apr 1824	John Carter b 01 Oct 1823 s/o William & Unity Carter; Sps: Cecilia Mattingly. -TR (p16)
26 Apr 1824	Lucy McKenzie b 21 Feb d/o Samuel & Margaret McKenzie; Sps: Lucy Mattingly. -TR (p16)
25 Jul 1824	Catherine Elizabeth Murphy b 24 Jun 1824 d/o James & Mary Murphy; Sps: John & Anastasia McKenzie. -TR (p16)
20 Aug 1824	Sylvester Nathan Frost b 20 Jun 1824 s/o Meshack & Catherine Frost; Sps: Miss Mary Arnold. -TR (p16)
22 Aug 1824	Francis Porter b 24 Jul 1824 s/o Henry & [Lydia] Mary Porter; Sps: Francis Dean & Miss Elizabeth Magers. -TR (p16)
22 Aug 1824	Elizabeth Burns b 25 Jun 1824 d/o Andrew & Margaret Burns; Sps: [Can't read]. -TR (p16)
22 Aug 1824	Honora Durbin b 02 Jul 1824 d/o John & Mary Durbin; Sps: James Durbin & Mary Durbin. -TR (p19)
23 Aug 1824	Mary Caroline Krigbaum b 10 Aug 1824 d/o Conrad & Priscilla Krigbaum; Sps: Mrs. Krigbaum. -TR (p19)
23 Nov 1824	Martha Emilia Ridgely b 09 Nov 1824 d/o Eli & Elinor Ridgely; Sps: Miss Elinor Ridgely & John Mattingly.-TR (p19)
28 Nov 1824	William Blubaugh b 08 Oct 1824 s/o Stephen & Honora Blubaugh; Sps: Mrs. Honora Blubaugh & William Logsdon. -TR (p19)
28 Nov 1824	Miss Baker, convert, in the 19 year of her age. -TR (p19)
22 Jan 1825	Henry Garlitz b 17 Jan 1825 s/o Christian & Sarah Garlitz; Sps: Jane McKenzie. -TR (p19)
30 Jan 1825	Sarah Ann McKenzie b 05 Dec 1823 d/o Jesse & Elisa McKenzie; Sps: Miss Catherine McKenzie. -TR (p20)
31 Jan 1825	Mrs. Mary Logsdon , a convert, bapt this morning -TR (p20)
27 Mar 1825	Adam James Hixonbaugh b 25 Feb 1825 s/o Wm & Catherine Hixonbaugh; Sps: Miss Anastasia McKenzie. -TR (p20)
20 May 1825	Elias Athey b 28 Apr 1823 s/o Bennett & Ruth Athey; Sps: Miss Cecilia Mattingly. -TR (p20)

85

20 May 1825	George Athey b 28 Nov 1824 s/o Bennett & Ruth Athey; Sps: Miss Mary Arnold. -TR (p20)
20 May 1825	Samuel McKenzie b 16 Feb 1825 Gabriel & Rachel McKenzie; Sps: Mary McKenzie & Moses McKenzie. -TR (p20)
22 May 1825	Anna O'Brien b 23 Mar 1825 d/o Daniel & Susanna O'Brien; Sps: Miss Anastasia McKenzie. -TR (p20)
23 May 1825	Margaret Blubaugh b 16 May 1825 d/o Ben & Honora Blubaugh; Sps: Margaret Arnold. -TR (p21)
23 May 1825	Margaret Trimble b 01 May 1820 d/o John & Elizabeth Trimble; Sps: Mrs. Margaret McKenzie -TR (p21)
23 May 1825	Anna Trimble b 03 Mar 1822 s/o John & Elizabeth Trimble; Sps: Mrs. Anna Clister. -TR (p21)
25 May 1825	Jane Frances Jameston b 22 Feb 1825 d/o Samuel & Priscilla Jameston; Sps: Miss Priscella Jameston. -TR (p21)
31 Jul 1825	Anna McKenzie b 09 Apr 1825 d/o John & Anna McKenzie; Sps: Miss Mary McKenzie. -TR (p21)
24 Sep 1825	Henrietta Porter b 12 Jul 1825 d/o Thomas & Nancy Porter; Sps: Miss Maria Porter. -TR (p21)
24 Sep 1825	Rachel Emandy [Amanda?] Porter b 06 Jun 1825 d/o John & Julianna Porter; Sps: Francis Dean. -TR (p21)
28 May 1825	Rachel McKenzie in 30 year of her age -TR (p22)
28 May 1825	Moses Wade b 28 Aug 1817 s/o Henry & Rachel Wade; Sps: Joseph & Priscilla McKenzie. -TR (p22)
28 May 1825	Jesse McKenzie b 05 May 1813 s/o Joe & Nancy McKenzie; Sps: Joseph McKenzie. -TR (p22)
28 May 1825	Sarah [Cora] b 07 Dec 1824 d/o Elias & Nancy Cora; Sps: Priscilla Johnson. -TR (p22)
28 May 1825	Priscilla Jefferys b 03 Feb 1825 d/o John & Margaret Jefferys; Sps: Priscilla Johnson. -TR (p22)
28 May 1825	Anna McKenzie b 29 Jan 1824 d/o Samuel & Rachel McKenzie; Sps: Elizabeth McKenzie. -TR (p22)
28 May 1825	Mary Anna Cora b 07 Dec 1824 d/o Elias & Nancy Cora; Sps: Priscilla Johnson. -TR (p22)
28 May 1825	Catherine Anna Wade b 13 Jun 1823 d/o Henry & Rachel Wade; Sps: Joseph McKenzie. -TR (p22)
02 Dec 1825	William Durbin b 19 Oct 1825 s/o John & Margaret Durbin; Sps: Mr. & Mrs. William Logsdon. -TR (p23)

28 Jan 1826	Henry Blubaugh b 28 Nov 1825 s/o Jacob & Honora Blubaugh; Sps: Johnzee Arnold. -TR (p23)
04 Jan 1826	Daniel Clister b 08 Dec 1825 s/o Peter & Anna Clister; Sps: Miss Catherine Durbin. -TR (p23)
09 Apr 1826	David John Logsdon b 08 Mar 1826 s/o Joseph & Mary Logsdon; Sps: Mr. & Mrs. John Mattingly. -TR (p23)
10 Apr 1826	Anna Mary Winters b 06 Nov 1825 d/o John & Easter Winters; Sps: Miss Mary Arnold. -TR (p23)
11 Apr 1826	Rebecca Ridgely b 11 Mar 1826 d/o Eli & Elinor Ridgely; Sps: Francis Dean. -TR (p23)
14 May 1826	Joseph Logsdon b 19 Apr 1826 s/o John & Patience Logsdon; Sps: Mary Coasson & Joseph Logsdon. -TR (p23)
14 May 1826	James Elias Carter b 14 Mar 1826 s/o William & Unity Carter; Sps: Mrs. John Logsdon. -TR (p24)
14 May 1826	Elizabeth Arnold b 14 Apr 1826 d/o Anthony & Mary Arnold; Sps: Miss Margaret Arnold. -TR (p24)
22 Jul 1826	John McKenzie b 02 Jun 1826 s/o Gabriel & Rachel McKenzie; Sps: Miss Margaret Arnold. -TR (p24)
22 Jul 1826	Lousia Trullinger b 27 Mar 1826 d/o George & Honora; Trullinger Sps: Francis Dean. -TR (p24)
21 Sep 1826	Euphemia Mattingly b 24 Jul 1826 d/o John & Nancy Mattingly; Sps: Francis Dean & Cecilia Mattingly, -TR (p24)
24 Sep 1826	Leonidas Logsdon b 25 Jul 1826 s/o William & Elizabeth Logsdon; Sps: Miss Margaret Arnold. -TR (p24)
24 Sep 1826	Joseph McKenzie b 04 Sep 1826 s/o John & Margaret McKenzie; Sps: Miss Anastasia McKenzie. -TR (p25)
24 Sep 1826	Margaret Burns b 22 May 1826 d/o Andrew & Margaret Burns; Sps: Alex & Miss M. O'Brien. -TR (p25)
24 Sep 1826	Rachel McKenzie b 13 Jun 1826 d/o Samuel & Rachel McKenzie; Sps: Miss Catherine McKenzie. -TR (p25)
27 Sep 1826	Sarah Carter b 01 Sep 1826 d/o Richard & Sarah Carter; Sps: Miss Margaret Arnold. -TR (p25)
28 Sep 1826	James Krigbaum b 09 Aug 1826 s/o Conrad & Priscilla Krigbaum; Sps: Mrs. Krigbaum. -TR (p25)
28 Sep 1826	Mary Jane Smith b 12 Sep 1825 d/o Isaac & Mary Smith; Sps: Mrs. Priscilla Krigbaum. -TR (p25)

01 Dec 1826   Moses Garlitz b 08 Jul 1826 s/o Christian & Sarah [Sally] Garlitz;   Sps: James Mattingly. -TR (p26)

03 Nov 1826   Cecilia Blubaugh b 29 Oct 1826 d/o Ben & Honora Blubaugh; Sps: Miss Cecilia Mattingly. -TR (p26)

08 Mar 1827   Mary McKenzie b 12 Nov 1826 d/o Sam & Margaret McKenzie; Sps: Miss Rebecca McKenzie -TR (p26)

11 Mar 1827   Mary Anna McKenzie b 01 Mar 1826 d/o Moses & Margaret (Porter) McKenzie; Sps: Miss Fanny Arnold. -TR (p26)

07 Mar 1827   Mary Anna Durbin b 05 Mar 1827 d/o John & Margaret Durbin; Sps: Miss Catherine [blank]. -TR (p26)

17 Mar 1827   Ambrose Meshack Frost b 05 Nov 1826 s/o Mesech & Cath Frost; Sps: Ambrose Magers & Miss Fanny Arnold. -TR (p27)

03 Jun 1827   Rebecca McKenzie b 24 Mar 1827 d/o John & Hanna McKenzie; Sps: Miss Rebecca Porter. -TR (p27)

03 Jun 1827   Thomas McGuire b 04 Mar 1825 s/o Thomas & Elizabeth McGuire; Sps: Edward Logsdon. -TR (p27)

03 Jun 1827   Catherine McGuire b 18 Jun 1826 d/o Thomas & Elizabeth McGuire; Sps: Mrs. Edward Logsdon. -TR (p27)

04 Jun 1827   Mary Jane Porter b 21 Feb 1827 d/o Henry & Lydia Porter; Sps: Mr. & Mrs. Dean. -TR (p27)

__ May 1827   _____ Smith b 19 Feb 1827 ?/o Isaac & Mary Smith; Sps: Miss Catherine McKenzie. -TR (p27)

10 Jun 1827   Susanna O'Brien b 05 Mar 1827 d/o Daniel & Susanna O'Brien; Sps: Mrs. John Winters. -TR (p27)

10 Jun 1827   Mary Durbin b 30 Mar 1827 d/o Elijah & Margaret Durbin; Sps: Miss Susanna Mattingly. -TR (p28)

10 Jun 1827   John Troutman in 14th year of his age Sps: Mr. Henry Mattingly. -TR (p28)

11 Jun 1827   George Washington Blubaugh s/o Jacob & Honora Blubaugh; Sps: Miss Mary Arnold. -TR (p28)

11 Aug 1827   Leonard Porter b 19 Feb 1827 s/o John Evan & Elizabeth Porter; Sps: Miss Mary Blubaugh. -TR (p28)

19 Aug 1827   Peter Blubaugh b 10 Jun 1827 s/o Ralph & Catherine Blubaugh; Sps: Mr. & Mrs. John McKenzie. -TR (p28)

19 Aug 1827   Mary Elinor Porter b 15 Jan 1827 d/o John & Julianna Porter; Sps: Mr. & Mrs. Francis Dean. -TR (p28)

BAPTISMS

23 Oct 1827	Thomas McClay b 04 Jul 1827 s/o Peter & Nancy McClay; Sps: Mr. Clifton BeGold. -TR (p29)
31 Oct 1827	Anna Elizabeth Murphy b 09 May 1827 d/o James & Mary Murphy; Sps: Rebecca McKenzie. -TR (p29)
19 Jan 1828	Mrs. Anna Mattingly, wife to James Mattingly, in the 19 year of her age. -TR (p29)
20 Jan 1828	Lucinda Agnes Mattingly b 13 Dec 1827 d/o George & Anna Mattingly; Sps: Miss Mary Mattingly. -TR (p29)
25 Apr 1828	John Mattingly b 24 Dec 1827 s/o Henry & Susanna Mattingly; Sps: Cecilia Mattingly. -TR (p29)
25 Apr 1828	William Mattingly b 20 Jan 1828 s/o James & Anna Mattingly; Sps: Mary Mattingly. -TR (p29)
27 Apr 1828	Taby Jane Crow b 14 Aug 1827 d/o George & Mary Crow; Sps: Mary McKenzie. -TR (p30)
28 Apr 1828	Jacob Ridgely b 11 Apr 1828 s/o Elijah & Nelly [Elinor] Ridgely; Sps: Elisa Ridgely. -TR (p30)
02 May 1828	Leonidas Porter b 10 Dec 1827 s/o Thomas & Nancy Porter; Sps: Mr. John Porter. -TR (p30)
02 May 1828	Josiah [Price] McKenzie b 09 Apr 1828 s/o Moses & Margaret McKenzie; Sps: [Gabriel Mc] Kenzie Porter. -TR (p30)
04 May 1828	Elias Winters b 20 Dec 1827 s/o John & Easter Winters; Sps: Cecilia Mattingly. -TR (p30)
04 May 1828	John Blubaugh b 08 Jan 1828 s/o Benjamin & Honora Blubaugh; Sps: Elizabeth Mattingly. -TR (p30)
04 May 1828	Bernard Joseph Garity b 24 Jan 1828 s/o James & Jane Garity; Sps: Rebecca Porter. -TR (p30)
17 Feb 1828	Ann Lovina Logsdon b 10 Feb 1828 d/o William & Elizabeth Logsdon; Sps: Mrs. John Durbin. -TR (p30)
11 Aug 1828	Joseph Logsdon b Jun 1828 s/o Joseph & Mary Logsdon; Sps: Mr. & Mrs. Francis Dean. -TR (p31)
11 Aug 1828	Julianna O'Brien b Apr d/o Daniel & Susanna O'Brien; Sps: Mrs. Jane Logsdon. -TR (p31)
20 Jan 1829	Emilia McKenzie d/o Gabriel & Rachel McKenzie; Sps: Mrs. Garlitz. -TR (p31)
22 Jan 1829	Henry Kemp b 05 Dec 1828 s/o William & Harietta Kemp; Sps: Honora Mattingly. -TR (p31)

22 Jan 1829	Christopher Mattingly b 08 Jan 1829 s/o James & Anna Mattingly; Sps: Cecilia Mattingly. -TR (p31)
25 Jan 1829	William Timothy O'Brien b 29 Nov 1828 s/o Daniel & Susanna O'Brien; Sps: Charles Mattingly & Julia Timmonds. -TR (p31)
25 Jan 1829	Emilia Sophia Creamer b Jun 1821 colored d/o Elia Creamer; Sps: Elia Mattingly. -TR (p31)
26 Jan 1829	Anna Cordelia Porter b 19 Nov 1828 d/o John & Julianna (Winters) Porter; Sps: Cecilia Mattingly. -TR (p33)
08 May 1829	William Smith b 01 Dec 1828 s/o Isaac or [John] & Mary Smith; Sps: Mrs. Krigbaum. -TR (p32) [See 28 Aug 1831]
09 May 1829	Demetrius Leonidas Krigbaum b 19 Mar 1829 s/o Henry & Fanny Krigbaum; Sps: Fanny Logsdon. -TR (p32)
10 May 1829	[Aaron] Sebastian Murphy , b 28 Feb 1289 s/o James & Mary Murphy; Sps: Miss Anastasia & James McKenzie. -TR (p32)
10 May 1829	Emilia Durbin b 08 Mar 1829 d/o Elijah & Margaret Durbin; Sps: Miss Elizabeth Mattingly & D. Logsdon. -TR (p32)
11 May 1829	Anna Elizabeth Porter b 31 Mar 1829 d/o Henry & Liddy Porter; Sps: Mrs. William Logsdon. -TR (p32)
19 Jul 1829	Leonidas Arnold b 30 Apr 1829 s/o William & Maria Arnold; Sps: Catherine McKenzie.-TR (p32)
19 Jul 1829	Leonidas Dean b 19 Jul 1829 s/o Francis & Mary Dean; Sps: Mrs. John Logsdon. -TR (p33)
19 Jul 1829	William Garlitz b 05 May 1829 s/o Christopher & Sally Garlitz; Sps: Mrs. Sam'l Durbin & Joe Logsdon. -TR (p33)
01 Aug 1829	Rebecca Porter d/o Moses Porter & wife, Emelia; Sps: Cecilia Mattingly. -FXM (p34)
30 Aug 1829	Rachel Ellen Crowe d/o John & Elizabeth Crowe; Sps: Anastasia McKenzie. -TR (p33)
27 Sep 1829	Helen Euphemia McKenzie d/o Samuel McKenzie & Catherine Durbin; Sps: John Durbin & Rebecca McKenzie. -Baptized by Father Francis Xavier Marshall (p34)
25 Oct 1829	Susanna Durbin b 04 Sep 1829 d/o John Durbin & Margaret Logsdon; Sps: Raphael Logsdon & Susanna Durbin. -FXM (p34)
27 Dec 1829	John Porter s/o Thomas & Nancy [Ann] Porter; Sps: Francis Dean & Cecilia Mattingly. -FXM (p34)

BAPTISMS

01 Jan 1830	Joseph Hardy Logsdon s/o John Logsdon & Elizabeth Hardy; Sps: Francis Dean & Mary Dean. -FXM (p34)
03 Jan 1830	Catherine Logsdon s/o William Logsdon & Elizabeth Magers; Sps: Frances & Mary Dean. -FXM (p34)
28 Mar 1830	Ignatius Mattingly s/o James & Hanna Mattingly; Sps: Levi [Marc] & Elizabeth Mattingly. -FXM (p34)
28 Mar 1830	Cecilia Mattingly d/o Henry & Susanna Mattingly; Sps: Baptist Mattingly & Cecilia Mattingly. -FXM (p34)
26 Feb 1830	Ann Hester Winters d/o John & Hester Winters; Sps: Mary McKenzie. -FXM (p35)
26 Feb 1830	Mary Porter d/o Evan & Elizabeth Porter; Sps: Susan Arnold. -FXM (p35)
13 Jun 1830	Ellen Maria Lowry d/o Daniel & Susan Lowry; Sps: William Logsdon & Honora Mattingly. -FXM (p35)
13 Jun 1830	Maria Jane Mattingly d/o George & Mary Ann Mattingly; Sps: Michael Mattingly & Elizabeth Mattingly. -FXM (p35)
30 Jul 1830	Abraham (Illegitimate) s/o of Sarah; Sps: Clotilda, all black. -FXM (p35)
01 Aug 1830	Harriet Elizabeth Porter d/o John & Mary Magdalin Porter; Sps: Elizabeth Porter. -FXM (p35)
26 Sep 1830	Gabriel Porter s/o Moses & Emilia Porter; Sps: Cecilia Mattingly. -FXM (p35)
26 Sep 1830	Gabriel McKenzie s/o Moses & Margaret McKenzie; Sps: Rachel Payne. -FXM (p35)
26 Sep 1830	Susanna Blubaugh d/o Raphael & Catherine Blubaugh; Sps: Mary Dean. -FXM (p35)
10 Dec 1830	Eli Logsdon s/o David & Rebecca Logsdon; Sps: William Arnold & Cecilia Mattingly. -FXM (p36)
10 Dec 1830	Leonard McKenzie s/o James & Mary McKenzie; Sps: John Durbin & Rachel Payne. -FXM (p36)
27 Mar 1831	Lydia McKenzie d/o Gabriel & Rachel McKenzie; Sps: Patience Logsdon. -FXM (p36)
27 Mar 1831	John Durbin s/o Elijah & Margaret Durbin; Sps: Raphael Logsdon & Rachel Payne. -FXM (p36)
31 Mar 1831	Francis Dean s/o Francis & Mary Dean; Sps: Patience Logsdon. -FXM (p36)

04 Apr 1831   Henrietta McKenzie d/o Samuel & Catherine McKenzie; Sps: Charles Mattingly & Honora Durbin. -FXM (p36)

04 Apr 1831   Mary Ann Hannah Sickel; Sps: Francis Dean & Ellen Mattingly. -FXM (p36)

04 Apr 1831   Rachel Crow, conditionally (who says she had been baptized by a Protestant minister). -FXM (p36)

24 Apr 1831   Thomas [Singer] Cross s/o William & Rebecca Cross; Sps: John & Ellen Mattingly. -FXM (p36)

31 Jul 1831   Frederick Crow s/o George & Mary Crow; Sps: Francis & Mary Dean. -FXM (p37)

31 Jul 1831   David (blank) s/o Robert & Rachel; Sps: [maybe] Milly and many other people. -FXM (p37)

28 Aug 1831   (blank) Smith, s/o John & Mary Smith; Sps: Priscilla Krigbaum. -FXM (p37) *(See 08 May 1829)*

25 Sep 1831   Mary Ann Elizabeth Blubaugh d/o Stephen & Honora Blubaugh; Sps: George Blubaugh & Cecilia Mattingly. -FXM (p37)

02 Oct 1831   James Logsdon s/o Archibald Logsdon; Sps: Raphael Logsdon & Fanny Logsdon. -FXM (p37)

02 Oct 1831   Mary Logsdon d/o Archibald Logsdon; Sps: John Logsdon & Ellen Mattingly. -FXM (p37)

23 Nov 1831   Raphael Logsdon s/o John & Patience Logsdon; Sps: Raphael Logsdon & Ellen Mattingly. -FXM (p37)

29 Mar 1832   John William Murphy s/o James & Mary Murphy; Sps: Francis Dean & Susanna Durbin. -FXM (p37)

29 Mar 1832   Jesse McKenzie s/o John & Hanna McKenzie; Sps: Mary Logsdon -FXM. (p37)

29 Mar 1832   Anna Marie Krigbaum d/o Henry & Fanny Krigbaum; Sps: Jeremiah Arnold & Mary Krigbaum. -FXM (p37)

29 Mar 1832   Catherine Logsdon d/o David & Rebecca Logsdon; Sps: Elizabeth Mattingly. -FXM (p38)

29 Mar 1832   Anastasia McKenzie d/o James & Mary McKenzie; Sps: Ann Logsdon. -FXM (p38)

22 Apr 1832   Ambrose Logsdon s/o William & Elizabeth Logsdon; Sps: Ambrose Magers & Susanna Durbin. -FXM (p38)

22 Apr 1832   Francis Logsdon s/o William & Elizabeth Logsdon; Sps: Francis Dean & Mary Dean. -FXM (p38)

BAPTISMS

22 Apr 1832	Joseph Jeremiah Garlitz s/o Soloman & Rebecca Garlitz; Sps: Samuel McKenzie & Mary McKenzie. -FXM (p38)
30 Apr 1832	Ann Fisher adopted d/o Joseph & Sarah Twigg; Sps: Jonathan Arnold & Susanna Durbin. -FXM (p38)
17 Jun 1832	Samuel McKenzie s/o Samuel & Margaret McKenzie; Sps: Jeremiah McKenzie & Honora Durbin. -FXM (p38)
11 Nov 1832	Ambrose McKenzie s/o Gabriel & Rachel McKenzie; Sps: Rachel Payne. -FXM (p38)
19 Nov 1832	Francis McKenzie s/o Samuel B. & Catherine McKenzie; Sps: George Mattingly & Susanna Durbin. -FXM (p38)
	[Records appear to be missing from 19 Nov 1832 through 19 Nov 1836, although the following baptisms are recorded on page 39 along with the arrival of Rev. H. Myers.]
13 Apr 1833	Susanna Dean d/o Francis & Mary Dean; Sps: Honora Durbin. -FXM (p39)
13 Apr 1833	Peter Porter s/o Evan & Elizabeth Porter; Sps: Rachel Payne. -FXM (p39)
20 Jun 1835	William Conrad Krigbaum s/o Henry & Fanny (Arnold) Krigbaum; Sps: Fanny Logsdon. -FXM (p39)
05 Nov 1836	Mary Ann Turner b 26 Oct 1836 d/o Bernard & Rachal Turner; Sps: Ann McGaity & Denis Hoane. -HM (p34)

>>>>>>>>>>>>>>>>>>>>>>>>>>><<<<<<<<<<<<<<<<<<<<<<<<<<

Rev. H. Myers arrived at the Mountain Church 20 Nov 1836

20 Nov 1836	Henry Krigbaum b 18 Sep 1836 s/o Frances & Henry Krigbaum; Sps: Frances Logsdon. -HM (p39)
20 Nov 1836	[W] John Trimbleson b 14 May 1836 s/o Jesse & Ann Trimbleson; Sps: Mary Mattingly. -HM (p39)
20 Nov 1836	Mary Porter b 05 Apr 1836 d/o Ann & Thomas Porter; Sps: Mary Haja (?). -HM (p39)
20 Nov 1836	Sarah Jane Simpson b 23 Jun 1834 d/o Nancy & David Simpson; Sps: E. Carter. -HM (p40)
20 Nov 1836	Catherine Elizabeth Simpson b 03 Jul 1836 d/o Nancy & David Simpson; Sps: Cecilia Arnold. -HM (p40)
20 Nov 1836	Eleanor Logsdon b 21 Aug 1836 d/o Mary & Joseph Logsdon; Sps: E. Mattingly. -HM (p40)
21 Nov 1836	Catherine Porter b 21 Jun 1836 d/o Lydia & Henry Porter; Sps: Honora Durbin. -HM (p40)

12 Jan 1837	James Thomas Mattingly b 29 Dec 1836 s/o James & Ann Mattingly; Godfather: H. Myers. -HM (p40)
12 Jan 1837	Baptist Mattingly b 16 Nov 1835 s/o James & Ann Mattingly; Sps: Cecilia Mattingly. -HM (p40)
	[missing data ?]
01 Mar 1837	Ellen Fealey b 19 Feb 1837 d/o Thomas & Jane Fealey; Sps: Mary Black & H Myers. -HM (p34)
01 Mar 1837	Rebecca Ellen Roberts b 22 Feb 1837 d/o Mary & W. Roberts; Sps: Rebecca Murrey. -HM (p34)
31 Mar 1837	Daniel Brosnahan b 21 Mar 1837 s/o Daniel & Catharine Brosnahan; Sps: Th Fealey & Jane Fealey. -HM (p34)
12 Apr 1837	John George Mullan b 25 Mar 1837 s/o E. & Ann Mullan; Sps: Cath Brown. -HM (p34)
16 Apr 1837	Samuel Garlitz b 14 Apr 1836 s/o Soloman & Rebecca Garlitz; Godmother: Sarah Garlitz. -HM (p40)
29 Apr 1837	Sarah Ann Holtzman b 08 Jan 1834 d/o Augustus & Mary Louisa Holtzman; Sps: Aladdin Lance & Th Marshall. -HM (p 35)
29 Apr 1837	John Thomas Holtzman b 13 Mar 1836 s/o Augustus & Mary Louisa Holtzman; Sps:[illegible]. -HM (p35)
16 Jun 1837	Sarah Ann Porter b 31 Mar 1837 d/o Mary & John Porter; Godmother: F. Logsdon. -HM (p40)
29 Jun 1837	James Walter Donahoe b 30 May 1836 s/o Patrick & Ann Donahoe; Sps: Thom Donahoe & Jane Donahoe. -HM (p34)
29 Jun 1837	James Dicken b 12 Oct 1836 [smeared] s/o Jesse & Mary Dicken; Sps: Thomas W Donahoe. -HM (p34)
29 Jun 1837	Mary Dicken b 23 Oct 1835 d/o Nathan & Judith Dicken; Sps: Pat Donahoe, Ann Donahoe. -HM (p35)
29 Jun 1837	Rebecca Ellen Dicken b 18 May 1837 d/o Nathan & Judith Dicken; Sps: Rebecca Donahoe, Pat Donahoe. -HM (p35)
03 Jul 1837	Mary Martha Kelly d/o James & E. Kelly; Sps Jane Kelly. -HM (p35)
16 Jul 1837	Enoch Winters b 29 May 1836 s/o John & Esther Winters; Sps: Elizabeth Porter. -HM (p40)
15 Aug 1837	Samuel Laurence Mattingly b 09 Aug 1837 s/o Nancy & Baptist Mattingly; Sps: Catharine Mulholand & Mich[l] Mulholand. -HM (p35)

94

BAPTISMS

19 Aug 1837	Anthony Logsdon b 07 Jun 1833 s/o Lawrence & Lendy Logsdon; Sps: Frances Logsdon. -HM (p41)
19 Aug 1837	Moses Logsdon b 23 Sep 1835 s/o Lawrence & Lendy Logsdon; Sps: Frances Logsdon. -HM (p41)
20 Aug 1837	Lucinda Crow b 27 Dec 1835 d/o George & Mary Crow; Sps: Lydia Porter. -HM (p41)
20 Aug 1837	John Percy b 26 May 1837 s/o Douglas & Mary Percy; Sps: Agnes Creggin. -HM (p41)
20 Sep 1837	Alexius Null b 31 Aug 1837 s/o Sarah & Joseph Null; Sps: Rebecca Wilson. -HM (p35)
10 Dec 1837	Bridget McGarity b 05 Dec 1837 d/o B. & Ann McGarity; Sps: John McGarity & Mary McGarity. -HM (p35)
06 Jan 1838	Samuel Ecclaston Holtzman b 13 Nov 1837 s/o Augustus & Mary Louisa Holtzman; Sps: Samuel Marshall & Nancy Marshall. -HM (p35)
11 Feb 1838	Elizabeth Carnay b 24 Jan 1838 d/o Pat & Mary Carnay; Sps: P. Daugherty, _____. -HM (p36)
01 Apr 1838	Johnzee Arnold b 06 Feb 1838 s/o Matila & G. Arnold; Sps: Margaret Logsdon. -HM (p38)
01 Apr 1838	Jacob Harmony b 17 Mar 1838 s/o Henry & Elizabeth Harmony; Sps: Jacob Smucks & Marg^t Rasman. -HM (p35)
11 Apr 1838	Catharine Amelia Mattingly b 15 Feb 1838 d/o Charles & Rachel Mattingly; Sps: Sarah Null. -HM (p36)
11 Apr 1838	Peter Mattingly b 23 Feb 1838 s/o James & Ann Mattingly; Sps: Henry Mattingly. -HM (p41)
11 Apr 1838	Mary Ann Mattingly b 12 Feb 1838 d/o Henry & Christina Mattingly; Sps: Ann Mattingly. -HM (p41)
18 Apr 1838	Mathew Coffey b 14 Apr 1838 s/o Mathew & Eliza Coffey; Sps: Mrs. Blocker, Mich^l Cones. -HM (p36)
20 Apr 1838	Michael Daley b 19 Apr 1838 s/o Anthony & Catharine Daley; Sps: Rosina M. Coffey, Thomas Kiveehan. -HM (p36)
22 Apr 1838	John Dressman b 29 Feb 1838 s/o John & Sally Dressman; Sps: Magdaline Caton & John Hemp. -HM (p37)
22 Apr 1838	Julian Clink b 23 Dec 1837 d/o Valentine & Mary Clink;Sps: Lidia Heyler. -HM (p37)
22 Apr 1838	Mary Donelly b 16 Apr 1838 d/o Hugh & Catharine Donelly; Sps: Dalitia Linch & H. Mulholand. -HM (p37)

95

23 Apr 1838   John Brofield b 21 Apr 1838 s/o Thomas & Sarah Brofield; Sps: Maria Ryan & Pet Mulholand. -HM (p36)

06 May 1838   Peter Miller abt. 9 weeks old s/o Peter & Elizabeth Miller; Sps: Margaret Reirigh. -BSP (p37)

13 May 1838   Johanna McKenzie b 13 Jan 1838 d/o George & Susanna McKenzie; Sps: Aug McKenzie. -BSP (p37)

20 May 1838   Mathew Rulof b 14 May 1838; Sponsor's names forgotten [parents as well]. -HM (p37)

20 May 1838   John Beale b 18 May 1838 s/o Charles & Margaret [Durbin] Beale; Sps: Samuel & Sara Durbin. -Baptized by Father Bertrand S. Piot (p42)

24 May 1838   William Nelson Porter b 25 Mar 1838 s/o John Evan & Elizabeth Porter; Sps: Mathilda Logsdon. -BSP (p42)

27 May 1838   Mary Ann Haganmyers b 17 Nov 1837 d/o Fred'k Haganmeyers & Elizabeth Cremer; Sps: Mary Ann Millman. -BSP (p37)

30 May 1838   Mary Elizabeth Turner b 19 Apr 1838 d/o David & Ellen Turner; Sps: Peter McClaier. -HM (p37)

01 Jun 1838   Mary Louise Krigbaum b 19 Apr 1838 d/o Henry & Frances Krigbaum; Sps: Louisa Swann & Rev. Henry Myers. -HM (p42)

03 Jun 1838   Barny Larkin b 29 May 1838 s/o Thomas & Margaret Larkin; Sps: Barny Monahan & Cath Roddy. -HM (p38)

14 Jun 1838   Peter Samuel Vonstreet b 15 Apr 1838 s/o Henry & Cath Vonstreet; Sps: Peter Rereick & Catherine Messman. -HM (p38)

14 Jun 1838   Eleanor Maria Porter b 21 Apr 1838 d/o Thomas & Nancy Porter; Sps: Honora Durbin. -BSP (p42)

14 Jun 1838   Margaret Dean b 01 Apr 1838 d/o Francis & Mary Dean; Sps: Nancy Arnold. -BSP (p42)

01 Jul 1838   Henry Timothy Mattingly b 1838 s/o George & Mary Ann Mattingly; Sps: Joseph Null & Sarah Null. -HM (p38)

01 Jul 1838   Mary Elizabeth Garlitz b 10 Mar 1838 d/o Solomon & Rebecca Garlitz; Sps: John Garlitz & Catherine McKenzie. BSP (p43)

08 Jul 1838   Enoch Stephen Porter b 04 Aug 1837 s/o Henry & Margaret Porter; Sps: John Mattingly Sr. & Hester Winters. -BSP (p43)

09 Jul 1838   Jacob Allbright b 24 Apr 1837 s/o Daniel & Catharine Allbright; Sps: Henry Mattingly Sr. -HM (p38)

BAPTISMS

16 Jul 1838	Ellen McManus b 13 Jul 1838 d/o Patrick & Rosa McManus; Sps: John McManus & Catharine Harmony. -HM (p38)
18 Jul 1838	Joseph Kuhn b 13 Feb 1838 s/o Joseph and Mary Kuhn; Sps: Josephine Wankel & Jacob Start. -HM (p41)
29 Jul 1838	James Maher b 24 Jul 1838 s/o Pat & Martha Maher; Sps: Mary Silk & John Egan. -HM (p38)
31 Jul 1838	Sarah Ann Catharine Brown b 25 Jun 1838 d/o Henry & Elizabeth Brown; Sps: Catharine Vonstreet. -HM (p38)
31 Jul 1838	Eva Benz b 24 Jul 1838 d/o Adam & Elizabeth Benz; Sps: Jno Bumbaughner. -HM (p39)
31 Jul 1838	Jermius Michael Bean b Nov 1837 s/o John & Mary Bean; Sps: John Levi & Polly Marshall (note: in Virginia added to margin). -BSP (p39)
31 Jul 1838	James William Ryan b 23 Apr 1838 s/o William & Rebecca Ryan; Sps: George Bean & Letty Marshall (note: in Virginia added to margin). -BSP (p39)
02 Aug 1838	Mary Ann Daugherty b 01 Aug 1838 d/o Patrick & Margaret Daugherty; Sps: John & Nancy Kenney. -HM (p39)
04 Aug 1838	Catharine Sachs b 02 Aug 1838 d/o John & Margaret Sachs; Sps: Cath Husan. -HM (p39)
05 Aug 1838	Sebastian Tomlinson b 10 Jun 1838 s/o Jesse & Ann Tomlinson; Sps: Samuel & Sara Durbin. -BSP (p43)
12 Aug 1838	William Carter b 09 Jun 1838 s/o Richard & Margaret Carter; Sps: Elizabeth Carter. -BSP (p43)
15 Aug 1838	Henry Dierich Kulman b 09 Aug 1838 s/o Henry & Mary Adelile Kulman; Sps Henry Dressman & Johanna Schrodek. -HM (p38)
19 Aug 1838	Mary Elizabeth Foglepole b 01 Aug 1838 d/o Henry & Eli'h Foglepole; Sps: Eliz Glick & Ber'd Foglepole. -HM (p39)
21 Aug 1838	Mary Cunningham b 09 Aug 1838 d/o John & Mary Cunningham; Sps: Rosina Martin & James Henry. -HM (p40)
25 Aug 1838	Edward Ryan b 17 Aug 1838 s/o Nathan & Mary Ryan; Sps: Mary McGin, William Welch. -HM (p40)
25 Aug 1838	James Fitzpatrick b 21 Aug 1838 s/o John & Ellen Fitzpatrick; Sps: Sophia Roney & John Fitzpatrick. -HM (p40)

25 Aug 1838	Anna Whelan b 21 Aug 1838 d/o James & Bridget Whelan; Sps: Rosina Martin. -HM (p40)
02 Sep 1838	Samuel George Baker Healy b 16 Aug 1838 s/o Thomas & Emily Healy; Sps: Patrick Healy. -HM (p40)
02 Sep 1838	Anna Clancy b 30 Aug 1838 d/o John & Elizabeth Clancy; Sps: Eliz Brenhan & Pet Mulholand. -HM (p40)
02 Sep 1838	John Lowry b 11 Dec 1837 s/o Robert & Julianna Lowry; Sps: Edward McDonald & Lucinda Porter. -BSP (p43)
09 Sep 1838	Ann Rebecca Logsdon b 23 Jul 1838 d/o Joseph & Mary Logsdon; Sps: Francis Mattingly & Teresa Logsdon. -BSP (p44)
09 Sep 1838	James Francis McMullen b 02 Sep 1838 s/o Laurence & Marg't McMullen; Sps: John Black & Lydia Ann Smith. -HM (p40)
11 Sep 1838	Michael Hevrin b 8 Sep 1838 s/o Andrew and Anna Hevrin; Sps: Thomas Brisco & Bridget Kearny. -HM (p41)
16 Sep 1838	Mary Logsdon b (?), d/o William and Elizabeth Logsdon; Sps: Elizabeth Krigbaum. Ceremonies supplied. -BSP (p41)
18 Sep 1838	Helena Myers b 17 Sep 1838 d/o Peter and Catharine Myers; Sps: Helena Battis & John Battis. -HM (p41)
23 Sep 1838	Thomas Bodam b 13 Sep 1838 s/o Jacob and Margaret Bodam; Sps: Thomas Gallagher & Ann McConnell. -HM (p41)
23 Sep 1838	Peter Maguire b 15 Sep 1838 s/o William & Nancy Maguire; Sps: Patrick Dimond & Catharine Downy. -HM (p42)
24 Sep 1838	Mary Jane M^CGill b 02 May 1837 d/o William & Ann Elizabeth M^CGill; Sps: James Logan & Margaret Hinder. -HM (p42)
24 Sep 1838	Isabella Menking b 14 Sep 1838 d/o John & Mary Menking; Sps: Isabella Daugherty & Anthony Lutman. -HM (p42)
26 Sep 1838	Anna Shummen b 25 Sep 1838 d/o John & Gertrude Shummen; Sps: Anna Quinn & Nicholas Baltis. -HM (p42)
27 Sep 1838	Michael Cain b 26 Sep 1838 s/o John & Debra Cain; Sps: James Cassey & Mary Shannon. -BSP (p42)
02 Oct 1838	Mary Jane Marshall b 22 Sep 1838 d/o Mary & Hanson Marshall; Sps: Polly Marshall. -HM (p43)
03 Oct 1838	Catherine Rivell b 22 Sep 1838 d/o Michael & Mary Rivell; Sps: Elizabeth Farrell & Patrick Carlis. -BSP (p43)

03 Oct 1838	Catherine Muldrony b 02 Oct 1838 d/o James & Cecilia Muldrony; Sps: Frances McCauley & Patrick Rush. -BSP (p43)
04 Oct 1838	Sylvandus Kelly b 25 Jan 1829, Hugh Kelly b 25 Jan 1831, Eliza Kelly b 04 Jan 1834 & Camilla Kelly b 06 Jan 1836, children of David & Susan Kelly, privately bapt. -BSP (p43)
06 Oct 1838	Bridget Coner b 28 Sep 1838 d/o John & Mary Coner; Sps: Mary Downey & Thomas Given. -HM (p43)
07 Oct 1838	Eliza Mary Ann Zury b 14 Sep 1838 d/o Francis & Sophia Zury; Sps: Mrs. Eleanor Mattingly. -BSP (p44)
09 Oct 1838	William Merkle b 06 May 1838 s/o Bernard & Catherine Merkle; Sps: Justina Stoyer. -BSP (p44)
14 Oct 1838	Joseph McKenzie b 26 Jul 1838 s/o Samuel & Margaret McKenzie; Sps: Samuel Durbin & Elizabeth McKenzie. -BSP (p44)
14 Oct 1838	John Coner b 04 Oct 1838 s/o Michael & Catherine Coner; Sps: Cath McCormick & Martin Haw. -HM (p44)
16 Oct 1838	William Peter Burke b 10 Oct 1838 s/o William & Eliza Burke; Sps: Bridget Mulveel & Pete Dillon. -HM (p44)
20 Oct 1838	James Hopkins b 03 Oct 1838 s/o Patrick & Mary Hopkins; Sps: Catherine & James Garahan. -BSP (p44)
20 Oct 1838	Margaret McGonigle b 02 Oct 1838 d/o Cornelius & Bridget McGonigle; Sps: Ann Quigley & Thos Larkin. -HM (p44)
20 Oct 1838	James Brisco b 20 Oct 1838 s/o Michael & Catherine Brisco; Sps: Catherine Quigley & Michael Monnelly. -HM (p44)
21 Oct 1838	Daniel Campbell b 17 Sep 1838 s/o Michael & Rebecca Campbell; Sps: Christopher & Ann McDonald. -HM (p44)
21 Oct 1838	Charles Washington (col^d) b Oct 1837 s/o Neal & Mary, of Mr. Huddleson's, privately bapt. -BSP (p44)
22 Oct 1838	Catharine Smising b 29 Sep 1838 d/o John & Mary Smising; Sps: Catharine Smidth. -HM (p45)
28 Oct 1838	Mary Eliza Victoria Smith b 10 Sep 1838 d/o Leonard & Eliza Smith; Sps: Charles Jenkins & Catharine Smith. -HM (p45)
28 Oct 1838	Teresa Reader (col^d) b 20 Aug 1838 d/o Alexius & Harriet Reader; Sps: Joanna Zeller. -HM (p45)
07 Nov 1838	Eliza Priscilla Porter b 08 May 1838 d/o Emilia & Moses Porter; Sps: Margaret McKenzie. -HM (p45)

11 Nov 1838   Mary Virginia Ervin Coulehan b (blank) d/o James &
               Martha Coulehan; Sps: W. Matthews & Ellen Kearney.
               -HM (p45)

12 Nov 1838   Catharine Lanehoff b 11 Nov 1838 d/o Fred & Margaret
               Lanehoff; Sps: John Shellhouse & Catharine Sneider. -HM
               (p45)

18 Nov 1838   Mary Catharine Rodgers b 07 Nov 1838 d/o Patrick &
               Sarah Rodgers; Sps: Hugh M^{C}Aleer & Mary M^{C}Aleer.
               -HM (p46)

01 Dec 1838   Peter M^{C}Glenn b 26 Oct 1838 s/o James & Margaret
               M^{C}Glenn; Sps: Michael Campbell & Mary Duffy. -HM
               (p46)

13 Dec 1838   Bridget Corboy b 11 Dec 1838 d/o James & Catharine
               Corboy; Sps: Patrick Cronan & Mary M^{C}Cormack. -HM
               (p46)

16 Dec 1838   James Kelly b 27 Nov 1838 s/o William & Mary Kelly;
               Sps: James & Marshall Hindes. -HM (p46)

17 Dec 1838   John Culdy b 17 Dec 1838 s/o John & Margaret Culdy;
               Sps: Mary Melman. -HM (p46)

08 Jan 1839   Patrick Ford b 07 Jan 1839 s/o Owen & Mary Ford;
               Sps: Anthony & Catherine Laughney. -HM (p46)

14 Jan 1839   Susan Ann Catharine Gramkey b 10 Jan 1839 d/o Henry &
               Eliza Gramkey; Sps: Frederick Meimon & Elizabeth
               Brown. -HM (p47)

28 Jan 1839   Henry Edgar Mudd b 12 Dec 1838 s/o Athanesius &
               Priscilla Mudd, at Blooming Rose; Sps: Jeremiah & Mary
               Jamison. -BSP (p47)

03 Feb 1839   Joseph Hipp b 27 Jan 1839 s/o Joseph & Helena Hipp;
               Sps: [none listed, different handwriting]. (p47)

07 Feb 1839   Mary Ann O'Conner b 07 Dec 1838 d/o Arthur & Ann
               O'Conner; Sps: Captn William Welsh & Mrs. Coffee. -HM
               (p47)

08 Feb 1839   Charles Leo b 23 Jan 1839 s/o Thomas & Sarah Leo;
               Sps: Anthony Cain & Catharine M^{C}Cormack. -HM (p47)

09 Feb 1839   John Allegany Warren b [not given] s/o Henry & Rebecca
               Warren, privately bapt., the ceremonies were supplied
               30 Jul 1839; Sps. in the cerm. Mrs. Null -BSP (p48)

10 Feb 1839   John Thomas Coulehan b 04 Feb 1839 s/o W. & Cath
               Coulehan; Sps: James Coulehan & Mary Ann Masters.
               -HM (p47)

17 Feb 1837	Charles Edward Snyder (col^d) b abt. Dec 1837 s/o Betsy Snyder, privately bapt. -BSP (p48)
17 Feb 1839	William Henry (col^d) b 09 Nov 1838 s/o John Paw & Nancy, privately bapt. -BSP (p48)
17 Feb 1839	Christian Kenop b 24 Jan 1839 s/o (blank) Kenop & Barbara Holt; Sps: Christian Waver & Elizabeth Afala. -BSP (p48)
24 Feb 1839	Mintey Ann Lucritia (col^d) b 11 Sep 1838 d/o Polly & Edward, servants of Athanasius Mudd; Sps: Sara, servant of Mr. L. .Smith. -BSP (p48)
24 Feb 1839	Margaret Ann (col^d) b 29 Sep 1838 d/o William & Sarah, servants of Leonard Smith; Sps: Ann of Mr. Smith. -BSP (p48)
24 Feb 1839	Margaret Kart b 07 Jan 1839 d/o Jacob & Barbara Kart; Sps: [blank]. -HM (p49)
25 Feb 1839	John McDonald b 25 Feb 1839 s/o Christopher & Nancy McDonald; Sps: James Riley & Catharine Dumire. -HM (p49)
01 Mar 1839	Mary Alice Sweeney b 23 Feb 1839 d/o Ed & Cath Sweeney; Sps: Phil & Bridget McDonald. -HM (p49)
02 Mar 1839	Anna Josephine Wankle b 05 Feb 1839 d/o Peter & Cath Wankle; Sps: Josephine Wankle. -HM (p49)
02 Mar 1839	John Charles Augustus Rosenberger b 30 Aug 1838 s/o John & Magdalen Rosenberger; Sps: Josephine Wankle. -HM (p49)
05 Mar 1839	John Callahan b 28 Feb 1839 s/o John & Ann Callahan; Sps: Pat O'Rouke & Bridget McGlenn. -HM (p49)
08 Mar 1839	Agnes Caroline Poste b 01 Mar 1839 d/o Yorick & Elizabeth Poste; Sps: Agnes Will. -HM (p50)
08 Mar 1839	Caroline Will b 03 Feb 1839 d/o Phillip & Agnes Will; Sps: Caroline Will. -HM (p50)
16 Mar 1839	Margaret Maher b 25 Dec 1838 d/o John & Ann Maher; Sps: Michael Kelly & his wife. -BSP (p50)
17 Mar 1839	William Henry Robinson b 30 Dec 1838 s/o Solomon & Ellen Robinson; Sps: Elizabeth McKenzie. -HM (p50)
17 Mar 1839	James McGowan b 19 Feb 1839 s/o James & Catharine McGowan; Sps: Ellen Fitzpatrick. -HM (p50)
21 Mar 1839	John Harkin b 20 Mar 1839 s/o Joseph & Nelly Harkin; Sps: Michael Linnehan & Mary Connody. -BSP (p50)

23 Mar 1839   Isabella Brady b 01 Mar 1839 d/o James & Margaret Brady; Sps: John Cannay & Cath Callahan. -HM (p51)

24 Mar 1839   Richard (col^d) abt. 4 mo old s/o Wallace, servant of Mr. Coddington @ Blooming Rose; Sps: [blank]. -BSP (p51)

28 Mar 1839   Joseph Wombhar b 23 Mar 1839 s/o John & Effa Wombhar; Sps: Nora David. -BSP (p51)

01 Apr 1839   Catharine Sible b 03 Apr 1837 d/o John & Gertrude Sible; Sps: Valentine Helfree & Catharine Helfree. -BSP (p51)

03 Apr 1839   Mary Ellen Kearney b 30 Mar 1839 d/o [blank] & Mary Kearney; Sps: Ellen Carroll. -BSP (p51)

03 Apr 1839   Catharine Mary Boyer b 30 Mar 1839 d/o Francis & Cunegunda Boyer; Sps: Cath Margaret Hoffman. -HM (p52)

03 Apr 1839   John Henry Wagoner b 29 Jan 1839 s/o Francis & Catharine Wagoner; Sps: John Havercamp & Margaret Schrhaff. -HM (p52)

14 Apr 1839   Thomas Hagan b 11 Apr 1839 s/o Hugh & Bridget Hagan; Sps: Edward Duffey & Cath Murray. -HM (p52)

21 Apr 1839   John Mulcahil b 20 Apr 1839 s/o John & Bridget Mulcahil; Sps: Matthew McCormick & Catharine Corboy. -BSP (p52)

23 Apr 1839   Rebecca Jane Garlitz b 02 Mar 1839 d/o Solomon & Rebecca Garlitz; Sps: Basil McKenzie & Jane Getty. -BSP (p45)

25 Apr 1839   Catharine Eliza Dougherty b 17 Apr 1839 d/o John & Mary Dougherty; Sps: Ed Harkins & Cath Sweeney. -HM (p52)

02 May 1839   Patrick Barrett b 29 Apr 1839 s/o widow Margaret Barrett, having lately lost her husband; Sps: Sally Colby. -HM (p52)

05 May 1839   Barbara Baltis b 25 Apr 1839 d/o John & Catharine Baltis; Sps: Peter Myers & Barbara Snueun. -HM (p53)

05 May 1839   Catharine Hendle b 07 Feb 1839 d/o Henry & Catherine Hendle; Sps: Francis Paulus & Catharine Willy. -HM (p53)

05 May 1839   Anna Leidemen b 02 Apr 1839 d/o Nicholas & Barbara Leidemen; Sps: John Baltis & Anna Snueun. -HM (p53)

05 May 1839   Mary Goulden b 30 Apr 1839 d/o Michael & Mary Goulden; Sps: John Manley & Mary Ford. -HM (p53)

09 May 1839   Ambrose Porter b 02 Feb 1839 s/o Henry M. & Lydia Porter; Sps: Mary Elizabeth Mattingly & Francis Mattingly. -BSP (p44)

09 May 1839	James Washington Porter b 08 Mar 1839 s/o John & Lana Porter; Sps: Mathilda Logsdon. -BSP (p45)
09 May 1839	Mary Veger b 30 Apr 1839 d/o [blank] Veger & Mary, his wife; Sps: Mary Backvout. -BSP (p45)
13 May 1839	Mary Ricker b 06 Apr 1839 d/o John & Mary Ricker; Sps: Mary Buckholtz. -HM (p45)
13 May 1839	Samuel Merkle b 23 Feb 1839 s/o Leopold & Elizabeth Merkle; Sps: Joseph & Christina Staube. -HM (p45)
13 May 1839	Francis Joseph Staube b 29 Jan 1839 s/o Joseph & Christina Staube; Sps: Leopold & Elizabeth Merkle. -HM (p45)
17 May 1839	Susan Logsdon b 02 Aug 1838 d/o Larence (sic) & Linda Logsdon; Sps: Polly Mattingly. -HM (p53)
19 May 1839	Peter Smith born middle of Nov 1838 s/o Tho^S & Susan Smith; Sps: Tho^S McGirr & Mary A. Smith. -HM (p53)
19 May 1839	Mary Ann Egan b 20 Apr 1839 d/o Patrick & Mary Egan; Sps: J^S Murphey & Ellen Callan. -HM (p54)
20 May 1839	Margaret Riley b 15 May 1839 d/o Judah & David Riley; Sps: John M^{C}Namara & Bridget Tuey. -HM (p54)
20 May 1839	Catharine M^{C}Girr b 17 May 1839 d/o Thomas & Mary M^{C}Girr; Sps: Ed Mullan & Cath Brown. -HM (p54)
24 May 1839	John Koin b 21 May 1839 s/o Pat & Cath Koin; Sps: Thomas Hevrin & Mary Ruddy. -HM (p54)
24 May 1839	Michael Carlis b 20 May 1839 s/o Pat & Elizabeth Carlis; Sps: Patrick Farrel & Mary Kululy. -HM (p54)
26 May 1839	Adam Keler b 01 Jan 1834 [or 1839] s/o Peter & Rosina Keler; Sps: Adam Roman. -HM (p55)
26 May 1839	Catharine Keler b 11 May 1836 d/o Peter & Rosina Keler; Sps: Catharine Roman. -HM (p55)
26 May 1839	John Horne b 25 [May] 1839 s/o Patrick & Mary Horne; Sps: Michael Horne & Sarah Conway. -HM (p55)
02 Jun 1839	John M^{C}Dermott b 15 May 1839 illeg. s/o Thomas & Mary M^{C}Dermott; Sps: James Reed & Margaret Muller. -HM (p55)
02 Jun 1839	John Durbin b 27 Apr 1839 s/o John & Margaret Durbin; Sps: George & Honora Durbin. -BSP (p46)
02 Jun 1839	Joseph Arnold b 10 May 1839 s/o Anthony & Margaret Arnold; Sps: Cecilia Mattingly. -BSP (p46)

09 Jun 1839   Joseph Aaron Coleman b 21 Aug 1838 s/o William & Eleanor Elizabeth Coleman; Sps: F. Mattingly & Mrs. F. Krigbaum (He was privately baptized by Mrs. Hixonbaugh towards the end of Oct 1838.) -BSP (p46)

09 Jun 1839   Catherine Dowd b 06 Jun 1839 d/o Patrick & Rosa Dowd; Sps: John McKale & Elizabeth Neuman. -HM (p55)

16 Jun 1839   John William McKenzie b 16 Mar 1839 s/o George & Susan McKenzie, bapt. privately in April last, ceremonies were supplied; Sps. at cerm: Ann Mary McKenzie. -BSP (p56)

23 Jun 1839   William Graham (col^d) b 1838 s/o Charles, servant of L. Smith, & Hetty, servant of Peter McClery -BSP (p56)

23 Jun 1839   Harriet (col^d) b Feb 1833 d/o Charles & Hetty above. -BSP (p56)

30 Jun 1839   Hanna Cavenaugh b 21 Jun 1839 d/o Charles & Rosey Cavenaugh; Sps: John Cornelius & Rosann Slavin. -BSP (p56)

06 Jul 1839   Mary Garlitz aged 16 years, d/o [blank], a convert. (Baptized privately). -BSP (p46)

06 Jul 1839   William Garlitz b 06 May 1839 s/o Samuel & Susan Garlitz; Sps: Leo McKenzie & Rebecca Garlitz. -BSP (p46)

06 Jul 1839   John Leonard Nefzker b 27 Apr 1839 s/o Michael & Catharine Nefzker; Sps: D. Frotz. -HM (p56)

07 Jul 1839   William Henry Hashbyer b 07 Apr 1839 s/o John & Mary Hashbyer; Sps: William Ryan & Mary Ryan. -HM (p56)

07 Jul 1839   James Shannon b 04 Jul 1839 s/o John & Mary Shannon; Sps: John Kitson & Nancy Hurley. -HM (p57)

07 Jul 1839   Adam Sebastian Gramlick b 01 Jul 1839 s/o Sebastian & Elizabeth Gramlick; Sps: Adam Moud & Teresa Moud. -HM (p57)

11 Jul 1839   John Carr b 05 Jul 1839 s/o James & Mary Carr; Sps: Patrick Meloy & Mary Burgess. -HM (p57)

14 Jul 1839   John Simpson b 08 May 1839 s/o David & Nancy Simpson; Sps: Mrs. Margaret Durbin. -BSP (p46)

16 Jul 1839   Harman Bernard Fullenkamp b 14 Jul 1839 s/o Henry & Mary Catharine Fullenkamp; Sps: Harman Bernard Droppek. -BSP (p57)

17 Jul 1839   Anna Nancy Mullan b 30 May 1839 d/o Anna & Edward Mullan; Sps: B. S. Piot & Anna Brown. -BSP (p57)

18 Jul 1839	John Deacon b 09 Jul 1834 [or 1839] s/o Nathan & Judith Deacon; Sps: Michael Kelly & Mary Deacon. -HM (p58)
18 Jul 1839	William Donahoe b 18 Jul 1839 (this day) s/o Patrick & Ann Donahoe; Sps: Rev. H. Myers & Jane Donahoe. -HM (p58)
19 Jul 1839	Anna Langman b 14 Jul 1839 d/o Michael & Mary Langman; Sps: Patrick Daley & Catharine Brisco. -HM (p58)
21 Jul 1839	Mary Pluck b 31 Mar 1839 d/o Joseph & Mary Pluck; Sps: Mary Melmon. -HM (p58)
22 Jul 1839	Catharine Fisher b 18 Jun 1839 d/o Joseph & Catharine Fisher; Sps: Catharine Brown. -HM (p58)
27 Jul 1839	Mary Ann Burkman b 16 Jul 1839 d/o Gerard & Margaret Burkman; Sps: Catharine Dierkes. -HM (p58)
27 Jul 1839	Patrick Henigan b 08 Jul 1839 s/o Bartholomy & Margaret Henigan; Sps: John Garvey & Bridget McNulty. -HM (p59)
28 Jul 1839	Thomas Byrns b 25 Jul 1839 s/o Patrick & Marcella Byrns; Sps: John Brady & Ann Newman. -HM (p59)
28 Jul 1839	Mary Jane Duffey b 25 Jul 1839 d/o William & Mary Duffey; Sps: Patrick Ward & Jane McNulty. -HM (p59)
28 Jul 1839	Anthony Rickman b 25 Jul 1839 s/o Henry & Elizabeth Rickman; Sps: Cath Dierkes. -HM (p59)
29 Jul 1839	Catharine Wina Gayner b 29 Jul 1839 d/o William & Elizabeth Gayner; Sps: Pat Landrigan & Bridget Murray. -HM (p59)
31 Jul 1839	James Britt b 07 Jul 1839 d/o John & Winefred Britt; Sps: James Corboy & Margaret McNulty. -HM (p59)
04 Aug 1839	James Francis Bisel b 03 Jul 1839 s/o Henry John & Anna Bisel; Sps: Henry & Frances Kreighbaum. -HM (p60)
11 Aug 1839	Mary Larkins b 04 Aug 1839 d/o Thomas & Margaret Larkins; Sps: Patrick Mooney & Bridget Conelly. -HM (p60)
11 Aug 1839	Johanna O'Brian b 10 Aug 1839 d/o Patrick & Ellen O'Brian; Sps: Anthony Cain & Ellen Atkins. -HM (p60)
11 Aug 1839	Lord Ervin [or Ewing] Francis Rice b 09 Feb 1839 s/o William & Barbara Rice; Sps: James Gorney & Julia Riley. -HM (p60)

11 Aug 1839   Samuel Charles Logsdon b 21 Jul 1839 s/o Raphael & Rebecca Logsdon; Bap 26 Jul 1839 by Cecilia Mattingly. (Fr. Poit supplied the ceremony 11 Aug 1839 with Cecilia Mattingly as sponsor.) -BSP (p47)

13 Aug 1839   Michael Henney b 09 Aug 1839 s/o Pat & Margaret Henney; Sps: Henry Fox & Bridget Whelan. -HM (p60)

15 Aug 1839   Margaret Karman b 09 Jul 1839 d/o Henry & Elizabeth Karmen; Sps: Adam Mead & Margaret Karman. -HM (p60)

24 Aug 1839   John Joseph Priel b 28 Jul 1839 s/o Conrad & Margaret Priel; Sps: John Hedrick & Joseph[a] Wungle. -BSP (p61)

30 Aug 1839   John Henry Brown born today [30 Aug 1839] s/o Henry & Elizabeth Brown, privately bapt. Sps: Catharine Vonstreet. -BSP (p61)

30 Aug 1839   Abner Ravenscraft age abt. 21, convert, was bapt. conditionally. -BSP (p61)

01 Sep 1839   Moses Wade b 28 Sep 1838 s/o Isaiah & Susan Wade, cerm. of baptism supplied; Sps: Ann Mary M[c]Kenzie. -BSP (p81)

05 Sep 1839   Anna Leidingner b 02 Sep 1839 d/o Nicholas & Barbara Leidingner; Sps: John Baltis & Anna [illegible].-HM (p61)

06 Sep 1839   Nicholas Baltis b 26 Aug 1839 s/o John & Catharine Baltis; Sps: Nicholas Baltis & Catharine Cliser. -HM (p61).

08 Sep 1839   Daniel Burke b 25 Aug 1839 s/o Eulick & Mary Burke; Sps: Patrick Brown & Margaret Brown. -HM (p62)

08 Sep 1839   John Francis Klink b 22 Aug 1839 s/o Windlein & Mary Klink; Sps: John Rickert. -BSP (p47)

09 Sep 1839   Mary Parker b 01 Aug 1839 d/o William & Ellen Parker; Sps: Robert Loftus & Mary Welsh. -HM (p62)

09 Sep 1839   Elizabeth Egan b 25 Aug 1839 d/o Peter & Catharine Egan; Sps: Pat M[c]Cauley & Ann Cullam. -HM (p62)

10 Sep 1839   Anna Barbara Schiffendecker b 30 Jul 1839 d/o Joseph & Teresa Schiffendecker; Sps: Mary Ann Schiffendecker. -HM (p62)

16 Sep 1839   Bridget Helena M[c]Cana b 19 Aug 1839 d/o Hugh & Ann M[c]Cana; Sps: John Flannigan & Mary Byrns. -HM (p62)

20 Sep 1839   John Joseph Hemer b 10 Sep 1839 s/o Adam & Elizabeth Hemer; Sps: John Joseph Pedrey & Anna Pedrey. -HM (p62)

21 Sep 1839   Michael Loftus b 19 Sep 1839 s/o John & Rosa Ellen Loftus; Sps: Pat Monahan & Juda Barrett. -HM (p63)

22 Sep 1839	Patrick Flynn b 13 Aug 1839 s/o John & Margaret Flynn; Sps: John Kearney & Mary Kearney. -HM (p63)
23 Sep 1839	Mary Ryan b 18 Sep 1839 d/o Michael & Margaret Ryan; Sps: Daniel Kain & Mary Burke. -HM (p63)
23 Sep 1839	Joseph Henry Plagman b 22 Aug 1839 s/o Joseph & Mary Plagman; Sps: Gerard Henry Remphe & Elizabeth Cross. -HM (p63)
26 Sep 1839	Ann M^{C}Donald b 25 Sep 1839 d/o Patrick & Jane M^{C}Donald; Sps: Anthony Monigan & Nelly Kevrin. -BSP (p63)
29 Sep 1839	Sara Catharine M^{C}Intire b 22 Sep 1839 d/o Owen M^{C}Intire (lately deceased) and Salley M^{C}Intire; Sps: James Riley & Rosanna Curnor. -BSP (p63)
29 Sep 1839	John Thomas Brown b 24 Aug 1839 s/o Charles & Latitia Brown, residing in Virginia; Sps: Aug Holtzman & Nancy Marshall. -HM (p64)
12 Oct 1839	Elizabeth Schrem b 06 Oct 1839 d/o Caspar & Elizabeth Schrem; Sps: Christian Weaver & Elizabeth Rode. -HM (p64)
13 Oct 1839	Joseph Helmsteder b 25 Sep 1839 s/o Francis & Thiela Helmsteder; Sps: Joseph Zeller. -HM (p64)
13 Oct 1839	John Fuller b 14 Aug 1839 s/o Michael & Susan Fuller; Sps: Daniel Cassidy & Sophia Rooney. **The day of the Ded^n of the Church.** -HM (p64)
16 Oct 1839	Mary Eliza Null b 30 Sep 1839 d/o Joseph & Sarah Null; Sps: Elizabeth Carter. -HM (p64)
20 Oct 1839	William Henry Fisher (col^d) b last June, s/o Samuel & Eleanor Fisher bapt. privately, the mother belongs to Mr. Worthington; Sps: Sophy Faulett. -BSP (p64) The Ceremonies of bapt. were supplied to this child 02 Aug 1840 Sps: M. Coffee. -HM (p64)
21 Oct 1839	Anna Burke b 20 Oct 1839 d/o James & Mary Burke; Sps: Philip Hussey & Clara Murray. -HM (p65)
21 Oct 1839	Carolina Baughman b 03 Oct 1839 d/o Nicholas & Elizabeth Baughman; Sps: Margaret Dierke. -HM (p65)
21 Oct 1839	Gerard William Melman b 19 Oct 1839 s/o Henry [or Harry] & Mary Melman; Sps: Anna Maria Brokeman & William Lutman. -HM (p65)
27 Oct 1839	Elenor Jane M^{C}Neer b 07 Nov 1838 d/o Andrew & Catherine M^{C}Neer, at Blooming Rose; Sps: Catherine Smith. -BSP (p65)

27 Oct 1839	Catharine Casey b 14 Oct 1839 d/o John & Mary Casey; Sps: Francis Higgins & Mary McCavoy. -HM (p65)

27 Oct 1839 Catharine Casey b 14 Oct 1839 d/o John & Mary Casey; Sps: Francis Higgins & Mary McCavoy. -HM (p65)

30 Oct 1839 Joseph Misal b 29 Oct 1839 s/o John & Barbara Misal; Sps: Joseph Brutterk & Catharine Brutterk. -HM (p65)

01 Nov 1839 Domonic Arnold b 31 Aug 1839 s/o Joseph & Matilda Arnold; Sps: Bapt Mattingly & Margaret Speelman. -HM (p66)

01 Nov 1839 James Kivlahan b 26 Oct 1839 s/o Thomas & Mary Kivlahan; Sps: Darboy Clark & Sarah Ryan. -HM (p66)

03 Nov 1839 Catharine Clancy b 09 Oct 1839 d/o John & Elizabeth Clancy; Sps: Patrick Cronon & Mary Vonstreet. -HM (p66)

03 Nov 1839 Julian Rereick b 09 Oct 1839 d/o Peter & Anna Margarita Rereick; Sps: Julian Rereick. -HM (p66)

06 Nov 1839 Joseph Aloysius Kelly b 04 Nov 1839 s/o Patrick & Mary Jane Kelly; Sps: Catharine Brazil. -HM (p66)

08 Nov 1839 Mary Aloysia Cross b 22 Oct 1839 d/o William & Elizabeth Cross; Sps: Henry Vercamp & Mary Anna Neman. -HM (p66)

25 Nov 1839 Michael Cain b 09 Nov 1839 s/o Thomas & Bridget Cain; Sps: Michael Hanigan & Bridget Muligan. -HM (p67)

05 Dec 1839 Adam Anthony Petre' b 03 Dec 1839 s/o Joseph & Anna Petre'; Sps: Adam Hammer & Elizabeth Hammer. -HM (p67)

05 Dec 1839 Nicholas Rereick b 19 May 1839 illeg. s/o Peter & Margaret Rereick; Sps: Nicholas Bereat. -HM (p67)

15 Dec 1839 Bernard Henry Helfrick b 29 Nov 1839 s/o Valentine & Eve Catharine Helfrick; Sps: Bernard Henry & Anna Maria Sumer. -HM (p67)

24 Dec 1839 Francis John Black b 22 Dec 1839 s/o John & Lydia Ann Black; Sps: E. Mullar & Mrs. Mary Smith. -HM (p67)

02 Jan 1840 Patrick Paddon b 26 Dec 1839 s/o John & Bridget Paddon; Sps: James Scanlan & Ellen Lavell. -HM (p67)

08 Jan 1840 Mary Coffey b 05 Jan 1840 d/o Mathew & Eliza Coffey; Sps: John Mulcahey & Mary O'Brian. -HM (p68)

09 Jan 1840 Mathew Ryan b 06 Jan 1840 s/o William & Mary Ryan; Sps: John Welsh & Caroline Mary McGee.-HM (p68)

18 Jan 1840 John Edward McIntire b 17 Dec 1839 illeg s/o Mary Jane McIntire; Sps: Alice McIntire & John McIntire. -HM (p68)

BAPTISMS

24 Jan 1840	Peter Farrell b 19 Jan 1840 s/o John & Ann Farrell; Sps: Andrew Conlon & Mary Conlon. -HM (p68)
27 Jan 1840	Bridget M^CCann b 02 Jan 1840 s/o Barney & Bridget M^CCann; Sps: Lawrence Mathews & Eliza Brown. -HM (p68)
27 Jan 1840	Mary Ann Murphey b 16 Jan 1840 d/o John & Rosa Murphey; Sps: Ed Gilney & Ann Brown. -HM (p68)
02 Feb 1840	John Kerdman b 05 Jan 1840 s/o Bernard Anthony & Anna Kerdman; Sps: John S Hashberger & Maria Moser. -HM (p69)
03 Feb 1840	Richard Leo b 22 Jan 1840 s/o Thomas & Sarah Leo; Sps: Pat Cronon & Mary M^CCormick. -HM (p69)
07 Feb 1840	Bridget Luddy b 06 Feb 1840 d/o Thomas & Catharine Luddy; Sps: Martin M^CCartey & Mary Corboy. -HM (p69)
19 Feb 1840	Catharine Downey b 17 Feb 1840 d/o Thomas & Mary Downey; Sps: Philip Gavin & Catharine Gavin. -HM (p69)
19 Feb 1840	Mary Catharine Brady d/o [blank] Brady; Sps: W. Welsh. -HM (p69)
20 Feb 1840	Joseph Mattingly b 14 Feb 1840 s/o Baptist & Nancy Mattingly; Sps: Ed Mullan & Lucinda Mattingly. -HM (p70)
23 Feb 1840	Margaret Butts b 03 Jan 1840 illeg, supplied ceremonies of bapt.; Sps: John Fitzpatrick. -HM (p70)
26 Feb 1840	John Riley b 03 Feb 1840 s/o Michael & Catharine Riley; Sps: David Murray & Mary Smithing. -HM (p70)
29 Feb 1840	John Roll b 20 Feb 1840 s/o Matthew & Mary Roll; Sps: John Crowley & Ellen M^CCann. -HM (p70)
29 Feb 1840	Frances Byrns b 25 Feb 1840 d/o Pierce & Frances Byrns; Sps: John Kearney & Frances Kearney. -HM (p70)
01 Mar 1840	Henry Crow b 02 Feb 1840 s/o George & Polly Crow; Sps: Matilda M^CQuicker. -HM (p70)
01 Mar 1840	Henry Ferle b 01 Feb 1840 s/o Valentine & Elizabeth Ferle; Sps: Henry Ferle & Catharine Cross. -HM (p71)
01 Mar 1840	Francis William Eggart b 18 Oct 1839 s/o John & Mary Eggart; Sps: Frances Gramlick & Elizabeth Gramlick. -HM (p71)
05 Mar 1840	Ellen M^CGovern b 05 Mar 1840 d/o Thomas & Ann M^CGovern; Sps: Pat O'Farrel & Ann Riley. -HM (p71)

07 Mar 1840   Michael Mattingly b 15 Dec 1839 s/o Henry & Christina Mattingly; Sps: James Mattingly. -HM (p71)

07 Mar 1840   Catherine Mattingly b 24 Feb 1840 d/o James & Ann Mattingly; Sps: H. Mattingly. -HM (p71)

14 Mar 1840   Thomas Hix, b 20 Jan 1840, illeg s/o Thoma[s] Hix & Mrs. Margaret Cahoe; Sps: Wm Foley & Margaret McAulty. -HM (p71)

14 Mar 1848   Mary Cain b 13 Mar 1840 d/o John & Debra Cain; Sps: Joseph Artkins. -HM (p72)

15 Mar 1840   Mary Martha Smith (col^d) b 11 Jun 1839 illeg. d/o Mary Martha Smith, servant of J. Black; Sps: John Black & Lydia Black. -HM (p72)

16 Mar 1840   Edward Dowling b 10 Mar 1840 s/o John & Margaret Dowling; Sps: Ed Dillon & Mrs. Kelly. -HM (p72)

20 Mar 1840   Joseph Bens b 02 Mar 1840 s/o Adam & Elizabeth Bens; Sps: Joseph Brutterk. -HM (p72)

25 Mar 1840   Thomas McGlenn b 23 Mar 1840 s/o James & Margaret McGlenn; Sps: Cath Garahan. -HM (p72)

25 Mar 1840   Margaret Garahan b 17 Nov 1839 d/o Peter & Catharine Garahan; Sps: Jeremiah Jamison & Mary Jamison. -HM (p73)

25 Mar 1840   Louisa Jamison b 03 Feb 1840 d/o Richard & Rosa Jamison; Sps: Mrs. Catharine Graham. -HM (p73)

27 Mar 1840   Bridget Flood b 19 Mar 1840 d/o Pat & Margaret Flood; Sps: Owen Cain & Margaret Row. -HM (p72)

31 Mar 1840   Mary Elizabeth Holtzman b 02 Dec 1839 d/o Aug & Mar^t Louisa Holtzman, in Virginia; Sps: Elizabeth Mulledy. -HM (p73)

02 Apr 1840   John Thomas Brown b 24 Oct 1839 s/o Latitia & Charles Brown, in Virginia; Sps: Aug Holtzman & Nancy Marshall. -HM (p73)

04 Apr 1840   John Albert Henkey b 25 Mar 1840 s/o John & Mary Elizabeth Henkey; Sps: Gerard Henkey & Mary Evas [Evisman?]. -HM (p73)

04 Apr 1840   Mary Magdalena Grisman b 13 Dec 1840 [1839] d/o John & Salome Grisman; Sps: Magdalena Soldel. -HM (p73)

05 Apr 1840   Ellen Colligan b 05 Mar 1840 d/o Daniel & Frances Colligan; Sps: Michael Lanan & Juliam Rereick. -HM (p74)

BAPTISMS

05 Apr 1840	Catharine M^CLaughlin b 02 Apr 1840 d/o Thomas & Honora M^CLaughlin; Sps: Michael Goulden & Teresa Healy. -HM (p74)
05 Apr 1848	Mary Brofield b 23 Mar 1840 d/o Thomas & Sarah Brofield; Sps: James M^CLaney & Mary Kennedy. -HM (p74)
14 Apr 1840	Bernard Henry Couleman b 09 Apr 1840 s/o Gerard Henry & Mary Adeleide Couleman; Sps: Bernard Henry Couleman & Anna Maria Summa. -HM (p74)
19 Apr 1840	John Martin b 18 Mar 1840 s/o James & Polly Martin; Sps: John Baltis & Catharina Snure. -HM (p74)
25 Apr 1840	John Kilduff b 08 Apr 1840 s/o Patrick & Rosa Kilduff; Sps: Pat Kearney & Anna Sheridan. -HM (p75)
27 Apr 1840	Mary Reynolds b 23 Apr 1840 d/o John & Honor Reynolds; Sps: Pat Gaughan & Catharine Kine. -HM (p75)
27 Apr 1840	Thomas Callahan b 31 Mar 1840 s/o John & Anna Callahan; Sps: John Traner & Mary Evisman. -HM (p75)
27 Apr 1840	Mary Barry b 26 Apr 1840 d/o John & Margaret Barry; Sps: Pat Barry & Mary Barry. -HM (p75)
27 Apr 1840	Mary M^CNalley b 26 Apr 1840 d/o John & Mary M^CNalley; Sps: Ed Barret & Rosa M^CNalley. -HM (p75)
28 Apr 1840	David Kelly b 05 Apr 1840 s/o Michael & Ann Kelly; Sps: Christopher Tolin. -HM (p76)
28 Apr 1840	Thomas Deacon b 1840 s/o Jesse & Mary Beacon; Sps: Thomas & Rebecca Donahoe. -HM (p76)
29 Apr 1840	Francis Durkey b 21 Apr 1840 s/o Francis & Ann Durkey; Sps: Arthur & Margaret M^CNulty. -HM (p76)
30 Apr 1840	John Whelan b 23 Apr 1840 s/o James & Bridget Whelan; Sps: Peter Lynch & Mary Sullivan. -HM (p76)
30 Apr 1840	Catharine Larkin b 23 Apr 1840 d/o Thomas & Mary Larkin; Sps: Francis Bergan & Cecilia Salmon. -HM (p76)
30 Apr 1840	Gertrude Hipp b 07 Apr 1840 d/o Joseph & Helena Hipp; Sps: Maria Anna Myers. -HM (p76)
04 May 1840	John Rey b 22 Dec 1840 [1839] s/o John & Valp Carolina Rey; Sps: Alley Coffey. -HM (p77)
19 May 1840	Altha Selmon Frances Creighbaum b 29 Mar 1840 d/o Henry & Fanny Creighbaum; Sps: Ann Bisel. -HM (p77)
21 May 1840	Anna Rooney b 18 May 1840 d/o James & Sabina Rooney; Sps: Thomas Rooney & Margaret Ryan. -HM (p77)

111

21 May 1840	Margaret Hughes b 21 May 1840 d/o Henry & Mary Hughes; Sps: Nicholas Hughes & Bridget Matthews. -HM (p77)
21 May 1840	Elizabeth Morgan b 15 May 1840 (twin) d/o James & Ann Morgan; Sps: Arthur Mills & Nancy Mills. -HM (p77)
21 May 1840	Ellen Morgan b 15 May 1840 (twin) d/o James & Ann Morgan; Sps: Michael Callan & Mary Ann Flanagan. -HM (p77)
24 May 1840	Mary Owens b 22 May 1840 d/o Gerard & Catharine Owens; Sps: Anna Mary Owens. -HM (p78)
25 May 1840	Catharine Carrol b 09 May 1840 d/o John & Mary Carrol; Sps: Ed Riley & Mary Row. -HM (p78)
25 May 1840	Adam Knetz b 10 May 1840 s/o Lawrence & Elizabeth Knetz; Sps: Adam Roman. -HM (p78)
25 May 1840	George Smith b 04 Feb 1840 s/o Jacob & Catharine Smith; Sps: George Roman. -HM (p78)
25 May 1840	Elizabeth Peter b 10 Oct 1839 d/o Henry & Sophia Peter; Sps: Elizabeth Retbroke. -HM (p78)
26 May 1840	Margaret Early b 16 May 1840 d/o Francis & Mary Early; Sps: Barney Courtney & Rosa McManus. -HM (p78)
02 Jun 1840	Jesse John Cross b 21 Jan 1840 s/o Uriah & Barbara Cross; Sps: Israel & Sarah Garlitz. -HM (p47)
02 Jun 1840	George Washington Robinson b 12 Mar 1840 s/o William & Priscilla Robinson; Sps: Samuel Garlitz & Jane Getty. -HM (p47)
02 Jun 1840	Samuel Peter Garlitz b 02 Feb 1840 s/o Samuel & Catherine Garlitz Sps: John Garlitz & Mary Garlitz. -HM (p47)
03 Jun 1840	Thomas Arkins b 26 May 1840 s/o Joseph & Ellen Arkins; Sps: James Corboy & Ellen O'Brian -HM (p78)
03 Jun 1840	Margaret Elizabeth Coner b 21 Apr 1840 d/o Arthur & Ann Coner; Sps: John Fitzgerald & Lucy McCormick. -HM (p78)
07 Jun 1840	(unnamed) Hopkins b 12 May 1840 s/o Patrick & Mary Hopkins; Sps: Patrick Farrell & Margaret Farrell. -HM (p79)
12 Jun 1840	Elizabeth Gillan b 04 Jun 1840 d/o Patrick & Winefred Gillan; Sps: Thomas Salmon & Ellen Kelly. -HM (p79)
14 Jun 1840	Thomas Burley b 09 Jun 1839 s/o John & Margaret Burley; Sps: Mary Porter. -HM (p79)

14 Jun 1840	Anna Porter b 25 Mar 1840 d/o John Evan & Elizabeth Porter; Sps: Elizabeth McKenzie. -HM (p47)
14 Jun 1840	[blank] Tomlinson b 15 May 1840 d/o Jesse & Ann Tomlinson; Sps: Catherine Hixonbaugh. -HM (p48)
21 Jun 1840	Eliza Porter b 15 Mar 1840 d/o Thomas & Nancy Porter; Sps: Desire Hoffman. -HM (p79)
26 Jun 1840	Thomas Michael Healey b 16 Jun 1840 s/o Thomas & Emily Healey; Sps: Wm Matthews & Zelie Hoffman. -HM (p79)
28 Jun 1840	Edward Rooney b 18 Jun 1840 s/o Brian & Mary Rooney; Sps: John Cough & Mary Welsh. -HM (p79)
05 Jul 1840	Winefred Toule b 04 Jul 1840 d/o John & Mary Toule; Sps: Anthony Barret & Bridget Flinn. -HM (p80)
12 Jul 1840	Henry Dean b 12 May 1840 s/o Francis & Polly [Mary] Dean; Sps: Mathilda Logsdon. -HM (p48)
12 Jul 1840	John Francis Buckholse b 16 Jun 1840 s/o William & Mary Buckholse; Sps: John Sr. & Ellen Mattingly. -HM (p48)
12 Jul 1840	Daniel Coleman b 05 Feb 1840 s/o William & Elizabeth Coleman; Sps: Catherine Elizabeth _____. -HM (p48)
12 Jul 1840	Anna Elizabeth Porter b 16 May 1840 d/o Henry & Margaret Porter; Sps: William & Elizabeth Logsdon. -HM (p48)
14 Jul 1840	Peter Hussey b 11 Jul 1840 s/o Mary Hussey, widow of the late Peter Hussey; Sps: John Hussey & Rosa Hussey. -HM (p80)
19 Jul 1840	John Caney b 18 Jun 1840 s/o Patrick & Mary Caney; Sps: John Caney & Mary Cusick. -HM (p80)
19 Jul 1840	Elizabeth Garahan b 12 Jun 1840 d/o Thomas & Elizabeth Garahan; Sps: Peter Kilduff & Mary Hopkins. -HM (p80)
19 Jul 1840	John Denis Sweeney b 02 Jul 1840 s/o Ed & Catharine Sweeney; Sps: James Dougherty & Sarah Dougherty. -HM (p80)
25 Jul 1840	Elizabeth Breuding b 22 Jul 1840 d/o Joseph & Catharine Breuding, conditionally; Sps: Margaret Hackin. -HM (p80)
26 Jul 1840	James Francis Burke b 14 Mar 1840 illeg. s/o [blank] Burke; Sps: James Hines & Margaret Hines. -HM (p81)
26 Jul 1840	Mary Brokman b 23 Jul 1840 d/o Gerard & Margaret Brokman; Sps: Dederick Coldey & Maria Owens. -HM (p81)

27 Jul 1840	Eliza Bremer b 25 Mar 1840 illeg. d/o Mira Bremer; Sps: Ludolph Bremer & Eliza Henkey. -HM (p81)
27 Jul 1840	Regina Cremer b 05 Jul 1840 illeg. d/o Carolina Cremer; Sps: Regina Cross. -HM (p81)
27 Jul 1840	Charles O'Neil b 26 Jul 1840 (twin) s/o Hugh & Mary O'Neil; Sps: John Dowling & Ciley Costello. -HM (p81)
27 Jul 1840	Edward O'Neil b 26 Jul 1840 (twin) s/o Hugh & Mary O'Neil; Sps: William Friel & Bridget Wade. -HM (p81)
04 Aug 1840	Mary Beal b 21 Jun 1840 d/o Charles & Margaret Beal; Sps: Francis Mattingly & Margaret Durbin. -HM (p48)
10 Aug 1840	John Sebastian Hersheberger b 03 Aug 1840 s/o John & Mary Ann Hersheberger; Sps: Wm & Mary Ryan. -HM (p81)
14 Aug 1840	John Bush Porter b 19 Aug 1839 s/o John & Ann Eliza Porter; Sps: Mary Agnes Creigan. -HM (p82)
22 Aug 1840	Charlotte Barrett b 19 Aug 1840, without ceremonies, d/o James & Maria Barrett. Ceremonies supplied 13 Sep 1840; Sps: Miles Barret & [blank]. -BSP (p82)
23 Aug 1840	Mary Ann Ryan b 20 Aug 1840 d/o William & Mary Ryan; Sps: Patrick Coffee & Alley Coffee. -BSP (p82)
23 Aug 1840	John Cratz b 20 Aug 1840 (twin) s/o Philip & Barbara Cratz; Sps: John Horton. -HM (p82)
23 Aug 1840	Maria Cratz b 20 Aug 1840 (twin) s/o Philip & Barbara Cratz; Sps: Maria Horney. -HM (p82)
23 Aug 1840	Joseph Sloviniskey b 24 May 1840 s/o Augustus & Agnes Sloviniskey; Sps; Joseph Rinehart & Margaret Gatenarin. -HM (p82)
24 Aug 1840	Nancy McQuiliams b 23 Aug 1840 illeg. d/o widow McQuiliams, the ceremonies were supplied on 06 Sep 1840; Sps: Brian & Margaret Monahan. -HM (p82)
24 Aug 1840	Anna Monahen b 18 Aug 1840 d/o Brian & Margaret Monahen; Sps: Tersy Malone & Margaret Larkin. -HM (p83)
29 Aug 1840	Christopher Garlitz b 03 Jun 1840 s/o John & Mary Garlitz; Sps: Israel Garlitz & Catharine McKenzie. -HM (p83)
01 Sep 1840	Jane Sophronia Turney b 1840 d/o Daniel & Ellen Turney; Sps: H. Myers. -HM (p83)

04 Sep 1840	Mary Smith b 02 Sep 1840 d/o Barney & Catharine Smith; Sps: Laughlin Clark & Jane McNalley. -HM (p83)
04 Sep 1840	Thomas Hughes b 04 Sep 1840 s/o William & Margaret Hughes; Sps: Thomas McGhee & Mary Hughes. -HM (p83)
04 Sep 1840	Jerome Lowry b 24 May 1840 s/o Robert & Julianne Lowry; Sps: Michael Sherry & Elizabeth Carter. -HM (p49)
12 Sep 1840	Mary Ann Fay b 08 Sep 1840 d/o Patrick & Ann Fay; Sps: John Welsh & Rosanna McCaffrey. -HM (p84)
12 Sep 1840	Anna Mary Nihouse b 11 Sep 1840 d/o Henry & Agnes Nihouse; Sps: John Ricker & Anna Maria Brown. -HM (p84)
13 Sep 1840	Rachel Honora Carter b 10 Apr 1840 d/o Richard & Margaret Carter; Sps: Mary Carter. -HM (p49)
13 Sep 1840	Peter McKenzie b 04 Apr 1840 s/o John & Barbara McKenzie; Sps: Mary McKenzie & Basil McKenzie. -HM (p49)
13 Sep 1840	Mary Smith b 02 Sep 1840 d/o Barney & Catharine Smith; Sps: Laughlin Clark & Jane McNalley. -HM (p49)
20 Sep 1840	Margaret Emelia McKenzie b 01 Apr 1840 d/o Moses & Margaret McKenzie; Sps: Michael Cavenaugh & Hanna Elizabeth McKenzie. -HM (p84)
20 Sep 1840	Michael Garvin b 16 [Sep] 1840 s/o Philip & Catherine Garvin; Sps: John White & Nancy Hurley. -HM (p84)
20 Sep 1840	Bernard Farrel b 08 Sep 1840 s/o Patrick & Bridget Farrel; Sps: Pat Carrol & Mary Hopkins. -HM (p84)
22 Sep 1840	Robert Bean b 20 Oct 1840 s/o Joshua & Almedy Bean, in Virginia; Sps: Nancy Marshall. -HM (p85)
23 Sep 1840	Mary Elizabeth Bean b 29 Sep 1839 d/o George & Margaret Bean, in Virginia; Sps: Polly Marshall. -HM (p85)
23 Sep 1840	James Solomon Shepler b 11 Dec 1839 s/o Henry & Letitia Shepler, in Virginia; Sps: James Bean & Latitia Brown. -HM (p85)
27 Sep 1840	Patrick Tuey b 23 Sep 1840 s/o Austin & Mary Tuey; Sps: Mrs. Richard Conelly & Ellen Lavell. -HM (p85)
01 Oct 1840	Charles Michael Gallagher b 20 Sep 1840 s/o Francis & Ann Gallagher; Sps: John McIntire & Alley McIntire. -HM (p85)
04 Oct 1840	Jerome Folat (col^d)c 01 Jun 1840 s/o Jushua & Sophia Folat, privately bapt. Ceremonies supplied [this date] Sps: Regina Kelly. -HM (p86)

04 Oct 1840   John Ricker b 24 Sep 1840 s/o John & Mary Ricker; Sps: John Hartman & Anna Couleman. -HM (p86)

04 Oct 1840   John Henry Brown b 24 Sep 1840 s/o Henry & Mary Brown; Sps: Henry Brown & Elizabeth Tokenback. -HM (p86)

04 Oct 1840   Thomas Garner b 15 Sep 1840 s/o James & Margaret Garner; Sps: Patrick Cole & Mrs. McCaffrey. -HM (p86)

04 Oct 1840   Harriet Ann Speelman b 31 Jul 1840 d/o Lorens & Margaret Speelman; Sps: Valentine Rereik & Susan Rereik. -HM (p86)

04 Oct 1840   Denis William Wade b 20 Jun 1840 s/o Isaia[h] & Susan Wade, privately bapt., ceremonies supplied [this date]; Sps: Elizabeth McKenzie. -HM (p87)

11 Oct 1840   Jacob Anthony Shriver b 02 Sep 1840 s/o Henry & Catherine Elizabeth Shriver; Sps: Valentine Klink. -HM (p49)

11 Oct 1840   Thomas Hanikan b 20 Sep 1840 s/o Francis & Mary Hanikan; Sps: Thomas Foliart & Bridget Hussey. -HM (p50)

11 Oct 1840   Ann Cain b 29 Sep 1840 d/o James & Mary Cain; Sps: Martin Bolan & Mary Sheridan. -HM (p50)

11 Oct 1840   John Conway b 27 Sep 1840 s/o Patrick & Bridget Conway; Sps: John Hawn & Elizabeth Logsdon. -HM (p50)

19 Oct 1840   Gerard Henry Barlage b 15 [Oct] 1840 s/o Henry & Catharine Barlage; Sps: Gerard Turline. -HM (p87)

21 Oct 1840   Mary Conner b 19 Oct 1840 d/o Michael & Catharine Conner; Sps: John McCormick & Margaret McCartey. -HM (p87)

22 Oct 1840   Mary Conelly b 20 Oct 1840 d/o Richard & Bridget Conelly; Sps: James Conway & Margaret Barrett. -HM (p87)

25 Oct 1840   James Dougherty b 19 Oct 1840 s/o Hugh & Catharine Dougherty; Sps: Pat McGarr & Mary Kelly. -HM (p87)

25 Oct 1840   Ellen Sullivan b 29 Sep 1840 d/o John & Mary Sullivan; Sps: James Thompson & Mary Carroll. -HM (p88)

26 Oct 1840   Mary Pilsing b 02 Oct 1840 d/o Harman & Elizabeth Pilsing; Sps: Mary Owens. -HM (p88)

01 Nov 1840   Mary Riley b 19 Oct 1840 d/o James & Susan Riley; Sps: Peter Dillon & Bridget Farrel. -HM (p88)

BAPTISMS

01 Nov 1840	Robert Emmet Coulehan b (blank) s/o James & Martha Coulhan; Sps: __ Coulehan & Sarah Dougherty. -HM (p88)
06 Nov 1840	Michael Flyn b 05 Nov 1840 s/o John & Margaret Flyn; Sps: Peter Lynch & Bridget Farrel. -HM (p88)
06 Nov 1840	Mary Farrel b 12 Oct 1840 d/o John & Mary Farrel; Sps: Michael Flannagan & Mary Gerity. -HM (p88)
06 Nov 1840	George Schrem b 26 (Oct?) 1840 s/o Casper & Elizabeth Schrem; Sps: George Hart & Juliam Rereich. -HM (p89)
08 Nov 1840	Mary Brisco b 07 Nov 1840 d/o Michael & Catharine Brisco; Sps: John Kelly & Sally Murray. -HM (p89)
08 Nov 1840	Mary Ann Slown [Sloan?] b 05 Nov 1840 d/o John & Margaret Slown; Sps: Philip M^{C}Cauley & Henrietta Arnold. -HM (p89)
12 Nov 1840	Henry Hanson M^{C}Kenzie b 08 Jul 1840 s/o David & Mary M^{C}Kenzie; Sps: Elizabeth Carter. -HM (p89)
13 Nov 1840	John Burkett, privately bapt, s/o [blank] Burkett, (parents Protestants). -HM (p89)
15 Nov 1840	Patrick Tuez [Tuey?] b 13 Nov 1840 s/o Patrick & Bridget Tuez; Sps: John M^{C}Namara & Jinny Burke. -HM (p90)
15 Nov 1840	John Henry Brown b 28 Oct 1840 s/o Henry & Elizabeth Brown; Sps: Henry Vonstreet & Elizabeth Tokenberger. -HM (p90)
15 Nov 1840	Elizabeth Myers b 08 Nov 1840 d/o Peter & Catharine Myers; Sps: Nicholas Baltis & Elizabeth Schrem. -HM (p90)
23 Nov 1840	Catharine Murray b 13 Nov 1840 d/o Patrick & Bridget Murray; Sps: Law Byrns & Mary Byrns. -HM (p90)
23 Nov 1840	Ellenor Ann Gadultig b 12 Oct 1840 d/o Esra & Nancy Gadultig; Sps: Peter Flanigan & Mary Ann Flanigan. -HM (p90)
25 Nov 1840	James Augustine Kirbey b 19 Nov 1840 s/o George & Margaret Kirbey; Sps: James Garner & Elizabeth Murphy. -HM (p91)
25 Nov 1840	Henry Myers b 24 Nov 1840 s/o Henry & Elizabeth Myers; Sps: Harry Luman. -HM (p91)
01 Dec 1840	Charles Mahoney (col^d) b 01 Nov 1840 s/o Charles & Esther Mahoney, at Blooming Rose; Sps: Nancy M^{C}Cleary. -HM (p91)

117

04 Dec 1840	Patrick Riley b 03 Dec 1840 s/o David & Judith Riley; Sps: Anthony Flanigan & Maria Kilborn. -HM (p91)
05 Dec 1840	John George Misal b 02 Dec 1840 s/o John & Barbara Misal; Sps: George Kuslan & Regina Keble. -HM (p91)
07 Dec 1840	Charles Cavenagh b 30 Nov 1840 s/o Charles & Rosa Cavenagh; Sps: James Kelly & Susan Riley. -HM (p92)
08 Dec 1840	Eliza Little b 01 Dec 1840 d/o John & Elizabeth Little; Sps: Thomas Carrol & Rosa Coners. -HM (p92)
11 Dec 1840	Elizabeth Baltis b 26 Nov 1840 d/o John & Catharine Baltis; Sps: Peter Myers & Elizabeth Snure. -HM (p92)
13 Dec 1840	Patrick Langhan b 30 Nov 1840 s/o Michael & Mary Langhan; Sps: Thomas Hevrin & Margaret McGurey. -HM (p92)
26 Dec 1840	Julia Murray b 19 Dec 1840 d/o Patrick & Mary Murray; Sps: Denis Hays. -HM (p92)
27 Dec 1840	John Rinehart b 09 Dec 1840 s/o Joseph & Catharine Rinehart; Sps: John Lanendorfer. -HM (p93)
27 Dec 1840	John Adam Meleberger b 24 Aug 1840 s/o Casper & Susan Meleberger; Sps: Teresa Fall. -HM (p93)
27 Dec 1840	Mary Bard b 12 Nov 1840 d/o Harman & Maria Bard; Sps: Maria Bard. -HM (p93)
27 Dec 1840	Ambrose Mertz b 25 Oct 1840 s/o Yorick & Catharine Mertz; Sps: Ambrose Plum. -HM (p93)
28 Dec 1840	Joseph Bernard Culdez b 15 Dec 1840 s/o Dederick & Margaret Couldz; Sps: Joseph Lacus & Margaret Dierka. -HM (p93)
28 Dec 1840	Nicholas Hughes illeg. s/o Nicholas Hughes & Neoma Boyd; Sps: John Fletcher. -HM (p93)
28 Dec 1840	Eliza Josephine Ryan b 01 Dec 1840 d/o Nicholas G. & Ann Ryan; Sps: Mary Garrighty. -HM (p94)
03 Jan 1841	Ann Dillon b 31 Dec 1840 d/o Peter and Mary Dillon; Sps: Patrick Farrel. -HM (p94)
03 Jan 1841	Bridget Fox b 27 Dec 1840 d/o Henry and Mary Fox; Sps: John Ruddy. -HM (p94)
10 Jan 1841	Edward Naughton b 24 Dec 1840 s/o John and Bridget Naughton; Sps: John Connelly. -HM (p94)
10 Jan 1841	Henry O'Beka b 06 Jan 1841 s/o Ferdinand and Agatha O'Beka; Sps: Lydia Gibe. -HM (p94)

BAPTISMS

10 Jan 1841	Henry Thomas Logsdon b 07 Jan 1841 s/o William and Elizabeth Logsdon; Sps: W. Arnold & Catherine McKenzie. -HM (p94)
22 Jan 1841	Ann Murry b 13 Sep 1840 d/o John & Rosann Murry; baptized privately; Sps: Mat Coffey. -HM (p95)
20 Feb 1841	Jane Davis b 04 Feb 1841 d/o William & Elizabeth Davis; Sps: Patrick Gorman & Ann McCauly. -HM (p95)
20 Feb 1841	John Kelly b 08 Feb 1841 s/o James & Catharine Kelly; Sps: Michael Kelly & Ellen Kelly. -HM (p95)
23 Feb 1841	John Salmon b 20 Feb 1841 s/o Thomas & Elizabeth Salmon; Sps: William Gallagher & Catharine Manly. -HM (p95)
23 Feb 1841	Bridget Clark b 05 Feb 1841 d/o Darby & Catharine Clark; Sps: Martin McDermot & Mary McDermot. -HM (p95)
23 Feb 1841	Elizabeth Myers b 28 Feb 1840 d/o Albert & Mary Myers; Sps: Mrs. Coffey. -HM (p96)
28 Feb 1841	John Harman Capeller s/o George Capeller, privately; Sps: Mrs. Kelle. -HM (p95)
28 Feb 1841	Laurence Jurdon b 23 Feb 1841 s/o Michael & Rose Jurdon; Sps: Thomas McCauley & Catharine Kelly. -HM (p96)
06 Mar 1841	Elizabeth Turner b 04 Mar 1841 d/o John & Anna Maria Turner; Sps: Elizabeth Brown & John Helshaus. -HM (p96)
11 Mar 1841	Mary McManus b 23 Feb 1841 d/o Michael & Nancy McManus; Sps: Anthony Barret & Bridget Flynn. -HM (p96)
11 Mar 1841	John Ford b 03 Feb 1841 s/o Owen & Mary Ford; Sps: Pat Daugherty & Catharine Kain. -HM (p96)
11 Mar 1841	Ellen Maginnis b 02 Mar 1841 d/o John & Mary Maginnis; Sps: John Madden & Mary Casey. -HM (p96)
13 Mar 1841	Patrick Mulcahaey b 11 Mar 1841 s/o John & Mary Mulcahey; Sps: Mathew Coffey & Mary McCormick. -HM (p97)
14 Mar 1841	Joseph Ferley b 16 Jan 1841 s/o Henry & Catharine Ferley; Sps: Joseph Ferley & Helena Battis. -HM (p97)
14 Mar 1841	Margaret Ferley b 18 Feb 1841 s/o _____ dalen & Elizabeth Ferley; Sps: Margaret _____. -HM (p97)
21 Mar 1841	Mary Ann McGran b 02 Jan 1841 d/o Patrick & Catharine McGran; Sps: James McManus & Ann Sheridan. -HM (p97)

119

21 Mar 1841   Patrick Culcanon b 07 Feb 1841 s/o Patrick & Mary Culcanon; Sps: Thomas Farrel & Elizabeth Farrel. -HM (p97)

21 Mar 1841   Ann McGan b 28 Feb 1841 d/o Patrick & Mary McGan; Sps: Pat Smith & Bridget Oneal. -HM (p97)

21 Mar 1841   Bridget Kearney b 04 Feb 1841 d/o John & Mary Kearney; Sps: Pat Kearney & Rose Kearney. -HM (p98)

21 Mar 1841   John Mootey b 12 Mar 1841 s/o John & Bridget Mootey; Sps: Pat Mootey & Catherine Lastley. -HM (p98)

22 Mar 1841   Mary Elizabeth Shenoff b 14 Jan 1841 d/o Joseph L. & Adelaide Shenoff; Sps: Dederick Culday & Margaret Culday. -HM (p98)

22 Mar 1841   Martine Constantine Masters b 15 Jan 1841 s/o Richard & Ann Masters; Sps: Mary McCann. -HM (p98)

23 Mar 1841   Mary Jane Cummiskey b 19 Feb 1841 d/o Patrick & Elizabeth Cumminkey; Sps: Michael Conlon & Margaret Crewans. -HM (p98)

25 Mar 1841   Mary Elizabeth Spade b 18 Mar 1841 d/o Francis & Cath Spade; Sps: Elizabeth Ganter. -HM (p98)

01 Apr 1841   Catharine Farrel b 12 Mar 1841 d/o Michael & Ann Farrel; Sps: Cat Cole & Ann Redmond. -HM (p99)

03 Apr 1841   Mary Ryan b 02 Apr 1841 d/o Philip & Catharine Ryan; Sps: William Darcy & Elizabeth Darcy. -HM (p99)

11 Apr 1841   James Flood b 06 Feb 1841 s/o John & Catharine Flood; Sps: James Farrel & Margaret Hern. -HM (p99)

11 Apr 1841   Elizabeth Murray b 12 Mar 1841 d/o Henri & Catharine Murray; Sps: John McKelup & Teresa Logsdon. -HM (p99)

11 Apr 1841   Henry William Wegus b 15 Jan 1841 s/o Harman & Mary Wegus; Sps: Henry Wickman & Mary Bookhulse. -HM (p99)

11 Apr 1841   Michael Finnigan b 26 Mar 1841 s/o Patrick & Bridget Finnigan; Sps: James Melia & Margaret Brown. -HM (p99)

11 Apr 1841   James Welsh b 16 Mar 1841 s/o Patrick & Mary Welsh; Sps: Wm Park & Ellen Park. -HM (p100)

11 Apr 1841   James Whelan b 22 Mar 1841 s/o Patrick & Mary Whelan; Sps: James Egan & Catharine Kelly. -HM (p100)

17 Apr 1841   John Gerard Henry Eggamyer b 11 Apr 1841 s/o Phillip Frederick & Catharine Maria Eggamyer; Sps: John G. H. Couleman & Anna M. Mertz -HM (p100)

18 Apr 1841 Denis Arnold b 07 Jan 1841 s/o Joseph & Matilda Arnold; Sps: Silvester Mattingly & Matilda McQuicker. -HM (p100)

27 Apr 1841 Margaret Amelia Donahoe b 09 Mar 1841 d/o Patrick & Anna Donahoe; Sps: William Welsh & Rebecca Donahoe. -HM (p100)

[At this time L. Obermyer took over and reorganized baptisms into a tabular form; however we will continue the previous format.]

01 May 1841 James Smith s/o John & Ann Smith; Sps: James Smith & Ann Maier. -BLO (p101)

01 May 1841 Bridget Dowd d/o Patrick & Rosa Dowd; Sps: James Brown & _____[smeared]. -BLO (p101)

01 May 1841 Mary Ann Gorman d/o John & Juliann Gorman; Sps: Pat^k Gorman & Cath Gorman. -BLO (p101)

02 May 1841 Rose Ellen Rodgers d/o Patrick & Sally Rodgers; Sps: Jno Maloy & Jane Laughlin. -BLO (p101)

02 May 1841 Lucy Margaret Rickelman d/o Henry & Mary Eliz^h Rickelman; Sps: John Witt & Lucy McDicker. -BLO (p101)

02 May 1841 Catharine Elizabeth Luttman d/o Garret & Rach^l Luttman; Sps: Henry Ott & Catharine Gers. -BLO (p101)

03 May 1841 Mary Mohlman d/o Henry & Mary Eliz^h Mohlman; Sps: Garret Luttman & Mary Mohlman. -BLO (p101)

08 May 1841 Mary Lydia Staub d/o Joseph & Christina Staub; Sps: Leop Merkle & Eliz^h Merkle. -BLO (p101)

09 May 1841 Margaret Matilda Durbin d/o John & Marg^t Durbin; Sps: Benedict Logsdon & Alice Logsdon. -BLO (p101)

09 May 1841 Mary Keenan b 30 Apr 1841 d/o Thomas & Betty Keenan; Sps: Wm Arnold. -BLO (p101)

09 May 1841 James Barry b 06 May 1841 s/o Patrick & Mary Barry; Sps: Jno Barry & Nancy Maguire. -BLO (p101)

09 May 1841 Barbara Eveline b 09 May 1841 d/o Mathias & Margaret Eveline; Sps: Jno Betz & Barbara Betz. -BLO (p101)

11 May 1841 Mary Wempi born 02 May 1841 d/o Francis & Mary Wempi; Sps: Jno B. Smesy & Mary A. Hinkleborn. -BLO (p102)

16 May 1841 John Kuhn b 08 Jun 1840 s/o Jos & Mary Kuhn; Sps: Elizabeth Smith. -BLO (p102)

20 May 1841	Mary Catharine Black b 10 May 1841 d/o Jno & Lydia Black; Sps: Pierce Byrne & ___ Byrne. -BLO (p102)
23 May 1841	Ellen McCloskey d/o Peter & Catharine McCloskey; Sps: Peter Chafe & Mary Manly. -BLO (p102)
23 May 1841	Peter Spallen b 22 Mar 1841 s/o Peter & Catherine Spallen; Sps: Marcus Mulligan & Marg^t Spallen. -BLO (p102)
24 May 1841	James Devenny b 13 May 1841 s/o Hugh & Margaret Devenny; Sps: Mary Flannagan. -BLO (p102)
24 May 1841	Catherine Trueman b 14 May 1841 d/o Michael & Bridget Trueman; Sps: Mary Farrel. -BLO (p102)
24 May 1841	Mary Hughes b 17 May 1841 d/o Henry & Mary Hughes; Sps: Pat^K Connor & Marg^t Riley. -BLO (p102)
28 May 1841	Caroline Zeller b 22 Feb 1841 d/o Anthony & Mary Zeller; Sps: Bridget Whelen. -BLO (p102)
30 May 1841	Mary Ann Rebecca Robinson d/o Solomon & Ellen Robinson; Sps: Elizabeth McKinsey. -BLO (p102)
30 May 1841	Andrew Thomas Howe b 14 Jan 1841 s/o James & Mary Ann Howe; Sps: Andrew Gonder & Elizab^h Gonder. -BLO (p102)
31 May 1841	Ann McDermot born 13 May 1841 d/o Thomas & Maria McDermot; Sps: Marga^t Mullen & Jerem. Burke. -BLO (p102)
03 Jun 1841	John Mattingly b 28 May 1841 s/o Francis & Jane Amelia Mattingly; Sps: Cecilia Mattingly. -BLO (p102)
03 Jun 1841	John Conlon b 29 May 1841 s/o Andrew & Mary Conlon; Sps: John Foylen & Cath Beatly. -BLO (p102)
03 Jun 1841	John Flaherty b 25 May 1841 s/o Michael & Catharine Flaherty; Sps: Ed McDermot & Cath Ryan. -BLO (p102)
06 Jun 1841	Catherine Hendle b 23 Feb 1841 d/o Henry & Catharine Hendle; Sps: Catharine William & Geo Bekenhaus. -BLO (p102)
09 Jun 1841	James Cain b 30 May 1841 s/o Tho^S & Bridget Cain; Sps: James Dunn & Mary Daly. -BLO (p102)
09 Jun 1841	Margaret Hanson b 08 Jun 1841 d/o Patrick & Margaret Hanson; Sps: Mary Karney. -BLO (p103)
09 Jun 1841	Francis Henry Hagan b 29 May 1841 s/o Hugh & Bridget Hagan; Sps: Andrew Kelly & Mary Smith. -BLO (p103)
13 Jun 1841	Henry Mattingly s/o Henry & Christina Mattingly; Sps: Ann Mattingly & Jno Mattingly. -BLO (p103)

BAPTISMS

13 Jun 1841	Elijah Simpson s/o David & Nancy Simpson; Sps: Edmond Morrison & Eliz[h] Morrison. -BLO (p103)
13 Jun 1841	Francis McKinzie b 24 Oct 1840 s/o Samuel & Sally McKinzie; Sps: Cath McKinzie & Isreal Garlitz. -BLO (p103)
14 Jun 1841	Thomas Brown, age abt. 50, an adult and baptized conditionally. He was of the Church of England and for a month has been wishing to join the church. His inkrepat present caused his early baptism. -BLO (p103)
15 Jun 1841	John Karney s/o Michael & Bridget Karney; Sps: Luke Clarke & Mary Mahan. -BLO (p103)
20 Jun 1841	John Helfach b 06 Jun 1841 s/o Valentine & Apl Catharine Helfach;. Sps: Jno Miller & Elizabeth Miller. -BLO (p103)
20 Jun 1841	Peter Rerik b 12 Apr 1841 s/o Peter & Margaret Rerik; Sps: Peter Rerick & Margaret Rerick. -BLO (p103)
27 Jun 1841	Patrick Clarke b 10 Jun 1841 s/o William & Catherine Clarke; Sps: Hugh McManus & Mary Clarke. -BLO (p103)
28 Jun 1841	Margaret Ligas b 18 Jun 1841 d/o Joseph & Elizabeth Ligas; Sps: Jno Fletcher & Margaret Golde. -BLO (p103)
05 Jul 1841	Daniel Marcellus Mullen b 29 Jun 1841 s/o Edward & Ann Mullen; Sps: Mary Mullen & Marcellus Brown. -BLO (p103)
05 Jul 1841	Martha Ann Bisely b 08 Apr 1841 d/o John & Ann Bisely; Sps: Valentine Reric & Susan Reric. -BLO (p103)
08 Jul 1841	Dorothea Herman d/o John & Dorothea Herman; Sps: Lewis Huft and Elizabeth Fink. -BLO (p103)
08 Jul 1841	Charles Huft s/o Lewis & Dorothea Huft; Sps: Jno Herman & Elizabeth Fink. -BLO (p103)
08 Jul 1841	Lewis Upperman s/o Jno & Gertrude Upperman; Sps: Lewis Hesen & Eliz[h] Fink. -BLO (p103)
08 Jul 1841	Bernardina Hesen b 06 Jul 1841 d/o Lewis & Christina Hesen; Sps: Catherine Hesen & Henry Hesen. -BLO (p104)
11 Jul 1841	Frances Stritz d/o John & Christina Stritz; Sps: Margaret Wiendre. -BLO (p104)
11 Jul 1841	John Werner s/o John & Barbara Werner; Sps: John Stritz & Frances Heskel. -BLO (p104)
11 Jul 1841	Sarah Ann Garlitz d/o Solomon & Rebecca Garlitz; Sps: Sarah Durbin & Sam[l] F. McKenzie. -BLO (p104)

123

11 Jul 1841 John Clarke s/o James & Catherine Clarke;
Sps: Peter Conell & Marg^t Logsden. -BLO (p104)

13 Jul 1841 Eliza Jane Cole illeg. d/o John Cole & Elizabeth
Taylor; Sps: Jno Trainer & Mary Curry. -BLO (p104)

17 Jul 1841 Peter Schelhouse b 16 Jul 1841 s/o John & Barbara
Schelhouse; Sps: Peter Schnur & Margaret Schelhouse.
-BLO (p104)

18 Jul 1841 Elizabeth Stiy b 01 Mar 1841 d/o Conrad & Caroline
Stiy; Sps: Valentine Fele & Eliza Fele. -BLO (p104)

18 Jul 1841 George Henry Marz s/o Georg H. & Mary Marz;
Sps: Henry Coleman & Mary Aderlhet. -BLO (p104)

25 Jul 1841 Bridget Reiley b 11 Jul 1841 d/o Francis & Catherine
Reiley; Sps: James McManus & Bridg^t Dolan. -BLO
(p104)

25 Jul 1841 Mary Ann Flanagan b 22 Jul d/o Francis & Julia Flanagan;
Sps: John Cain & Julia Daugherty. -BLO (p104)

26 Jul 1841 Margaret Keller b 25 May 1841 d/o Peter & Rosina Keller;
Sps: Margaret Blume & Jno Blume. -BLO (p104)

26 Jul 1841 Peter Francis Flanagan b 02 Feb 1841 s/o William & Ann
Flanagan; Sps: Jno McGevit & Cath Keene. -BLO (p104)

26 Jul 1841 Julian Wigger b 17 Jul 1841 s/o Bar & Catherine Wigger;
Sps: Nancy Doyle & James Kelly. -BLO (p104)

26 Jul 1841 Mary Baltes b 13 Jul 1841 d/o Patrick & Mary Baltes;
Sps: Jno Boran & Mary Fox. -BLO (p104)

26 Jul 1841 James Corboy b 15 Jul 1841 s/o James & Catherine Corboy;
Sps: Mich^l Bolden & Mary McCormack. -BLO (p104)

26 Jul 1841 Elizabeth McDonel d/o Jno & Grace McDonel;
Sps: Rannel McDonel & Mary Lyon. -BLO (p104)

26 Jul 1841 Margaret & William Malone, twins, b 04 Jul 1841 children
of Terence & Mary Malone; Sps: Hugh Maguire, Ann
Maguire, Thos Larkin & Margaret Fowler. -BLO (p105)

28 Jul 1841 Maria Hanney b 23 Jul 1841 d/o John & Margaret Hanney;
Sps: Law Quorgan & Eliza Gerner. -BLO (p105)

01 Aug 1841 Cecilia McDonald b 29 Jul 1841 d/o Patrick & Jane
McDonald; Sps: Martin Flatly & Rose Flatly. -BLO (p105)

01 Aug 1841 Elizabeth Coffey b 23 Jul 1841 d/o Mathew & Alley
Coffey; Sps: Philip Ryan & Mary Corvan. -BLO (p105)

BAPTISMS

04 Aug 1841   Agnes Roberts abt. 25 Jul 1841 d/o [blank]; Sps: Lucinda Mattingly (note added ceremonies supplied 06 Sep 1842). -BLO (p105)

08 Aug 1841   Barbara Leitung b 04 Jul 1841 d/o Nicholas & Barbara Leitung; Sps: Barbara Holtz & Mich[l] Stump. -BLO (p105)

08 Aug 1841   Elizabeth Cath Hicksenbaugh b 12 Mar 1840 d/o Aaron & Rachel Hicksenbaugh; Sps: Cath E Hicksenbaugh. -BLO (p105)

08 Aug 1841   John Henry Winter b 19 Oct 1840 s/o John & Esther Winter; Sps: Wm Arnold, Eliz[h] Porter. -BLO (p105)

08 Aug 1841   Ellen Brogan b 25 Jul 1841 d/o Thomas & Mary Brogan; Sps: Tho[s] McGee & Bridget Higgins. -BLO (p105)

09 Aug 1841   Ann Ryan b 20 Jul 1841 d/o Michael & Margaret Ryan; Sps: Cath Egan & Michael Cooney. -BLO (p105)

10 Aug 1841   James Gillise b 07 Aug 1841 s/o Michael & Sarah Gillise; Sps: Christ McDonald & Bridg[t] Laughlin. -BLO (p105)

17 Aug 1841   Ann Elizabeth Brown b 08 Jan 1841 d/o Charles & Letitia Brown; Sps: Benj Henson Tucker & Mary Marshall. -BLO (p105)

23 Aug 1841   Catherine Murphy b 08 Aug 1841 d/o James & Catherine Murphy; Sps: Terrance Riley & Marg Naylor. -BLO (p105)

23 Aug 1841   George Nalus b 07 Aug 1841 s/o George & Nancy Nalus; Sps: Tho[s] Connor & Marg Riley. -BLO (p105)

23 Aug 1841   James Oneill s/o Bernard & Bridget Oneill; Sps: Ed Riley & Ellen Buckleman. -BLO (p105)

28 Aug 1841   Rachel McKinzie b 16 Jul 1840 d/o Samuel & Margaret McKinzie; Sps: Samuel F. McKinzie & Cath McKinzie. -BLO (p105)

29 Aug 1841   Hugh McNally b 17 Jun 1841 s/o Patrick & Ann McNally; Sps: John Smith & L. Teresa Jenkins. -BLO (p106)

29 Aug 1841   Lavina McNair b 25 Apr 1841 d/o Andrew & Catherine McNair; Sps: Charles Smith & Ellen Turney. -BLO (p106)

29 Aug 1841   Eliza Jane Thomson (black) d/o Wm & Sarah Thomson; Sps: Tho[s] Jackson & Catherine Thomson. -BLO (p106)

29 Aug 1841   Margaret Jane Follard b 13 Aug 1841 d/o Thomas & Rose Follard; Sps: James Edwards & Ann Hussey. -BLO (p106)

05 Sep 1841   Mary Ann Luddy b 29 Aug 1841 d/o Thos & Cathar Luddy; Sps: Mrs. Welsh & Ellen Aiken. -BLO (p106)

05 Sep 1841	Mary Elizabeth Arnold b 20 Jun 1841 d/o Nathan & Ellen Arnold; Sps: Mrs. Welsh & Eliz McKinzie. -BLO (p106)
11 Sep 1841	Wilhelmina Christina Merkel b 19 Jul 1841 d/o Leopold & Elizabeth Merkle; Sps: Jos Staub & Christina Staub. -BLO (p106)
12 Sep 1841	Andrew Carney b 27 Jul 1841 s/o Michael & Lorinda Carney; Sps: Den Mullany & Mrs. Durbin. -BLO (p106)
12 Sep 1841	Geo Washington Matter b 11 Jul 1841 s/o John & Margaret Matter; Sps: Andrew MacKengles. -BLO (p106)
19 Sep 1841	William Ryan s/o Peter & Eliza Ryan; Sps: Mrs. Ryan & Mary Murry. -BLO (p106)
19 Sep 1841	George Henry McKinzee s/o George & Susan McKinzee; Sps: Mat Coffey & Ann McKinzee. -BLO (p106)
19 Sep 1841	Emanuel Walter (col) s/o Greenberry & Mary Sps: Jane Worth. -BLO (p106)
19 Sep 1841	George Henry Dressman b10 Sep 1841 s/o Henry & Catherine Dressman; Sps: Henry Wonstreet & Ann Kohlman. -BLO (p106)
25 Sep 1841	Michael Murry b 07 Sep 1841 s/o Matthew & Sarah Murry; Sps: Michael Golen & Honna Golen. -BLO (p106)
26 Sep 1841	John William Wissinger (il) 1 yr old s/o Mary Wampe & Geo Wissinger; Sps: Jno B Schmease & Cath Clarke. -BLO (p106)
26 Sep 1841	Mary Callahan b 5 Sep 1841 d/o John & Catherin Callahan; Sps: Pat^K Roach & Marg^t Himes. -BLO (p106)
27 Sep 1841	Elizabeth Brown b 24 Aug 1841 d/o Cornelius & Mary Brown; Sps: Jno Crowley & Mary Kanny. -BLO (p106)
01 Oct 1841	John Frederick Fletcher b 01 Oct 1841 s/o John & Teresa Fletcher; Sps: Joseph Legus & Mary Dillon. -BLO (p107)
03 Oct 1841	Ellen Hopkins b 13 Sep 1841 d/o Patrick & Mary Hopkins; Sps: Mary Dillon & Thos Cunningham. -BLO (p107)
03 Oct 1841	Catharine Fallen b 07 Sep 1841 d/o Michael & Susan Fallen; Sps: Pat^K Fallen & Mary Sheridan. -BLO (p107)
03 Oct 1841	Mary Ellen Heard b 30 Sep 1841 d/o William (dec'd) and Esther Heard; Sps: James Kearney & Marg^t Kearney. -BLO (p107)
09 Oct 1841	Catherine Rody b 01 Oct 1841 d/o John & Mary Rody; Sps: Mich^l Lavelle & Jane Burke. -BLO (p107)

BAPTISMS

10 Oct 1841	James Monahan b 04 Oct 1841 s/o Michael & Margaret Monahan; Sps: Mart McLaughlin & Miss McAvoy. -BLO (p107)
10 Oct 1841	Michael Hogan b 25 Sep 1841 s/o Garret & Catherine Hogan; Sps: Thos Larkin & Cath Kealty .-BLO (p107)
11 Oct 1841	Thomas Conway b 08 Oct 1841 s/o Patrick & Sarah Conway; Sps: Pat^K Bartlett & Mary Lruves. -BLO (p107)
11 Oct 1841	Mary Ellen Gallaher b 25 Sep 1841 d/o Thomas & Mary Gallaher; Sps: Jo^S Farrell, Pat^K Cauly, Eliza Kilben & Mary Kenady. -BLO (p107)
24 Oct 1841	Thomas Heney b 01 Oct 1841 s/o Edward & Jane Heney; Sps: Francis McCormick & Rose McManus. -BLO (p107)
03 Nov 1841	Henry Heip b 30 Oct 1841 s/o (blank) & Joseph Heip; Sps: (blank). -BLO (p107)
06 Nov 1841	Martha Ray, an adult married today. -BLO (p107)
07 Nov 1841	Marcellus Hilary Better b 27 Aug 1841 s/o Marcellus & Catherine Better; Sps: Edward Mullen & Mrs. Mullen. -BLO (p107)
10 Nov 1841	Mary Guest Semmes b 14 Oct 1841 d/o Samuel M & Elenora Semmes; private bapt. Died Jun 1842. -BLO (p107)
13 Nov 1841	Hannah Brodrock b 11 Nov 1841 d/o Michael & Catherine Brodrock; Sps: Pat^K McCormack & Cath O'Brien. -BLO (p107)
14 Nov 1841	Joseph Alexan^r Coleman b 19 Aug 1841 s/o William & Honor Coleman; Sps: Bend^t Logsdon & Susan Durbin. -BLO (p107)
14 Nov 1841	Daniel Samons b 12 Nov 1841 s/o Thomas & Margaret Samons; Sps: Pat^K Carlin & Marg^t Hoame, -BLO (p107)
15 Nov 1841	Sarah Henoghen b 21 Oct 1841 d/o Francis & Mary Henoghen; Sps: Ed Coin & Cath Neff, -BLO (p108)
15 Nov 1841	John Heilman 5½ years old s/o Mordica Heilman (dead) & Lorinda (now Mrs. Carney); Sps: Francis Henoghen, -BLO (p108)
15 Nov 1841	Mary Margaret S. Rerig born 09 Oct 1841 d/o Valentine & Susan Rerig; Sps: Margaret Rerig. -BLO (p108)
21 Nov 1841	Catherine Teresa Petri b 04 Nov 1841 d/o Joseph & Ann Petri; Sps: Cath Roman & Martin Roman. -BLO (p108)
24 Nov 1841	Mary Ann McCauley b 16 Nov 1841 d/o Thomas & Ann McCauley; Sps: Pat^K Gennen & Bridget Gennen. -BLO (p108)

27 Nov 1841   James Larkin b 16 Oct 1841 d/o Thomas & Mary Larkin;
Sps: Jno Callahan & Mary Monahan. -BLO (p108)

28 Nov 1841   William Kelly b 04 Nov 1841 s/o Thomas & Jane Kelly;
Sps: Jno Flynn & Marg^t McNulty. -BLO (p108)

28 Nov 1841   Ja^S Gerrety b 09 Nov 1841 s/o Michael & Mary Gerrety;
Sps: Jno Gerrety & Mrs. Ryan. -BLO (p108)

28 Nov 1841   Bernard Smith b 13 Nov 1841 s/o Bernard & Susan Smith;
Sps: Pat^k Riley & Cath Welsh. -BLO (p108)

29 Nov 1841   John O'Neill Jamison b 15 Aug 1841 s/o Francis & Eliza
Ann Jamison; Sps: Henry A. Jamison & Frances Howard.
-BLO (p108)

29 Nov 1841   Eliza Jane (col^d, ill) slave of Henry Jamison;
Sps: Lucy & Aaron. -BLO (p108)

08 Dec 1841   Owen (ill-col^d) b 21 Nov 1841 s/o Charlotte, slave of Dom
O'Donnel; Sps: Dom A. O'Donnel. -BLO (p108)

13 Dec 1841   Catherin Parks b 06 Dec 1841 d/o William & Ellen Parks;
Sps: Jno Nelson & Giles Cortellg. -BLO (p108)

17 Dec 1841   Sarah McCann b 12 Dec 1841 d/o Charles & Margaret
McCann; Sps: Mrs. McNulty. -BLO (p108)

19 Dec 1841   Garity Henry Brokand b 12 Dec 1841 s/o Herman &
Elizabeth Brokand; Sps: Henry Tuckenbey & Mary
Wonstreet. -BLO (p108)

27 Dec 1841   Jane Kelly b 12 Dec 1841 d/o Mich^l Kelly & Ann Kelly;
Sps: Owen Victory & Cecilia Samon. -BLO (p108)

28 Dec 1841   David O'Brien b 28 Dec 1841 s/o Pat^k O'Brien & Mrs.
O'Brien; Sps: Tho^S Mahony & Mary Coffy. -BLO (p108)

05 Jan 1842   John Daniel Kane b 02 Jan 1842 s/o Anthony & Maria
Kane; Sps: Jno Hershberger & Mrs. Mary A. Hershberger.
Prem supplied Dec 25. -BLO (p108)

06 Jan 1842   Hugh O'Neill b 22 Dec 1841 s/o Hugh & Mary O'Neill;
Sps: Pat^k Gainer & Maria Gainer. -BLO (p109)

06 Jan 1842   Thomas Reynolds b 22 Dec 1841 s/o John & Honor
Reynolds; Sps: Pat^K Cueick & Mary Kelly. -BLO (p109)

07 Jan 1842   Mary Susan Manion b 29 Aug 1841 d/o Patrick & Ellen
Manion; Sps: Mich^l Riley & Ann Maguire. -BLO (p109)

09 Jan 1842   Agnes McAleuse b 29 Dec 1841 d/o Danl & Agnes
McAleuse; Sps: Ja^S McHenry & Bridget McKellup. -BLO
(p109)

128

BAPTISMS

09 Jan 1842	Catherin Coulter (Ill) b 07 Oct 1841 d/o Marg^t Blubaugh & Saml Coulter; Sps: Cath Murry & Danl McAluse. -BLO (p109)
09 Jan 1842	Daniel McWilliams b 30 Dec 1841 s/o Daniel & Catherine McWilliams; Sps: John Campbell & Mary Clark. -BLO (p109)
10 Jan 1842	Anthony Riley b 09 Jan 1842 s/o David & Julia Riley; Sps: Miles Barrot & Honor Barrot. -BLO (p109)
12 Jan 1842	Herman Schrep b 06 Jan 1842 s/o Caspar & Elizabeth Schrep; Sps: Herman Luthman & Eliz^h Hack. -BLO (p109)
22 Jan 1842	John Loftus b 20 Jan 1842 s/o John & Rose Loftus; Sps: Ant Monihan & Rose Monihan. -BLO (p109)
23 Jan 1842	Margaret Jane Murry b 05 Dec 1841 d/o Daniel & Sally Murry; Sps: Jno Murry & Cath McCusker. -BLO (p109)
23 Jan 1842	Michael Tims b 30 Nov 1841 s/o Thomas & Catherine Tims; Sps: Pat Farrel & Bridget Turne. -BLO (p109)
30 Jan 1842	Bernard Riley b 28 Nov 1842 s/o Bernard & Margaret Riley; Sps: Leo^d Smith Jr. & Bridget Garahan. -BLO (p109)
31 Jan 1842	Julia Solphina Edwards, about 2 years old, d/o James & Ann Edwards; Sps: Fran B. Jamison & Cath Jamison; bapt. ceremonies were today supplied. -BLO (p109)
31 Jan 1842	Margaret Ann McCleery b 19 Nov 1841 d/o John & Maria McCleery; Sps: Peter McCleery & Nancy McCleery. -BLO (p109)
01 Feb 1842	John Leo b 07 Jan 1842 s/o Thomas & Sarah Leo; Sps: Pat^k Cronin & Nancy his wife. -BLO (p109)
07 Feb 1842	William Farrall b 03 Feb 1842 s/o John & Ann Farrall; Sps: Pat^k Hopkins & Mary Hopkins. -BLO (p109)
23 Feb 1842	Margaret Fitzpatrick (il.) b 12 Jan 1842 s/o Pat^k Fitzpatrick & Margaret Calahan; Sps: Marg^t McCabe. -BLO (p109)
27 Feb 1842	Patrick Welsh b 08 Feb 1842 s/o Thomas & Catharin Welsh; Sps: Pat^k Manion & Marg^t Kitzmiller. -BLO (p110)
27 Feb 1842	John Alexander Clarke b 14 Feb 1842 s/o Peter & Jane Clarke; Sps: Leonidas McLeer & Ellen McCusker. -BLO (p110)
27 Feb 1842	Catherin Flannigan b 18 Feb 1842 d/o Michael & Mary Flannigan; Sps: Christ McDonnel & Catherine Tims. -BLO (p110)

27 Feb 1842   Catherin Grube b 26 Jan 1842 d/o Bernard & Elizabeth Grube; Sps: Cath Williams. -Rev. Mr. Rumpler (p110)

01 Mar 1842   Patrick McNally b 09 Feb 1842 s/o Thomas & Mary McNally; Sps: Anthony Waughhan & Susan McNally. -Rev. Mr. Rumpler (p110)

01 Mar 1842   Eliza Mitchell d/o Thomas & Catherine Mitchell; Sps: Joseph Betz & Eliz[h] Schmidt. -Rev. Mr. Rumpler (p110)

04 Mar 1842   Ellen McKitrick b 20 Feb 1842 d/o Patrick & Jane McEntyee McKitrick; Sps: Mary McDermot & John Nealy. -BLO (p110)

06 Mar 1842   Patrick Ryan b 04 Mar 1842 s/o William & Mary Ryan; Sps: Philip Garvin & Ellen McGir. -BLO (p110)

06 Mar 1842   Nicholas Kreller b 03 Mar 1842 s/o George & Margaret Kreller; Sps: Nicholas Shue & Susan Shue. -BLO (p110)

08 Mar 1842   Joseph McGir b 07 Mar 1842 s/o Thomas & Mary McGir; Sps: Patrick Fay & Mary M Mattingly. -BLO (p110)

11 Mar 1842   Thomas McAndrass b 10 Feb 1842 s/o Mark & Bridget McAndrass; Sps: Thomas Farrell & Bridget McCormack. -BLO (p110)

14 Mar 1842   Patrick Barrot b 04 Mar 1842 s/o Antony & Ellen Barrot; Sps: Ed Barrot & Ellen Ford. -BLO (p110)

14 Mar 1842   Peter McGarey b 09 Mar 1842 s/o Peter & Marg[t] McGarey; Sps: Martin McGarey & Ann McGarey. -BLO (p110)

14 Mar 1842   John Connor b 06 Mar 1842 s/o Thomas & Catherin Connor; Sps: James McCune & Ann Cummings. -BLO (p110)

14 Mar 1842   Mary Ann Byrne b 13 Mar 1842 d/o Patrick & Jane Byrne; Sps: Jno Downey & Mary Riley. -BLO (p110)

14 Mar 1842   Patrick Lalley b 11 Mar 1842 s/o Michael & Bridget Lalley; Sps: And. Curley & Ellen Lalley. -BLO (p110)

18 Mar 1842   Josephine Null b 09 Mar 1842 d/o Joseph & (blank)Null; died. -BLO (p110)

Baptisms continuing from the back part of this record -L. Obermyer

18 Mar 1842   Mary Eliza Weisel b 23 Feb 1842 d/o Michael & Eve Weisel; Sps: Ann Yekell. -BLO (p25)

23 Mar 1842   Margaret McGovin b 24 Feb 1842 d/o Thomas & Ann McGovin; Sps: Mich[l] McNulty & Bridg[t] McDermot. -BLO (p25)

BAPTISMS

27 Mar 1842   George Henry Mutts b 20 Mar 1842 s/o Adam & Teresa Mutts; Sps: Geo Lemer & Mary Lemer. -BLO (p25)

27 Mar 1842   Rose Kennedy b 24 Mar 1842 d/o John & Bridget Kennedy; Sps: James Reed & Mary Garret. -BLO (p25)

27 Mar 1842   Mary Leonard b 03 Mar 1842 d/o James & Mary Leonard; Sps: Lawrence Byrne & Mary Byrne. -BLO (p25)

03 Apr 1842   Mary Adelaid Baller b 14 Feb 1842 d/o John & Mary Elizabeth Baller; Sps: Ch Swallenhaus & Mary Coulman. -BLO (p25)

04 Apr 1842   John Slokase b 02 Apr __ s/o John & Margaret Slokase; Sps: James Dolen & Mrs. Flaherty. -BLO (p25)

04 Apr 1842   Bridget Slokase b 15 Mar ____ s/o John & Margaret Slokase; Sps: James Dolen & Mrs. Flaherty. -BLO (p25)

05 Apr 1842   John and William Larkins, twins, b 03 Apr 1842, children of Thomas & Margaret Larkins; Sps: Brian Monahan. -BLO (p25)

06 Apr 1842   Henry Edmund Mattingly b 19 Feb 1842 s/o James & Ann Mattingly; Sps: Henry Mattingly. -BLO (p25)

10 Apr 1842   Mary Josephine Bucholtz b 07 Mar 1842 d/o William & Mary Bucholtz; Sps: Henry ____ & Mary Weger. -BLO (p25)

10 Apr 1842   Sarah Ellen Porter b 10 Dec 1841 d/o Henry & Lydia Porter; Sps: Elizabeth Logsdon. -BLO (p25)

10 Apr 1842   Joseph Anthony Klink b 06 Mar 1842 s/o Vandeline & Mary Klink; Sps: Lydia Porter. -BLO (p25)

11 Apr 1842   Mary Coyne b 10 Apr 1842 d/o Patrick & Catherine Coyne; Sps: Pat[k] Daley & Mary Nilan. -BLO (p25)

11 Apr 1842   Bridget Hevsen b 26 Mar 1842 d/o Andrew & Nancy Hevsen; Sps: Michael & Mrs. McDermot. -BLO (p25)

11 Apr 1842   Ann Tuen b 03 Apr 1842 d/o Austin & Mary Tuen; Sps: Pat[k] Tuen & Mary Narrow. -BLO (p25)

22 Apr 1842   Rose Flalty b 21 Apr 1842 d/o Martin & Rose Flalty; Sps: Pat McNallen & Brig[t] Burke. -BLO (p26)

23 Apr 1842   Margaret Beall b 06 Mar 1842 d/o Charles & Margaret Beall; Sps: Mat Coffey. -BLO (p26)

24 Apr 1842   Louisa Frances Holtzman b 26 Jan 1842 d/o Augustine & Louisa Holtzman; Sps: Hugh McAleer & Mary McAleer. -BLO (p26)

26 Apr 1842   Edward O'Connor b 08 Mar 1842 s/o Arthur & Ann
O'Connor; Sps: Ellen O'Brien. -BLO (p26)

01 May 1842   Catherin Miller b 16 Apr 1842 d/o Michael & Mary Miller;
Sps: Cath Breting. -BLO (p26)

01 May 1842   Elizabeth Gramlick b 29 Mar 1842 d/o Francis & Elizabeth
Gramlick; Sps: Elizabeth Gonder. -BLO (p26)

01 May 1842   Loretta Catherin Smith b 10 Feb 1835 d/o Fat^r dead & Mrs.
Holtaman (now); Sps: Math Coffey. -BLO (p26)

05 May 1842   Catherin Brophee b 02 May 1842 d/o Thomas & Sarah
Brophee; Sps: Mich^l Degnan & Sarah Ryan. -BLO (p26)

08 May 1842   Stephen McBride Kriegbaum b 04 Dec 1841 d/o Henry &
Fanny Kriegbaum; Sps: Susan Rerig. -BLO (p26)

08 May 1842   Sarah Raney b 12 Apr 1842 d/o Patrick & Mary Raney;
Sps: Ant Daley & Cath Daley. -BLO (p26)

08 May 1842   Luke Clarke b 07 May 1842 s/o Luke & Mary Clarke;
Sps: Jo^S McKelup & Cath McKelup. -BLO (p26)

08 May 1842   Catherin Reynolds b 06 May 1842 d/o Francis & Catherin
Reynolds; Sps: Ber^d Reynolds & Ellen Welsh. -BLO (p26)

09 May 1842   Alexander Coulter b 24 Feb 1842 s/o Samuel & Matilda
Coulter; Sps: Mary A. Carter. -BLO (p26)

09 May 1842   John Thomas Porter b 28 Apr 1842 s/o George & Margaret
Porter; Sps: Mary A. Carter. -BLO (p26)

11 May 1842   Elizabeth Fealy b 07 May 1842 d/o Patrick & Ann Fealy;
Sps: Ja^S Mahan & Marcella Cain. -BLO (p26)

15 May 1842   Mary Catherin Brown b 24 Apr 1842 d/o Herman & Ann
Mary Brown; Sps: Jo^S Cremer & Cath Wonstreet. -BLO
(p26)

22 May 1842   William Ryan b 15 May 1842 s/o William & Mary Ryan;
Sps: Jno Daugherty & Cath Clark. -BLO (p26)

29 May 1842   John Henry Carter b 09 Apr 1842 s/o Richard & Margaret
Carter; Sps: Mary A Carter. -BLO (p27)

29 May 1842   William Lilly b 15 Apr 1842 s/o Joshua & Teresa Lilly;
Sps: Ann Logsdon. -BLO (p27)

29 May 1842   Michael Devron s/o John & Honor Devron; Sps: Mich^l
Notten & Ellen Parks. -BLO (p27)

29 May 1842   Mary Morrison (col convert) b 23 Feb 1816 d/o Charles &
Sophia Morrison; Sps: Bern^d Reynolds. -BLO (p27)

BAPTISMS

30 May 1842	John Barry b 16 May 1842 s/o John & Margaret Barry; Sps: Pat[k] Swift & Bridget Finneyern. -BLO (p27)
30 May 1842	John McDonnald b 14 May 1842 s/o David & Honor McDonnald; Sps: Jno Ruddy & Cath Daugherty. -BLO (p27)
05 Jun 1842	Eliza Rerig b 06 Feb 1842 d/o Peter & Margaret Rerig; Sps: Elizabeth Ferley & Ben[d] Ferley. -BLO (p27)
05 Jun 1842	Philip Shea b 19 Apr 1842 s/o John & Mary Shea; Sps: Mrs. Ryan & Marg[t] Murphy. -BLO (p27)
17 Jun 1842	John Ward b 11 Jun 1842 s/o John & Mary Ward; Sps: Jonathan Staff & Maria Laughnay. -BLO (p27)
20 Jun 1842	Michael Fitzpatrick b 01 Jun 1842 s/o Jno & Ellen Fitzpatrick; Sps: Thomas Maloy & Ann McKinzee. -BLO (p27)
25 Jun 1842	Basil Marcellus McKinzie b 22 Mar 1842 s/o Samuel & Catherin McKinzie; Sps: Israel Garlitz. -BLO (p27)
25 Jun 1842	Ellen Garlitz b 05 Mar 1842 d/o John & Mary Garlitz; Sps; Israel Garlitz & Ann McKinzie. -BLO (p27)
25 Jun 1842	Ellen Frost (ill) b 05 Feb 1842 d/o Catherine McKinzie; Sps: Sam[l] Garlitz & Jane Gettune. -BLO (p27)
25 Jun 1842	Julius Zeller b 12 Apr 1842 s/o Joseph & Mary Zeller; Sps: John Glap & Mary Garlitz. -BLO (p27)
26 Jun 1842	Michael Manning b Jan? 1842 s/o Richard & Elizabeth Manning; Sps: Pat[k] Conway & Sally Conway. -BLO (p27)
26 Jun 1842	Cecilia Josephine Jamison b 13 Apr 1842 d/o Richard B & Rosila Ann Jamison; Sps: Louisa T. Jenkins & Dan[l] Brown. -BLO (p27)
26 Jun 1842	Athenosius Nethkin b 17 Nov 1841 s/o Adam & Sarah Nethkin; Sps: Mich[l] Mulholand & Ann Edwards. -BLO (p27)
26 Jun 1842	Priscilla Ann Gant b 25 Mar 1842 d/o Maria & Levi Gant; Sps: L. Teresa Jenkins. -BLO (p28)
29 Jun 1842	Mary Jane Nugent d/o Ally & Patrick Nugent; Sps: John Donolly & Mary Conlon. -BLO (p28)
02 Jul 1842	Catherine Kain b 28 Jun 1842 d/o John & Debora Kain; Sps: Patrick Coffee and Mrs. O'Brien. -BLO (p28)
03 Jul 1842	Margaret Catherine Brown b 27 May 1842 d/o Henry & Elizabeth Brown; Sps: Henry Hufman & Catherine Wonstreet. -BLO (p28)

133

05 Jul 1842   Susan Meyer b 27 Jun 1842 d/o Peter & Catherine Meyer; Sps: Susan Bart. -BLO (p28)

10 Jul 1842   Augustine Miller b 30 Jul 1838 s/o William and Catherine Miller; Sps: Fanny Krigbaum and Wm Arnold. -BLO (p28)

10 Jul 1842   Mary Ann Cross b 6 Jun 1842 d/o Thomas and Elizabeth Cross; Sps: Mary Ann Carter. -BLO (p28)

10 Jul 1842   Agnes Porter b __ May 1842 d/o John and Ellen Porter; Sps: Lucinda Porter. -BLO (p28)

11 Jul 1842   William Logsdon b 22 Jun 1842 s/o William and Elizabeth Logsdon; Sps: Margaret Durbin. -BLO (p28)

11 Jul 1842   Peter Conway b 20 Jun 1842 s/o Patrick and Bridget Conway; Sps: William Foley & Mrs. Rock. -BLO (p28)

17 Jul 1842   Elizabeth Whelen b 19 Jun 1842 d/o James and Bridget Whelen; Sps: Thomas Whelen & Sophia Roony. -BLO (p28)

23 Jul 1842   Catharine Cavenaugh b 10 Jun 1842 d/o Charles and Rose Cavenaugh; Sps: Michael Kelly and Ann Kelly. -BLO (p28)

24 Jul 1842   Mary Ann Callahan b 3 Apr 1842 d/o John and Ann Callahan; Sps: Francis Bergen & Mary Forrest. -BLO (p28)

24 Jul 1842   Mary Garvin b 17 Jul 1842 d/o Philip and Catherine Garvin; Sps: Thomas Samons and Bridget McCormick. -BLO (p28)

26 Jul 1842   John Flood b 23 Jun 1842 s/o Patrick and Margaret Flood; Sps: Charles Flood and Ann Timmons. -BLO (p28)

26 Jul 1842   Ann Tierney b 10 May 1842 d/o John Tierney & Mary Brady; Sps: Patrick Hoye and Margaret Flood. -BLO (p28)

31 Jul 1842   William Morrison b 19 Jun 1842 s/o Edmond and Elizabeth Morrison; Sps: Richard Manning. -BLO (p28)

31 Jul 1842   Mary Jane Read (col) b 15 Feb 1842 d/o Alexus and Harriet Read; Sps: Betsy Thompson. -BLO (p28)

31 Jul 1842   Louisa Teresa Jenkins (conditionally) adult; Sps: Leon Smith. -BLO (p28)

06 Aug 1842   Ellen Fitzmorris b 23 Jul 1842 d/o Michael & Mary Fitzmorris; Sps: Ed McDermot & Margart McNully. -BLO (p29)

13 Aug 1842   Julia Ann Porter b 10 May 1842 d/o Thomas & Ann Porter; Sps: Cecilia Matingly. -BLO (p29)

BAPTISMS

14 Aug 1842	Mary Ellen Porter b 18 Jun 1842 d/o John & Elizabeth Porter; Sps: Mary Ann Carter. -BLO (p29)
16 Aug 1842	Catherin Gillmartin b 17 Jul 1842 d/o James & Mary Gillmartin; Sps: Pat Smith & Br^t Cavanaugh. -BLO (p29)
21 Aug 1842	Michael Ryan b 17 Aug 1842 s/o Philip & Catherin Ryan; Sps: John White & Biddy Mulcaha. -BLO (p29)
24 Aug 1842	George Porter b 21 Jun 1838 s/o Moses & Emily Porter; Sps: Priscilla McKinzie. -BLO (p29)
24 Aug 1842	Lydia Porter b 14 May 1841 s/o Moses & Emily Porter; Sps: Priscilla McKinzie. -BLO (p29)
25 Aug 1842	Henry Dyer b 24 Aug 1842 s/o Henry & Bridget Dyer; Sps: Thos Reynolds. -BLO (p29)
26 Aug 1842	Charles Augustine Mattingly b 19 Aug 1842 s/o Baptist & Nancy Mattingly; Sps: Marg^t Kearney & Jno Kearney. -BLO (p29)
27 Aug 1842	Anthony Augustus Rucker b 08 Aug 1842 s/o John & Adelaid Rucker; Sps: Augustin <u>Schafer</u> & Adelaid Kulman. -BLO (p30)
27 Aug 1842	Catherine Wilger (ill) b 16 Aug 1842 d/o Catherine Wilger; Sps: Mary Sali. -BLO (p30)
27 Aug 1842	Mary Joanna Cammel b 14 Aug 1842 d/o Michael & Sali Cammel; Sps: Cath Turnert. -BLO (p30)
28 Aug 1842	Mary Clostermann b 04 Jul 1842 d/o Barney & Mary Clostermann; Sps: And Butkey & Mary Brogman. -BLO (p29)
28 Aug 1842	Michael Daugherty b 11 Jun 1842 s/o Michael & Mary Daugherty; Sps: Thos Timms & Cath Murry. -BLO (p29)
28 Aug 1842	Mary Ellen Schmessey b 30 Jun 1842 d/o John & Ann Schmessey; Sps: Barny Tolbeck & Sarah Roger. -BLO (p29)
28 Aug 1842	Margaret Rhinehart b 10 Jun 1842 d/o Joseph & Catherine Rhinehart; Sps: Margaret Gertner. -BLO (p29)
28 Aug 1842	Charles O'Neill b 06 Aug 1842 s/o Hugh & Bridget O'Neill; Sps: Thos Winslow & Mary Clarke. -BLO (p29)
28 Aug 1842	Mary Catherin Smith b 14 Jul 1842 d/o Jacob & Mary G. Smith; Sps: Jno Weyend & Mary Halbeck. -BLO (p29)
28 Aug 1842	Teresa Roseann Fletcher b 13 Aug 1842 d/o John & Teresa Fletcher; Sps: Pat^k Flood & Teresa Full. -BLO (p29)

28 Aug 1842   Isabella Burke conditionally bapt and received into the church being dangerously ill. -BLO (p29)

07 Sep 1842   Maurice Healey b 04 Aug 1842 s/o Thomas & Emily Healey; Sps: Pat[k] Healey & Zelei Hoffman. -BLO (p30)

07 Sep 1842   Michael and John Langen, twins, b 26 Aug 1842 s/o Michael & Mary Langen; Sps: Cath Ruddy & Mich[l] Rooney, James Mealey & Mary Barret respectifully (sic) -BLO (p30)

08 Sep 1842   Cha[s] Augustine Smith b 03 Sep 1842 (Illeg) s/o Mary Jane Smith; Sps: Catherin Brazil. -BLO (p30)

09 Sep 1842   Catherin Maguire b 11 Aug 1842 d/o Michael & Mary Ann Maguire; Sps: Thos Beatty & Cath Beatty. -BLO (p30)

11 Sep 1842   Henrietta Petronilla Hicksenbaugh b 31 May 1842 d/o Aaron & Rachel Hicksenbaugh; Sps: Susan Durbin. -BLO (p30)

11 Sep 1842   William Enock McKinzie b 03 Jan 1842 s/o John & Barbara McKinzie; Sps: Mary Logsdon. -BLO (p30)

11 Sep 1842   Rebecca Simpson b 17 Jul 1842 d/o David & Nancy Simpson; Sps: Mary Ann Carter. -BLO (p30)

12 Sep 1842   Michael Carney b 09 Sep 1842 s/o Michael & Bridget Carney; Sps: Jno Carney & Cath Kelly. -BLO (p30)

12 Sep 1842   Catherin Langen b 11 Sep 1842 d/o Michael & Ann Langen; Sps: Pat[k] Daugherty & Ellen Barrott. -BLO (p30)

17 Sep 1842   Dennis Lewis Garlitz b 18 Aug 1842 s/o Solomon & Rebecca Garlitz; Sps: Sam[l] F. McKinzie & Cath McKinzie. -BLO (p30)

18 Sep 1842   Matilda McAtee b 05 Sep 1842 d/o Michael & Martha McAtee; Sps: Pat[k] Brady & Cath Garahan. -BLO (p30)

25 Sep 1842   Maria Louisa Howell (convert) abt. 20 yrs; Sps: Mat Coffee. -BLO (p30)

28 Sep 1842   Teresa (colord-illeg.) b Jun 1842 d/o Lucy, ___ing to Mrs. Byran Jamison; Sps: Cath Jamison. -BLO (p30)

02 Oct 1842   Antony Meyer b 24 Sep 1842 s/o Henry & Elizabeth Meyer; Sps: Antony Helson. -BLO (p31)

07 Oct 1842   Joseph Breting b 04 Oct 1842 s/o Joseph & Catherin Breting; Sps: Joseph Hodel & Margart Killen. -BLO (p31)

09 Oct 1842   Christina Verner b ___ Jul 1842 s/o John & Barbara Verner; Sps: Jno Shethen & Christ[na] Shethen. -BLO (p31)

09 Oct 1842	Denis McKinzie b 26 Aug 1842 s/o Basil & Elizabeth McKinzie; Sps: Mary Logsdon. -BLO (p31)
10 Oct 1842	Daniel King b 25 Sep 1842 s/o Edward & Bridget King; Sps: Denis Mullady. -BLO (p31)
10 Oct 1842	Mary Barrot b 12 Sep 1842 d/o James & Maria Barrot; Sps: Pat Manahan & Julia Barrot. -BLO (p31)
10 Oct 1842	James Kelly b 29 Sep 1842 s/o John & Catherin Kelly; Sps: Ant Herrogen & Alice Young. -BLO (p31)
13 Oct 1842	Sarah Monahan b 20 Aug 1842 d/o Brien & Mary Monahan; Sps: Thos Sinod & Ann Redmon. -BLO (p31)
13 Oct 1842	Sarah Jane Murphy b 18 Jul 1842 d/o William & Caroline Murphy; Sps: Ann Heyer. -BLO (p31)
16 Oct 1842	Bridget Ford b 11 Oct 1842 d/o Jeremia & Mary Ford; Sps: Cha^S McCan & Mrs. Ward. -BLO (p31)
17 Oct 1842	Elizabeth Atkinson b 30 Sep 1842 d/o Alexander & Rose Ann Atkinson; Sps: Margrt McCafrey & James McCafrey. -BLO (p31)
19 Oct 1842	Mary Ann Garlan b 23 Sep 1842 d/o James & Margaret Garlan; Sps: Thos Brady & Mary Brady. -BLO (p31)
29 Oct 1842	Henry Kercher b 26 Sep 1842 s/o Henry & Adelaid Kercher; Sps: Francis Shuldt. -BLO (p31)
30 Oct 1842	John Barney Weiger b 08 Sep 1842 s/o Barney & Catherin Weiger; Sps: Bar^d Coleman & Cath Bruchman. -BLO (p31)
30 Oct 1842	Nicholas Haek b 23 Oct 1842 s/o John & Elizabeth Haek; Sps: Nich^S Haek & Ann Snair. -BLO (p31)
30 Oct 1842	Jane Downey b 28 Oct 1842 d/o Thomas & Mary Downey; Sps: Pat Coleman & Honora Gorman. -BLO (p31)
31 Oct 1842	John Martin Rosenberger b 15 Oct 1842 s/o Baldesa & Elizabeth Rosenberger; Sps: Mr. Weisel, Eve Weisel. -BLO (p32)
13 Nov 1842	Catherin Flynn b 25 Oct 1842 d/o Michael & Mary Flynn; Sps: Jno Briscoe & Cath Hogen. -BLO (p32)
14 Nov 1842	James Rooney b 10 Nov 1842 s/o James & Sabrina Rooney; Sps: Mich^l Harris & Winey Hart. -BLO (p32)
14 Nov 1842	John Padin b 26 Oct 1842 s/o John & Bridget Padin; Sps: Jno McCormick & Mary Scott. -BLO (p32)
20 Nov 1842	Mary Ann Byrne b 20 Oct 1842 d/o Pierce & Frances Byrne; Sps: Mich^l Kerney & Martha Matingly. -BLO (p32)

20 Nov 1842   Michael Jackson, b abt. 11 Nov 1842, s/o Father dead & widow Eliz[th] Jackson, (ceremonies to be supplied, they were supplied 19 Feb 1843); Sps: Sarah Ryan. -BLO (p32)

27 Nov 1842   Catherin McGran b 25 Sep 1842 d/o Patrick & Catherin McGran; Sps: Edward Ruddy & Ellen McCusker. -BLO (p32)

27 Nov 1842   John Daley b 03 Nov 1842 s/o Patrick & Mary Daley; Sps: Mich[l] McDermot & Bridget Rogers. -BLO (p32)

27 Nov 1842   Joseph Moody b 18 Nov 1842 s/o John & Bridget Moody; Sps: Tho[s] Conly & Bridg[t] McGee. -BLO (p32)

04 Dec 1842   Mary Cronin b 17 Nov 1842 d/o Philip & Julia Cronin; Sps: Jno Barrot & Mary Mohan. -BLO (p32)

04 Dec 1842   Mary Samons b 27 Nov 1842 d/o Thomas & Cecilia Samons; Sps: Tho[s] Ward & Mrs. Sheridan. -BLO (p32)

09 Dec 1842   Elizabeth Hart b 06 Dec 1842 d/o George & Juliann Hart; Sps: Eliz[h] Heack for another woman. -BLO (p32)

11 Dec 1842   Mary Jane Lavinski b 22 Nov 1842 d/o Augustine & Agnes Lavinski; Sps: Wm Gallaher & Mary Lynn. -BLO (p32)

12 Dec 1842   Catherin Brogan b 30 Nov 1842 d/o Thomas & Maria Brogan; Sps: Tho[s] Hegen & Miss Kelley. -BLO (p32)

12 Dec 1842   Margaret Lowry b 10 May 1842 d/o Robert & Juliann Lowry; Sps: Mich[l] Nugent & Mary Nugent. -BLO (p32)

18 Dec 1842   Elizabeth Berkheart b 06 Dec 1842 d/o Nicholas & Elizabeth Berkheart; Sps: Eliz[th] Ferley. -BLO (p32)

24 Dec 1842   Charles Black b 13 Dec 1842 s/o John & Lydia Ann Black; Sps: Bap Mattingly & Martha Mattingly. -BLO (p32)

25 Dec 1842   Douglas Ferley b 27 Sep 1842 s/o Henry & Catherin Ferley; Sps: Nic Berkhart & Josephine Wendel. -BLO (p33)

25 Dec 1842   William Henry Howe b 21 Nov 1842 s/o James & Mary Howe; Sps: Wm Lepold & Mrs. Gondor. -BLO (p33)

25 Dec 1842   Mary Magdalen Hershberger b 03 Dec 1842 d/o Jno & Mary Elizabeth Hershberger; Sps: Fran Gramlick & Eliz Gramlick. -BLO (p33)

30 Dec 1842   Mary Catherin Staizen b 21 Dec 1842 d/o George & Lenah Staizen; Sps: George Lerfred & Cath Danner. -BLO (p33)

01 Jan 1843   Patrick Coffey b 28 Dec 1842 s/o Patrick & Mary Coffey; Sps: Mat Coffey & Mr. Carin. -BLO (p33)

01 Jan 1843   Ellen McCan b 23 Dec 1842 d/o Charles & Margaret McCan; Sps: Jno Bowry & Mrs. Mealy. -BLO (p33)

BAPTISMS

08 Jan 1843   John Briscoe b 25 Dec 1842 s/o Michael & Catherin Briscoe; Sps: Tho^S Rooney & Honor Cavanagh. -BLO (p33)

10 Jan 1843   John McCabe b 27 Dec 1842 s/o James & Margaret McCabe; Sps: Pat Kanagh & Eliz^h Nunan. -BLO (p33)

15 Jan 1843   Keern Kirby b 21 Dec 1842 s/o George & Margaret Kirby; Sps: Keern Farrel & Mary Rourke. -BLO (p33)

22 Jan 1843   Eliza Weber b 09 Dec 1842 d/o Francis & Mary Weber; Sps: Mary Bucholtz. -BLO (p33)

22 Jan 1843   Francis Thomas Arnold b 28 Aug 1842 s/o Joseph & Matilda Arnold; Sps: Tho^S Halpin & Mat^a McVigor. -BLO (p33)

28 Jan 1843   Mary Butts b 05 Jan 1843 d/o Margaret Butts; Sps: Mary Kelley & Pat Crow. -BLO (p33)

29 Jan 1843   Ann Gouldin b 04 Apr 1842 d/o John & Ellen Gouldin; Sps: Danl McNally & Cath McNally. -BLO (p33)

29 Jan 1843   Patrick McManus b 28 Dec 1842 s/o Patrick & Rose McManus; Sps: Jno McManus & Cath McGrass. -BLO (p33)

29 Jan 1843   Francis McCusker b 30 Nov 1842 s/o John & Margaret McCusker; Sps: Wm McLaughlin & Frances Ryan. -BLO (p33)

29 Jan 1843   Sarah Florence Ryan b 03 Jan 1843 d/o Nicholas P & Ann Ryan; Sps: Sarah Garrhity. -BLO (p33)

               1843 BAPTISMS. Since 01 Jan 1843 there were 12 bapt^S whose names are recorded in the old book. -BLO (p03) [Those presented above]

02 Feb 1843   James Kelley b 26 Jan 1843 s/o Thomas & Mary Kelley; Sps: Peter & Mary Dillon. -BLO (p04)

05 Feb 1843   Catherine Ann Riley b 25 Jan 1843 d/o James & Susan Riley; Sps: William Davy & May Campbell. -BLO (p03)

05 Feb 1843   Valentine Knighthart b 29 Jan 1843 d/o Titus & Gertrude Knighthart; Sps: Val Helfing & Eliza Rosenberger. -BLO (p03)

05 Feb 1843   Nicholas Ferley b 10 Jan 1843 s/o Wendland & Elizabeth Ferley; Sps: N. Berkhart & Eliz Berkhart. -BLO (p03)

08 Feb 1843   John Wallace b 16 Feb 1836 s/o Daniel Wallace, decea^d, and his wife Elizabeth now widow Jackson; Sps: Mat Coffy. -BLO (p04)

13 Feb 1843	Jane McDonald b 16 Jan 1843 d/o Patrick & Jane McDonald; Sps: Jno & Mary Loftus. -BLO (p04)
13 Feb 1843	Anthony Ford b 31 Jan 1843 s/o Owen & Mary Ford; Sps: Mich[l] Angen & Ann Ford. -BLO (p04)
13 Feb 1843	Patrick Manly b 05 Feb 1843 s/o James & Bridget Manley; Sps: Pat[k] Gallaher & Honor Gahan. -BLO (p04)
13 Feb 1843	Patrick Raferty b 16 Jan 1843 s/o Patrick & Mary Raferty; Sps: Dan[l] Kine & Mary Melarkey. -BLO (p05)
15 Feb 1843	Juliann Miller b 03 Jan 1843 d/o Peter & Elizabeth Miller; Sps: Margaret Rerig. -BLO (p05)
19 Feb 1843	Mary Magdalen Better b 09 Dec 1842 d/o Marcelle & Catharin Better; Sps: Marg[t] Kerney & Tho[s] Quinn. -BLO (p05)
19 Feb 1843	Mary McDermot b 23 Jan 1843 d/o Thomas & Maria McDermot; Sps: Ch McLaughlin & Mrs. Le Massle. -BLO (p05)
19 Feb 1843	John Henry Mattingly b 28 Jan 1843 s/o George & Ann Mattingly; Sps: Jno & Margrt Kerney. -BLO (p06)
20 Feb 1843	Joan Bern Knapp b 17 Oct 1842 s/o Henry & Catharine Knapp (conj); Sps: Bern Marburg & Cath Wanidiass. -P. Joan Neumann (p06)
26 Feb 1843	John Frederic Kramer b 14 Feb 1843 s/o John F. Kramer & Anna Mary Joergen; Sps: Jos Kramer & Eliz Schreiber. -P. Joan Neumann (p06)
26 Feb 1843	Frederick William Legermeister, 18 yr old, rexertims ex heresi lutheran, conditionally, s/o Henri Arimini Legermeister & (xchatry women spin Grotmn); Sps: fmt Francis Kremlich. -P. Joan Neumany (p06)
26 Feb 1843	Catharine Gorman b 10 Feb 1843 d/o John & Juliann Gorman; Sps: Dan[l] Flynn & Ellen Callen. -BLO (p07)
26 Feb 1843	Francis Keyho b 19 Feb 1843 s/o Thomas & Ann Keyho; Sps: Pat[k] Brady & Eliz[h] Brown. -BLO (p07)
05 Mar 1843	James Garrahan b 01 Feb 1843 s/o Thomas & Elizabeth Garrahan; Sps: Bar Rabit & Mary Cusick. -BLO (p07)
05 Mar 1843	John Clarke b 26 Feb 1843 s/o Darby & Catherine Clarke; Sps: Mich[l] Graham & Sal Samon. -BLO (p07)
12 Mar 1843	Catharine Keenan b 24 Feb 1843 d/o Thomas & Elizabeth Keenan; Sps: Mary A. Carter & Mich[l] Cummerford. -BLO (p08)

BAPTISMS

13 Mar 1843	Margaret Hoarn b 18 Feb 1843 d/o Pat^k & Mary Hoarn; Sps: Lawrence Coulehan & Jane Gallaher. -BLO (p08)
13 Mar 1843	Patrick Barrot b 20 Feb 1843 s/o Miles & Mary Barrot; Sps: John & Sarah McNally .-BLO (p08)
13 Mar 1843	John Roach b 01 Mar 1843 s/o Michael & Jane Roach; Sps: Jno Healy & Lydia Miller. -BLO (p09)
13 Mar 1843	Ann Gallaher b 12 Mar 1843 d/o Edward & Elizabeth Gallaher; Sps: Hugh Gallaher & Cath Hogan. -BLO (p09)
27 Mar 1843	Ellen Lee b 23 Mar 1843 d/o Cornelius & Ellen Lee; Sps: Pat^k O'Brien & Judy Murphy. -BLO (p09)
02 Apr 1843	John Henry Mahoney (col^d) b 29 Nov 1842 s/o Chas & Hetty, slaves; Sps: Ja^s Karney & Ellen McCleery. -BLO (p09)
02 Apr 1843	Martha Ellen Watson (col^d) b 3 mo ago d/o Greenbury (free) & Mary, slave of J. Hudelson; Sps: Jno McCaffrey. -BLO (p09)
02 Apr 1843	Francis Costello b 29 Oct 1842 s/o William & Mary Costello; Sps: Michael Hopkins. -BLO (p09)
03 Apr 1843	Margaret Cunningham b. Feb 1843 d/o Michael & Cath Cunningham; Sps: Danl Morgan. -BLO (p10)
05 Apr 1843	Richard Thompson Semmes b 02 Jan 1843 s/o Saml M. Semmes & his wife Elenora; bapt. privately. -BLO (p10)
06 Apr 1843	George Marks age abt. 20 yrs, a convert, was conditionally & privately baptized, being in danger of death, dec^d soon after. -BLO (p10)
11 Apr 1843	Ann Maria Gessner b 31 Mar 1843 d/o (blank) Gessner; Sps: Cath Breting. -BLO (p10)
13 Apr 1843	Ann McGerry b 22 Mar 1843 d/o Patrick & Margaret McGerry; Sps: Peter Mealue & Ellen Crowe. -BLO (p11)
23 Apr 1843	Mary Fealey b 19 Mar 1843 d/o Pat^k & Ann Fealey; Sps: William & Margaret Hoarne. -BLO (p11)
23 Apr 1843	Mary Ann Daley b 18 Mar 1843 d/o Anthony & Catherin Daley; Sps: Hugh Mulholand & Mary Rainey. -BLO (p11)
24 Apr 1843	Mary Ann Kelley b 10 Apr 1843 d/o John & Honora Kelley; Sps: Mich^l McLaughlin & Ann Riley. -BLO (p11)
24 Apr 1843	James Tuey b 09 Apr 1843 s/o Pat^k & Bridg^t Tuey; Sps: Mich^l Barro & Susan McNally. -BLO (p11)
04 May 1843	Mary Ann Shriber b 21 Apr 1843 d/o Henry & Elizabeth Shriber; Sps: Mary Ann Heyer. -BLO (p12)

07 May 1843	William Thomas Mullen b 06 Apr 1843 s/o Edward & Ann Mullen; Sps: Tho^S Healey & Sar Brod. -BLO (p12)
07 May 1843	Sarah Degnon b 29 Apr 1843 d/o Tho^S & Mary Degnon; Sps: James Ganon & Mary Ryan. -BLO (p12)
11 May 1843	John Fay b 30 Apr 1843 s/o Patrick & Ann Fay; Sps: Tho^S & Ann Maria McGir. -BLO (p12)
14 May 1843	Francis Strutmueller b 06 Mar 1843 s/o Henry & Catharine Strutmueller; Sps: Nich^S Lestung & Cath Shuelrick. -BLO (p12)
14 May 1843	James Turley b 20 Mar 1843 s/o Richard & Rose Turley; Sps: Pat^K & Mary Whalen. -BLO (p13)
14 May 1843	Susanna Leitinger b 11 Apr 1843 d/o Mich^l & Barbara Leitinger; Sps: Geo Hosneu & Susan Knapp. -BLO (p13)
14 May 1843	George Fisher b 15 Apr 1843 s/o Joseph & Catharine Fisher; Sps: Geo Hosneu. -BLO (p13)
15 May 1843	Catherin Dean b 04 May 1843 d/o Francis & Mary Dean; Sps: Henrietta Arnold. -BLO (p13)
15 May 1843	Ellen Naughten b 25 Apr 1843 d/o John & Jullia Naughten; Sps: Michael Madden & Margrt Coskery. -BLO (p13)
15 May 1843	Catherin Ruddy b 25 Apr 1843 d/o Anthony & Cath Ruddy; Sps: Mich^l Finney & Mary Sheriden. -BLO (p14)
18 May 1843	John Fox b 11 Mar 1843 s/o Henry & Mary Fox; Sps: Rosana Martin & Edward Sick. -BLO (p14)
21 May 1843	William Mulcahey b 15 May 1843 s/o John & Bridget Mulcahey; Sps: Pat^K & Marg^t Mulcahey. -BLO (p14)
21 May 1843	William Folk b 13 Apr 1843 s/o Peter & Barbara Folk; Sps: Mrs. Gessner. -BLO (p14)
25 May 1843	Petrus Bompacher b 04 Jan 1843 s/o John Bompacher & Eva _____. -P. Newmann (p14)
25 May 1843	John Schellhaus b 16 Apr 1843 s/o John Peter Shellhaus & Barbara G. Schnurr.-P. Newmann (p15)
25 May 1843	Julian Loftus b 13 May 1843 s/o John & Mary Loftus; Sps: Michael Ruddy & Mary Howe. -BLO (p15)
27 May 1843	Rose Ann Larkin b 19 Apr 1843 d/o Tho^S & Mary Larkin; Sps: Francis Brogan & Mary [blank]. -BLO (p15)
28 May 1843	Thomas William Lasley b 01 Sep 1842 s/o Rich^d & Cath Lasley; Sps: Ja^S Thompson & Bridg^t McLaughlin. -BLO (p15)

28 May 1843	Mary Trainer b 17 May 1843 d/o John & Roseanna Trainer; Sps: Cha[S] Denny & Mary Kelley. -BLO (p15)
28 May 1843	Catherin Carney b 27 Feb 1843 d/o Jno & Mary Carney; Sps: Pat Kilduf & Cath Bordin. -BLO (p16)
28 May 1843	Patrick McGar b 25 Apr 1843 s/o Pat[k] & Mary McGar Sps: Hugh Brady & Brdg[t] Doherty. -BLO (p16)
28 May 1843	William McCue b 10 May 1843 s/o Ja[s] & Mary McCue; Sps: Barney & Bridg[t] Murphy. -BLO (p16)
28 May 1843	George Wash[n] Windel b 10 Apr 1843, s/o Mary E. Windel bpt privately-it being not likely to live long. -BLO (p16)
04 Jun 1843	Francis Ott b 07 Apr 1843 s/o Valentine & Elizabeth Ott; Sps: Francis & Eliz[h] Gramlich. -BLO (p16)
04 Jun 1843	Mich[l] Thomas Sinnet b 11 Mar 1843 s/o Bridg[t] McNally; Sps: Pat Connor & Mrs. Larkin. -BLO (p17)
04 Jun 1843	Solomon Jacob Robinson b 28 Feb 1843 s/o Solomon & Ellen Robinson; Sps: Sarah Ann McKinzie. -BLO (p17)
06 Jun 1843	Ann & Mary Smith, twins b 02 Jun 1843, children of Pat[k] & Ann Smith; Sps. of Ann: Christ[r] O'Rouke & Mary King, Sps. of Mary: Owen Victory & Cath FitzPatrick. -BLO (p17)
11 Jun 1843	William Spesinger b 13 Mar 1843 s/o Joseph & Catherine Spesinger; Sps: Leop & Eliz[h] Larkey. -BLO (p17)
11 Jun 1843	Ann Elizabeth Tumlinson b 07 Apr 1843 d/o Jesse & Ann Tumlinson; Sps: Jo[s] Stoup & Mary Logsdon. -BLO (p17)
11 Jun 1843	John Dempsey b 29 May 1843 s/o Thomas & Ann Dempsey; Sps: Mich[l] Hanon & Mary Horne. -BLO (p18)
11 Jun 1843	Jane McGan b 09 Jun 1843 d/o Richard & Marcella McGan; Sps: Pat Keegan & Cath Beaty. -BLO (p18)
13 Jun 1843	Sarah Ann Weitsel b 03 Sep 1840 d/o Elias & Fanny Weitsel; Sps: Sarah Garlitz. -BLO (p18)
13 Jun 1843	Susan Weitsel b 01 Jan 1843 sister of above (d/o Elias & Fanny Weitsel); Sps: Nancy McKenzie. -BLO (p18)
13 Jun 1843	William Andrew Robison b 18 Nov 1842 s/o William & Rody Resella Robison; Sps: Jeremiah & Cath McKenzie. -BLO (p18)
13 Jun 1843	Baptist Mattingly b 08 May 1843 s/o William & Eva Mattingly; Sps: Henry Mattingly & Sam[l] F. McKenzie. -BLO (p19)

15 Jun 1843	James Hanna b 03 Jun 1843 s/o Jno & Margrt Hanna; Sps: Jer Ford & Mary Sheriden. -BLO (p19)
17 Jun 1843	Mary McMohan b 24 Dec 1842 d/o John & Mary McMohan; Sps: Tho^S Cox & Mary Brady. -BLO (p19)
20 Jun 1843	Mary Helen Masters b 27 Jan 1843 d/o Richard & Ann Masters; Sps: Michael & Margaret Kearney. -BLO (p19)
25 Jun 1843	Elizabeth Ellen Mattingly b 03 Apr 1843 d/o Dominick & Nancy Mattingly; Sps: Mary Jamison & Henry McKehan. -BLO (p19)
25 Jun 1843	John Henry Hardy aged nearly 6 years and Elizabeth Hardy b 10 May 1842 (colored children) children of Grafton & Valet Hardy; Sps: Peggy Miller. -BLO (p20)
25 Jun 1843	Mary Jane Logsdon b 07 May 1843 d/o Joseph & Margaret Logsdon of the Blooming Rose Congregation; Sps: Peter & Nancy McCleery. -BLO (p20)
26 Jun 1843	Simon Cronin b 17 Jun 1843 s/o Patrick and Nancy Cronin; Sps: Mary Ann Cragen. -BLO (p20)
26 Jun 1843	Ann Jane Hagen b 19 Jun 1843 d/o Hugh & Bridg^t Hagen; Bapt by Bishop Chance of Natches; Sps: Michael & Ann McVay. -BLO (p21)
26 Jun 1843	Catherine Barry b 12 Jun 1843 d/o Pat^k & Mary Barry; Bapt by Bishop Chance; Sps: Mart Ruddy & Mary Naily. -BLO (p21)
26 Jun 1843	John Ruddy b 13 Jun 1843 s/o Jno & Mary Ruddy; bapt. by Bishop Chance; Sps: Pat^k & Cath Coyne. -BLO (p21)
26 Jun 1843	John Callahan b 24 Jun 1843 s/o Peter & Ann Calahan; Bpt. by Bishop Chance; Sps: James & Catherine McKellup. -BLO (p22)
02 Jul 1843	Ann Maria Gannon b 18 Jun 1843 d/o Patrick & Bridget Gannon; Sps: Jno McNeff & Margaret King. -BLO (p20)
02 Jul 1843	Jno McCall b 24 Jun 1843 s/o John & Mary McCall; Sps: Jno Smith and Elizabeth King. -BLO (p20)
03 Jul 1843	Catherin Bulsing b 27 Apr 1843 d/o Herman & Eliz^h Bulsing; Sps: Hen Sulkdt. -BLO (p21)
03 Jul 1843	Mary Shulte b 02 Jun 1843 d/o Christian & Julia Shulte; Sps: Mary Rickelanan & Hen Weiger. -BLO (p21)
04 Jul 1843	William Land b 02 Jul 1843 s/o Michael & Julia Land; Sps: Jno White & Margt Moran -BLO (p21)
05 Jul 1843	Jerome Deacon b 19 Feb 1843 s/o Jesse & Mary Deacon; Sps: Dr. Tho^S Healy. -BLO (p21)

09 Jul 1843	Ann Wegas b 28 Jan 1843 d/o Herman & Mary Wegas; Sps: Ann Logsdon & Henry Neiman. -BLO (p22)
09 Jul 1843	Cornelius Shura b 09 Feb 1843 s/o Mathias & Luisa Shura; Sps: Jo[S] Shura. -BLO (p22)
09 Jul 1843	Samuel McKinzie b 11 Oct 1842 s/o Patrick McKinzie & Lavina; Sps: Cath McKinzie. -BLO (p22)
10 Jul 1843	Mary Coreran b 10 Jul 1843 d/o Martin & Biddy Coreran; Sps: Danl McAlice & Ag McKellup. -BLO (p22)
10 Jul 1843	Michael Barry b 03 Jul 1843 s/o Jno & Margaret Barry; Sps: Danl Haslin & B. M. Kelly. -BLO (p22)
10 Jul 1843	Michael Riley b 07 Jul 1843 s/o David & Julia Riley; Sps: Mich[l] Williams & J Bryne. -BLO (p23)
10 Jul 1843	Stanislaus Kostta Kreighbaum b 31 Mar 1843 s/o Henry & Frances Kreighbaum; Sps: Eliz[h] Kreighbaum. -BLO (p23)
10 Jul 1843	Demetrius Leonidas Beisel b 09 Apr 1843 s/o Jno & Ann Biesel; Sps: Frances Kreighbaum. -BLO (p23)
16 Jul 1843	Juliana Helfri b 25 Jun 1843 d/o Valentine & Mary Helfri; Sps: Geo & Juliana Hart. -BLO (p23)
16 Jul 1843	Margaret Catherine Shultz b 06 Jun 1843 d/o Garret & Mary Shultz; Sps: Jno Cookey & Mary Weget. -BLO (p23)
16 Jul 1843	Mary Catherin Rerig b 22 May 1843 d/o Peter & Mary Rerig; Sps: Geo & Juliana Hart. -BLO (p23)
16 Jul 1843	James Null s/o Jo[S] & (blank) Null was privately baptized being sick, cermonies supplied Sep 24; Sps: Mrs. O'Rouke. -BLO (p23)
24 Jul 1843	Arnold Henry Messman b 11 Jun 1843 s/o Henry & Cath[n] Messman; Sps: Hen Wonstreet & Mrs. Gramber. -BLO (p24)
29 Jul 1843	Jane Darake b 28 May 1843 d/o John & Mary Darake; Sps: Hen Matingly & Mary Garlits. -BLO (p24)
05 Aug 1843	Michael Nathan b 25 Jun 1843 s/o Peter & Margaret Nathan; Sps: James Sherry & Jane Garlitz. -BLO (p24)
05 Aug 1843	Mathew Farrell b 24 Jul 1843 s/o John & Ann Farrell; Sps: Francis & Bridg[t] McCormack. -BLO (p24)
06 Aug 1843	Nicholas Shea b 23 Apr 1843 s/o Jno & Mary Shea; Sps: Nic Murphy & Ann Fay. -BLO (p24)
06 Aug 1843	Daniel Dillon b Jan 22 1843 s/o Edward & Luisa Dillon; Sps: James Kelly & Cath Kelly. -BLO (p24)

06 Aug 1843	Mary McNulty b 23 Jul 1843 d/o Mich[l] and Margret McNulty; Sps: John & Mary Mealy. -BLO (p24)
11 Aug 1843	Bernard Murphy b 17 Jun 1843 s/o Pat[k] & Bridget Murphy; Sps: Jno & Mary Timmons. -BLO (p25)
11 Aug 1843	John Haney b 29 Jul 1843 s/o Edward & Jane Haney; Sps: And McMohan & Mary McCan. -BLO (p25)
13 Aug 1843	Herman Wetmuller b __ June 1843 s/o Denis & Cath Wetmuller; Sps: Hen Shutmuller. -BLO (p25)
13 Aug 1843	Thomas Reynolds b 28 Jul 1843 s/o Jno & Biddy Reynolds: Sps: Fr Reynolds & widow Murry. -BLO (p25)
13 Aug 1843	Hugh McWilliams b 13 Jul 1843 s/o Daniel & Cath McWilliams; Sps: Wm & Bridget McKellup. -BLO (p25)
13 Aug 1843	William Briscoe b 19 Jul 1843 s/o Jno & Sarah Briscoe; Sps: Mary Welan. -BLO (p25)
13 Aug 1843	James Mattingly b 02 Aug 1843 s/o Francis & Jane Mattingly; Sps: Reb Donahoe. -BLO (p25)
13 Aug 1843	Mary Ann Finley b 02 Aug 1843 d/o John & Ann Finley; Sps: Pat[k] Mitchel & Ann Brown. -BLO (p26)
14 Aug 1843	Thomas Landers b 28 Dec 1842 s/o Maurice & Joanna Landers; Sps: Timothy & Ellen Murathy. -BLO (p26)
15 Aug 1843	Elizabeth Mallen b 22 Apr 1843 d/o Jno & Rosanna Mallen; Sps: Ja[s] Reed & Brig[t] Murtogh. -BLO (p26)
15 Aug 1843	Ann Mallen b 13 Sep 1840 of same parents [d/o Jno & Rosanna Mallen] bapt soon after had ceremonies supplied; Sps Tho[s] Murtogh. -BLO (p26)
20 Aug 1843	Ann Maria Dorothy Koleman b 01 Aug 1843 d/o Henry & Mary A. Koleman; Sps: Geo & Cath Dressman. -BLO (p26)
20 Aug 1843	John George Mertz b 11 Aug 1843 s/o Geo & Ann Mary Mertz; Sps: Jno Egast & Eliz[h] Eckmyer. -BLO (p26)
20 Aug 1843	Bridget Fitzmaurice b 09 Aug 1843 d/o Mich[l] & Mary Fitzmaurice; Sps: Jno Bucker & Mary Hughs. -BLO (p26)
21 Aug 1843	George Dorner b 15 Aug 1843 s/o Jno & Ann M Dorner; Sps: Geo Steveser & Magln Steveser. -BLO (p27)
27 Aug 1843	John Golden b 12 Aug 1843 s/o John & Ellen Goulden; Sps: Pat Kilbucher & Jane Fitzmaurice. -BLO (p27)
27 Aug 1843	Mary Jane Fitzmorris b 15 Aug 1843 d/o Michael & Jane Fitzmorris; Sps: Jno McGowan & Joana Murphy. -BLO (p27)

27 Aug 1843	Josephine Botke b 17 Aug 1843 d/o Geo & Mary Botke; Sps: And Botke & Mary Falls. -BLO (p27)
	[Inserted in the microfilm is a scrap of paper containing baptisms, in Latin, of 27 Aug 1843, in a strange hand, unsigned.]
27 Aug 1843	Ludoviaes Linx b 21 Jun 1843 s/o Ant Linx & Elis Hesen; Patrinus [Godfather] Ludos Hesm. (p27a)
27 Aug 1843	Elisabeth _____ adopted d/o Anton Fuke & Elizabetha; Sps: Matrina [Godmother] Jer & And^W Oppermann. (p27a)
27 Aug 1843	M. Elizabeth Oppermann b 19 Jul 1843 d/o Joan Oppermann & Andrus Hesse; Matrina [Godmother] Eliz Fuke. (p27a)
27 Aug 1843	M. Magd Wagner b 19 Jul 1842 d/o Franc Wagner & Catha^{II} Slieger; Matrina [Godmother] Maria Mag Fasin. (p27a)
27 Aug 1843	M. Cath Frady b 15 Nov 1842 d/o Bern Frady & M. Magd Jassner; Matrina [Godmother] M. Cath Wagner. (p27a)
27 Aug 1843	Ann Mary Eliz Hammer b 26 Dec 1842 d/o Adam Hammer & Elizab Iresslein; Matrina [Godmother] Ann Padrin & Joseph Padrin. (p27a)
27 Aug 1842	Maria Langer b 01 Jun 1843 d/o Eliz Felly & Mar Cass Langer; Matrina [Godmother] Eliz Felly.
27 Aug 1842	Joan Eberhardus Spats b 11 May 1843 s/o F Spats & Cath Kaufmann; Patrinus [Godfather] Joan Eberhard _____ hmer & Josepha Wonnel.
05 Sep 1843	Elizabeth Ann Hughes b 04 Sep 1843 d/o Henry & Mary Hughes; Sps: Pat McCauley & Cath Collins. -BLO (p27)
10 Sep 1843	Mary Ann Merkel b 01 Aug 1843 d/o Leopald & Elizabeth Merkel; Sps: Jo^S & Christ^a Staub. -BLO (p27)
10 Sep 1843	Elizabeth Mary Stoub b 04 Aug 1843 d/o Joseph & Christina Stoub; Sps: La^d & Eliz Merkel. -BLO (p28)
10 Sep 1843	Rose Ann Carey b 28 Jul 1843 d/o Danl & Mary Carey; Sps: And & Ann Heorrn. -BLO (p28)
10 Sep 1843	Margaret Mattingly b 03 Jul 1843 d/o Henry & Christina Mattingly; Sps: Fancis & Cecelia Matingly. -BLO (p28)
10 Sep 1843	James Donelly b 24 ___ 1843 s/o Wm & Mary Donelly; Sps: Jno Briscoe. -BLO (p28)
10 Sep 1843	Ann Teresa Arnold b 10 Jul 1843 d/o Anthony & Elizabeth Arnold; Sps: Wm & Mary Donelly. -BLO (p28)

147

11 Sep 1843   Bridget Gallaher b 30 Aug 1843 d/o Tho[S] & Mary Galaher; Sps: Th Larkin & M. Gala__. -BLO (p28)

11 Sep 1843   Peter Murry b 19 Aug 1843 s/o Jno & Hannah Murry; Sps: Pat[K] & Kitty Levin. -BLO (p28)

11 Sep 1843   Peter Murphy b 10 Sep 1843 s/o Wm & Ellen Murphy; Sps: Ant Gala & Jane Burk. -BLO (p29)

17 Sep 1843   Abraham Thayer b 20 Aug 1842 s/o Stephen & Rebecca Thayer; Sps: Peter & Nancy McCleery. -BLO (p29)

24 Sep 1843   Mary Morgan b __ Aug 1843 d/o James & Ann Morgan; Sps: Jno McCall & Ann Callahan. -BLO (p29)

24 Sep 1843   John Garrot Dressman b 23 Apr 1843 s/o Henry & Cath Dressman; Sps: Hen Kolman & Cath Wonstreet. -BLO (p29)

24 Sep 1843   Martha Ellen Spelman b __ Jul 1843 d/o Laurence & Margrt Spelman; Sps: Peter & Margaret Rerig. -BLO (p29)

24 Sep 1843   Margaret Ann Smith b 02 Sep 1843 d/o Tho[S] & Elizabeth Smith; Sps: Tho[S] Harpin & <u>Maty Dunger.</u> -BLO (p29)

15 Oct 1843   John Dillon b 28 Sep 1843 s/o Peter & Mary Dillon; Sps: Tho[S] Dunham & Mrs. Hopkins. -BLO (p30)

15 Oct 1843   Margaret Elizabeth Hudson b 10 Aug 1843 d/o Jacob & Rebecca Hudson; Sps: Geo Roman. -BLO (p30)

15 Oct 1843   Elizabeth McKinzie b 08 Aug 1843 d/o Moses & Margaret McKinzie; Sps: Pracilla Johnson. -BLO (p30)

22 Oct 1843   John Henry Mibuck b 05 Oct 1843 s/o Bernard & Ann Mibuck; Sps: H. Wonstreet & Mary Brown. -BLO (p30)

22 Oct 1843   Joshua Francis McKinzie b 30 Sep 1842 s/o Geo & Susan McKinzie; Sps: Sara A. McKinzie. -BLO (p30)

22 Oct 1843   Jonathan Albert McKinzie b 08 Mar 1843 s/o Sarah & Jeremiah McKinzie; Sps: Geo Roman & Mr. Ne__. -BLO (p30)

26 Oct 1843   Philip Goulden b 08 Oct 1843 s/o Mich[l] & Mary Goulden; Sps: Mic Linan & Eliza Gainer. -BLO (p31)

29 Oct 1843   John McGowan b 01 Jun 1843 s/o Mich[l] & Ann McGowan; Sps: Mich[l] Murry & Ann Mahan. -BLO (p31)

29 Oct 1843   Catherin Mahan b 21 Sep 1843 d/o James & Ann Mahan; Sps: Mich[l] McDermot & Ann McGorva. -BLO (p31)

29 Oct 1843   Michael Conly b 06 Sep 1843 s/o Tho[S] & Biddy Conly; Sps: Pat Murphy & Brg Tuman. -BLO (p31)

BAPTISMS

29 Oct 1843	Denis Lynch b 29 Oct 1843 s/o Pat & Biddy Lynch; Sps: Teddy Gorman & Mary A McCusker. -BLO (p31)
01 Nov 1843	Francis Thomas Farrel b 30 Sep 1843 s/o Neal & Mary Farrel; Sps: Mary Laughney. -BLO (p31)
01 Nov 1843	John Henry Brokeman b 31 Oct 1843 s/o Herman & Elizabeth Brokeman; Sps: Henry & Mary Brown. -BLO (p31)
04 Nov 1843	Rosanna Cusick b 01 Oct 1843 d/o Jno & Mary Cusick; Sps: B Kerney & Nick Bowfee. -BLO (p32)
06 Nov 1843	Mary Ann Stammer b 19 Aug 1843 d/o Averet and Adeline Stammer; Sps: Mary A. Smith. -BLO (p32)
11 Nov 1843	Mary Yerkel b 19 Sep 1843 d/o Jno and Elizabeth Yerkel; Sps: Ann Saturday. -BLO (p32)
11 Nov 1843	Elizabeth McGir b 01 Nov 1843 d/o Thomas & Mary McGir; Sps: P. Donly & Reg Cabel. -BLO (p32)
12 Nov 1843	Martha Logsdon b 26 Sep 1843 d/o Joseph & Mary Logsdon; Sps: Susan Durbin. -BLO (p32)
13 Nov 1843	Pat[k] Dermoty b 4 Nov 1843 s/o John & Honor Dermoty; Sps: Math Clarke and Mrs. Loftus. -BLO (p32)
13 Nov 1843	Daniel Carney b 20 Oct 1843 s/o Michael & Bridget Carney; Sps: Dav McDonel & Honor Burke. -BLO (p32)
13 Nov 1843	Bridget Ryan b 20 Oct 1843 d/o Michael & Margaret Ryan; Sps: Thos Mulasky & Mrs. Gallahan. -BLO (p33)
14 Nov 1843	Thomas Edward Gondor b 12 Nov 1843 s/o Andrew & Catherin Gondor (privately bapt), ceremonies supplied 22 Jul 1844; Sps: Rev. H. Myers & Margrt Kearney.-BLO (p33)
15 Nov 1843	Bernardina Werveler b 08 Jan 1842 d/o Marcus & Catherin Werveler; Sps: Hen Knabb & Eliz[h] Ferley. -BLO (p33)
19 Nov 1843	Michael Ryan b 21 Sep 1843 s/o Wm & Mary Ryan; Sps: Darby Monahan. -BLO (p33)
25 Nov 1843	Roseanna Mattingly b 17 Oct 1843 d/o James & Ann Mattingly; Sps: Martha Mattingly. -BLO (p33)
26 Nov 1843	William Loftus b 17 Nov 1843 s/o John & Rose Loftus; Sps: Pat McEnally & Mary Lavelle. -BLO (p33)
26 Nov 1843	Elizabeth Ann Rerig b 01 Oct 1843 d/o Valentine & Susanna Rerig; Sps: Pet Kreighbaum & Eliz Miller. -BLO (p34)

30 Nov 1843	Bridget Linen b 20 Nov 1843 d/o Mich[l] & Sarah Linen; Sps: Jno Kelly & Ann Brien. -BLO (p34)
10 Dec 1843	Andrew Arklie, convert, adult, b __ Apr 1818; Sps: August[e] Breuler. -BLO (p34)
11 Dec 1843	James Quinn b 03 Dec 1843 s/o Ja[s] & Bridgt Quinn; Sps: Jno Murry & Mary Jones. -BLO (p34)
11 Dec 1843	Roseanna Byrne d/o Ber[d] & Ann Byrne; Sps: Jo[s] Laughlin & Mary Murry. -BLO (p34)
11 Dec 1843	Patrick Brown b 30 Nov 1843 s/o James & Margaret Brown; Sps: Mich[l] Cosway & Hon <u>Nactin.</u> -BLO (p34)
11 Dec 1843	Ellen Kruse b 30 Nov 1843 d/o Arthur & Elenora Kruse; Sps: Ja[s] Walsh & Mag McGerry. -BLO (p34)
11 Dec 1843	John Rerig b 08 Nov 1843 s/o Peter & Mary Rerig; Sps: Jno Mueller & Barbara Knap. -BLO (p35)
17 Dec 1843	Mary Luisa Arnold b 06 Oct 1843 d/o Joseph & Matilda Arnold; Sps: Margrt Mulcahi. -BLO (p35)
17 Dec 1843	John Brodrick b 05 Dec 1843 s/o Mich[l] & Cath Brodrick; Sps: Patrick Coffey & his wife. -BLO (p35)
19 Dec 1843	William & Honora Higgins, twins b 19 Dec 1843, children of father Miles Higgins & mother (blank) Higgins. Privately bapt., ceremonies to be sup. -BLO (p35)
25 Dec 1843	Cornelius Collins b 14 Dec 1843 s/o John & Mary Collins; Sps: Jno Murry & widow Mahany. -BLO (p35)
31 Dec 1843	Henry Cross b 15 Nov 1843 s/o Thomas & Elizabeth Cross; Sps: Mary Ann Carter. -BLO (p35)
01 Jan 1844	Andrew Porter b 19 Nov 1843 s/o John of Henry & Mary Ann Porter; Sps: Mich[l] Laughlin & M. A. Carter. -BLO (p36)
01 Jan 1844	Margaret Hannehan b 31 Dec 1843 d/o Anthony & Mary Hannehan; Sps: Jno M[c]Cormack & Rose Monahan. -BLO (p36)
01 Jan 1844	Edward Tafe b 13 Sep 1843 s/o Peter & Bridget Tafe; Sps: Tho[s] Carrol & Cath Smith. -BLO (p36)
01 Jan 1844	Ann Smith b 06 Jun 1843 d/o Barney & Catherine Smith; Sps: Tho[s] Carroll & Bridg[t] Tafe. -BLO (p36)
03 Jan 1844	Mary Ann Carr b 30 Oct 1843 d/o James & Sarah Carr; Sps: Caroline Herendon. -BLO (p37)
06 Jan 1844	Francis Wempe b 11 Nov 1843 s/o Francis & Mary Wempe; Sps: Francis Laing & Mary Schmeising. -BLO (p37)

BAPTISMS

07 Jan 1844	Elizabeth Powlus b 22 Dec 1843 d/o Francis & Anna Powlus; Sps: Jno Shellhouse & Eliz Heck. -BLO (p37)
07 Jan 1844	Mary Ann O'Neill b 07 Dec 1843 d/o Hugh & Mary O'Neill; Sps: Ch McLaughlin & Sop Rooney. -BLO (p37)
14 Jan 1844	Ann Maguire b 10 Jan 1844 d/o James & Mary Maguire; Sps: Jno Keegan & Ann Quinn. -BLO (p38)
14 Jan 1844	Bridget Henagan b 06 Jan 1844 d/o Francis & Mary Henagen; Sps: Mich^l Coney & Marg^t Henagen. -BLO (p38)
14 Jan 1844	Bridget Noctin b 08 Jan 1844 d/o John & Bridget Noctin; Sps: Thos Rhoney & Mar Rhoney. -BLO (p38)
20 Jan 1844	Charles Warren b 04 Nov 1843 s/o James & Margaret Warren; Sps: Mich^l McCarthy & Bridg^t McCarr. -BLO (p38)
21 Jan 1844	Mary Ann Byrne b 04 Jan 1844 d/o Joseph & Petronella Byrne; Sps: Mich^l King & Mary Dumfrey. -BLO (p39)
21 Jan 1844	Margaret Schremp b 08 Jan 1844 d/o Casper & Elizabeth Schremp; Sps: Pet Rerig & Mag^t Rerig. -BLO (p39)
22 Jan 1844	John Toughey b 20 Jan 1844 s/o Austin & Mary Toughey; Sps: And Curley & Sarah McEnally. -BLO (p39)
23 Jan 1844	Dennis Cavanagh b 02 Jan 1844 s/o Charles & Rose Cavanagh; Sps: Chas Noland & Mrs. Murphy. -BLO (p39)
24 Jan 1844	John Zaub b 14 Jan 1844 s/o Conrad & Catherine Zaub; Sps: Jno Breting. -BLO (p40)
28 Jan 1844	Mary Riley b 27 Jan 1844 d/o Miles & Ann Riley; Sps: Bern^d Reynolds & Honora Kelly. -BLO (p40)
28 Jan 1844	Bridget Langen b 16 Jan 1844 d/o Michael & Ann Langen; Sps: Thos Hefren & Mary Gould. -BLO (p40)
30 Jan 1844	Thomas Carroll b 11 Jan 1844 s/o Thomas & Ann Carroll; Sps: Jno Dunant & Eliza Brown. -BLO (p40)
30 Jan 1844	John Henry Grebruch b 10 Aug 1843 s/o Henry & Catherin Grebunch; Sps: Jno & Teresa Falei. -BLO (p41)
30 Jan 1844	James Hughes b 16 May 1843 s/o Nicholas & Omey Hughes: Sps: Pat^k Byrne & Mary Duffy. -BLO (p41)
30 Jan 1844	Edward Luttman b 21 Jan 1844 s/o Garret & Frederica Luttman; Sps: Ed Cassidy & Ann Mcguire. -BLO (p41)
02 Feb 1844	George Callahan b 25 Nov 1843 s/o Jno & Ann Callahan; Sps: Mich^l Collins & Cath Askins. -BLO (p42)

04 Feb 1844   Mary Ann Daugherty b 03 Jan 1844 d/o Jno & Margaret
               Daugherty; Sps: Mich[l] Degnon & Mary M[c]Donald. -BLO
               (p42)

05 Feb 1844   Catherin Greller b 07 Jan 1844 d/o George & Margaret
               Greller; Sps: Cath Breting. -BLO (p42)

11 Feb 1844   Lavina Jane Carney b 04 Feb 1844 d/o Michael & Lorinda
               Carney; Sps: Wm Carney & Mary Hegen. -BLO (p43)

21 Feb 1844   Mary Louisa Topper b 07 Jun 1841 in Virginia, d/o Samuel
               L. & Julia Ann Topper; Sps: Henry & Louisa Spicer. -BLO
               (p43)

21 Feb 1844   James Thomas Spicer b 11 Dec 1842 and Mary Elizabeth
               Spicer b 06 Jan 1844, both in Virginia, children of Henry &
               Hannah Spicer; Sps: S. L. Topper & Luisa Spicer. The
               parents having been legitimately married a few moments
               before, their marriage by the preacher not being valid on
               account of Dispentus Cultus. -BLO (p43)

22 Feb 1844   Mary M[c]Donald b 11 Feb 1844 d/o Christopher & Mary
               M[c]Donald; Sps: Pat[k] Crow & Mary E. M[c]Girk. -BLO
               (p44)

23 Feb 1844   Ellen Conners b 11 Feb 1844 d/o Jno & Mary Conners;
               Sps: Martin Loftus & Mary Clarke. -BLO (p44)

25 Feb 1844   James Henry Arnold b 23 Jun 1843 s/o Nathaniel & Ellen
               Arnold; Sps: Mary Arnold. -BLO (p44)

25 Feb 1844   Thomas Fallen b 07 Oct 1843 s/o Thomas & Mary Fallen;
               Sps: Tho[s] Cox & Mary Brogan. -BLO (p45)

25 Feb 1844   Eliza Jane M[c]Donald b 26 Oct 1843 d/o John & Grace
               M[c]Donald; Sps: Ja[s] Cavanagh & Rose Doud. -BLO (p45)

26 Feb 1844   George B. Casius May b 29 Dec 1843 s/o Peter Philip &
               Eva May; Sps: Geo B. & Josephine Wandel. -BLO (p45)

27 Feb 1844   Philip M[c]Mahan b 27 Feb 1844 s/o Andrew & Mary
               M[c]Mahan; Sps: Bernard M[c]Kenna & Julia Gorman. -BLO
               (p46)

03 Mar 1844   Ann Elizabeth Gramlick b 12 Feb 1844 d/o Francis &
               Elizabeth Gramlick; Sps: Win Ferle & wife. -BLO (p46)

03 Mar 1844   Margaret Ryan b 20 Jan 1844 d/o Philp & Catherin Ryan;
               Sps: Jno Collins & Mary Mahoney. -BLO (p46)

03 Mar 1844   Alice Ryan b 19 Feb 1844 d/o Wm & Mary Ryan; (not the
               butcher)?; Sps: Tho[s] Downey & Ellen O'Brien. -BLO (p47)

03 Mar 1844   Mary Louisa Wade b 23 May 1843 d/o Isreal & Susanna
               Wade; Sps: Elizabeth M[c]Kinzie. -BLO (p47)

BAPTISMS

03 Mar 1844	Maurice Condon b 21 Feb 1844 s/o Thomas & Margaret Condon; Sps: Jno McCarthy & Honora Crowly. -BLO (p47)
10 Mar 1844	Honora Ellen Bare b 17 Aug 1843 d/o Peter & Mary Bare; Sps: Cecilia Mattingly. -BLO (p48)
10 Mar 1844	John McCormack b 01 Mar 1844 s/o Patrick & Mary McCormack; Sps: Anses McDonald & Martha McDonald. -BLO (p48)
10 Mar 1844	Ann Handle b 10 Dec 1843 d/o Henry & Catherin Handle, by Rev. Mr. Chakert; Sps: Ann Rodener. -BLO (p48)
11 Mar 1844	Peter Joseph Petre b 01 Mar 1844 s/o Joseph & Anna Petre, by Rev. Mr. Chakert; Sps: Peter Freidhof by Rev. Mr. Chakert. -BLO (p49)
17 Mar 1844	Bridget McCauley b 09 Mar 1844 d/o Thomas & Ann McCauley; Sps: Pat^k McCauly & Mary Quinn. -BLO (p49)
17 Mar 1844	Ellen Elizabeth Campbell b 15 Mar 1844 d/o James & Mary Campbell; Sps: James Morgan & Susan Reilley. -BLO (p49)
17 Mar 1844	Ann Casey b 27 Feb 1844 d/o Thomas & Mary Casey; Sps: Thos Nolan & Mary Buckley. -BLO (p50)
24 Mar 1844	Jane McAleer b 22 Mar 1844 d/o Daniel & Agnes McAleer; Sps: Danl McWilliams & Cath McGrogan. -BLO (p50)
24 Mar 1844	Michael Ryder b 08 Jul 1843 s/o Peter & Eliza Ryder; Sps: Martin Flatly & Grace Jones. -BLO (p50)
24 Mar 1844	John Barrot b 15 Mar 1844 s/o Anthony & Ellen Barrot; Sps: Miles & Honora Barrot. -BLO (p51)
24 Mar 1844	Michael Reynolds b 20 Mar 1844 s/o Michael & Eliza Reynolds; Sps: Hugh Scott & Mary Harrison. -BLO (p51)
24 Mar 1844	Elizabeth Hughes b 21 Mar 1844 d/o Terence & Mary Hughes; Sps: Francis Carlin & Mary A. Barbara. -BLO (p51)
25 Mar 1844	Bridget Kennedy b 20 Feb 1844 d/o John & Bridget Kennedy; Sps: James Lee & Cath Ennis. -BLO (p52)
27 Mar 1844	Augustine Parsons O'Donnell b 13 Feb 1844 s/o Dominic A & Mary Ann O'Donnell; Sps: L. Obermyer & Mary Parsons. -BLO (p52)
27 Mar 1844	Alexander (col^d) b 30 Nov 1843 s/o Charlotte, negress of Dr. O'Donnell; Sps: D. A. O'Donnell. -BLO (p52)
06 Apr 1844	John Welsh b 04 Apr 1844 s/o Mich^l & Ellen Welsh; Sps: Mich^l Brady & Cath Reynolds. -BLO (p53)

07 Apr 1844   Frances Foley b 03 Apr 1844 d/o Michael & Ellen Foley; Sps: Tho[S] Condon & Joanna Flynn. -BLO (p53)

07 Apr 1844   Teresa Helmstetter b 25 Feb 1844 d/o Antony & Mary Helmstetter; Sps: Jno Smith & Teresa Keble. -BLO (p53)

08 Apr 1844   Henry Joseph Emmel b 17 Mar 1844 s/o Joseph & Kunigunda Emmel; Sps: Michael Weisel. -BLO (p54)

09 Apr 1844   Mary Ann O'Brien b 20 Mar 1844 d/o Patrick & Ellen O'Brien; Sps: Geo Mattingly & Mary A. Murry. -BLO (p54)

13 Apr 1844   Mary Ann Ennis b 05 Apr 1844 d/o John & Catherin Ennis; Sps: Tho[S] Harpin & Mary Kenedy. -BLO (p54)

14 Apr 1844   Martha M[C]Kinzie b 19 Dec 1843 d/o Leo & Ann M[C]Kinzie; Sps: Augustine Breler [Brailer] & Mary Arnold. -BLO (p55)

14 Apr 1844   Catherine Gately b 07 Apr 1844 d/o Patrick & Margaret Gately; Sps: Jno Kelly & Marg[t] Mitchell. -BLO (p55)

14 Apr 1844   Ellen Reynolds b 09 Sep 1843 d/o James & Mary Reynolds; Sps: Jno Kelly & Eliza Ryan. -BLO (p55)

14 Apr 1844   William Parks b 25 Mar 1844 s/o William & Ellen Parks; Sps: Wm Finnity & Honora Dermedy. -BLO (p56)

14 Apr 1844   Ann Doyle b 02 Feb 1844 d/o Terry & Ann Doyle; Sps: Mich[l] & Honora Mehenny. -BLO (p56)

14 Apr 1844   George Carter b 07 Feb 1844 s/o Richard & Margaret Carter; Sps: Jeremiah Arnold & Elisb[h] Cross. -BLO (p56)

14 Apr 1844   Catherin Maloney b 05 Dec 1843 d/o Thomas & Bridget Maloney; Sps: Tho[S] Danen & Susana Blubach. -BLO (p57)

14 Apr 1844   Catherin M[C]Bride b 20 Nov 1843 d/o Patrick & Mary M[C]Bride; Sps: Mich[l] Laughlin & Cath Murry. -BLO (p57)

15 Apr 1844   Rose Connor b 05 Apr 1844 d/o Thomas & Catherin Connor; Sps: William Fox & Cath Collins. -BLO (p57)

15 Apr 1844   Ellen Kink [King] b 15 Apr 1844 d/o Edward & Bridget King; Sps: Hugh M[C]Ginn & Ellen M[C]Cusker. -BLO (p58)

15 Apr 1844   Francis Mulvaney b 29 Nov 1843 s/o Tho[S] & Ann Mulvaney; Sps: Mich[l] Murry & Rose Collins. -BLO (p58)

15 Apr 1844   Sarah Byrne b 11 Apr 1844 d/o Pat[k] & Jane Byrne; Sps: Denis Mullady & Mary Moran. -BLO (p58)

16 Apr 1844   Ann Maria Kane b 05 Apr 1844 d/o Anthony & Maria Kane, privately baptized. -BLO (p59)

21 Apr 1844	James Forrest Maguire b 08 Mar 1844 s/o Michael & Mary Maguire; Sps: Pat^K Nugent & Rose Cavanagh. -BLO (p59)
21 Apr 1844	Mary Adelia Ryan b 08 Apr 1844 d/o William & Mary Ryan; Sps: Jno White & Ellen Murry. -BLO (p59)
21 Apr 1844	Ann Kane b 17 Apr 1844 d/o John & Deborah Kane; Sps: Maurice Murphy & Ann Stapleton. -BLO (p60)
21 Apr 1844	Ellen M^{C}Cormack b 04 Apr 1844 d/o John & Mary M^{C}Cormack; Sps: John Hughes & Martha Mattingly. -BLO (p60)
21 Apr 1844	Patrick Cunningham b 05 Apr 1844 s/o Thomas & Ann Cunningham; Sps: Michael Cunningham & Celilia Samon. -BLO (p60)
22 Apr 1844	Anselm Hughes Holtzman b 28 Mar 1844 s/o John & Cath Holtzman; Sps: Mary & James Kelly. -BLO (p61)
01 May 1844	Bernard Brady b 01 Apr 1844 s/o Hugh & Ann Brady; Sps: Alex M^{C}Coy & Catherin Spallen. -BLO (p61)
05 May 1844	Valentine Schremp b 24 Apr 1844 s/o Evald & Elizabeth Schremph; Sps: Valent Helfrey & Eva his wife. -BLO (p61)
05 May 1844	Thomas Gordon b 01 Apr 1844 s/o Edward & Bridget Gordon; Sps: Ant Glesty & Alice M^{C}Gir. -BLO (p62)
12 May 1844	Mary Zeller b 25 Mar 1844 d/o Jos A & Mary Zeller; Sps: Jno Koub & Barbara Madden. -BLO (p62)
13 May 1844	Ellen Byrne b 24 Apr 1844 d/o Jno & Ellen Byrne; Sps: Wm Welsh & Ellen M^{C}Auley. -BLO (p62)
16 May 1844	Catherin Shinock b 15 May 1844 d/o Michael & Mary Shinock; Sps: Jno Ambrose & Marg^t Condon. -BLO (p63)
16 May 1844	Windlin Erlberth Gerdiman b 29 Apr 1844 s/o Ant & Ann Gerdiman; Sps: Wind Ferle & Mary Stammers. -BLO (p63)
16 May 1844	Elizabeth Slohan b 12 May 1844 d/o John & Mary Slohan; Sps: Jno Farrell & Elizabeth Keenan. -BLO (p63)
18 May 1844	Francis M^{C}Kinzie b 05 Oct 1843 s/o John & Barbara M^{C}Kinzie; Sps: Saml F. M^{C}Kinzie & Reb Garlitz. -BLO (p64)
18 May 1844	James Alexander M^{C}Kinzie b 08 Jan 1844 s/o Pat^k & Lavina M^{C}Kinzie; Sps: James & Jane Getty. -BLO (p64)
18 May 1844	Peter Cunningham b 07 Mar 1844 s/o Michael & Cath Cunningham; Sps: Jno M^{C}Caffrey & Cath M^{C}Kinzie. -BLO (p64)

18 May 1844   Lucy Garlitz b 25 Mar 1844 d/o John & Mary Garlitz; Sps: Basil McKinzie & Lucy Garlitz. -BLO (p65)

18 May 1844   Henry McKinzie b 21 Mar 1844 s/o Basil & Elizabeth McKinzie; Sps: Isreal Garlitz & Cath McKinzie. -BLO (p65)

18 May 1844   Norman Farrell b 30 Nov 1843 s/o John & Nancy Farrell; Sps: Wm Sigeron & Cath McKinzie. -BLO (p65)

19 May 1844   Michael Conway b 23 Oct 1843 s/o Patrick & Sarah Conway; Sps: John & Rosanna Conors. -BLO (p66)

19 May 1844   Helen Jenkins Mullholland b 23 Nov 1843 d/o Michael & Louisa Teresa Mullholland; Sps: Henry McKeon & Cath Smith. -BLO (p66)

19 May 1844   Elizabeth Ellen McClery b 17 Oct 1843 d/o John & Maria McClery; Sps: Peter & Nancy McClery. -BLO (p66)

19 May 1844   Cornelia Victoria Turney b 20 May 1842 d/o Daniel & Ellen Turney; Sps: Jo^s Logsdon & Fanny Howard. -BLO (p67)

19 May 1844   William Henry [col^d] b 30 Sep 1843 s/o Betsey, slave of Leonard Smith; Sps: Peter McClery .-BLO (p67)

22 May 1844   Michael Hughes b 14 May 1844 s/o William & Margaret Hughes; Sps: John Hone & Mary Hughes. -BLO (p67)

27 May 1844   Francis Heinart b 10 Mar 1844 s/o Joseph & Catherin Heinart; Sps: Francis & Teresa Fall. -BLO (p68)

27 May 1844   Thomas Duffy b 22 Apr 1844 s/o John & Mary Duffy; Sps: Thos Murray & Ann Cullen. -BLO (p68)

27 May 1844   Thomas Timms b 09 Feb 1844 s/o Thomas & Catherin Timms; Sps: Pat^k & Margaret A. Hanson. -BLO (p68)

27 May 1844   Bridget Hanson b 24 Feb 1844 d/o Patrick & Margaret Hanson; Sps: Thos Timms & Mary Carney. -BLO (p69)

06 Jun 1844   James Ward b 20 Feb 1844 s/o John & Mary Ward; Sps: Pat^k McCormack & Ann Brien. -BLO (p69)

06 Jun 1844   Joseph Chrysostom Black b 04 May 1844 s/o John & Lydia Black; Sps: Richd Masters & Mary Black. -BLO (p69)

09 Jun 1844   Robert 4 mos & Margaret 4 yrs [col^d], slaves of John Porter; Sps: Mary Craig & Mrs. Porter. -BLO (p70)

09 Jun 1844   Francis Smith b 04 Mar 1844 s/o Elizabeth Smith; Sps: Francis Smith. -BLO (p70)

09 Jun 1844	James Flannagan b in Nov 1843 s/o Francis & Julia Flannagan; Sps: Pat^K Handly & Mary M^{C}Cormack. -BLO (p70)
09 Jun 1844	Elizabeth M^{C}Can b in Apr 1844 d/o Georgesee & Ann M^{C}Can; Sponsors being two persons not legible in the pocket ven^d. -BLO (p71)
09 Jun 1844	Michael Keenan b 05 May 1844 s/o Mich^l & Catherin Keenan; Sps: Jno M^{C}Enally & Marg^t O'Brien. -BLO (p71)
09 Jun 1844	John Morgan b 31 May 1844 s/o William & Mary Morgan; Sps: Mich^l Naughtin & Mary Noland. -BLO (p71)
09 Jun 1844	Thomas Fox b 09 May 1844 s/o Henry & Mary Fox; Sps: Pat^K Levan & Cath M^{C}Cusker. -BLO (p72)
09 Jun 1844	Mary Ann Sharp b 18 Apr 1844 d/o Geo Henry & Mary Sharp; Sps: Herman Lotman & Martha M^{C}Creary. -BLO (p72)
10 Jun 1844	Heinrich Klostermann b 20 Feb 1844 s/o Johanis Bernhard Klostermann; Sps: Francis Xav Qein [unsigned, different handwriting]. (p72)
10 Jun 1844	Aloysius Germann b mense Jul 1838 s/o a German Lutheran; Sps: Karl Kehnful [unsigned, different handwriting]. (p72)
15 Jun 1844	Harriett Hayden, adult & convert, (wife of Wm Hayden) was conditionally baptized, she had been in her early years bap^d by a Lutheran; Sps: Mrs. Masters. -BLO (p73)
15 Jun 1844	Joseph Hershberger b 17 May 1844 s/o John & Mary Ann Hershberger; Sps: Francis & Mrs. Gramlick. -BLO (p73)
15 Jun 1844	Peter Hard b 01 Jun 1844 s/o Geo & Julian Hard; Sps: Peter & Margaret Rerig. -BLO (p73)
15 Jun 1844	Mary Elizabeth Eggemyer b 13 Jun 1844 d/o John F & Mary S. Eggemyer; Sps: Henry & Elizabeth Brokeman. -BLO (p74)
15 Jun 1844	Elizabeth M^{C}Govern b 16 May 1844 d/o Tho^S & Ann M^{C}Govern; Sps: Pat^K Reily & Mary Kirby. -BLO (p74)
23 Jun 1844	John Zacheas Lilly b 05 May 1844 s/o Joshua & Teresa Lilly; Sps: Susan Durbin & Aug Breeler [Brailer]. -BLO (p74)
23 Jun 1844	Catherin Cockeran b 02 Apr 1844 d/o James & Ann Cockeran; Sps: Wm Healy & Ann Brady. -BLO (p75)

29 Jun 1844	Patrick Theodore Garlitz b 27 Jun 1844 s/o Henry & Lucy Garlitz; Sps: Saml F. McKinzie & Cath McKenzie. -BLO (p75)
29 Jun 1844	Levi Hilary Staunton b 10 Jul 1843 s/o William & Mary Staunton; Sps: Basil McKinzie & Ellen Ridgely. -BLO (p75)
30 Jun 1844	Richard Manning b 31 May 1844 s/o Rich^d & Betsy Manning; Sps: Peter & Cath Garahan. -BLO (p76)
30 Jun 1844	Margaret Priscilla Banford b 26 Aug 1843 d/o Jonathan & Melvana Banford Sps: Sara Ann R. Kreg. -BSP (p50)
04 Jul 1844	James Campbell Donahoe b 27 Oct 1843 s/o Thos & Elizabeth Donahoe; Sps: Wm Ryan & Mary McCune. - BLO (p76)
04 Jul 1844	Edward Donahoe b 27 Apr 1844 s/o Pat^k & Ann Donahoe; Sps: Tim Clancy & Sar A. Donahoe. -BLO (p76)
04 Jul 1844	Mary Ellen Fitzpatrick b 27 Apr 1844 d/o John & Ellen Fitzpatrick; Sps: Robt Maloy & Mrs. Whelan. -BLO (p77)
04 Jul 1844	Ellen Landers b 01 May 1844 d/o Maurice & Joanna Landers; Sps: Jno Cavanagh & Julia Fitzgerald. -BLO (p77)
14 Jul 1844	John Peter Eggart b 24 May 1844 s/o Jno & Mary Eggart; Sps: Peter Rerig & Margrt [Rerig?]. -BLO (p77)
14 Jul 1844	John Doughery b 02 Jul 1844 s/o Thomas & Ellen Doughery; Sps: Thos Kelly & Mary Fallen. -BLO (p78)
14 Jul 1844	John Hefren b 04 Jul 1844 s/o Andrew & Nancy Hefren; Sps: Ed Gallahan & Sarah Davis. -BLO (p78)
14 Jul 1844	Bridget Reynolds b 05 Jul 1844 d/o John & Honora Reynolds; Sps: Mich^l Rickad & Ellen Manly. -BLO (p78)
14 Jul 1844	Ellen Killduff b 05 Jun 1844 d/o Pat^k & Rose Killduff, by Rev. Mr. Myers; Sps: Peter Carney & Ann Farrell. -BLO (p79)
20 Jul 1844	Bernard Maguire b 14 Jan 1839 & Josiah Mcguire b 04 Aug 1842 children of Thos Maguire, dec'd, and Elizabeth his wife, were privately baptized. -BLO (p79)
20 Jul 1844	Giles Dyer Augustine Kreighbaum b 24 Jun 1844 s/o Henry & Fanny Kreighbaum by Rev. H. Myers; Sps: Giles B. & Catherin Dyer. -BLO (p80)
21 Jul 1844	Sarah Ann Catherin Myers b 17 Jun 1844 d/o Peter & Cath Myers; Sps: J. P. Shellhouse & Sarah A. McKinzie. -BLO (p79)

BAPTISMS

21 Jul 1844	James Henry Lenden b 01 Mar 1844 s/o James & Cath Lenden; Sps: Arthur McGir & Mary O'Rouke. -BLO (p80)
21 Jul 1844	Elizabeth Ann Brown (negress) b 09 May 1844 d/o James & Mary Brown; Sps: Celeste Cook. -BLO (p80)
21 Jul 1844	Michael Flatley b 20 Jul 1844 s/o Martin & Rose Flatley by Rev. Henry Myers; Sps: Ant Ruddy & Mary Barrot. -BLO (p81)
04 Aug 1844	Joshua Robinson b 22 Mar 1844 s/o Charles & Ellender Robinson; Sps: Joshua & Sarah A. McKinzie. -BLO (p81)
04 Aug 1844	Sarah Ann Kenny b 29 Jun 1844 d/o William & Rose Kenny; Sps: Pat^k McAulty & Ann Maguire. -BLO (p81)
04 Aug 1844	Mary Elizabeth Firley b 29 Jun 1844 d/o Henry & Cath Firley; Sps: Wind & Elisb^h Ferley. -BLO (p82)
04 Aug 1844	Anna Maria Kirker b 21 Jul 1844 d/o Henry & Mary Kirker; Sps: Pet Frithof & Mary Rickelman. -BLO (p82)
07 Aug 1844	James Reader (negro) b 30 Apr 1844 s/o Harriett & Alexius Reader; Sps: Jno R. Brook. -BLO (p82)
18 Aug 1844	Ann Maria Roman b 10 Nov 1843 d/o John A. & Ann Roman; Sps: Susanna O'Brien. -BLO (p83)
18 Aug 1844	Catherin McAtee b 31 Jul 1844 d/o Michael & Martha McAtee; Sps: Bridget Garahan. -BLO (p83)
24 Aug 1844	Mary Guess Semmes b 08 Aug 1844 d/o Samuel M. & Elenora Semmes; Sps: Sarah Carroll. -BLO (p83)
25 Aug 1844	James McGerry b 21 Aug 1844 s/o Pat^k & Margaret McGerry; Sps: Hugh & Bridget Doyle. -BLO (p84)
25 Aug 1844	James McDonald b 31 Jul 1844 s/o Mich^l & Honora McDonald; Sps: Thos Larkin & Mary Toy. -BLO (p84)
27 Aug 1844	Mary Ann Brown b 10 Feb 1844 in Va d/o Cornelius & Mary Brown; Sps: Elizabeth Garahan. -BLO (p84)
28 Aug 1844	Lawrence Kelley b 27 Aug 1844 s/o Michael & Ann Kelley; Sps: James Carney & Mrs. Rabet. -BLO (p85)
01 Sep 1844	Emily Ambrosia Healey b 20 Jul 1844 d/o Emily & Thos Healey; Sps: Pat^k Healey & Mrs. Hoffman. -BLO (p85)
01 Sep 1844	Rose Ann Kelley b 06 Aug 1844 d/o James & Catherin Kelley; Sps: Ch Kavanagh & Mary Kenedy. -BLO (p85)
08 Sep 1844	Martha Ann Logsdon b 24 Jul 1844 d/o George and Mary Logsdon; Sps: Ann Logsdon. -BLO (p86)

08 Sep 1844	Ellen Lynch b 08 Feb 1844 d/o Thomas and Mary Lynch; Sps: John & Mary Conlon. -BLO (p86)
08 Sep 1844	William Edmond Sheehy b 27 Nov 1843 s/o John and Rachel Sheehy; Sps: Mrs. Fox. -BLO (p86)
08 Sep 1844	Thomas Dillon b 31 Aug 1844 s/o Edward & Louisa Dillon; Sps: James Reed & Margaret McNulty. -BLO (p87)
08 Sep 1844	Adam Hammer b 23 Jun 1844 s/o Adam & Elizabeth Hammer; Sps: Adam Hartt. -BLO (p87)
09 Sep 1844	John Heck b 04 Sep 1844 s/o John & Elizabeth Heck; Sps: J. P. Shellhouse & Cath Schner. -BLO (p87)
22 Sep 1844	Cecilia Klink b 26 Aug 1844 d/o Windel & Mary Klink; Sps: Augustine Breeler [Brailer] & Cecilia Mattingly. -BLO (p88)
22 Sep 1844	Elizabeth Kohlman b 16 Aug 1843 d/o William & Elenora Kohlman; Sps: Wm Arnold & Mary A. Carter. -BLO (p88)
22 Sep 1844	Ann Carlis b 17 Sep 1844 d/o Pat^k & Betty Carlis; Sps: Wm Morgan & Mary Morgan. -BLO (p88)
22 Sep 1844	Michael Harrison b 13 Sep 1844 s/o William & Mary Harrison; Sps: Mich^l Ruddy & Mary McElroy. -BLO (p89)
28 Sep 1844	Catherin Snyder b 03 Mar 1844 d/o Jacob & Elizabeth Snyder; Sps: Mary Garlitz. -BLO (p89)
28 Sep 1844	John Smith b 17 Oct 1843 s/o Michael & Elizabeth Smith; Sps: Jno White. -BLO (p89)
06 Oct 1844	Leo Sampson Hicksenbaugh [Hixonbaugh] b 11 Apr 1844 s/o Adam & Rachel Hicksenbaugh; Sps: Mary A. McKinzie & Jno Wonstreet. -BLO (p90)
08 Oct 1844	Peter George Dentz b 05 Apr 1844 s/o John & Catherin Dentz; Sps: Peter Heime. -BLO (p90)
11 Oct 1844	Mary Kean, wife of Ant. Kean, adult & convert, was conditionally baptized. She was baptized by a Lutheran preacher formerly. -BLO (p90)
13 Oct 1844	Cath Elizabeth Steigmuller b 17 Jul 1844 d/o Henry & Philomena Steigmuller; Sps: Jno Mennert & Cath Vickers. -BLO (p91)
18 Oct 1844	Maria Lynch b 15 Oct 1844 d/o John & Biddy Lynch; Sps: John Locks & Susan McEnally. -BLO (p91)
20 Oct 1844	Ann Elizabeth Asklie b 02 Sep 1844 d/o Andrew & Druscilla Asklie; Sps: August Breeler [Brailer] & Maria McCleery. -BLO (p91)

BAPTISMS

20 Oct 1844	Margaret Reynolds b 28 Sep 1844 d/o Francis & Catherin Reynolds; Sps: Wm McLaughlin & Bridg^t Reynolds. -BLO (p92)
20 Oct 1844	Julia Raney (twin) b 06 Oct 1844 d/o Pat^k & Mary Raney; Sps: Mich^l Maden & Rose Turley. -BLO (p92)
20 Oct 1844	Mary Raney (twin) b 06 Oct 1844 d/o Pat^k & Mary Raney; Sps: Thos Smith & Mary Nolen. -BLO (p92)
20 Oct 1844	William Gallaher b 06 Oct 1844 d/o Edward & Elisb^h Gallaher; Sps: Wm Kelly & Ann Carmine. -BLO (p92)
27 Oct 1844	Ann Slavinski b 19 Oct 1844 d/o Augustus & Agnes Slavinski; Sps: Pat^k McVey & Anna his wife. -BLO (p93)
27 Oct 1844	Mary Ann Reynolds b 19 Oct 1844 d/o Thomas & Bridget Reynolds; Sps: Thos Follen & Allen Doherty. -BLO (p93)
27 Oct 1844	Elizabeth Gillmartin b 20 Oct 1844 d/o James & Mary Gillmartin; Sps: Pat^k Clarke & Bridg^t Cockeran. -BLO (p93)
01 Nov 1844	John Joseph Vigor b 13 Sep 1844 s/o Bernard & Catherin Vigor; Sps: Jno I Wegman & Elisb^h Gramlick. -BLO (p94)
03 Nov 1844	Mary Ann McCue b 13 Oct 1844 d/o James & Mary McCue; Sps: Pat^k Brady & Mary O'Rourke. -BLO (p94)
03 Nov 1844	Jeremiah Murry b 07 Oct 1844 s/o Jeremiah & Ellen Murry; Sps: Jno Murry & Mary Quigg. -BLO (p94)
07 Nov 1844	Christina Mary Meyers b 04 Nov 1844 d/o Henry & Elizabeth Meyers; Sps: Jo^s Wegman & Christina Hays. -BLO (p95)
10 Nov 1844	Lydia Ann Porter b 21 Jun 1844 d/o John & Ellen Porter; Sps: Jeremiah & Hannah Arnold. -BLO (p95)
10 Nov 1844	John Sheridan b 30 Oct 1844 s/o John & Nancy Sheridan; Sps: David Riley & Mary Sheridan. -BLO (p95)
10 Nov 1844	Bridget Conroy b 07 Nov 1844 d/o Peter & Nancy Conroy; Sps: Pat O'Brien & Rose Hoye. -BLO (p96)
10 Nov 1844	Mary Ann McDonald b 26 Oct 1844 d/o Pat^k & Mary McDonald; Sps: Jno Carroll & Ann McDonel. -BLO (p96)
13 Nov 1844	William Shulten b 16 Sep 1844 s/o Christian & Julia Shulten; Sps: Casper Clize & Cath Dinnerman. -BLO (p96)
17 Nov 1844	Mary Ann Coffey b 11 Nov 1844 d/o Pat^k & Mary Coffey; Sps: Mich^l Gormon & Mrs. Askins. -BLO (p97)

17 Nov 1844   John Davey b 12 Nov 1844 s/o William & Elizabeth Davey; Sps: Hugh O'Neill & Cath Ryan. -BLO (p97)

17 Nov 1844   Harriett Catherin Twigg b 03 Jan 1844 d/o Jesse & Mary Ann Twigg; Sps: Jo^S Hodel & Alice M^{C}Gir. -BLO (p97)

17 Nov 1844   Rose Ann Brady b 19 Oct 1844 d/o Pat^k & Rose Ann Brady; Sps: Ja^S M^{C}Dermot & Mary Connor. -BLO (p98)

21 Nov 1844   Harriet Luisa [col^d] b in Oct 1844 d/o Sarah, slave of Francis Jamison; Sps: negress Linny. -BLO (p98)

23 Nov 1844   James Lally b 22 Nov 1844 s/o Michael & Bridget Lally; Sps: William Murphy. -BLO (p98)

01 Dec 1844   Ellen M^{C}Laughlin b 14 Nov 1844 d/o Michael & Julia M^{C}Laughlin; Sps: Mich^l M^{C}Laughlin & Julia Sheridan. -BLO (p99)

01 Dec 1844   Thomas M^{C}Call b abt. 12 days ago s/o John & Mary M^{C}Call; Sps: Jno Fitzpatrick & Teresa Healey. -BLO (p99)

01 Dec 1844   Elizabeth Keenan b 26 Aug 1844 d/o Peter & Bridget Keenan; Sps: Mich^l M^{C}Donald & Mary Barnett. -BLO (p99)

01 Dec 1844   Patrick Brofee b 20 Nov 1844 s/o Thomas & Sarah Brofee; Sps: Tho^S Beatty & Rosan M^{C}Manus. -BLO (p100)

08 Dec 1844   Mary [Reynolds] wife of Ber^d Reynolds, convert fron the Ch. of England, was conditionally baptized. She was born in Ireland. -BLO (p100)

08 Dec 1844   Catherin Barrot b 15 Nov 1844 d/o Miles & Mary Barrot; Sps: Ant Barrot & Ellenora Lavelle. -BLO (p100)

08 Dec 1844   Catherin Galvin b 26 Nov 1844 d/o Pat^k & Jane Galvin; Sps: Martin Clarke & Mary Henogen. -BLO (p101)

08 Dec 1844   Margaret Horne b 26 Nov 1844 d/o Martin & Mary Horne; Sps: Pat^k Carroll & Cath M^{C}Kenna. -BLO (p101)

08 Dec 1844   Thomas Lyons b 18 Nov 1844 s/o Michael & Mary Lyons; Sps: Tho^S Farrell & Ann Ford. -BLO (p101)

09 Dec 1844   James Larkin b 19 Nov 1844 in Virginia s/o Michael & Mary Larkin; Sps: Patrick & Roseanna Brady. -BLO (p102)

10 Dec 1844   John Erskin b 02 Nov 1844 s/o William & Catherin Erskin; Sps: Ja^S M^{C}Kenna & Marg^t King. -BLO (p102)

15 Dec 1844   John Tuman b 25 Nov 1844 s/o Mich^l & Bridget Tuman; Sps: Pat^k & Ann Riley. -BLO (p102)

BAPTISMS

15 Dec 1844	Thomas Fitzmorris b 05 Nov 1844 s/o Michael & Mary Fitzmorris; Sps: Margaret & Jno McCafrey. -BLO (p103)

15 Dec 1844   Thomas Fitzmorris b 05 Nov 1844 s/o Michael & Mary Fitzmorris; Sps: Margaret & Jno McCafrey. -BLO (p103)

15 Dec 1844   James Patrick McEntire b 20 Jul 1844 s/o Pat^k & Jane McEntire; Sps: Patrick Kennedy & Brdg^t McDonald. -BLO (p103)

20 Dec 1844   Catherine Howard b 03 Dec 1844 d/o Thomas & Catherin Howard; Sps: Cornel Kelley & Teresa Cable. -BLO (p103)

22 Dec 1844   Ellen Flaherty b 01 Dec 1844 d/o Owen & Catherin Flaherty; Sps: Maurice Fite & Cath Connors. -BLO (p104)

22 Dec 1844   Charles Flood b 11 Dec 1844 s/o Patrick & Margaret Flood; Sps: Pat^k Rhooney & Mary Rhooney. -BLO (p104)

25 Dec 1844   Henry Hyer b 14 Dec 1844 s/o Francis & Ann Hyer; Sps: Henry Greser & Mary Berkman. -BLO (p104)

29 Dec 1844   John Degnon b 02 Dec 1844 s/o Thomas & Margaret Degnon; Sps: John & Sarah Ryan. -BLO (p105)

218 [baptized] in 1844.

[Page 106 is blank.]

__ Jan 1845   James Barry b 04 Sep 1844 s/o John & Hulda Barry, baptized about New Years by Rev. James O'Donnel, OSA; Sps: Jno Ambrose & Ann Mallerin. -BLO (p108)

__ Jan 1845   Bridget Ford b 28 Dec 1844 d/o Owen & Mary Ford, baptized about New Years by Rev. Ja^s O'Donnel. OSA; Sps: Pat^k Hughes & Cath Hughes. -BLO (p108)

__ Jan 1845   Martin Clarke b 26 Dec 1844 s/o Luke & Mary Clarke, baptized about New Years by by Rev. Ja^s O'Donnel. OSA; Sps: Mart Padin & Bridg^t Farley. (p109)

05 Jan 1845   Thomas Clarke b 13 Dec 1844 s/o Darby & Catherin Clarke; Sps: Pat^k & Mrs. Coffey. -BLO (p107)

06 Jan 1845   Henry Joseph Rosenberger b 18 Oct 1844 s/o Belthafier & Elizabeth Rosenberger; Sps: Michael Weisel & Eve Weisel, -BLO (p107)

10 Jan 1846   Ellen Dailey b 03 Nov 1844 d/o Pat^k & Mary Dailey; Sps: Jno Long & Rosan Murphy, -BLO (p107)

11 Jan 1845   Mary Margaret Muller b 02 Jan 1845 d/o Peter & Elizabeth Muller; Sps: Margaret Rerig, -BLO (p108)

24 Jan 1845   Margaret Ann Kirby b 23 Jan 1845 d/o George & Margaret Kirby; Sps: Pat^k Nutny & Brdg^t Nutny, -BLO (p109)

26 Jan 1845   William Kelly b 24 Jan 1845 s/o John & Honora Kelly; Sps: Mich^l Norton & Ann E Dean, -BLO (p109)

26 Jan 1845   Patrick Henagen b 21 Jan 1845 s/o Antony & Mary Hennagen; Sps: Ant Monahan & Mary Murry, -BLO (p110)

26 Jan 1845   Patrick Murry b 07 Jan 1845 s/o John & Ann Murry; Sps: Peter Medley & Honor McTee, -BLO (p110)

26 Jan 1845   Catherin Harrison b 14 Jan 1845 d/o Mich^l & Mary Harrison; Sps: Hugh & Winny Scott. -BLO (p110)

26 Jan 1845   Eliza Healey b 12 Jan 1845 d/o William & Bridget Healey; Sps: Pat^k Tracey & Sara Quigg. -BLO (p111)

02 Feb 1845   Eliza O'Brien b 10 Feb 1844 d/o Edward & Ellen O'Brien; Sps: Mich^l Collin & Mary Ryan. -BLO (p111)

02 Feb 1845   Eliza Gormon b 13 Jan 1845 d/o Jno & Julien Gormon; Sps: Ch Dinney & Marg^t Gormon. -BLO (p111)

02 Feb 1845   Ellenora McGran b 17 Nov 1844 d/o Patrick & Catherin McGran; Sps: [none listed]. -BLO (p112)

09 Feb 1845   James Nolan b 30 Jan 1845 s/o Thomas & Mary Nolan; Sps: Mark Mulligan & Eliza Brady. -BLO (p112)

09 Feb 1845   Catherin Elizabeth Loftus b 03 Feb 1845 d/o Jno & Mary Loftus; Sps: Thos Nolan & Marg^t Cuningham. -BLO (p112)

09 Feb 1845   Margaret O'Sullivan b 07 Feb 1845 d/o Timothy & Ellen O'Sullivan; Sps: Danl Sullivan & Mrs. Shinick. -BLO (p113)

16 Feb 1845   James Polk Conor b 06 Aug 1844 s/o Arthur & Ann Conor; Sps: Jno Wonstreet & Eliz Brown. -BLO (p113)

16 Feb 1845   John Stoeser b 05 Feb 1845 s/o George & Ellen Stoeser; Sps: Geo Lifre & Emma Daner. -BLO (p113)

23 Feb 1845   Patrick Carney b 16 Feb 1845 s/o Michael & Bridget Carney; Sps: Mrs. Murphy & Cath Carney. -BLO (p114)

23 Feb 1845   Patrick Reiley b 17 Feb 1845 s/o David & Judith Reiley; Sps: Edward Barrott & Mary Sheridan. -BLO (p114)

23 Feb 1845   Bridget Quigley b 01 Feb 1845 d/o Peter & Mary Quigley; Sps: Hil Garvin & Brdg Laughlin. -BLO (p114)

23 Feb 1845   Francis Melchive Ferli b 22 Jan 1845 s/o Windly & Elizabeth Ferli; Sps: Francis & Elisb^h Gramlick. -BLO (p115)

02 Mar 1845   Ann Hopkins b 06 Feb 1845 d/o Pat^k & Mary Hopkins; Sps: Mich^l Handlin & Cath Carney. -BLO (p115)

03 Mar 1845	Francis Romauld Better b 07 Feb 1845 s/o Marcellus & Cath Better; Sps: Lew Leopold & Elisb^h Hakil. -BLO (p115)
09 Mar 1845	Mary Ann Flynn b 29 Jan 1845 d/o Pat^k & Brdg^t Flynn; Sps: Robt Hunt & Ann Riley. -BLO (p116)
09 Mar 1845	John Muller b 01 Feb 1845 s/o John & Margaret Muller; Sps: Jo^s A Celler & Margaret Lidinger. -BLO (p116)
09 Mar 1845	Margaret Dempsey b 05 Mar 1845 d/o Thos & Ann Dempsey; Sps: Wm Coulehan & Nancy Galvin. -BLO (p116)
09 Mar 1845	Mary Foy b 27 Feb 1845 d/o James & Elizabeth Foy; Sps: Ja^s Welsh & Mary Ford. -BLO (p117)
09 Mar 1845	Hugh Gerrity b 26 Feb 1845 s/o Patrick & Margrt Gerrity; Sps: Mich^l Cosgrove & Mary Rhooney -BLO (p117)
09 Mar 1845	Sarah Kelley b 08 Mar 1845 d/o John & Catherin Kelley; Sps: Ed Kelley & Mary Lavelle -BLO (p117)
11 Mar 1845	Mary Ann Zaup b 26 Feb 1845 d/o Conrad & Catherin Zaup; Sps: Ann Maria Bruting -BLO (p118)
13 Mar 1845	Maria Eva Thilde b 29 Dec 1844 d/o John & Wilhelmina Thilde, privately baptized -BLO (p118)
16 Mar 1845	Margaret McMahan b 01 Mar 1845 d/o John & Mary McMahan; Sps: Jno Welsh & Luc^{da} Lentz -BLO (p118)
16 Mar 1845	Daniel Cook (negro of Mr. Semmes) b five weeks previously s/o Celeste & Thos Cook, was privately baptized. -BLO (p119)
16 Mar 1845	Michael Garnier b 20 Jan 1845 s/o James & Margrt Garnier; Sps: John & widow Mealy. -BLO (p119)
17 Mar 1845	Patrick Farley b 15 Mar 1845 s/o Patrick & Ann Farley; Sps: Pat^k Casey & Brdg Kenedy. -BLO (p119)
17 Mar 1845	Patrick Crowly b 16 Mar 1845 s/o Patrick & Johanna Crowly; Sps: Timothy O'Sullivan & Mrs. Conlon. -BLO (p120)
24 Mar 1845	Patrick Gallaher b 17 Mar 1845 s/o John & Bridget Gallaher; Sps: Pat^k & Mary Gallaher. -BLO (p120)
24 Mar 1845	John Patrick Shea b 17 Mar 1845 s/o John & Mary Shea; Sps: Thos Dunbar & Cath McKenna. -BLO (p120)
25 Mar 1845	John Bernard Joseph Brown b 16 Mar 1845 s/o Henry & Elisb^h Brown; Sps: Ber^d Mibuck & Cath Dressman. -BLO (p121)

25 Mar 1845   Sarah Jane Roberts b 22 Feb 1845 d/o William & Mary Roberts; Sps: Susan Mattingly. -BLO (p121)

25 Mar 1845   Joseph Washington Howe b 01 Mar 1845 s/o Ja[S] & Mary Howe; Sps: Lew Leopold & Mary Burnett. -BLO (p121)

27 Mar 1845   Mary Ellen Davis b 25 Mar 1845 d/o Michael & Sarah Davis; Sps: Thomas & Mary Gallaher. -BLO (p122)

29 Mar 1845   Frances Burton, adult & convert from Church of England was conditionally baptized. -BLO (p122)

30 Mar 1845   Mary Neithart b 14 Mar 1845 d/o Titus & Gertrude Neithart; Sps: Peter & Margaret Rerig. -BLO (p122)

30 Mar 1845   Margaret Porter b 23 Aug 1844 d/o John E. & Elizabeth Porter; Sps: Mary Logsdon. -BLO (p123)

01 Apr 1845   Susan Smith b 08 Feb 1845 d/o Bernard & Susan Smith; Sps: Nancy Donavan. -BLO (p123)

02 Apr 1845   Charles Henry Rinehart b 16 Feb 1845 s/o Sam[l] & Eliza Rinehart, baptized in Hancock; Sps: Dr. O'Donnell & Eveline Bevans. -BLO (p123)

03 Apr 1845   John Mahoney b 28 Feb 1845 s/o Thomas & Mary Mahoney; Sps: Mich[l] Shea & Margaret Murphy. -BLO (p124)

05 Apr 1845   Drusa Emily Garlitz b 29 Sep 1844 d/o Solomon & Rebecca Garlitz; Sps: Isreal & Sarah Garlitz. -BLO (p124)

05 Apr 1845   Rachel Catherine M[c]Kenzie b 25 Feb 1845 d/o Samuel & Cath M[c]Kinzie; Sps: Henry & Lucy Garlitz. -BLO (p124)

05 Apr 1845   Noah Sylvester Garlitz b 27 Oct 1844 s/o Isreal & Ellen Garlitz; Sps: Isadore M[c]Kinzie & Lucy Garlitz. -BLO (p125)

05 Apr 1845   Nancy Elizabeth Garlitz b 20 Mar 1845 d/o Sam[l] & Susan Garlitz; Sps: Sam[l] M[c]Kinzie & Rebecca Garlitz. -BLO (p125)

05 Apr 1845   William Costello b 20 Oct 1844 s/o William & Mary Costello; Sps: Peter & Margaret Nathan. -BLO (p125)

06 Apr 1845   Charles Henry Mullholland b 27 Dec 1845 [1844] s/o Michael & Teresa Mullholland; Sps: Leonard & Eliza Smith. -BLO (p126)

06 Apr 1845   Francis Samuel Jamison b 11 Aug 1844 s/o Rich[d] & Rosella Jamison; Sps: Jno R. Brook & Henrietta Jamison. -BLO (p126)

BAPTISMS

06 Apr 1845	Elizabeth Ann Riley born abt. 4 mo ago; d/o Bernard & Margaret Riley; Sps: Sam[l] Jamison & Mary Conors. -BLO (p126)
07 Apr 1845	John Thomas Thayer b 07 May 1844 s/o Stephen and Rebecca Thayer; Sps: Peter & Nancy McCleery. -BLO (p127)
07 Apr 1845	Elizabeth Logsdon b 30 Nov 1844 d/o Joseph and Margaret Logsdon; Sps: John & Margaret McCleery. -BLO (p127)
07 Apr 1845	Susan Beall b 24 Mar 1845 d/o Charles and Margaret Beall; Sps: Luisa (sic) Cross. -BLO (p127)
10 Apr 1845	John Kelley b 12 Mar 1845 s/o Patrick & Bridget Kelley; Sps: James Darkey & Ann Redmon. -BLO (p128)
13 Apr 1845	Mary Turley b 10 Apr 1845 d/o Richard & Rose Turley; Sps: Mich[l] Byrne & Elizabeth M[c]Ginnis. -BLO (p128)
13 Apr 1845	Mary Agnes Cronin b 28 Mar 1845 d/o Patrick & Nancy Cronin; Sps: James Kelley & Cecilia Arnold. -BLO (p128)
13 Apr 1845	John [Arnold] b 27 Jan 1845 s/o Mary Arnold; Sps: Hanna Arnold & Ber[d] Brady. -BLO (p129)
14 Apr 1845	John Kennan b 04 Apr 1845 s/o Thomas & Elizabeth Kennan; Sps: Ja[s] Gregory & Mary Campbell. -BLO (p129)
14 Apr 1845	John Francis Mootey b 06 Apr 1845 s/o John & Bridget Mootey; Sps: Ja[s] Murphy & Ann Kockeran [Cockeran]. -BLO (p129)
14 Apr 1845	Thomas John Higgins b 06 Apr 1845 s/o Miles & Margaret Higgins; Sps: Patrick Carlis & Betsey Carlis. -BLO (p130)
14 Apr 1845	Ellen Christy b 07 Apr 1845 d/o James & Ellen Christy; Sps: Mich[l] Leonard & Mary Jones. -BLO (p130)
17 Apr 1845	Francis Henry Jamison b 28 Jan 1845 s/o Francis & Eliza Ann Jamison; Sps: Cecilia & Tho[s] Jamison. -BLO (p130)
20 Apr 1845	George William Mattingly b 22 Mar 1845 s/o George & Ann Mattingly; Sps: Baptist Mattingly & Frances Kerney. -BLO (p131)
20 Apr 1845	John Francis Rosey b 07 Apr 1845 s/o Ant & Margaret Rosey; Sps: Jno Mann & Ellen Nugent. -BLO (p131)
27 Apr 1845	Joseph Porter b 18 Mar 1845 s/o George & Margaret Porter; Sps: Mary A. Carter. -BLO (p131)
27 Apr 1845	Ellen M[c]Gan b 18 Apr 1845 d/o Rich[d] & Marcella M[c]Gan; Sps: John Donelly & Ann Keegan. -BLO (p132)

28 Apr 1845   Mary Brennan b 26 Apr 1845 d/o Patrick & Ellenora Brennan; Sps: Mich^{l}Beheny & Mary Harris. -BLO (p132)

28 Apr 1845   Amilia Quigg b 23 Apr 1845 d/o James & Maga Quigg; Sps: Fr McLucky & Mary Handly. -BLO (p132)

28 Apr 1845   Rose McCabe b 23 Apr 1845 d/o James & Margaret McCabe; Sps: Jno Doonan & Ann Doyle. -BLO (p133)

28 Apr 1845   Bridget Lehey b 19 Apr 1845 d/o Cornelius & Ellen Lehey; Sps: Mary Keller. -BLO (p133)

29 Apr 1845   Andrew Gondor b 27 Mar 1845 s/o Andrew & Catherin Gondor; Sps: Fanny Burton & L. Obermyer. -BLO (p133)

04 May 1845   Martina Whelan b 10 Mar 1845 d/o James & Bridget Whelan; Sps: Pat^k Byrne & Elizabeth Davy. -BLO (p134)

04 May 1845   Francis Clarke b 25 Apr 1845 s/o Bern^d Clarke, dec'd, & his wife Elisb^h; Sps: Fran Hyer & Ann Petre. -BLO (p134)

04 May 1845   John (Morrissy) b 14 May 1844 s/o widow Morrissy; Sps: Wm Ryan & Ellen Hogan. -BLO (p134)

05 May 1845   Mary Cramer b 15 Apr 1845 d/o Frederick & Ann M. Cramer; Sps: Frederick Yeiker & Mary Trumpeter. -BLO (p135)

11 May 1845   Maurice Cavanagh b 03 May 1845 s/o Mathew & Cath Cavanagh; Sps: Jno Cavanagh & Mary Harvey. -BLO (p135)

11 May 1845   Ann Donelly b 02 May 1845 d/o William & Mary Donelly; Sps: Ja^s McGan & Mary J. Shehey. -BLO (p135)

11 May 1845   Bridget Welsh b 10 May 1845 d/o Michael & Ellen Welsh; Sps: John Brennen & Mary Brogan. -BLO (p136)

11 May 1845   James Callahan b 11 May 1845 s/o Peter & Nancy Callahan; Sps: Martin Cockeran & Margaret McMahan. -BLO (p136)

12 May 1845   Ellen Ruddy b 09 May 1845 d/o Anthony & Cath Ruddy; Sps: Peter Levelle & Sar McNally. -BLO (p136)

12 May 1845   John Nolan b 04 May 1845 s/o Charles & Catherin Nolan, ceremonies supplied 25 May 1845; Sps: Mich^l & Mary Carney. -BLO (p137)

17 May 1845   Vincent Mattingly b 05 Apr 1845 s/o James & Ann Mattingly; Sps: Joseph Null. -BLO (p137)

25 May 1845   William Dunn b 22 Oct 1843 s/o Owen & Mary Dunn; Sps: Henry Garvin & Mary Shehey. -BLO (p137)

BAPTISMS

25 May 1845	Bernard Raferty b 16 May 1845 s/o Patrick & Mary Raferty; Sps: Thomas Mullarky & Marg^t Farrel. -BLO (p138)
25 May 1845	Mary Elizabeth King b 13 May 1845 d/o Michael & Mary King Sps: John Hughes & Ann McHeron. -BLO (p138)
25 May 1845	Ellen Hoye b 13 May 1845 d/o Peter & Rose Hoye; Sps: Ja^s Cumerford & Grace McDonald. -BLO (p138)
25 May 1845	Peter Murphy b 18 May 1845 s/o Patrick & Bridget Murphy; Sps: Terry & Mary Hughes. -BLO (p139)
25 May 1845	Thomas Lynch b 07 May 1845 s/o Thomas & Catherin Lynch; Sps: Ja^s Gilmartin & Eliza Ryan. -BLO (p139)
25 May 1845	John Madden b 23 May 1845 s/o Michael & Bridg^t Madden; Sps: John & Honora Kelley. -BLO (p139)
25 May 1845	Rachel Carey b 23 Mar 1845 d/o Danl & Mary Carey; Sps: Jno Sheridan & Ann Sheridan. -BLO (p140)
25 May 1845	Michael Thomas Clarke b 17 May 1845 s/o Peter & Jane Clarke; Sps: Mich^l Laughran & Mary Clarke. -BLO (p140)
26 May 1845	Ellen White b 24 May 1845 d/o Maurice & Mary White by Rev. Rd Fox; Sps: Jno Kerby & Marg^t Bagley. -BLO (p140)
01 Jun 1845	Casper Henry Gers b 27 May 1845 s/o Henry & Adelaid Gers; Sps: Henry Dressman & Alet Kohlman. -BLO (p141)
08 Jun 1845	Catherin McWilliams b 29 May 1845 d/o Daniel & Cath McWilliams; Sps: Denis McWilliams & Elisb^n Banter. -BLO (p141)
08 Jun 1845	Mary Frances Beisel b 12 Apr 1845 d/o Jno & Ann Beisel; Sps: Ann M Kreighbaum. -BLO (p141)
22 Jun 1845	Patrick McDonald b 09 Jun 1845 s/o David & Honor McDonald; Sps: Mich^l Ruddy & Ann Manly. -BLO (p142)
22 Jun 1845	Richard McCormack b 15 Jun 1845 s/o Thomas & Catherin McCormack; Sps: John Shehey & Mary Loftus. -BLO (p142)
22 Jun 1845	Rachel Buscella Arnold b 01 Mar 1845 d/o Nathan & Ellen Arnold; Sps: Jer & Cath McKinzie. -BLO (p142)
28 Jun 1845	James Ryder b 20 Jun 1845 s/o Peter & Eliza Ryder; Sps: Saml F McKinzie & Marg^t Beal. -BLO (p143)
30 Jun 1845	Elizabeth Knight b 08 Apr 1844 d/o Laurence & Elizabeth Knight; Sps: Cecilia Jamison. -BLO (p143)
30 Jun 1845	Catherin Rose b 05 Apr 1845 d/o Michael & Barbara Rose; Sps: Cath Blume. -BLO (p143)

30 Jun 1845	Catherin Knight b 08 Apr 1845 d/o Laurence & Elizabeth Knight; Sps: Cath Blume. -BLO (p144)
30 Jun 1845	John Nathan b 10 Apr 1842 s/o Peter & Margaret Nathan; Sps: William & Mary Costello. -BLO (p144)
30 Jun 1845	Mary Shinick b 22 Jun 1845 d/o Michael & Mary Shinick; Sps: Tim Colahan & Ann Scanlan. -BLO (p144)
03 Jul 1845	Mary Mulcahey b 24 Jun 1845 d/o John & Bridget Mulcahey; Sps: Judith Collins. -BLO (p145)
04 Jul 1845	Mary Jane Lastly b 04 Oct 1844 d/o Richard & Cath Lastley; Sps: Ja^S Carney & Mary Carroll. -BLO (p145)
04 Jul 1845	Mary Ann Cunningham b 24 Jun 1845 d/o John & Catherin Cunningham; Sps: Pat^K Fealy & Judy Handy. -BLO (p145)
05 Jul 1845	Mary Kenny b 02 Feb 1845 d/o Patrick & Mary Kenny; Sps: Owen Mathew & Margaret (?). -BLO (p146)
06 Jul 1845	Catherin Kenedy b 17 Jun 1845 d/o William & Mary Kenedy; Sps: Kearn Farrel & Elisb^h Noonan. -BLO (p146)
06 Jul 1845	Thomas Hennigan b 17 Jun 1845 s/o Thomas & Mary Hennagen; Sps: Catherine & John Ennis. -BLO (p146)
06 Jul 1845	James McDermot b 04 May 1845 s/o Tho^S & Maria Burns; Sps: Tho^S Garahan & Marg^t Garner. -BLO (p147) [Could be James McDermot Burns].
06 Jul 1845	David O'Neil b 24 May 1845 s/o Hugh & Mary O'Neil; Sps: Hugh Griffin & Teresa Healy. -BLO (p147)
12 Jul 1845	Michael Scanlin b 28 Nov 1844 s/o Maurice & Ann Scanlin; Sps: Pat^K & Brdg^t Murry. -BLO (p147)
13 Jul 1845	John Kelly b 07 Jul 1845 s/o Edward & Brdg^t Kelley; Sps: Martin Ruddy & Mary Barrot. -BLO (p148)
13 Jul 1845	William Rhoney b 07 Jul 1845 s/o Patrick & Mary Rhoney; Sps: Peter Shelly & Cath Hines. -BLO (p148)
13 Jul 1845	Ellen Naughtin b 10 Jul 1845 d/o John & Honor Naughtin; Sps: Bridget & Mich^l Healy. -BLO (p148)
16 Jul 1845	Sarah Rogers b 13 Jul 1845 d/o Patrick & Cath Rogers; Sps: Andrew Curley & Mary Carroll. -BLO (p149)
16 Jul 1845	Josephine Lenora Cusick b 29 May 1845 d/o Jno & Mary Cusick; Sps: John Egan & Rose Dolan. -BLO (p149)
16 Jul 1845	Daniel Collins b 30 Jun 1845 s/o John & Mary Collins; Sps: Jno Kelly & Honor Ambrose. -BLO (p149)

16 Jul 1845	Mahala Catherin Dicken b 28 Jan 1845 d/o Jesse & Mary Dicken; Sps: Wm & Catherin Ryan. -BLO (p150)
20 Jul 1845	Charles Constantine Masters b 24 Jun 1845 s/o Richard & Ann Masters; Sps: J. B. Byrne & Harriet Hayden. -BLO (p150)
20 Jul 1845	John Peter Smith b about a month ago s/o Issack & Mary Ann Smith; Sps: Jno Brumbacher & Eva his wife. -BLO (p150)
20 Jul 1845	John Baptist Mattingly b 04 Jul 1845 s/o Baptist & Ann Mattingly; Sps: Ja^S Mattingly & Ellen Hogan. -BLO (p151)
20 Jul 1845	Michael Gessner b 03 Jul 1845 s/o William & Margaret Gessner; Sps: Mich^l Wisel & Elizabeth Kolb. -BLO (p151)
20 Jul 1845	John McNulty b 02 Jul 1845 s/o Michael & Margaret McNulty; Sps: Cath Farrel & Michael Byrne. -BLO (p151)
27 Jul 1845	Thomas Glisin Porter b 20 Feb 1845 s/o Thomas & Ann E. [Nancy] Porter; Sps: Pat^k Cronin & Cath Coners. -BLO (p152)
27 Jul 1845	James Reynolds b 08 Jul 1843 s/o John & Bridget Reynolds; Sps: James & Catherin Reynolds. -BLO (p152)
27 Jul 1845	Thomas Finnegan b 19 Jul 1845 s/o Patrick & Mary Finnegan; Sps: Mich^l Richard & Mary Rafety. -BLO (p152)
27 Jul 1845	Mary Murphy b 18 Jul 1845 d/o William & Ellen Murphy; Sps: Ph Canfield & Brdg^t Malowny. -BLO (p153)
27 Jul 1845	Mary Conway b 22 Jul 1845 d/o James & Margaret Conway; Sps: Pat^k Conway & Rose Monahan. -BLO (p153)
27 Jul 1845	Mary Mooney b 07 Jul 1845 d/o Pat^k & Mary Mooney; Sps: Ja^S Gannon & Mary Mooney .-BLO (p153)
27 Jul 1845	Catherin Hagan b 25 Jul 1845 d/o Hugh D & Bridg^t Hagan; Sps: Owen Daugherty & Cath Hagan. -BLO (p154)
27 Jul 1845	Maria Keenan b 05 Jul 1845 d/o Thomas & Margaret Keenan; Sps: Martin & Mary Nolan. -BLO (p154)
03 Aug 1845	Thomas Leo b in Apr 1845 s/o Thomas & Cath Leo; Sps: Tim Sullivan & Sab Kenedy. -BLO (p154)
03 Aug 1845	John Martin Gramlick b 19 Jul 1845 s/o Martin & Elisb^h Gramlick; Sps: Francis & Elisb^h Gramlick. -BLO (p155)
03 Aug 1845	Francis Martin Gramlick b 21 Jul 1845 s/o Francis & Elisb^h Gramlick; Sps: Martin & Elizabeth Gramlick. -BLO (p155)

08 Aug 1845	Joseph Peter Weisel b 20 Jul 1845 s/o M. & Eva Weisel; Sps: Peter Hein & Elisb^h Yeagle. -BLO (p155)
10 Aug 1845	Mary Flatly b 08 Aug 1845 d/o Martin & Rose Flatly; Sps: Jno Murphy & Mary Fire. -BLO (p156)
10 Aug 1845	Owen Quinn b 04 Aug 1845 s/o Owen & Mary Quinn; Sps: Ja^s Cavanagh & Mary Cavanagh. -BLO (p156)
10 Aug 1845	Sarah McNally b 01 Aug 1845 d/o John & Mary McNally; Sps: Dan & Elizabeth McNally. -BLO (p156)
10 Aug 1845	Ann Cockeran b 10 Aug 1845 d/o Martin & Bridg^t Cockeran; Sps: Pat^k & Brdg^t Cockeran. -BLO (p157)
10 Aug 1845	Julia O'Connell b 23 Jun 1845 d/o William & Ellen O'Connell; Sps: Jno Murphy & Ellen Hanglin. -BLO (p157)
10 Aug 1845	Bridget Monahan b 28 Jul 1845 d/o Michael & Ellen Monahan; Sps: Pat^k Coyle & Mary Hashton. -BLO (p157)
10 Aug 1845	Honora Ellen Mattingly b 01 Aug 1845 d/o Francis & Jane Mattingly; Sps: Cecilia Mattingly. -BLO (p158)
10 Aug 1845	William Gallaher b 01 Aug 1845 s/o Thomas & Mary Gallaher; Sps: Hugh Gallaher & Sara Davis. -BLO (p158)
10 Aug 1845	Peter Williams b 07 Aug 1845 s/o Michael & Catherin Williams; Sps: Thos Donelan & Judy Riley. -BLO (p158)
14 Aug 1845	Sarah Ann Wiensten b 27 May 1845 d/o Herman & Mary Weinsten; Sps: Cath Mintruss. -BLO (p159)
14 Aug 1845	William Mintruss b 27 Nov 1844 s/o Henry & Cath Mintruss; Sps: Henry Myers. -BLO (p159)
15 Aug 1845	Michael Kelly b 20 Jul 1845 s/o James & Mary Kelly; Sps: Mich^l McCormack & Mary Gardner. -BLO (p159)
15 Aug 1845	James Kelly b 31 Jul 1845 s/o Christopher & Mary Kelly; Sps: Thos O'Reilly & Mrs. Kennedy. -BLO (p160)
15 Aug 1845	Edward Laurence Byrne b [blank] s/o Pierce & [blank] Byrne; Sps: John & Margaret Karney. -BLO (p160)
16 Aug 1845	Rosina Monahan b 21 Nov 1844 d/o Brian & Mary Monahan; Sps: Pet Carney & widow Kelley. -BLO (p160)
17 Aug 1845	Anastasia Arnold b 19 Apr 1845 d/o Joseph & Matilda Arnold; Sps: Ann Pitman. -BLO (p161)
17 Aug 1845	George Wade b 26 Feb 1845 s/o Isreal & Susan Wade; Sps: Edward Silk & Elisb^h McKinzie. -BLO (p161)

BAPTISMS

20 Aug 1845	James Bohan b 30 Jul 1845 s/o James & Catherin Bohan; Sps: Ja^S ____ & Ellen Byrne. -BLO (p161)
24 Aug 1845	Mary M^{C}Kandriss b 19 Aug 1845 d/o Mark & Brdg^t M^{C}Kandriss; Sps: Tho^S Ruddy & Mary Kenedy. -BLO (p162)
24 Aug 1845	Bridget Fitzmorris b 14 Aug 1845 d/o Mich^l & Jane Fitzmorris; Sps: Pat^K & Mary O'Brien. -BLO (p162)
24 Aug 1845	Denis Murphy b 19 Aug 1845 s/o James & Mary Murphy; Sps: Pat Murphy & Mary Farrel. -BLO (p162)
24 Aug 1845	James Barry b 11 Aug 1845 s/o Jno & Marg^t Barry; Sps: John Cumins & Jane [or Jessie] Roach. -BLO (p163)
24 Aug 1845	Catherin Casey b 01 Aug 1845 d/o Thomas & Mary Casey; Sps: James Riley & Mary Dooley. -BLO (p163)
24 Aug 1845	Ellen Reiley b 10 Aug 1845 d/o James & Susan Riley Sps: Hugh Riley & Cath Kenedy. -BLO (p163)
24 Aug 1845	Joseph Shannohan b 15 Aug 1845 s/o Christopher & Bridget Shanohan; Sps: Pat Donahoe & Marcella M^{C}Graw. -BLO (p164)
24 Aug 1845	Henry Berkhard b 05 Aug 1845 s/o Nicholas & Elizabeth Berkhart; Sps: Wind Ferle & Elisb^h Firle. -BLO (p164)
24 Aug 1845	John Leidiger b 16 Jun 1845 s/o Nicholas & Barbara Leidiger; Sps: Jno Muller & Mary Brunner. -BLO (p164)
24 Aug 1845	David Sloan b 03 Jul 1845 s/o Mathew & Ann Sloan; Sps: Danl M^{C}Williams & Cath M^{C}Grogan. -BLO (p165)
24 Aug 1845	Catherin Keegan b 22 Aug 1845 d/o Patrick & Ann Keegan; Sps: Mark Mulligard & Cath Maguire. -BLO (p165)
28 Aug 1845	Mary Downey b 22 Aug 1845 d/o Thomas & Mary Downey; Sps: Ant Cain & Mary Coffey. -BLO (p165)
30 Aug 1845	Mary Magdalena M^{C}Kinzie b 22 Jul 1845 d/o Leo & Ann M^{C}Kinzie; Sps: Cath M^{C}Kinzie & Isreal Garlitz. -BLO (p166)
31 Aug 1845	Isaac Augustine Holtzman b 27 Mar 1845 s/o Aug & Mary Holtzman; Sps: Peter & Ann M^{C}Cleery. -BLO (p166)
31 Aug 1845	Caroline Glass b 25 Oct 1844 d/o John & Mary Glass; Sps: Pet Garahan & Mrs. Conors. -BLO (p166)
	Mr. Brenen now takes charge of Mt. Savage mission.
03 Sep 1845	Eva Neus b 29 Aug 1845 d/o John & Barbara Neus; Sps: Eva Heldifer. -BLO (p167)

07 Sep 1845   James Monahan b 25 Aug 1845 s/o Darbey & Mary Monahan; Sps: Thomas Samon & Sabrina Kenedy. -BLO (p167)

07 Sep 1845   Mary Shultz b abt. 5 months ago d/o Bernard & Elizabeth Shultz; Sps: Mary Ortman. -BLO (p167)

07 Sep 1845   Elizabeth Brofey b 29 Aug 1845 d/o Corn & Eliza Brofey; Sps: Cha^S Kenna & Marg^t Cabe. 1-BLO (p168)

07 Sep 1845   John Henry Mohlman b 17 Aug 1845 s/o Hen & Mary Mohlman; Sps: Jno Wonstreet & Mary Rickelman. -BLO (p168)

07 Sep 1845   Garet James Steigmuller b 05 Aug 1845 s/o Hen & Mary Steigmuller; Sps: Pat Shultz & Adel Geis. -BLO (p168)

07 Sep 1845   Mary Elizabeth Weiner b 04 Jul 1845 d/o Henry & Cath Weimer; Sps: Jno Wonstreet & Elizabeth Fink. -BLO (p169)

10 Sep 1845   Martha Mattingly b 27 Jul 1845 d/o Henry & Christina Mattingly; Sps: Martha Mattingly. -BLO (p169)

21 Sep 1845   Francis Anthony Rucker b 19 Jun 1845 s/o Jno & Helena Rucker; Sps: Ant Fink. -BLO (p169)

21 Sep 1845   Mary Sabrina Haberkamp b 14 Jul 1844 d/o Jno & Cath Haberkamp; Sps: Xavier Haberkamp & Helena Rucker. -BLO (p170)

21 Sep 1845   Francis Patrick Donelly b [blank] s/o Francis & [blank] Donelly; Sps: Jno Welsh & Teresa Healey. -BLO (p170)

05 Oct 1845   John James Byrne b 28 Sep 1845 s/o Bern^d & Ann Byrne; Sps: Jno Sheridan & Marg^t Riley. -BLO (p170)

05 Oct 1845   James Reiley b 03 Sep 1845 s/o Francis & Cath Reilley; Sps: Tho^S McAuley & Mary Cody. -BLO (p171)

12 Oct 1845   William Henry Hayden b 03 Oct 1845 s/o Wm J. Hayden, dec'd, and his wife Harriett; Sps: Rch^d Masters & Cath Garlan. -BLO (p171)

13 Oct 1845   Mary Mahan b 29 Sep 1845 d/o Tho^S & Mary Mahan; Sps: Ant & Cath Swift. -BLO (p171)

13 Oct 1845   Hugh Lyon b 08 Oct 1845 s/o Patrick & Ann Lyon; Sps: Tho^S Lyon & Mar Kelly. -BLO (p172)

13 Oct 1845   Michael Fay b 29 Sep 1845 s/o Patrick & Ann Fay; Sps: Pat^k Farrel & Mrs. Ganer. -BLO (p172)

14 Oct 1845   Frances Cunningham b 28 Aug 1845 d/o James & Eliza Cunningham; Sps: Danl Shannon & Sab^a Kenedy. -BLO (p172)

14 Oct 1845	John Joseph Fate b 16 Sep 1845 s/o Ja^S & Cath Fate; Sps: Jo^S Wegman & Christine Rollin. -BLO (p173)
16 Oct 1845	John Heldinfer b 14 Oct 1845 s/o John & Eva Heldinfer; Sps: Jno & <u>Barb</u> <u>Knivis.</u> -BLO (p173)
19 Oct 1845	Hannah Lutman b 18 Jul 1845 d/o Geret H & Frederica Lutman; Sps: Mich^l Lautler & Cath McLaughlin. -BLO (p173)
19 Oct 1845	Andrew Flaherty b 23 Aug 1843 s/o Mich^l & Elizabeth Flaherty; Sps: Denis & Marg^t Murphy. -BLO (p174)
19 Oct 1845	Joseph Flaherty b 27 Aug 1845 Mich^l & Elizabeth Flaherty; Sps: Mich^l Bolen & Mary McMahan. -BLO (p174)
19 Oct 1845	Philomena Catherin Shriver b 11 Oct 1845 d/o Henry & [blank] Shriver; Sps: Philom[ena] Cath Driver. -BLO (p174)
26 Oct 1845	Rachel McKinzie b 25 Dec 1844 d/o Jeremiah & Sarah McKinzie; Sps: Ann E. McKinzie. -BLO (p175)
26 Oct 1845	Martin Kelley b 07 Oct 1845 s/o Tho^S & Jane Kelley; Sps: Jno Kelley & Cath McKenna. -BLO (p175)
28 Oct 1845	John Mullin b 25 Oct 1845 s/o Jno & Rosanna Mullin; Sps: Jno Conly & Ann Mallen. -BLO (p175)
02 Nov 1845	Ann Maria Elizabeth Brokeman b 28 Oct 1845 d/o Herman & Elisb^h Brokeman; Sps: Ber^d Kohlman & Eliz^h Eggmyer. -BLO (p176)
06 Nov 1845	Ellen Fitzgerald b 15 Oct 1845 d/o James & Julia Fitzgerald; Sps: Ellen Stapleton. -BLO (p176)
11 Nov 1845	Henry Bevans b 06 Nov 1845 s/o James & Eveline Bevans; Sps: Dom & Mary A. O'Donnell. -BLO (p176)
16 Nov 1845	Charles Lewis Kerful b 01 Oct 1845 s/o Charles & Phebe Kerful; Sps: Lewis Leopold. -BLO (p177)
07 Dec 1845	John Julius Barleger b 19 Nov 1845 s/o Henry & Elizabeth Barleger; Sps: Jno Cokey & Regina Cabel. -BLO (p177)
07 Dec 1845	Edward Mathew Roe b 21 Nov 1845 s/o Rich^d & Cath Roe; Sps: Peter Carney & Cath Rigney. -BLO (p177)
14 Dec 1845	Lewis Edward Watmyer b 24 Nov 1845 s/o Jno & Maryann Watmyer; Sps: Mr. & Mrs. Masters. -BLO (p178)
14 Dec 1845	Mary Elizabeth, negress, b in May 1845 d/o Cecilia, slave of Adel Jamison, privately baptized. -BLO (p178)
19 Dec 1845	Mary Elizabeth Clotze b 31 Oct 1845 d/o Casper & Ann Clotze; Sps: Elisb^h Yeager. -BLO (p178)

25 Dec 1845   John Johnson b 18 Dec 1845 s/o Robt & Mary Johnson; Sps: Jno Smith & Mrs. Smith. -BLO (p179)

25 Dec 1845   Elizabeth Shelhouse b 03 Dec 1845 d/o Jno P & Mrs. Shelhouse; Sps: Elisb^h Hack & Frances Paulis. -BLO (p179)

25 Dec 1845   Mary Ann Dunn b 29 Sep 1845 d/o Owen & Mary Dunn; Sps: Peter Ennis & Mrs. O'Brien. -BLO (p179)

219 [baptized] in 1845, [page 180 is blank.]

01 Jan 1846   James Lynch b 07 Dec 1845 s/o Pat^k & Bridg^t Lynch; Sps: Owen Daugherty & Mrs. Colvin -BLO (p181

04 Jan 1846   Elizabeth Sanders b 31 Dec 1845 d/o Henry & Mary Sanders; Sps: Victoria Acre. -BLO (p181

06 Jan 1846   Catherine Ryan b 02 Nov 1845 d/o Philip & Cath Ryan; Sps: Mat Coffey & Mary Casey. -BLO (p181

11 Jan 1846   Michael Draper b 26 Sep 1845 s/o George & Mary Draper; Sps: Lew Bartell & Frances Ryan. -BLO (p182)

11 Jan 1846   Bridget Heaney b 10 Aug 1845 d/o Edward & Jane Heaney; Sps: Pat Doyle & Mary A. Hanson. -BLO (p182)

11 Jan 1846   Thomas McGir b 15 Oct 1844 s/o Pat^k & Mary McGir Sps: George Brown & Brdg^t Brady. -BLO (p182)

11 Jan 1846   Edward Anthony Gillespy b 30 Nov 1845 s/o William & Elizabeth Gillespy; Sps: Pat Gillespy & Christina Larkin. -BLO (p183)

12 Jan 1846   Casper Knap b 10 Jan 1846 s/o Jno & Barbara Knap; Sps: Casp Shrimp & Cat Snure. -BLO (p183)

18 Jan 1846   Mary McDermot b 03 Jan 1846 d/o Ed & Bridget McDermot; Sps: Mich^l Tierney & Mrs. Brofey. -BLO (p183)

18 Jan 1846   Mary Ann Kelley b 31 Dec 1845 d/o Pat^k & Cath Kelley; Sps: Bar Hanon & Mary O'Coner. -BLO (p184)

25 Jan 1846   Eliza Brady b 15 Jan 1846 d/o Hugh & Ann Brady; Sps: Rh^d Lastly & Bridget Cockeran. -BLO (p184)

01 Feb 1846   Ellen Kelley b 08 Oct 1845 d/o Wm & Mary Kelley; Sps: Thos & Mary Ward. -BLO (p184)

08 Feb 1846   Peter Cavanagh b 22 Dec 1845 s/o Charles & Rose Cavanagh; Sps: Jno Beatty & Margaret McNulty. -BLO (p185)

BAPTISMS

15 Feb 1846	Anthony Bernard Stephan b 08 Feb 1846 s/o Anthony & Mary Stephan, by Rev. Mr. Petech; Sps: Ant Ber Mechler. -BLO (p185)
16 Feb 1846	Henry Augustine Heckert b 21 Aug 1842 s/o Henry & Cath Heckert, by Rev. Mr. Petech; Sps: Eliz Teckel. -BLO (p185)
16 Feb 1846	John Heckert b 18 Mar 1845 s/o Henry & Cath Heckert, by Rev. Mr. Petech; Sps: Eliz Teckel. -BLO (p186)
16 Feb 1846	George Helmsteter b 03 Jan 1846 s/o Fran A. & Maria T. Helmsteter; Sps: Geo Lifred -BLO. (p186)
20 Feb 1846	Michael Baker b 05 Feb 1846 s/o Nich^s & Catherin Baker; Sps: Jno Shea & Mary Garvey. -BLO (p186)
22 Feb 1846	Mary Ann Rerig b 22 Jan 1846 d/o Peter & Margaret Rerig; Sps: Peter & Margrt Rerig. -BLO (p187)
25 Feb 1846	Eva [blank] b 23 Feb 1846 d/o [blank] Sps: Eva Hagar. -BLO (p187)
01 Mar 1846	Sarah Ann Clarke b 06 Aug 1845 d/o William & Mary Clarke; Sps: Math Maguire & Mary Ann Colvin. -BLO (p187)
05 Mar 1846	Mary Elizabeth Dressman b 02 Mar 1846 d/o Henry & Catherin Dressman; Sps: Hen Dressman Sr. & Elizabeth Brown. -BLO (p188)
06 Mar 1846	Mary Ann Dermody b 25 Jan 1846 d/o Jno & Honor Dermody; Sps: Peter Flatly & Mary Murry. -BLO (p188)
07 Mar 1846	Ellen Barbara Sawmuller b 05 Mar 1846 d/o Geo & Barbara Sawmuller; Sps: Ann Brown. -BLO (p188)
20 Mar 1846	Kate Middleton Semmes b 10 Mar 1846 d/o Saml M. & Elenora Semmes, ceremonies to be supplied. -BLO (p188)
22 Mar 1846	Ellen Cunningham b 02 Mar 1846 d/o Thos & Ann Cunningham; Sps: Pat^k & Mary Brady. -BLO (p189)
22 Mar 1846	Ellen Jane Stewart b 28 Dec 1845 d/o Jos & Matilda Stewart; Sps: Susan Mattingly. -BLO (p189)
22 Mar 1846	Mary Ann Regen b 26 Jan 1846 d/o Pat^k & Cath Regen; Sps: Marg^t Spelman. -BLO (p189)
29 Mar 1846	Patrick Black b 18 Mar 1846 s/o Jno & Lydia Black; Sps: Jno Coulehan & Margrt Kearney. -BLO (p189)
29 Mar 1846	Bridget Goulden b 10 Aug 1845 d/o Mich^l & Mary Goulden; Sps: Pat Cusick & Cath McCauley. -BLO (p189)

12 Apr 1846	Alexander Calahan,b 22 Nov 1845 s/o John & Ann Calahan; Sps: Ber[d] Lynch & Cath Welsh. -BLO (p190)
13 Apr 1846	Peter Louis Emel b 24 Jan 1846 s/o Jos & Kunigunda Emel; Sps: Peter Hein. -BLO (p190)
13 Apr 1846	Margaret Glob b abt. last Jan d/o Geo & Catherin Glob; Sps: Ant Hoctren & Marg[t] Hembling. -BLO (p190)
15 Apr 1846	Margaret Ann Hein b 26 Feb 1846 d/o Peter & Matilda Hein; Sps: Ann Eckels. -BLO (p190)
19 Apr 1846	Caroline Berkey b 07 Mar 1846 d/o Geo & Mary Berkey; Sps: And[W] Berkey & Elizb[h] Foley. -BLO (p190)
19 Apr 1846	Catherin Elizabeth Wempe b 10 Mar 1846 d/o Francis & Mary Wempe; Sps: Jo[s] Loeing & Mary Loeing. -BLO (p191)
19 Apr 1846	Thomas Quillen b 11 Apr 1846 s/o Andrew & Cath Quillen; Sps: Thomas Sheridan & Cath Murray. -BLO (p191)
19 Apr 1846	Patrick Thompson b 22 Mar 1846 s/o James & Mary Thompson; Sps: Geo Brown & Ann Doyle. -BLO (p191)
26 Apr 1846	Julia Dillon b 11 Apr 1846 d/o Peter & Sarah Dillon; Sps: Mich[l] Hanlen & Honor Kelley. -BLO (p191)
26 Apr 1846	Mary Moore b 17 Mar 1846 d/o Levi & Lucinda Moore; Sps: Lucinda Lentz. -BLO (p191)
03 May 1846	Mary Eliza Kane b 26 Mar 1846 d/o John & Debra Kane; Sps: Jno Mulcahy & Mary Brown. -BLO (p192)
03 May 1846	John Stephen Kuhlman b 27 Apr 1846 s/o Jno G. & Adelaid Kuhlman; Sps: Jno S. Schelenberg & Mary E. Barker. -BLO (p192)
03 May 1846	Julia Patricia Rerig b 25 Jan 1846 d/o Valentine & Susan Rerig; Sps: Geo & Julia Hardt. -BLO (p192)
03 May 1846	Emily Cecilia Mullen b 02 Apr 1846 d/o Edward & Ann Mullen; Sps: Tho[s] Mahony & Sarah Mullen. -BLO (p192)
03 May 1846	Catherin Ann Clarke b 02 Apr 1846 d/o Darby & Cath Clarke; Sps: Likel Clark & Mary Monahan. -BLO (p192)
03 May 1846	Caspar Schrimp b 23 Apr 1846 s/o Caspar & Elizabeth Schrimp; Sps: Caspar & Ann Cloze. -BLO (p193)
03 May 1846	Samuel Sampson M[c]Kinzie b 06 Nov 1845 s/o Geo & Susan M[c]Kinzie; Sps: Jno S. Schelenberg & Rody M[c]Kinzie. -BLO (p193)
05 May 1846	Robert (negro) b in Apr s/o negroes Hanna & Alectus, slaves of H. A. Jamison; Sps: negro Daniel. -BLO (p193)

BAPTISMS

06 May 1846	John Joseph Meiberg b 03 May 1846 s/o Ber^d & Mary Meiberg; Sps: Henry Winkelman & Cath Wonstreet. -BLO (p193)
11 May 1846	Sarah Ann Twigg b 11 Apr 1846 d/o Jesse & Harriet Twigg; Sps: John Welsh & Mary A. McGir. -BLO (p193)
17 May 1846	Patrick Fallon b 24 Jan 1846 s/o Mich^l & Susan Fallon; Sps: Wm Leopold & Bridg^t McWilliams. -BLO (p194)
17 May 1846	Mary Catherin Finke b 23 Dec 1845 d/o Ant & Elisb^h Finke, by Rev. Mr. Petech; Sps: John Menne & Mary C Hasen. -BLO (p194)
17 May 1846	Mary Christina Opperman b 28 Jan 1846 d/o John & Gertrude Opperman by Rev. Mr. Petech; Sps: Jo^s Wegnon & Mary C. Hasen. -BLO (p194)
17 May 1846	Caroline Kientzberg b 05 Apr 1846 d/o Wilhelm & Mary Kientzberg, by Rev. Mr. Petrech; Sps: Caroline I. Shallen & Bern^d Viger. -BLO (p194)
17 May 1846	Mary Margaret Ruptwegt b 29 Sep 1844 d/o Frederick & Barbara Ruptwegt, by Rev. Mr. Petrech; Sps: Peter Rerig & Mary Rerig. -BLO (p194)
17 May 1846	Arthur Fallon b 23 Dec 1844 s/o Mich^l & Susan Fallon, by Rev. Mr. Petech; Sps: Arthur McQuaid. -BLO (p195)
17 May 1846	Caroline Mary Wegaman, adult & convert, baptized by Rev. Mr. Petech; Sps: Car M. Weber. -BLO (p195)
19 May 1846	Mary Norris b 10 May 1846 d/o Pat^k & Cath Norris; Sps: Ja^s & Mary Norris. -BLO (p195)
20 May 1846	John Hammer b abt. 07 Jan last [1846] s/o Adam & Elisb^h Hammer; Sps: Jno B. Rosenberger. -BLO (p195)
21 May 1846	Mathias Hendle b 05 Apr 1846 s/o Henry & Cath Hendle; Sps: Martin Roman & Elizabeth Heck. -BLO (p195)
24 May 1846	Mary Ann Erskin b 27 Apr 1846 d/o William & Cath Erskin; Sps: Jno White & Mary O'Rouke. -BLO (p196)
24 May 1846	Christina Shane b 27 Apr 1846 d/o Jno & Marg^t Shane; Sps: Cecilia Ware. -BLO (p196)
24 May 1846	Rody Ellen Robinson b 19 Aug 1846 d/o Solⁿ & Ellen Robinson; Sps: Rody Ann McKinzie. -BLO (p196)
24 May 1846	Daniel Porter b 24 Jan 1846 s/o Jno B. & Elisb^h Porter; Sps: Pierce Byrne & Rody E. McKinzie -BLO (p196)
24 May 1846	George Myers b 14 Apr 1846 s/o Peter & Cath Myers; Sps: Jno & Rosanna Mullen -BLO (p196)

24 May 1846	David Dignon b 05 May 1846 s/o Tho^S & Marg^t Dignon; Sps: Thomas Brofey & Rose Ann M^{C}Manus -BLO (p197)
01 Jun 1846	John Murphy b 23 Jun 1845 s/o Ja^S & Cath Murphy; Sps: Pat Connors & Mary M^{C}Mahan -BLO (p197)
01 Jun 1846	Thomas Murphy in Jan 1843 s/o Ja^S & Cath Murphy; Sps: Ja^S Smith & Mrs. Mathews -BLO (p197)
01 Jun 1846	Ellen Murphy b 17 Mar 1844 d/o Ja^S & Cath Murphy; Sps: Joanna Buckley -BLO (p197)
07 Jun 1846	Mary Lohan b 31 May 1846 d/o Jno & Mary Lohan; Sps: Pat^k Lohan & Sally Dillon -BLO (p197)
07 Jun 1846	Margaret Ann Campbell b 13 May 1846 d/o James & Mary Campbell; Sps: Francis & Marg^t Riley -BLO (p198)
07 Jun 1846	Catherin Morgan b 13 Apr 1846 d/o James & Ann Morgan; Sps: Ed Cassidy & M. A. Colvin -BLO (p198)
07 Jun 1846	Bridget Kelley b 23 May 1846 d/o Pat^k & Mary Kelley; Sps: Pat^k M^{C}Neil & Rose Dolon -BLO (p198)
07 Jun 1846	Mary Gonnon b 22 May 1846 d/o Ja^S & Rose Gonnon; Sps: Jno Leonard & Amanda Barret -BLO (p198)
08 Jun 1846	Mary Elizabeth Johnson b 04 May 1846 d/o Wm & Elisb^h Johnson; Sps: Jno Mallon & Mary Brown-BLO (p198)
15 Jun 1846	Thomas Gibson Holtzman b 11 Jul 1841 s/o Jno & [blank] Holtzman; Sps: P. J. Cahill -BLO (p199)
17 Jun 1846	Patrick Malone b 28 May 1846 s/o Tho^S & Brdg^t Malone; Sps: Tho^S C___han & Mary Kennedy -BLO (p199)
21 Jun 1846	James Dayly b 24 Mar 1846 s/o Jno & Mary Dayly; Sps: Jno Cavanagh -BLO (p199)
04 Jul 1846	Sylvester DeKon b 09 May 1846 s/o Jesse & Mary DeKon; Sps: Tho^S Brofey -BLO (p199)
11 Jul 1846	Susan Sigerson b 01 Dec 1823, adult & convert, was baptized conditionally-BLO (p199)
12 Jul 1846	Mary Ann M^{C}Manus b 23 Jun 1846 d/o Edward & Ellen M^{C}Manus; Sps: Ja^S Thompson & Elisb^h King -BLO (p200)
12 Jul 1846	John Smith b 18 Jun 1846 s/o Jno L & Margaret Smith; Sps: Ant Helmstetter & Mary Lastfred -BLO (p200)
13 Jul 1846	John Hughes b 10 May 1846 s/o Ja^S & Mary Hughes; Sps: P. J. Cahill & Cecilia Dougherty -BLO (p200)
14 Jul 1846	Caspar Freith b 13 Jul 1846 s/o Peter & Eva Freith; Sps: Caspar Brown & his wife -BLO (p200)

BAPTISMS

18 Jul 1846	Mary Jane Donelly, married, was conditionally baptized -BLO (p200)
19 Jul 1846	John Schrimp b 25 Jun 1846 s/o Evalt & Elisb^h Schrimp; Sps: Jno Miller & Elisb^h Miller-BLO (p201)
26 Jul 1846	Maurice Arkins b 22 Jun 1846 s/o Jo^s & Ellen Arkins; Sps: Jer Shea & Ellen Sullivan -BLO (p201)
26 Jul 1846	Ellen Smith b 06 Jul 1846 d/o Pat^k & Ann Smith; Sps: Thos Brady & Margrt Murphy -BLO (p201)
26 Jul 1846	Bridget McGovern b 22 Jun 1846 d/o Thos & Ann McGovern; Sps: Henry McKeen & Marg^t King -BLO (p201)
26 Jul 1846	Catherin Ennis b 29 Jun 1846 d/o Jno & Cath Ennis; Sps: Pat^k Murphy & Nancy Hol___ -BLO (p201)
02 Aug 1846	Mary Catherin Humel b 24 Jul 1846 d/o Geo & Magdal Humel; Sps: Gertrude Knytelhardt -BLO (p202)
02 Aug 1846	Mary Elizabeth Egmeyer b 19 Jul 1846 d/o Fred^k & Mary E. Egmeyer; Sps: Hen Kulker & Mary E Burleigh -BLO (p202)
04 Aug 1846	Mary Zaup b 04 Jul 1846 d/o Conrad & Cath Zaup; Sps: Mary Breting -BLO (p202)
09 Aug 1846	George Henry Schulde b 22 Jul 1846 s/o Garet & Mary A. Schulde; Sps: Ber^d Weiges & Arle Moelman -BLO (p202)
09 Aug 1846	Rose Ann Byrne b 19 Jul 1846 d/o Mich^l & Cath Byrne; Sps: Pat^k & Ann Fay -BLO (p202)
09 Aug 1846	Charles Lenden b 04 Apr 1846 s/o Ja^s & Cath Lender; Sps: Mich^l & Mary A. McGir -BLO (p203)
09 Aug 1846	Thomas Oregon H. Price b 27 Jul 1846 s/o Wm & Honora Price; Sps: Henry McKeen -BLO (p203)
14 Aug 1846	Margaret McCoy, adult & convert, was conditionally baptized -BLO (p203)
22 Aug 1846	Ann Donahoe b 04 Nov 1845 d/o Thos & Elizabeth Donahoe; Sps: Sarah Owings-BLO (p203)
23 Aug 1846	Dan Paulus b 29 Dec 1845 d/o Ann_m Francis Paulus & Ann Likmur; Sps Johan Fack & Actxxs Radermattel, -Q. Pappert, CSR. (p203)
23 Aug 1846	Catharina Kreller b 01 Aug 1846 d/o George Kreller & Margaret Ruebelin; Sps: Catharina Prellinger -Q. Pappert, CSR. (p204)

23 Aug 1846   Johannan Petrim Mey b 12 Jul 1846 s/o Petris Phil Mey & Eva Lehman; Sps: Johann Lebart Herschberger -Q. Pappert, CSR. (p204)

23 Aug 1846   John Tumen b 24 Jun 1846 s/o Mich^l & Biddy Tumen; Sps: Jno Doonan & Mary Winslow -BLO (p204)

23 Aug 1846   Catherin Skelly b 22 Mar 1846 d/o Jno & Mary Skelly; Sps: Jno Smesing & Brdg^t Tumen-BLO (p204)

25 Aug 1846   Mary Elizabeth Gondor b 30 Jul 1846 d/o And^W & Cath Gondor; Sps: Mary Gondor -BLO (p205)

28 Aug 1846   William Monahan b 04 Jan 1844 s/o Mich^l & Margaret Monahan; Sps: Mich^l McLaughlin & Mary Casey -BLO (p205)

28 Aug 1846   Margaret Murry b 22 Aug 1846 d/o Pat^k & Brdg^t Murry; Sps: Hugh McAleer & Jane Heaney -BLO (p205)

30 Aug 1846   Mary Wonstret b 20 Aug 1846 d/o Chas & Elizabeth Wonstret; Sps: Henry Wonstret & Mary Brown -BLO (p205)

06 Sep 1846   Martin Vigor b 03 Aug 1846 d/o Ber^d & Cath Vigor; Sps: Martin Gramlick & Mary Steigmuller -BLO (p205)

06 Sep 1846   Bridget Swift b 19 Aug 1846 d/o Ant & Cath Swift; Sps: Pat Kelly & Mary Kelly -BLO (p206)

06 Sep 1846   Mary Catherin Danner b 26 Aug 1846 d/o Jno & Ann Maria Danner; Sps: Hen Snibely & Mary Shindler -BLO (p206)

09 Sep 1846   William Condon b 30 Aug 1846 s/o Thos & Marg^t Condon; Sps: Ed Flynn -BLO (p206)

09 Sep 1846   Margrt Kerby & Mary Kerby (twins) b 30 Aug 1846 d/o [not given]; Sps: D. Lane & Nan Donavan -BLO (p206)

13 Sep 1846   Mary Elizabeth Sigerson b 16 Aug 1846 d/o Wm & Mary Sigerson; Sps: Martin Harris & Old Mrs. Gondor -BLO (p206)

24 Sep 1846   Michael Riley b 07 Sep 1846 s/o Peter & Jane Riley; Sps: Jno Nugent & Cath Riley -BLO (p206)

27 Sep 1846   James Kenny b 25 Mar [May?] 1846 s/o Wm & Rose Kenny; Sps: Hugh Maguire & Rose Forester -BLO (p207)

04 Oct 1846   Jeremiah Desmon b 15 Sep 1846 s/o Jno & Honor Desmon; Sps: Cor Kelley & Mary A. Murry -BLO (p207)

04 Oct 1846   Catherin Lynch b 17 Sep 1846 d/o Jno & Brdg^t Lynch; Sps: Mich^l Brodrick & Marg^t Kearney -BLO (p207)

05 Oct 1846	Frederick Hoffman Healey b 13 Sep 1846 s/o Tho[S] & Emily Healey; Sps: Henrietta <u>Larrison</u> & P. Healy -BLO (p207)
11 Oct 1846	Margrt Murry b 01 Oct 1846 d/o Jeremiah & Ann Murry; Sps: Jno Long & Mary Mahoney -BLO (p207)
11 Oct 1846	Catherin Fitzpatrick b 26 Apr 1846 d/o Jno & Ellen Fitzpatrick; Sps: Mich[l] Gorman & Mary Ward -BLO (p208)
19 Oct 1846	James Thomas Whelan b 26 Sep 1846 s/o Ja[S] & Brdg[t] Whelan; Sps: Wm Roach & Cath Whelan -BLO (p208)
15 Nov 1846	Maria Teresa Hamer b 12 Oct 1846 d/o Simeon & Cath Hamer; Sps: Maria Leibfred -BLO (p208)

[Next four entries, by Ja[S] or Jo[S] Reamey, are in Latin, with a difficult handwriting compounded with multiple ink blotches. The authors have chosen to not include a probable mis-interpretation.]

15 Nov 1846	John Mulcahey b 03 Nov 1846 s/o Jno & Brdg[t] Mulcahey; Sps: Michael & Honor Mulcahey -BLO (p209)
15 Nov 1846	Honora Margaret Goche b 08 Nov 1846 d/o Jno & Honora Goche; Sps: Hen Rickelman & Hon Heyer -BLO (p209)
15 Nov 1846	Joseph Peter Hager b 03 Nov 1846 s/o Albert & Eva Hager; Sps: Pet Hein & Eliza Brown -BLO (p209)
-- Nov 1846	James M[c]Laughlin b 31 Oct 1846 s/o Mich[l] & Julia M[c]Laughlin; Sps: Roger M[c]Laughlin & Mary Sheridan -BLO (p210)
17 Nov 1846	Mary Elizabeth [negress] b in Aug 1846 d/o Harriett, slave of ___ Brook; Sps: Mrs. Brook -BLO (p210)
22 Nov 1846	Richard Welsh b five weeks ago s/o Edward & Mary Welsh, by Rev. Henry Myers; Sps: Jno Ambrose & Mary Haring -BLO (p210)
22 Nov 1846	Caroline Clusterman b 01 May 1846 d/o Ber[d] & Mary Clusterman; Sps: widow Ryan -BLO (p210)
22 Nov 1846	Basil Dairz, negro, abt. 5 years old, s/o Jesse & Nancy; Sps: Henry Jackson -BLO (p210)
22 Nov 1846	William Henry Jackson b 25 Aug 1846 s/o Henry Jackson & wife, privately baptized -BLO (p211)
29 Nov 1846	John Thomas Benfrid b [not listed] s/o Jno & Melvina Benfrid was privately baptized -BLO (p211)
29 Nov 1846	John Sculley b 22 Nov 1846 s/o Jno & Joanna Sculley; Sps: Pat[k] Mulcahey & Ellen O'Brien -BLO (p211)

01 Dec 1846   Robert Johnson b 26 Nov 1846 s/o Robt & Mary Johnson; Sps: Peter Fallon & Fanny Burton -BLO (p211)

13 Dec 1846   Ellen Conley b 20 Nov 1846 d/o Thos & Brdg^t Conley; Sps: Wm Callahan & Mary A King -BLO (p211)

25 Dec 1846   Thomas Samon b 14 Dec 1846 s/o Thos & Cecilia Samon; Sps: Pat^k Cosgrove & Sab Kennedy -BLO (p212)

25 Dec 1846   John Hardt b 20 Dec 1846 s/o Geo & Juliann Hardt; Sps: Jno Muller & Cath Schn___ -BLO (p212)

25 Dec 1846   John McGir b 06 Dec 1846 s/o Thos & Mary McGir; Sps: Pat^k Farrel & Mary Hodel -BLO (p212)

25 Dec 1846   Thomas Gilmartin b 10 Dec 1846 s/o Ja^s & Mary Gilmartin; Sps: Arthur & Mary Gilmartin -BLO (p212)

26 Dec 1846   Francis Steffler Laing b 18 Dec 1846 s/o Jo^s & Mary Laing; Sps: Fr Laing & Cath Trumpter -BLO (p212)

27 Dec 1846   Francis George Lentz b 19 Dec 1846 s/o Jo^s & Lucinda Lentz; Sps: Geo & Mary Mattingly -BLO (p213)

27 Dec 1846   Francis Hershberger b 11 Nov 1846 s/o John & Elizabeth Hershberger; Sps: Fr M & Elisb^h Gramlick -BLO (p213)

147 [baptized in 1846]

See the first pages of this book for tabular statements of Baptisms, Marriages, etc.

For Baptisms previous to 1847, see baptismal records in two smaller books. - -BLO (p36)

01 Jan 1847   George & Margaret Richsteiger, twins, b 01 Jan 1847, c/o Geo & Ann Richsteiger; Sps: Geo & Margrt Metzger -BLO (p36, p214)

03 Jan 1847   Caspar Miller b 18 Nov 1846 s/o Mich^l & Mary Miller; Sps: Caspar & Elizabeth Brown -BLO (p36, p214)

10 Jan 1847   Ellen Howard b 30 Nov 1847 d/o Thos & Cath Howard; Sps: Thos Samon & widow Gainer -BLO (p36, p214)

10 Jan 1847   Michael Davy b 06 Dec 1846 s/o Wm & Elizabeth Davy; Sps: Mat Coffey & Cath O'Neill -BLO (p36, p214)

26 Jan 1847   Anthony Hoelsten b 06 Jan 1847 s/o Ant & Eliz^h Hoelsten; Sps: Valentine & Eva Helfrick -BLO (p36, p215)

02 Feb 1847   Elizabeth Ambrosia O'Brien b 31 Oct 1846 d/o Pat & Ellen O'Brien; Sps: Wm Askins & Marg^t Redmond -BLO (p36, p215)

BAPTISMS

For subsequent baptism see large folio 130 BAPTISMAL RECORD -L Obermyer, Pastor of Cumberland

06 Feb 1847   John Brofey b 23 Jan 1847 s/o Kaun & Elizabeth Brofey; Sps: Timothy Sullivan & Mary Ann McGir -BLO (p37)

06 Feb 1847   Agnes Better b 12 Jan 1847 d/o Marcellus & Cath Better; Sps: Mich^l Bolan & Mary Mullen -BLO (p37)

21 Feb 1847   John Pembroke (negro) b 24 Dec 1846 s/o Jno & Susan Pembroke, (privately baptized) -BLO (p37)

28 Feb 1847   Francis Leibfrid b 08 Feb 1847 s/o Geo & Teresa Leibfrid; Sps: Francis & Elizb^n Gramlick -BLO (p37)

28 Feb 1847   Mary Dorothea Mertz b 15 Feb 1847 d/o George H & Anna Mertz; Sps: Mary D. Pull by Rev. Hoderbreck -BLO (p37)

28 Feb 1847   Mary Margaret Rosenberger b 02 Feb 1847 d/o Ball^s & Eliz^n Rosenberger; Sps: Mary Roth by Rev. Hoderbreck -BLO (p37)

28 Feb 1847   Geo William Kane b 08 Feb 1847 s/o Ant & Mary Kane; Sps: M Weisel by Rev. Mr. Hoderbreck -BLO (p37)

28 Feb 1847   Mathias Bertrand b 02 Feb 1847 s/o M. & Christ^r Bertrand; Sps: Mat Schner by Rev. Mr. Hoderbreck -BLO (p37)

28 Feb 1847   John Haeck b ___ Nov 1846 s/o Nich^s & Cath Haeck; Sps: Jno Haeck & Rev. Mr. Hoderbreck -BLO (p37)

28 Feb 1847   Mary Ellen Tims b 11 Dec 1846 d/o Thos & Cath Tims; Sps: Mat Turman & Elizabeth Pira -BLO (p37)

05 Mar 1847   Julia Ann McMahan b 03 Mar 1847 d/o And^w & Mary McMahan; Sps: Ch Denny & Alice McGir -BLO (p38)

08 Mar 1847   Edward Keenan b 14 ___ 1847 s/o Peter & Bridget Keenan; Sps: Mich^l & Mary Brady -BLO (p38)

21 Mar 1847   Mary Catherin Dressman b 14 Mar 1847 d/o Geo & Mary Dressman; Sps: H Dressman & Cath Fren__ -BLO (p38)

21 Mar 1847   Mary Ann Kulker b 17 Mar 1847 d/o Henry & Mary Kulker; Sps: Hen Burley & Mary Gramlick -BLO (p38)

23 Mar 1847   George Shingle b 14 Mar 1847 s/o Jno & Mary Shingle; Sps: Geo Beckenborn & Helen Hipp -BLO (p38)

23 Mar 1847   Rose Ann Roe b ___ Mar 1847 d/o Richard & Catherin Roe; Sps: Ch Denny & Cath McLaughlin -BLO (p38)

28 Mar 1847   Martin Stigemuler b 16 Mar 1847 s/o Henry & Mary Stigemuler; Sps: Martin Gramlick & Mary Wige -BLO (p38)

28 Mar 1847   Catherin Barbara Gramlick b 17 Mar 1847 d/o Martin & Rosetta Gramlick; Sps: Hen Stigemuler & C. B. Wige -BLO (p38)

04 Apr 1847   Mary Louisa Hein b 19 Mar 1847 d/o Peter & Matilda Hein; Sps: Margaret Roth -BLO (p39)

04 Apr 1847   Elenora Kelley b 02 Apr 1847 d/o Jno & Honora Kelly; Sps: Timothy Sullivan & Mary Colvin -BLO (p39)

12 Apr 1847   Patrick Leo b 30 Mar 1847 s/o Tho^S & Cath Leo; Sps: Eli R Plowman & Cath McAuley -BLO (p39)

16 Apr 1847   Margaret Arnold b 13 Aug 1846 d/o Jos & Matilda Arnold; Sps: Mary Logsdon -BLO (p39)

18 Apr 1847   Patrick Byrne b 18 Mar 1847 s/o John & Ellen Byrne; Sps: Jno Kelley -BLO (p39)

18 Apr 1847   Jno Tho^S Cook (negro) b 01 Jan 1847 s/o Tho^S & Celestia Cook; Sps: Henry Jackson -BLO (p39)

25 Apr 1847   Michael Celestine Mattingly b 06 Apr 1847 s/o Geo & Ann Mattingly; Sps: Jno & Martha Kerney -BLO (p39)

25 Apr 1847   Margaret McCauly b 16 Apr 1847 d/o Tho^S & Ann McCauly; Sps: Jno McCofrey & Cath Askins. -BLO (p39)

27 Apr 1847   Charles William _____, b_ Mar 1847 s/o Ellen, slave of Francis Jamison; Sps: Danl & Harret, slave _____ -BLO (p40)

27 Apr 1847   Mary Ann Stoeser b 27 Feb 1847 d/o Geo & Mary M. Stoeser; Sps: Ann Danner -BLO (p40)

09 May 1847   Ellen Sullivan b ___ Apr 1847 d/o Timothy & Ellen Sullivan; Sps: Denis Delay & Margrt King -BLO (p40)

10 May 1847   Matilda Hein adult & convert was conditionally baptized -BLO (p40)

11 May 1847   Mary Julian Shulda b 16 Mar 1847 d/o Christian & Julian Shulda; Sps: Cas Closs & Mary Gr_____ -BLO (p40)

11 May 1847   John Cunningham b 23 Apr 1847 s/o Tho^S & Ellen Cunningham; Sps: Jno Mulcahy & Mary McLaughlin. -BLO (p40)

13 May 1847   Margaret Kenny b ___ Apr 1847 d/o William & Ann Kenny; Sps: Jno Scully & Nancy Donavan. -BLO (p40)

16 May 1847   Thomas Brofey b 2_ May 1847 s/o Tho^S & Sarah Brofey; Sps: Pat^K Kenedy & Brg^t Donavan. -BLO (p40)

18 May 1847   John Henry Schminhler b 11 May 1847 s/o Henry & Mary Schminhler; Sps: Hen Daly & Mary Kohlman. -BLO (p41)

18 May 1847	Honora Frances Bradford b 18 Apr 1847 d/o J. S. & Honora Bradford; Sps: Francis Sumner. -BLO (p41)
19 May 1847	Ann Kollman b 30 Apr 1847 d/o Wm H. & Christina Kohlman; Sps: Fred[k] Laing & Anna Closs. -BLO (p41)
23 May 1847	Mary Ann Elizabeth Miberg b 16 May 1847 d/o Ber[d] & Mary Miberg; Sps: Herman & Elizabeth Brown. -BLO (p41)
26 May 1847	Henry Wolff b 26 May 1847 s/o Martin & Elizabeth Wolff; Sps: Hen Babijar & Mary Kohlman. -BLO (p41)
30 May 1847	Susan Catherin Smith b 18 Feb 1847 d/o Jacob & Cath Smith; Sps: Au[t] Burkee & Cath Rebroke. -BLO (p41)
10 Jun 1847	Mary Catherin Rupert b 03 Mar 1847 d/o Fred[k] Rupert (deceased) and Mary his wife; Sps: Peter & Mary Rerig. -BLO (p41)
10 Jun 1847	Frederick Rupert b 10 Jun 1841 d/o Fred[k] Rupert (deceased) and Mary his wife; Sps: Peter & Mary Rerig. -BLO (p41)
13 Jun 1847	Mary Madden b 23 May 1847 d/o Mich[l] & Bridget Ann Madden; Sps: Pat[K] & Mary Maden. -BLO (p41)
13 Jun 1847	Ann Cahill b 21 May 1847 d/o John & Mary Cahill; Sps: Francis & Jane Riley. -BLO (p42)
27 Jun 1847	Joseph Roh b 25 May 1847 s/o Casper & Elizabeth Roh; Sps: Jos Honadt & Honor Gerdman. -BLO (p42)
27 Jun 1847	John Malon b 12 Jun 1847 s/o Jno & Rose Malon; Sps: Jno & Marg[t] Myers. -BLO (p42)
18 Jul 1847	Mary Elizabeth Donelly b 05 Jun 1847 d/o Francis & Mary Jane Donelly; Sps: Mich[l] Gorman & Honor Ambrose. -BLO (p42)
01 Aug 1847	Ellen Bohan b 13 Jun 1847 d/o Ja[s] & Cath Bohan; Sps: Tho[s] Carroll & Ellen Bohan. -BLO (p42)
01 Aug 1847	James Falkner b 24 Jul 1847 s/o Tho[s] & Marg[t] Falkner; Sps: Ja[s] Farrell & Cath King. -BLO (p42)
01 Aug 1847	George Knighthardt b 20 Jul 1847 s/o N. T. & Gertrude Knighthardt; Sps: Geo Humil & Magdl[a] Humil. -BLO (p42)
03 Aug 1847	Mary Ellen Brook b 22 Jul 1847 d/o Jno & Cath Brook; Sps: Wash Howard & Cecilia Jamison. -BLO (p42)
08 Aug 1847	Joseph Byrne b 04 Jul 1847 s/o Jos M. & Petronella Byrne; Sps: Rose Ann Mattingly. -BLO (p43)

15 Aug 1847	Enoch Carter b 12 Jun 1847 s/o Jno & Rose A. Carter; Sps: Geo Mattingly. -BLO (p43)
15 Aug 1847	Frances Elizabeth Faughtman b 01 Aug 1847 d/o Henry & Mary Faughtman; Sps: Fr Faughtman & Mary E Berkman. -BLO (p43)
21 Aug 1847	Rebecca Ellen Donaho b 28 Jun 1847 d/o Pat[k] & Ann Donaho; Sps: Francis Mattingly. -BLO (p43)
22 Aug 1847	William Augustus Kornhoff b 16 Aug 1847 s/o Jno & Frederika Korhnoff; Sps: Fr Becker & Cath Helfrich. -BLO (p43)
25 Aug 1847	Elizabeth Lavin b 19 Jul 1847 d/o Mich[l] & Betty Lavin; Sps: Tho[S] Folkman & Cath Slautery. -BLO (p43)
25 Aug 1847	Jane Null b 22 Aug 1847 d/o Jos & Sarah Null; Sps: Mary Jane Morrison. -BLO (p43)
30 Aug 1847	Catharin Zaupt b 26 Aug 1847 d/o Conrad & Cath Zapt; Sps: Cath Breting, was baptized by Rev. Mr. Hildberger. -BLO (p43)
31 Aug 1847	Jerome Joseph Mattingly b 17 Jul 1847 s/o James & Ann Mattingly; Sps: Tho[S] & Mary A. McGir. -BLO (p43)
05 Sep 1847	John Baptist Gillespy b 30 Aug 1847 s/o Wm & Elizabeth Gillespy; Sps: Jos & Mary Hodel. -BLO (p44)
05 Sep 1847	Charles Joseph Sanders b 02 Sep 1847 s/o Henry & Mary Sanders; Sps: Cha[S] & Ann M. Suntaben. -BLO (p44)
06 Sep 1847	Andrew Jackson Lee (negro), abt. 4 mo, s/o Rob[t] & Lee. -BLO (p44)
12 Sep 1847	Anne Magdalen Metzger b __ Aug 1847 d/o Geo & Margrt Metzger; Sps: And & Margr[t] Helwig. -BLO (p44)
19 Sep 1847	Catherin Quigly b 25 Aug 1847 d/o Peter & Mary Quigly; Sps: Peter Boyle & Cath Heaney. -BLO (p44)
19 Sep 1847	Mary Jane Hudson b 28 May 1846 d/o Jacob & Rebecca Hudson; Sps: Mary Brokeman. -BLO (p44)
19 Sep 1847	Ann McKinzie b 24 Feb 1847 d/o Moses & Mary McKinzie; Sps: Mary Moelman. -BLO (p44)
21 Sep 1847	Rose Bevans b 20 Sep 1847 d/o James H. & Eveline Bevans; Sps: L. Obermyer & Rose McDonald. -BLO (p45)
28 Sep 1847	Rebecca Ann O'Brien b 18 Jan 1847 d/o Edward & Ellen O'Brien; Sps: Pat[k] McAuley & Ann Mulhaney. -BLO (p45)

BAPTISMS

30 Sep 1847	James Alexander O'Neil b 27 Sep 1847 s/o Hugh & Mary O'Neil; Sps: Philip T Cahill & widow Elizabeth Davey. -BLO (p45)
03 Oct 1847	Catherin Dermody b 22 Sep 1847 d/o Jno & Honor Dermody; Sps: Michael & Bridget Madden. -BLO (p45)
09 Oct 1847	Elizabeth Euphrasinia Doonan, adult & convert from Methodism. -BLO (p45)
17 Oct 1847	Margaret Mahony b 14 Oct 1847 d/o Tho^S & Mary Mahony; Sps: Mat Coffey & Margrt Rice. -BLO (p45)
17 Oct 1847	William Kennedy b 20 Sep 1847 s/o Wm & Mary Kennedy; Sps: Tho^S Kelley & M S Cahill. -BLO (p45)
24 Oct 1847	Bernard Brady b 10 Sep 1847 s/o Hugh & Ann Brady; Sps: Ed Keegan & Mary Gorman. -BLO (p45)
24 Oct 1847	Waldburga Beriga b 14 Oct 1847 d/o Jos & Ann Beriga; Sps: Mich^l Leonard & Waldg^a Loisnier. -BLO (p46)
31 Oct 1847	Joseph William Minnon b 22 Oct 1847 s/o Jos & Mary Minnon; Sps: Jos Butke & Mrs. Goche. -BLO (p46)
31 Oct 1847	Elizabeth Ann Howe b 16 Sep 1847 d/o Ja^S & Mary Howe; Sps: Louis Leopold & Mrs. Gondor. -BLO (p46)
31 Oct 1847	John Kennagh b 18 Oct 1847 s/o Pat^k & Cath Kannagh; Sps: Jno Cassidy & Mary Brown. -BLO (p46)
31 Oct 1847	John William Kelly b 04 Sep 1847 s/o Pat^k & Bridget Kelly; Sps: Pat^K Kelly & Ann Smith. -BLO (p46)
07 Nov 1847	Susan Wade b 01 May 1847 d/o Iser & Susan Wade; Sps: Jno & Marg^t Myers. -BLO (p46)
09 Nov 1847	Elenora Jamison b 13 Jul 1847 d/o Francis & Eliza Ann Jamison; Sps: Tho^S Jamison & widow Byrne. -BLO (p46)
14 Nov 1847	Joseph Martin Erich b 03 Nov 1847 s/o Jos & Christina Erich; Sps: Martin Gramlick & Mary A. Hamermilk. -BLO (p46)
21 Nov 1847	Laurence Byrne b 17 Nov 1847 s/o Bernard & Ann Byrne; Sps: Laurence & Mary Byrne. -BLO (p47)
21 Nov 1847	Joseph Thomas Dolan b 18 Oct 1847 s/o Tho^S & Mary Dolan; Sps: Tim Manion & widow Gainer. -BLO (p47)
21 Nov 1847	Elizabeth Ann Rosen b 13 Nov 1847 d/o Ant & Martha Rosen; Sps: Jno Cooney & Ellen Shriver. -BLO (p47)
21 Nov 1847	Nicholas George Gessner b 29 Oct 1847 s/o Wm & Marg^t Gesner; Sps: Nich^S & Gertrude Knighthaldt. -BLO (p47)

25 Nov 1847   Bernard Francis Laing b 24 Nov 1847 s/o Francis & Mary
               Laing; Sps: Fr Vempe & Mary Laing. -BLO (p47)

28 Nov 1847   Ann Gondor b 18 Nov 1847 d/o Andrew & Cath Gondor;
               Sps: Ber^d Daugherty & Martha Masters. -BLO (p47)

28 Nov 1847   Lucinda Downey b 29 Oct 1847 d/o Thos & Mary Downey;
               Sps: Th Ryan & Mrs. Fay. -BLO (p47)

28 Nov 1847   Herman Seifen b 22 Nov 1847 s/o Mary Seifen;
               Sps: Herman Greter & Mrs. Goche. -BLO (p47)

28 Nov 1847   Augustine Black b 15 Nov 1847 s/o Jno & Lydia Black;
               Sps: Thos & Amanda Coulehan. -BLO (p48)

30 Nov 1847   Mary Jane Owens b 15 Sep 1847 d/o Jonathan & Sarah
               Owens; Sps: Thos Brofey & Bridgt Byrne. -BLO (p48)

05 Dec 1847   Michael Flanigan b 8 Nov 1847 s/o Mich^l & Margrt
               Flanigan; Sps: John Nertney. -BLO (p48)

18 Dec 1847   John Thomas Brown b 10 Dec 1847 s/o Henry & Elizabeth
               Brown; Sps: Jno Wonstreet & Mary Brown. -BLO (p48)

19 Dec 1847   Mary Margaret Clarke b 20 Aug 1847 d/o Wm & Margaret
               Clarke; Sps: Jno Cassidy & M. A. Colvin. -BLO (p48)

25 Dec 1847   Mary Ann Draper b 8 Dec 1847 d/o Geo & Mary Draper;
               Sps: Richd Lorenzo & Elizbh Ryan. -BLO (p48)

01 Jan 1848   Margaret Cunningham b 18 Nov 1847 d/o James & Eliza
               Cunningham; Sps: Thos Samon & Marg^t Cunningham.
               -BLO (p49)

09 Jan 1848   Daniel Hagerty b 25 Nov 1847 s/o Pat^k & Mary Hagerty;
               Sps: Fer Shea & M. A. McGir. -BLO (p49)

16 Jan 1848   Catherin Shellhouse b 02 Jan 1848 d/o J P & Barbara
               Shellhouse; Sps: Jno Groskins & Cath Clise. -BLO (p49)

22 Jan 1848   Catherin Lavina Hofner b 22 Jul 1847 d/o Jos & Ann Maria
               Hofner; Sps: Cath Brown. -BLO (p49)

23 Jan 1848   Dennis Lynch age abt. 3 mo s/o Dennis & Mary Lynch;
               Sps: Tim Clary & Cath Firm. -BLO (p49)

23 Jan 1848   George Peter Klink b 24 Dec 1847 s/o Windlen & Mary
               Klink; Sps: Peter Rerig. -BLO (p49)

23 Jan 1848   John Henry Kremer b 11 Jan 1848 s/o Fred^k & Mary A.
               Kremer; Sps: Jos Wegman & Elizbh Shriver. -BLO (p49)

25 Jan 1848   Laura Josephine Muller b 04 Dec 1847 d/o Ed^d & Ann
               Muller; Sps: Denton Brown & Mary Muller. -BLO (p49)

BAPTISMS

27 Jan 1848	Dennis Sheridan b 22 Jan 1848 s/o Thos & Mary Sheridan; Sps: Peter Lavin & Margaret Donely. -BLO (p50)
06 Feb 1848	Catherin Glosse b 22 Jan 1848 d/o Caspar & Ann Glosse; Sps: Catherin Hoop. -BLO (p50)
08 Feb 1848	Negro Edward b 05 Feb 1848 s/o a slave of Adolphus Jamison; Sps: Negro Henry & Fanny Howard. -BLO (p50)
08 Feb 1848	Negro Henry Thomas b 31 Dec 1847 s/o a slave of Henrietta Jamison; Sps: Negro Hectius & Fanny Howard. -BLO (p50)
13 Feb 1848	Rachel Kerful b 04 Feb 1848 d/o Chas & Phebe Ann Kerful; Sps: Jno & Ann Groskup. -BLO (p50)
15 Feb 1848	Bridget Kelly b 25 Jan 1848 d/o Pat^k & Mary Kelly; Sps: Ed McDermot & Ann Noonen. -BLO (p50)
20 Feb 1848	Francis Thompson b 27 Feb 1848 s/o James & Mary Thompson; Sps: Tho^S Nolan & Cath Wicker. -BLO (p50)
20 Feb 1848	Michael Turner b 31 Oct 1847 s/o Mich^l & Brdg^t Turner; Sps: P. Hopkins & Cath Muny. -BLO (p50)
27 Feb 1848	John McAtee b 25 Jan 1848 s/o Mich^l & Martha McAtee; Sps: Jno Brady & Cecelia Dougherty. -BLO (p51)
27 Feb 1848	John Mallon b 21 Feb 1848 s/o Henry & Ann Mallon; Sps: Peter & Margaret Myers. -BLO (p51)
11 Mar 1848	John Frederick Wempe b 22 Feb 1848 s/o Francis & Maria Wempe, by Rev. Mr. Helmpract; Sps: Fred Lahing. -BLO (p51)
12 Mar 1848	Sarah Catherin Rebo b 11 Feb 1848 d/o Henry & Cath Rebo; Sps: And^W Pritke & Cath Heck. -BLO (p51)
12 Mar 1848	Juliana Haeck b 27 Feb 1848 d/o John & Elizabeth Haeck, by Rev. Mr. Helmpract; Sps: Geo Hardt. -BLO (p51)
12 Mar 1848	Eva Catherin Schrimp b 19 Feb 1848 d/o Ewald & Elizabeth Schrimp, by Rev. Mr. Helmpract; Sps: Valentine Helfrick. -BLO (p51)
12 Mar 1848	Elizabeth Purcell b 18 Feb 1848 d/o Tho^S & Johana Purcell, by Rev. Mr. Helmpract; Sps: Tho^S Murphy. -BLO (p51)
18 Mar 1848	Ann Maria Tross b 10 Feb 1848 d/o Adam & Barbara Tross, by Rev. Mr. Helmspract; Sps: Ann M.Smith. -BLO (p51)
19 Mar 1848	Patrick Sculley b 03 Mar 1848 s/o Jno & Joanna Sculley; Sps: Jno Kane & Marg^t O'Brien. -BLO (p52)

19 Mar 1848	John Henry Hassen b 06 Feb 1848 s/o Jos & Martha M. Hassen; Sps: Pierce Byrne & Mary Adelsberger. -BLO (p52)
26 Mar 1848	Mary Celestia Emel b 19 Jan 1848 d/o Jos & Cunagunda Emel; Sps: Henry Turner & Mary Kemp. -BLO (p52)
26 Mar 1848	John Donlon b 17 Feb 1848 s/o Thos & Bridget Donlon; Sps: Mich^l Nortney & Mary Ward. -BLO (p52)
27 Mar 1848	William Henry Bradford b 30 Mar 1847 s/o Melvina & Jon^n Bradford; Sps: Hen Rickelman & Mrs. Wonstreet. -BLO (p52)
09 Apr 1848	Thonas Coulehan b 23 Mar 1848 s/o Thos & Amanda Coulehan; Sps: Ja^s & Martha McHenry. -BLO (p52)
09 Apr 1848	John Moore b 07 Mar 1848 s/o Levi & Lucinda Moore; Sps: Geo & Jane Mattingly. -BLO (p52)
13 Apr 1848	Susan Matilda McKinzie b 05 Nov 1847 d/o Geo & Susan McKenzie; Sps: Roda A. Morris. -BLO (p52)
16 Apr 1848	Alectium Masters b 23 Mar 1848 d/o Rich^d & Ann Masters; Sps: Andrew & Cath Gondor. -BLO (p53)
23 Apr 1848	Wendelin Joseph Gramlick b 07 Apr 1848 s/o Francis & Elizabeth Gramlick; Sps: Wend^n & Elisabeth Ferley. -BLO (p53)
23 Apr 1848	Elisabeth Ryan b 26 Feb 1848 d/o Philip & Cath Ryan; Sps: Jno & Joanna Sculley. -BLO (p53)
23 Apr 1848	John Hope b 20 Jan 1848 s/o Conrad & Maria Hope; Sps: Jno & Cath Hope. -BLO (p53)
30 Apr 1848	Lewis Edwin McLaughlin b 05 Apr 1848 s/o Henry & Harriet McLaughlin; Sps: P. J. Cahill & Mrs. Cath Harett. -BLO (p53)
06 May 1848	Elizabeth Jerret, age abt. 45, adult & convert, was conditionally baptized. [No sponsors listed.] -BLO (p53)
06 May 1848	George Tippett age abt. 15 was conditionally baptised, having been baptised by a Meth preacher. -BLO (p53)
07 May 1848	Mary Ann Malone b 04 May 1848 d/o James & Mary Malone; Sps: Christ^r & Mary Malone. -BLO (p53)
09 May 1848	Mary Adelia Cusick b 16 Jan 1848 d/o Jno & Mary Cusick; Sps: Thos Coulehan & Mary Brofey. -BLO (p54)
09 May 1848	Daniel (negro) b 08 Mar 1848 s/o Harriet slave of Jno Brooke; Sps: negro Henry. -BLO (p54)

15 May 1848	Joseph Breting b 13 Feb 1848 s/o Jos & Cath Breting; Sps: Jo^S Hodel. -BLO (p54)

15 May 1848   Joseph Breting b 13 Feb 1848 s/o Jos & Cath Breting; Sps: Jo^S Hodel. -BLO (p54)

16 May 1848   John Knois b 13 May 1848 s/o Jno & Barbara Knois; Sps: Jno & Honor Grosskupp. -BLO (p54)

20 May 1848   James & Mary Catherine Monahan, twins, b 14 Mar 1848, children of Brian & Mary Monahan; Sps: Pierce Byrne, _____ McNeff & D. McNauly. -BLO (p54)

21 May 1848   Ellen Shingle b 19 May 1848 d/o Jno & Mary Shingle; Sps: Geo Beckerbaum & Ellen Hipp. -BLO (p54)

21 May 1848   George William Meyers b 17 Mar 1848 s/o Henry & Elizabeth Meyers; Sps: Gertrude & Mr. Obecker. -BLO (p54)

26 May 1848   Michael Smith b 26 May 1848 s/o Mich^l & Christina Smith; Sps: Jos Hoffner. -BLO (p54)

28 May 1848   James Goulden b 24 Feb 1845 s/o Jno & Ellen Goulden; Sps: Ed Cassidy & Mrs. Maguire. -BLO (p55)

28 May 1848   Thomas Goulden b 07 Dec 1847 s/o Jno & Ellen Goulden; Sps: Tho^S Bolan & Elizabeth McAuley. -BLO (p55)

28 May 1848   Mary Luisa Regen b 05 May 1848 d/o Pat^k & Cath Regen; Sps: Tim Regen & Honor Ambrose. -BLO (p55)

28 May 1848   James Dillon b 10 May 1848 s/o Peter & Sally Dillon; Sps: Pat^K McCollough & Margaret Faulkner. -BLO (p55)

01 Jun 1848   Ann Elisabeth Dressman b 31 May 1848 d/o Henry & Cath Dressman; Sps: Jno Wonstreet & Mary Dressman. -BLO (p55)

01 Jun 1848   John Hann b 03 Feb 1847 s/o Miles & Ann Hann; Sps: Jno Wonstreet & Cath Wicker. -BLO (p55)

01 Jun 1848   Ann McGovern b 23 May 1848 d/o Tho^S McGovern, deceased, and his wife Ann; Sps: Cha^S Cavnagh & Brdg^t Kelley. -BLO (p55)

08 Jun 1848   Benedict Francis Lutman b 13 Nov 1847 s/o Henry & Frederica Lutman; Sps: Benedict & Gertrude Knighthardt. -BLO (p55)

10 Jun 1848   Margaret Ann Hughes b 12 Nov 1847 d/o Nicholas Hughes & Ome _____; Sps: R. Masters & Brdg^t Tuman. -BLO (p56)

12 Jun 1848   Catherine Elisabeth Morlman b 25 Apr 1848 d/o Henry & Maria Morlman, bapt. by Rev. Mr. Helmspact; Sps: C. R. Wonstreet. -BLO (p56)

12 Jun 1848	Mary Ann Putky b 27 May 1848 d/o Geo & A Maria Putky, bapt by Rev. Mr. Helmspact; Sps: F. Lahey & A. Putky. -BLO (p56)
12 Jun 1848	Rebecca Holtzer b 27 Mar 1848 d/o Jacob & Rebecca Holtzer, bapt by Rev. Mr. Helmspact; Sps: Ant Gateman & A. N. Merlman. -BLO (p56)
12 Jun 1848	John Larkin b 07 Jan 1848 s/o Tho^S & Mary Larkin; Sps: Pierce Byrne & Ann McGir. -BLO (p56)
15 Jun 1848	Joseph Fink b 28 Apr 1848 s/o Anthony & Elizabeth Fink; Sps: Jos Faith & Christina Hasen. -BLO (p56)
21 Jun 1848	Catherin Fisher b 26 Apr 1848 d/o Jo^S & Cath Fisher, bapt. by Rev. Mr. Helmspact; Sps: Cath Spree. -BLO (p57)
22 Jun 1848	Bernard Knoble b 04 Jun 1848 s/o Henry & Cath Knoble, bapt by Rev. Mr. Helmspact; Sps: Fred^K Meyer. -BLO (p57)
22 Jun 1848	Alexander King Rerig b 10 May 1848 s/o Valentine & Susan Rerig; Sps: Valentine Rerig & Margt Rerig. -BLO (p56)
23 Jun 1848	Henry Spiker b 14 Jun 1847 s/o Henry & Louisa Spiker, bapt. by Rev. Mr. Helmspact; Sps: Ant Finke. -BLO (p56)
25 Jun 1848	John Joseph Mintrup b 12 Apr 1848 s/o Jno & Cath Mintrup; Sps: Jos Wegman & Cath Blume. -BLO (p57)
02 Jul 1848	Mary Ann Kilmartin b 26 Apr 1848 d/o Jo^S & Mary Kilmartin; Sps: Jno Larel & Cath Dougherty. -BLO (p57)
13 Jul 1848	Mary Ann Ohr age abt. 1 yr was privately baptised. -BLO (p57)
16 Jul 1848	William Henry Burke b 01 Jul 1848 s/o James & Ann Burke; Sps: Ch McDermot & Brdg^t Shanen. -BLO (p57)
17 Jul 1848	Ellen Gallaher b 09 Jul 1848 d/o Margaret Gallaher; Sps: Luisa Brinker -BLO (p57)
23 Jul 1848	John Thomas Monahan b 22 Jun 1848 s/o Darby & Mary Monahan; Sps: Pat Kenedy & Brdg^t Degman. -BLO (p57)
24 Jul 1848	Margaret Weisel b 23 Jul 1848 (twin) d/o Michael & Eva Weisel; Sps: Margrt Roth -BLO. (p58)
24 Jul 1848	John Weisel b 23 Jul 1848 (twin) d/o Michael & Eva Weisel; Sps: Peter & Matilda Hein. -BLO (p58)
26 Jul 1848	Amos [Johnson], negro of Lemuel Cross, age abt. 4 yrs s/o Mimi Johnson; Sps: Jo^S H. Bevans. -BLO (p58)

BAPTISMS

26 Jul 1848	George Lewis [Hockins], negro of L[emuel] Cross, b Jun 1848, s/o Molly Hockins; Sps: Jo^S H. Bevans. -BLO (p58)
30 Jul 1848	Francis Gray b 17 Jul 1848 s/o Hermann & Mary Gray; Sps: Fr Gray & Mary Caphus. -BLO (p58)
05 Aug 1848	Adelin Meyers, age abt. 22, adult & convert was conditionally baptised. -BLO (p58)
06 Aug 1848	Henry Herman Gochey b 13 Jul 1848 s/o Jno & Mary C. Gochey; Sps: Jno Rickelman & Christina Bedler. -BLO (p58)
06 Aug 1848	Elisabeth Ferley b 27 Jul 1847 d/o Henry & Cath Ferley; Sps: Titus & Gertrude Knighthardt. -BLO (p58)
06 Aug 1848	Christina Leininger b 25 Jul 1848 d/o Mich^l & Weldbinga Leininger; Sps: Math^S & Christina Belion. -BLO (p59)
06 Aug 1848	John Weges b Jun 1848 s/o Herman & Mary Weges; Sps: Fr Gramlick & Susan Welds. -BLO (p59)
06 Aug 1848	Mary M^{C}Gee b 18 Jul 1848 d/o Tho^S & Elisb^h M^{C}Gee; Sps: Ja^S Noonan & Mary A M^{C}Gir. -BLO (p59)
06 Aug 1848	Mary Riley b 19 Jul 1848 d/o Francis & Cath Riley; Sps: Jno Cahill & Mary Cahill. -BLO (p59)
13 Aug 1848	Martin Welsh b 08 Aug 1848 s/o Martin & Mary Welsh; Sps: Wm & Sarah Doyle. -BLO (p59)
15 Aug 1848	Mary Brady b 02 Aug 1848 d/o Edward & Orfine Brady; Sps: Jared Brofey. -BLO (p59)
15 Aug 1848	James Francis Healey b 25 Jun 1848 s/o Jno & Ann Healey; Sps: James & Ann Carey. -BLO (p59)
15 Aug 1848	Mary Hopkins b 15 Jul 1848 d/o Pat^k & Mary Hopkins; Sps: Miss Cunningham & Mary Hopkins. -BLO (p59)
20 Aug 1848	John Porter b 23 Jan 1848 s/o Jno E. & Elizabeth Porter; Sps: Geo Byrne & Mary Buckley. -BLO (p60)
27 Aug 1848	Elenora Clarke b 22 Jul 1848 d/o Darby & Cath Clarke; Sps: Thos Dunbar & Mary A Dolan. -BLO (p60)
27 Aug 1848	Catherin Whelen b 30 Jun 1848 d/o Ja^S & Bridget Whelen; Sps: Thos M Cauly & Mary Black. -BLO (p60)
02 Sep 1848	Francis Donahoe b 26 Nov 1847 s/o Thos & Elisabeth Donahoe; Sps: Pierce & Brdg^t Byrne. -BLO (p60)
03 Sep 1848	Maria Luisa Stepp b 11 Jun 1847 d/o Cha^S & Magd^a Stepp; Sps: Appelonia Onx. -BLO (p60)

03 Sep 1848   Mary Cath Stepp, age 2½ yrs d/o Cha^S & Magd^a Stepp; Sps: Mary Baker. -BLO (p60)

05 Sep 1848   Catherin Tierny b 07 Jul 1848 d/o Ja^S & Elisab^h Tierny; Sps: Brdg^t Dunigan. -BLO (p60)

10 Sep 1848   William Drish b Dec 1846, s/o John & Genevia Drish, baptised by Rev. Mr. Cronenberger; Sps: Chas Steppes. -BLO (p60)

10 Sep 1848   Herman Myer b 10 Sep 1848 s/o Henry & Ann Marie Myer, baptised by Rev. Mr. Cronenberger; Sps: Henry Frass. -BLO (p61)

11 Sep 1848   Michael Mary O'Brien 5 mo old d/o Mich^l & Ruth O'Brien; Sps: Ant Gilespie & Mary Shields. -BLO (p61)

24 Sep 1848   Margaret Ellen Kelly b 15 Sep 1848 d/o Tho^S & Jane Kelley; Sps: Mich^l Kearney & Mary Dowling. -BLO (p61)

24 Sep 1848   Margaret Degnon b 04 Sep 1848 d/o Tho^S & Marg^t Degnon; Sps: Mich^l Flanegan & M. Ann McGir -BLO (p61)

30 Sep 1848   John Henry Heldefer b 26 Sep 1848 s/o Jno & Cath Heldefer; Sps: Jno H. Brokeman & Mary Sefus. -BLO (p61)

01 Oct 1848   Thomas Mulcahey b 09 Sep 1848 s/o Jno & Brdg^t Mulcahey; Sps: Mich^l Kerney & Mary E. Cahill. -BLO (p61)

08 Oct 1848   Mary Elisabeth Burlar b 29 Sep 1848 (twin) d/o Ber^d & Christina Burlar; Sps: Henry Winder & Elisb^h Burlar. - BLO (p61)

08 Oct 1848   Ann Maria Burlar b 29 Sep 1848 (twin) d/o Ber^d & Christina Burlar; Sps: Henry Burlar & Helen Winder. -BLO (p61)

08 Oct 1848   Mary Ann Murry b Jun 1848 d/o Mich^l & Elisabeth Murry; Sps: Ch McLaughlin & Mary E. Lowes. -BLO (p62)

22 Oct 1848   George Morris b 14 Sep 1848 s/o Granshaw & Rody Morris; Sps: Pat O'Brien & Elisb^h McKinzie. -BLO (p62)

29 Oct 1848   Mary Handle b 14 Jul 1848 d/o Henry & Cath Handle; Sps: Geo Rickstiger & Mary Shingle. -BLO (p62)

29 Oct 1848   Lewis Faith b 25 Oct 1848 s/o Jos & Cath Faith; Sps: Lewis & Christina Hesen. -BLO (p62)

29 Oct 1848   Francis William Becker b 20 Oct 1848 s/o Francis & Helena Becker; Sps: Jno Kornhof & Engle Barlagh. -BLO (p62)

BAPTISMS

29 Oct 1848	Ellen Catherin Kelley b 26 Sep 1848 d/o Pat^k & Cath Kelley; Sps: Thos Kelley & Maria Gainer. -BLO (p62)
05 Nov 1848	Patrick Mathews b 28 Oct 1848 s/o Pat^k & Ellen Mathews; Sps: Jno Cassidy & M. A. Plowman. -BLO (p62)
05 Nov 1848	Mary Ann Gillespy b 01 Nov 1848 d/o Wm & Elisb^h Gillespy; Sps: Jno & Ellen Gillespy. -BLO (p62)
16 Nov 1848	Sarah Jane Smith b 26 Oct 1848 d/o Pat^k & Ann Smith; Sps: Wm Smith & Mary Healy. -BLO (p63)
19 Nov 1848	Mary Dina Honist b 24 Oct 1848 d/o Jos & Dina Honist; Sps: Fred^k Missel & Mary Laing. -BLO (p63)
19 Nov 1848	John Julius Pilsin b 03 Oct 1848 s/o Henry & Elisabeth Pilsin; Sps: Jno Gochey & Mary Laing. -BLO (p63)
26 Nov 1848	Frances Shane b 09 Nov 1848 d/o Jno & Margaret Shane; Sps: Susan C. Tippett. -BLO (p63)
28 Nov 1848	John Meyer bapt privately s/o Thomas & Adeline Meyer. -BLO (p63)
03 Dec 1848	Peter Larkin b 23 Sep 1848 s/o Thos & Cath Larkin; Sps: Henry McKerr & Brdg^t Dillon. -BLO (p63)
05 Dec 1848	Sarah Ellen Alectius Brown b 02 Sep 1848 d/o Denton D. & Ann M. Brown; Sps: Leon^d & Mrs. Smith per Mary Mullin. -BLO (p63)
05 Dec 1848	Bridget Cawlis b 27 Nov 1848 d/o Ja^s & Ann Cawlis; Sps: Mich^l Kelley & Mary Madden. -BLO (p63)
17 Dec 1848	Mary Barbara Rerig b 09 Nov 1848 d/o Peter & Marg^t Rerig; Sps: Pet^r Muller & Barb Rerig. -BLO (p64)
17 Dec 1848	Charles Lynch b 18 Nob 1848 s/o James & Madgey Lynch; Sps: Mich^l Brodrick & Cath Collins. -BLO (p64)
24 Dec 1848	Catherin Myers b 17 Sep 1848 d/o Peter & Cath Myers; Sps: Geo Keller & Mrs. Schnor. -BLO (p64)
24 Dec 1848	John Johnson b 06 May 1848 s/o William & Elisabeth Johnson; Sps: Pierce Byrne & Cath Murphy. -BLO (p64)
	125 [baptised in 1848]
	[page 65 blank]
01 Jan 1849	John Schrimp b 15 Dec 1848 s/o Casper & Elizabeth Schrimp; Sps: Jno & Ther Dore. -BLO (p43)
02 Jan 1849	John Crittenden, negro abt. 5 wks old, in danger of death, privately baptised. -BLO (p43)

197

07 Jan 1849	John Sefas b 29 Dec 1848 s/o Herman & Johana Sefas; Sps: Herman Brokeman & Frederica Kornhof. -BLO (p43)
07 Jan 1849	John Malone b 25 Oct 1848 s/o Tho^S & Bridget Malone; Sps: Michael & Mary Malone. -BLO (p43)
21 Jan 1849	Nicholas Kenny b 21 Dec 1848 s/o Wm & Rose Kenny; Sps: Tho^S Falkner & Ann Delay. -BLO (p43)
21 Jan 1849	Emily Frances Morrison b 01 Dec 1848 d/o Jno & Teresa Morrison; Sps: Thos Adelsberger & Ann Goulin. -BLO (p43)
21 Jan 1849	Mary Ann Curren b 03 Jan 1849 d/o Pat^k & Brdg^t Curren; Sps: Jno Gaffner & Mary A. Dolen. -BLO (p43)
28 Jan 1849	Mary Catherin McHenry b 16 Jan 1849 d/o Ja^S & Martha McHenry; Sps: Bern^d Daugherty & Cath Masters. -BLO (p43)
04 Feb 1849	Margaret Healey b 31 Aug 1848 d/o Tho^S & Emily Healey; (conditionally) [bapt] Sps: Fanny Howard & Tho^S Healey Jr. -BLO (p67)
18 Feb 1849	Catherin Heldefer b 14 Feb 1849 d/o Jno & Margaret Heldefer; Sps: Jno & Cath Heldefer. -BLO (p67)
05 Mar 1849	William Nevins b 29 Jan 1849 d/o James & Marcella Nevins; Sps: Jno Coulehan & Mary Carney. -BLO (p67)
08 Mar 1849	Elenora Louisa Wolf b 08 Mar 1849 d/o Martin & Elizabeth Wolf; Sps: Henry Kohlman & Eleanora Furslenberg. -BLO (p67)
11 Mar 1849	Ann Clarke b 23 Feb 1849 d/o Jno & Ennis Clarke; Sps: Jno Riley & Nancy Paden. -BLO (p67)
11 Mar 1849	Henry Spetz b Jan 1849 s/o Francis & Cath Spetz, baptised by Rev. Mr. Rumpler; Sps: Hen Ferley & C. N. Kraus -BLO (p67)
11 Mar 1849	William Haps b Feb 1849 s/o Jon & Cath Haps; Sps: Jno Speagle & Elisb^h Kerman. -BLO (p67)
11 Mar 1849	Teresa Zoeller b 15 Dec 1848 d/o Jo^S Anton & Mary Zoeller, baptised by Rev. Mr. Rumpler; Sps: Francis A. Helmstetler & Mary Fackler Kohler. -BLO (p67)
11 Mar 1849	Mary Ann Frances Wegman b 15 Feb 1849 d/o Jos & Frances Wegman, baptised by Rev. Mr. Rumpler; Sps: Dut Wegman & Mary A Bossci. -BLO (p68)
18 Mar 1849	Emma Gondor b 26 Feb 1849 d/o Andrew & Cath Gondor; Sps: Mat^h Holoms & Petronilla Byrne. -BLO (p68)

BAPTISMS

22 Mar 1848	John Dunn age abt. 40, adult & convert from Church of England, conditionally baptised on his sick bed. -BLO (p68)
25 Mar 1849	Melinda, negress age abt. 6 mo, child of Sarah slave of S. M. Semmes; Sps: Celestia, a slave. -BLO (p68)
26 Mar 1849	Willomina Electra Haffnet b 05 Dec 1848 d/o Jos & Ann Haffnet; Sps: Alexina Garland. -BLO (p68)
30 Mar 1849	Peter Wise b 15 Jun 1848 s/o Peter & Mary Ann Wise; Sps: Jos Emel & Mary Cahill. -BLO (p68)
30 Mar 1849	Margaret Wise b 10 May 1843 d/o Peter & Mary Ann Wise; Sps: Sophia Cahill. -BLO (p68)
05 Apr 1849	George Michael Schultz b Feb 1849 s/o Gerhard & Mary Schultz; Sps: M. Wiesel & Maria Gevans. -BLO (p68)
15 Apr 1849	James Tims b 17 Mar 1849 s/o Tho[s] & Cath Tims; Sps: Mich[l] Menagh & Brdg[t] Daugherty. -BLO (p69)
15 Apr 1849	John M[c]Cormack b 10 Apr 1849 s/o Wm & Margaret M[c]Cormack; Sps: Peter Quigly & Mary Brady. -BLO (p69)
15 Apr 1849	Thomas O'Donnel b 04 Apr 1849 s/o Hugh & Mary O'Donel; Sps: Pat[K] Reiley & Sibey Monahan. -BLO (p69)
15 Apr 1849	Anthony Reilley b 30 Mar 1849 s/o Jno & Lulia Riley; Sps: Ja[s] Ginelly & Margaret M[c]Donell. -BLO (p69)
17 Apr 1849	John Henry Dressman b 11 Apr 1849 s/o Geo & Hillary Dressman; Sps: Henry Frever & Cath Dressman. -BLO (p69)
17 Apr 1849	Mary Ann Reilley b 31 Jan 1849 d/o Peter & Jane Reilley; Sps: Thos Duffy & Rose Kelley. -BLO (p69)
29 Apr 1849	James Farrell b 23 Apr 1849 s/o Jno & Ann Farrell; Sps: Ja[s] Farrell & Marg[t] Kearney. -BLO (p69)
29 Apr 1849	Mary Ann Boland b 25 Mar 1849 d/o Mich[l] & Mary Boland; Sps: Mich[l] O'Connor & Cath McLaughlin. -BLO (p69)
01 May 1849	Henry Gerken b 22 Feb 1849 s/o Fred[k] & Rebecca Gerken; Sps: Henry Gerken. -BLO (p70)
13 May 1849	James Moses Brant b 13 Feb 1849 s/o Cha[s] & Mary Ann Brant; Sps: Jno & Elisabeth Doonen. -BLO (p70)
20 May 1849	Mary Ann McDermot b 08 Mar 1849 d/o Cha[s] & Ann McDermot; Sps: Jno Coulehan & Elisa Cunningham. -BLO (p70)
27 May 1849	Emma Regina Windel b 01 Dec 1848 d/o Jno & Mary Windel; Sps: Regina Cabel. -BLO (p70)

27 May 1849	John James Hughes b 15 Apr 1849 s/o James & Isabella Hughes; Sps: Mich[l] Mallon & Ann Holton. -BLO (p70)
27 May 1849	Margaret Ann Allen b 18 Mar 1849 d/o William & Cecilia Allen; Sps: Pat[k] Honsoly & Mary Lynch. -BLO (p70)
10 Jun 1849	John Dermody b 12 May 1849 s/o Jno & Honora Dermody baptised by Rev. Urbancheck; Sps: Darby Clarke & Mary Mahan. -BLO (p70)
21 Jun 1849	John Moran b 17 Jun 1849 s/o Pat[k] & Cath Moran; Sps: James & Cath Galvin. -BLO (p70)
22 Jun 1849	Peter Rock b 27 Jan 1849 s/o Martin & Mary Rock; Sps: Pat[k] & Brdg[t] Gagligan. -BLO (p71)
22 Jun 1849	Michael Rock b 12 Jun 1849 s/o Andrew & Sibilian Rock; Sps: Anthony Merrick. -BLO (p71)
23 Jun 1849	Judith Flatly b 22 Jun 1849 d/o Martin & Rose Flatly; Sps: Brdg[t] Conelly. -BLO (p71)
24 Jun 1849	Mary Elisabeth Cahill b 04 Jun 1849 d/o Jno & Mary Cahill; Sps: Dan[l] McKenna & Cath Reilly. -BLO (p71)
02 Aug 1849	Daniel Murphy, infant & dangerously ill, was privately baptised. -BLO (p71)
05 Aug 1849	Ruth Ellen Arnold b 06 Oct 1848 d/o Jos & Matilda Arnold; Sps: Marg[t] Logsdon. -BLO (p71)
10 Aug 1849	Michael Paden b 10 Aug 1849 s/o Pat[k] & Sarah Paden was privately baptised. -BLO (p71)
11 Aug 1849	Margaret Ellen Mattingly b 26 Jun 1849 d/o James & Ann Mattingly; Sps: Mary C. Cahill. -BLO (p71)
12 Aug 1849	John Beatty b 23 Jul 1849 s/o Pat[k] & Mary Beatty; Sps: Jno Clarke & Sarah Garity. -BLO (p72)
12 Aug 1849	William Leo b 15 Jul 1849 s/o Tho[s] & Cath Leo, baptised by Rev. Mr. Urbancheck; Sps: Mich[l] Gormon & Elis[h] McAuley. -BLO (p72)
26 Aug 1849	Anthony Thomas Mattingly b 08 Aug 1849 s/o Geo & Ann Mattingly; Sps: L. Obermyer & Jane Mattingly. -BLO (p72)
26 Aug 1849	Patrick White b 03 Aug 1849 s/o Ja[s] & Mary White; Sps: Ja[s] McAlee & Elisb[h] McGeer. -BLO (p72)
29 Aug 1849	Jerome Jeremiah McKenzie b 11 Jul 1848 s/o Jer & Sarah McKenzie; Sps: Sam[l] A. & Clara Walker. -BLO (p72)
31 Aug 1849	Louisa Ellen O'Brien b 09 May 1849 d/o Ed & Ellen O'Brien; Sps: Bern[d] Reynolds & Cath Marr. -BLO (p72)

BAPTISMS

02 Sep 1849	James William Hann b 30 Dec 1848 s/o Miles & Ann Hann; privately baptised. -BLO (p72)
02 Sep 1849	Mary Buckley b 01 Sep 1849 d/o Denis & Mary Buckley; Sps: Mich^l & Cath Ambrose. -BLO (p72)
16 Sep 1849	Mary Ellen Donahoe b 29 Apr 1849 d/o Ja^s & Mary Donahoe; Sps: Jno Byrne & Marg^t Degnon. -BLO (p73)
16 Sep 1849	John Henry Meyers b 12 May 1849 s/o Henry & Louisa Myers; Sps: Ja^s Donahoe & Elisb^h Galvin. -BLO (p73)
07 Oct 1849	Margaret Ennis b 14 Sep 1849 d/o John & Cath Ennis; Sps: Wm Maguire & Ellen Stapleton. -BLO (p73)
07 Oct 1849	James Francis Horan b 08 Sep 1849 s/o Martin & Mary Horan; Sps: Ber^d Smith & Marg^t Irwin. -BLO (p73)
07 Oct 1849	Catherin Elizabeth (negro) b 24 May 1849 d/o Thos & Celestia, slaves of S. M. Semmes; Sps: Fanny Jones. -BLO (p73)
14 Oct 1849	Mary Ellen McAleer b 23 Sep 1849 d/o Geo & Mary Ann McAleer; Sps: Chas McGovern & Ellen Colvin. -BLO (p73)
14 Oct 1849	Ellen Ferguson b 11 Aug 1849 d/o James & Mary Ferguson; Sps: Laurence & Mary Byrne. -BLO (p73)
14 Oct 1849	John Stanton b 27 Sep 1849 s/o James & Mary Stanton; Sps: Ja^s & Brdg^t Farrell. -BLO (p73)
14 Oct 1849	Mary Ann Brown b 26 Sep 1849 d/o Pat^k & Mary Brown; Sps: Martin Moran & Ann McDermott. -BLO (p74)
15 Oct 1849	Bernard Augustine Twigg b 21 Aug 1849 s/o Jesse & Mary A. Twigg; Sps: Pat^k Donelan & Cath Cushmaugh. -BLO (p74)
19 Oct 1849	Mary Kenney b 14 Oct 1849 d/o Wm & Ann Kenney; Sps: Jno Burke & Nancy Donavan. -BLO (p74)
19 Oct 1849	George Donahoe b 15 Mar 1849 s/o Pat^k & Ann Donahoe; Sps: Thos McGir & Mary Ann Cox. -BLO (p74)
27 Oct 1849	Lawrence Hughes b 22 Apr 1849 s/o Nich^s & Omah Hughes; Sps: Peter & Jane Reilly. -BLO (p74)
28 Oct 1849	Charles William Stuart b 14 Jun 1849 s/o Jos & Matilda Stuart; Sps: Ann Rehy & Hen Gerderman. -BLO (p74)
28 Oct 1849	John Carney b 22 Oct 1849 s/o Peter & Mary Carney; Sps: Sarah Welsh & Mat Coffey Jr. -BLO (p74)
28 Oct 1849	Bridget Hagan b 28 Sep 1849 s/o Thos & Cath Hagan; Sps: Peter Carney & Jane Carney. -BLO (p74)

06 Nov 1849   Mary Ann Ryan b 29 Oct 1849 d/o Pat[k] & Brdg[t] Ryan; Sps: Mich[l] Cregan & Cath Owens. -BLO (p75)

11 Nov 1849   James Early b 01 Nov 1849 s/o Pat[k] & Abby Early; Sps: Mich[l] Dolan & Cath McAuley. -BLO (p75)

11 Nov 1849   James Turney b 29 Oct 1849 s/o Ant & Winfred Turney: Sps: Cha[s] & Mary Durkin. -BLO (p75)

11 Nov 1849   Owen Connor b 18 Oct 1849 s/o John Winifred Connor; Sps: Mich[l] Hayden & Cath Kerney. -BLO (p75)

11 Nov 1849   Honora Cook b 02 Nov 1849 d/o James & Mary Ann Cook; Sps: Ezekeal White & Rose Mattingly. -BLO (p75)

12 Nov 1849   Thomas O'Melia b 31 Oct 1849 s/o Tho[s] & Margaret O'Melia; Sps: Martin Kneelan & Mary Morrison. -BLO (p75)

15 Nov 1849   Mary Jane Mooty b 20 Aug 1849 d/o John & Brdg[t] Mooty; Sps: Peter Thurman & Marg[t] Faulkner. -BLO (p75)

16 Nov 1849   Mary Feeney b 13 Oct 1849 d/o Mich[l] & Judith Feeney; Sps: Timothy & Julia Welsh. -BLO (p75)

18 Nov 1849   Mary Dolan b 03 Nov 1849 d/o John & Susan Dolan; Sps: Pat[k] Hagan & Ann Welsh. -BLO (p76)

18 Nov 1849   Mary Alice Boyle b 11 Nov 1849 d/o Peter & Mary Boyle; Sps: Pat[k] Galager & Cath Mclaughlin. -BLO (p76)

25 Nov 1849   Mary Ann Byrne b 04 Nov 1849 d/o Bern[d] & Ann Byrne; Sps: Mich[l] Cumerford & Mary O'Donel. -BLO (p76)

25 Nov 1849   John Henry Ambrose Donelly b 10 Nov 1849 s/o Henry & Ann Donelly; Sps: Jno McKenna & Rose Mattingly. -BLO (p76)

25 Nov 1849   Madga Foley b 21 Nov 1849 child of Brien & Mary Foley; Sps: Michael Foley & Hannah Conley. -BLO (p76)

28 Nov 1849   Sylvester (negro) b 29 Oct 1849 s/o Harriet & Alextius, slaves of H. A. Jamison; Sps: Th Jamison & Fanny Howard. -BLO (p76)

29 Nov 1849   Mary Elisabeth Healy b 26 Nov 1849 d/o Mich[l] & Brdg[t] Healy; Sps: Laughlin Healy & Marg[t] Howard. -BLO (p76)

03 Dec 1849   Anthony Ganty b 17 Nov 1849 s/o Jno & Ellen Ganty; Sps: Ant Mangun & Ann Kane. -BLO (p76)

08 Dec 1849   Phobe Ann Kerful, adult & convert conditionally baptised; Sps: Ann Grosh___. -BLO (p77)

09 Dec 1849   Owen Dunleavy b 26 Nov 1849 s/o Martin & Brdg[t] Dunleavy; Sps: Mich[l] Early & Jane Carson. -BLO (p77)

20 Dec 1849	Ellen Richards b 30 Nov 1849 d/o James & Joanna Richards; Sps: Mich[l] Tulley & Brdg[t] Welsh. -BLO (p77)
23 Dec 1849	John James Sylvester McNair b 24 Oct 1849 s/o James & Mary McNair; Sps: Jno McNair & Susan C. Tippett. -BLO (p77)
30 Dec 1849	Sarah M[c]Cormack b 21 Dec 1849 d/o John & Cath M[c]Cormack; Sps: Ja[s] McCormack & Ann <u>Kallala</u>. -BLO (p77)
30 Dec 1849	Mary Ann Thompson b 27 Nov 1849 d/o Ja[s] & Mary A. Thompson; Sps: Ch McKenna & Brdg[t] Dillon. -BLO (p77)
30 Dec 1849	Mary Margaret Carney b 21 Dec 1849 d/o Wm & Mary Carney; Sps: James & Cath Carney. -BLO (p77)

95 [baptised in 1849]

06 Jan 1850	Margaret Helen Donelly b 13 Oct 1849 d/o Fra[s] & Jane Donelly; Sps: Mich[l] & Marg[t] Kerney. -BLO (p78)
06 Jan 1850	Andrew Thomas White b 29 Dec 1849 s/o Ezechial & Ellen White; Sps: Ja[s] Cook & Harriet Kemp. -BLO (p78)
09 Jan 1850	Bridget Battle b 06 Jan 1850 d/o Roger & Ann Battle; Sps: Elisabeth Galvin. -BLO (p78)
12 Jan 1850	Mary Jane Healey b 11 Jan 1850 d/o James & Maria Healey; Sps: Ann Healey & Jno Jordon. -BLO (p78)
12 Jan 1850	Barbara Conelly b 11 Jan 1850 d/o Mark & Hannah Conelly; Sps: Brian & Mary Foley. -BLO (p78)
13 Jan 1850	Ann Gertrude Gilespie b 07 Jan 1850 d/o William & Elizabeth Gilespie; Sps: Tho[s] & Ann Adelsberger. -BLO (p78)
18 Jan 1850	Hannah Mahoney b 17 Jan 1850 d/o Mich[l] & Ellen Mahoney; Sps: Donel Hart & Cath Mahoney. -BLO (p78)
20 Jan 1850	Mary Carr b 12 Jan 1850 d/o Hugh & Mary Carr; Sps: Tho[s] Hanon & Mary Welsh. -BLO (p78)
21 Jan 1850	Ellen Doran b 12 Jan 1850 d/o John & Honora Doran; Sps: Ellen Sullivan. -BLO (p79)
26 Jan 1850	Daniel Cain b 21 Jan 1850 s/o Pat[k] & Elisa Cain; Sps: R N Henisy & Ellen Russel. -BLO (p79)
27 Jan 1850	George Washington McLean Wood b 07 Jan 1850 s/o Wm P. & Harriet Wood; Sps: Jno Cassidy & Mary Adelsberger. -BLO (p79)
27 Jan 1850	Philip Ryan b 16 Jan 1850 s/o Philip & Cath Ryan; Sps: Tim Clery & Johanny Coffey. -BLO (p79)

29 Jan 1850	Bridget Hanlon b 24 Jan 1850 d/o Pat^k & Cath Hanlon; Sps: Jno Gegehan & Mary Maginnis. -BLO (p79)
31 Jan 1850	Honora Richards b 30 Jan 1850 d/o Jno & Mary Richards; Sps: Owen Mahony & Margaret Penny. -BLO (p79)
02 Feb 1850	Bridget Purcell b 15 Jan 1850 d/o Robt & Mary Purcell Sps: Ed Nee & Sili Burke. -BLO (p79)
03 Feb 1850	James Brofey b 21 Jan 1850 s/o Thos & Sarah Brofey; Sps: Hugh Mcguire & Brdg^t McDermot. -BLO (p79)
17 Feb 1850	Harriet Margaret McLaughlin b 22 Nov 1849 d/o Henry & Harriet McLaughlin; Sps: Bern^d Dougherty & Mary Kerne. -BLO (p80)
24 Feb 1850	Mary Margaret Coulehan b 21 Feb 1850 d/o Thos & Amanda Coulehan; Sps: Jno Coulehan & Margaret Coulehan. -BLO (p80)
24 Feb 1850	John Shields b Jan 1850 s/o Jno & Margaret Shields; Sps: Thos Heller & Margaret King. -BLO (p80)
03 Mar 1850	Mary Moran b 08 Feb 1850 d/o William & Ellen Moran; Sps: Pat^k Maguire & Mary Mangion. -BLO (p80)
09 Mar 1850	Peter Wise adult & convert baptised conditionally. -BLO (p80)
17 Mar 1850	Margaret Ann Fallon b 03 Mar 1850 d/o Peter & Brdg^t Fallon; Sps: Brdg^t & John Fallon. -BLO (p80)
17 Mar 1850	Catherin Lawler b 01 Jan 1850 d/o Thos & Mary Lawler; Sps: Mich^l & Elisabeth Hickey. -BLO (p80)
17 Mar 1850	Mary Ann Keenan b 15 Mar 1850 d/o Francis & Margaret Keenan; Sps: Elisabeth Galvin. -BLO (p80)
24 Mar 1850	Catherine Kelley b 18 Mar 1850 d/o Pat^k & Cath Kelley; Sps: Jno O'Brien & Cath Collins. -BLO (p81)
24 Mar 1850	Mary Foley b 12 Mar 1850 d/o Mich^l & Mary Foley; Sps: Thos McKay & Winnie Tuney. -BLO (p81)
24 Mar 1850	Mary Caton b 18 Mar 1850 d/o Robt & Maria Caton; Sps: Pat^k & Honor Gorman. -BLO (p81)
24 Mar 1850	Marcellus Gondor b 15 Mar 1850 s/o Andrew & Cath Gondor; Sps: B. Dougherty & M. Culehan. -BLO (p81)
31 Mar 1850	Edward O'Neill b 03 Mar 1850 s/o Hugh & Mary O'Neill Sps: Saml Mattingly & Elisa Gaines. -BLO (p81)
03 Apr 1850	Catherine O'Neill b 06 Mar 1850 d/o Henry & Honor O'Neill; Sps: Pat^k Dolan & Rosilia Walker. -BLO (p81)

03 Apr 1850	Michael Cassily b 02 Apr 1850 s/o James & Ellen Cassily; Sps: Jno & Margaret McMannus. -BLO (p81)
12 Apr 1850	Mary Ann Larkin b Mar 1850 d/o Tho[S] & Mary Larkin; Sps: Mich[l] Kigney & Ann Fox.. -BLO (p81)
12 Apr 1850	James McManus b 25 Jan 1850 s/o James & Eliza McManus; Sps: Martin Hopkins. -BLO (p45)
14 Apr 1850	Catherin Brofey b 30 Mar 1850 d/o Cornelius & Eliza Brofey; Sps: Jno & Rose A. Melon. -BLO (p45)
14 Apr 1850	James McCullough b 01 Apr 1850 s/o Jno & Mary McCullough; Sps: Dom Dowling & Rose Carney. -BLO (p45)
16 Apr 1850	Michael Kilroy b 14 Apr 1850 s/o Pat[k] & Marg[t] Kilroy; Sps: Peter Egan & Ann Kane. -BLO (p45)
20 Apr 1850	John Wise age abt. 15 yrs was baptised. -BLO (p45)
21 Apr 1850	Barbara Howe b 01 Apr 1850 d/o Pat[k] & Julia Howe; Sps: Tho[S] Carson & Honor M[c]Cormack. -BLO (p45)
27 Apr 1850	John Dolan b 15 Mar 1850 s/o Mich[l] & Mary Dolan; Sps: Tho[S] Gormerly & Winifred Heyden. -BLO (p45)
27 Apr 1850	John Staunton b 11 Apr 1850 s/o Pat[k] & Nancy Staunton; Sps: Edward Manion. -BLO (p45)
28 Apr 1850	Catherin M[c]Cue b 28 Mar 1850 d/o James & Mary M[c]Cue; Sps: Pat & Margaret Dunn. -BLO (p46)
28 Apr 1850	Thomas Kilduf b 12 Apr 1850 s/o Pat & Mary Kilduf; Sps: Pat Garrity & Mary M[c]Candriss. -BLO (p46)
29 Apr 1850	Mary Ann Donelon b 09 Apr 1850 s/o Tho[S] & Bridget Donelon; Sps: James Delay & Ann Timms. -BLO (p46)
02 May 1850	Mary Schroder b 17 Feb 1850 d/o Henry & Ann Schroder; Sps: Anna M. Schwaite. -BLO (p46)
06 May 1850	Philip Lynch b 20 Mar 1847 s/o Pat & Cath Lynch, conditionally & privately baptised. -BLO (p46)
12 May 1850	Francis Doonan b 04 May 1850 s/o Jno & Brdg[t] Doonan; Sps: Peter Kenny & Marg[t] Falkner. -BLO (p46)
13 May 1850	Ellen Burke b 19 Apr 1850 d/o Wm & Mary Burke; Sps: Mich[l] Ruddy & Mary Wood. -BLO (p46)
14 May 1850	Edward Shehey b 05 May 1850 s/o Bern[d] & Ann Shehey; Sps: Pat[k] Lynch & Mary Hayden. -BLO (p46)
16 May 1850	Mary Josephine Jamison b 20 Mar 1850 d/o Francis A. & Eliza A. Jamison; Sps: Ellen Byrne. -BLO (p84)

| 19 May 1850 | James Dorsey b 06 May 1850 s/o James & Mary Dorsey; Sps: Tho[S] Farrel & Ann Rhone. -BLO (p84) |

19 May 1850 James Dorsey b 06 May 1850 s/o James & Mary Dorsey; Sps: Tho[S] Farrel & Ann Rhone. -BLO (p84)

26 May 1850 Christina Mulligan b 13 May 1850 s/o James & Jane Mulligan; Sps: Mark Doyle & Martha Finnigan. -BLO (p84)

26 May 1850 Edward Madden b 15 May 1850 s/o Jno & Mary Maden; Sps: Pat[k] & Brdg[l] Lynch. -BLO (p84)

30 May 1850 Mary O'Hagan b 25 Mar 1850 d/o Pat[k] & Ann O'Hagan; Sps: Hugh & Mary Carr. -BLO (p84)

02 Jun 1850 Charles Henry Ways b 22 May 1850 s/o Jos H. & Elisb[h] Ways; Sps: Mich[l] Burke & Cecilia Ways. -BLO (p84)

09 Jun 1850 Margaret Burke b May 1850 d/o Michael & Ellen Burke; Sps: Jno O'Donnel & Ellen Lynch. -BLO (p84)

18 Jun 1850 Catherin Callahan b 31 Mar 1850 d/o John & Ann Callahan; Sps: Jo[S] Maguire & Ann Conway -BLO (p84)

19 Jun 1850 Joseph Peter Coffey b 13 Jun 1850 s/o Mat[W] & Johanna Coffey; Sps: Ph Ryan & Bridget Leibz. -BLO (p85)

14 Jul 1850 Catherin Hagerty b 16 Jun 1850 d/o Pat[k] & Mary Hagerty; Sps: Pat[k] Sheehan & Julia Collins. -BLO (p85)

14 Jul 1850 Elisabeth Clarkson b 28 Jun 1850 d/o Edward & Catherin Clarkson; Sps: Tho[S] & Elisabeth Gleason. -BLO (p85)

14 Jul 1850 Owen Mulvey b 29 Jun 1850 s/o Mich[l] & Margaret Mulvey; Sps: Martin Murry & Elisb[h] Keech. -BLO (p85)

19 Jul 1850 Bridget Scully b 13 Jul 1850 d/o Timothy & Mary Scully; Sps: Pat Ford & Mary Clarke. -BLO (p85)

21 Jul 1850 Mary Teresa Wolverton b 16 Jul 1850 d/o J. W. & Cath M. Wolverton; Sps: Alexina Garland. -BLO (p85)

21 Jul 1850 James Ford b 14 Jul 1850 s/o Bart[W] & Ellen Ford; Sps: Wm & Catherin Murphy. -BLO (p85)

23 Jul 1850 Patrick Kelley b 29 Jun 1850 s/o Wm & Julia Kelley; Sps: Pat Kelley & Ann Sheridan. -BLO (p85)

23 Jul 1850 John McEnally b 01 Jul 1850 s/o Jno & Bridget McEnally; Sps: Jno Cumins & Elisb[h] Melia. -BLO (p86)

28 Jul 1850 Patrick Mallin b 10 Jul 1850 s/o Mich[l] & Alice Mallin; Sps: Jno M[c]Namara & Ann Lohan. -BLO (p86)

02 Aug 1850 Margaret Lynch b 26 Jun 1850 d/o Pat & Cath Lynch; Sps: M. A. Gouldin & Jno Grady. -BLO (p86)

BAPTISMS

03 Aug 1850	John Gallaher b 28 Jul 1850 s/o Jno & Nancy Gallaher; Sps: Ann Healey. -BLO (p86)
04 Aug 1850	John Patrick Kerwick b 23 Jul 1850 s/o Keirn & Mary A. Kerwick; Sps: Sus C. Tippet & Ja^S Forester. -BLO (p86)
08 Aug 1850	Michael Gouldin b in 1848 s/o Jno & Ellen Gouldin; Sps: Arthur M^{C}Gir & Mary Brew. -BLO (p86)
11 Aug 1850	William Robert Myers b 15 Jun 1850 s/o Tho^S & Adel Myers; Sps: Mich^l Dolan & Cath Ryan. -BLO (p86)
15 Aug 1850	Ellen Regan b 04 Aug 1850 d/o Pat & Cath Regan; Sps: Bart^W Kain & Cath Regan. -BLO (p86)
16 Aug 1850	Michael Courdin b 16 Aug 1850 s/o Pat^k & Elis^h Courdin; Sps: Pat^k Donahu & Ann McCouley. -BLO (p87)
18 Aug 1850	Elten Riley b 12 Oct 1849 s/o Ber^d & Mary Riley; Sps: J. P. M^{C}Manus & Mary Horan. -BLO (p87)
18 Aug 1850	James Nagle b 01 Aug 1850 s/o Mich^l & Juliana Nagle; Sps: Ed Burke & Mary Moran. -BLO (p87)
18 Aug 1850	Joseph M^{C}Mahan b 14 Aug 1850 s/o Pat^k & Sarah M^{C}Mahan: Sps: Mich^l Lavin & Brdg^t Maguire. -BLO (p87)
18 Aug 1850	John Albert Demeris b 12 May 1843 s/o Jo^S & Ann Demeris, both deceased; Sps: S. D. & Cecilia Ways. -BLO (p87)
18 Aug 1850	Ann Josephine Demeris b 17 Aug 1847 d/o Jo^S & Ann Demeris; Sps: S. D. & Cecilia Ways. -BLO (p87)
18 Aug 1850	James Murphy b 17 Aug 1850 s/o Jer & Susan Murphy; Sps: Den & Cath Murphy. -BLO (p87)
18 Aug 1850	Thomas Mahon b 15 Aug 1850 s/o Jno & Brdg^t Mahon; Sps: Pat^k Gill & Ellen Masters. -BLO (p87)
25 Aug 1850	John Boland b 15 Aug 1850 s/o Mich^l & Mary Boland; Sps: Darly M^{C}Donugh & Cath M^{C}Gittyan. -BLO (p88)
28 Aug 1850	Elisa Keeley b 20 Jul 1850 d/o Jno & Mary Keeley; Sps: Tho^S M^{C}Laughlin & Sarah Lanahan. -BLO (p88)
28 Aug 1850	Dahlia Kane b 17 Aug 1850 d/o John (of Virginia) & Ann Kane; Sps: James O'Connor & Marg^t Kilroy. -BLO (p88)
31 Aug 1850	William Henry Mix b 17 Feb 1849 s/o B & Mary Mix; Sps: Peter & Emily Wise. -BLO (p88)
01 Sep 1850	John James Beers b 17 Jul 1850 s/o Rich^d & Mary A. Beers; Sps: Mich^l & Mary Gibson. -BLO (p88)

07 Sep 1850   Michael King b 02 Sep 1850 s/o Pat^k & Ann King;
Sps: Hugh King & Mary McTague. -BLO (p88)

08 Sep 1850   John Tracey b 25 Aug 1850 s/o Malachy & Mary Tracey;
Sps: Hugh Tracey & Ellen Duffy. -BLO (p88)

11 Sep 1850   Mary Minnogue b 11 Sep 1850 d/o Mich^l & Ann
Minnogue; Sps: __ Faulkner & Cath Barron. -BLO (p88)

11 Sep 1850   Frances Rebecca Wise b 22 Jul 1850 d/o Peter & Mary
Wise; Sps: P. J. Cahill & Emily Wise. -BLO (p89)

11 Sep 1850   Teresa McLaughlin b 09 Sep 1850 d/o Ann & Jno
McLaughlin; Sps: Ed Sweeney & Ellen Laurence. -BLO
(p89)

22 Sep 1850   Mary Ann Culheem b 09 Sep 1850 d/o Pat^k & Brdg^t
Culheem; Sps: widow Ann Ryan. -BLO (p89)

23 Sep 1850   Elisabeth Carlos b 03 Sep 1850 d/o Pat^k & Elisb^h Carlos;
Sps: Pat^k Kelly & Ann Hedyan [Hayden?]. -BLO (p89)

29 Sep 1850   Thomas Mahony b 25 Sep 1850 s/o Thos & Mary Mahony;
Sps: Jno & Honora Ambrose. -BLO (p89)

29 Sep 1850   Robert Emmett Whelen b 21 Aug 1850 s/o Ja^s & Brdg^t
Whelen; Sps: John Byrne. -BLO (p89)

29 Sep 1850   Rose Ann Conell b 18 Sep 1850 s/o Ed & Honor Conell;
Sps: Ber^d Mullen & Elis^h Davey. -BLO (p89)

04 Oct 1850   Michael Conelly b 19 Sep 1850 s/o Mich^l & Brdg^t Conelly;
Sps: Henry Loftus & Kale Shehan. -BLO (p89)

13 Oct 1850   John Henry Kelley b 29 Sep 1850 s/o Pat^k & Fanny Kelley;
Sps: Jno Cavenagh & Mary Kelly. -BLO (p90)

13 Oct 1850   George Patrick Carney b 01 Oct 1850 s/o Pat^k & Jane
Carney; Sps: Hugh Lynch & Ann Wallace. -BLO (p90)

13 Oct 1850   William Purcell b 01 Sep 1850 s/o Thos & Johanna Purcell;
Sps: Pat^k & Cath Kelley. -BLO (p90)

20 Oct 1850   Catherin Healey b 26 Sep 1850 d/o Jno & Ann Healey;
Sps: Maria Gainer. -BLO (p90)

27 Oct 1850   Mary Ann Gorman b 20 Oct 1850 d/o Pat^k & Honora
Gorman; Sps: Robt Caton & Ellen Mandy. -BLO (p90)

02 Nov 1850   Thomas Edward Sheridan b 30 Oct 1850 s/o Thos & Mary
Sheridan; Sps: Jno Sheridan & Cath Welsh. -BLO (p90)

03 Nov 1850   Selie Barry b 27 Sep 1850 child of Philip & Margaret
Barry; Sps: Pat^k Healey & widow Hoffman. -BLO (p90)

BAPTISMS

03 Nov 1850	Stephen (negro) b 31 Dec 1848 s/o Susan & John slaves of Mr. Russel; Sps: Tho^S Cook. -BLO (p90)
03 Nov 1850	Patrick Ryan b 26 Sep 1850 s/o Wm & Mary Ryan; Sps: Ja^S Maloney & Cath Dolon. -BLO (p91)
10 Nov 1850	Mary Ann Dolon b 23 Oct 1850 d/o Peter & Mary A.Dolon; Sps: Terrance Curren & Ellen Murray. -BLO (p91)
10 Nov 1850	Edward Duffy b 03 Nov 1850 s/o Tho^S & Rose Duffy; Sps: Frances & Jane Reilly. -BLO (p91)
10 Nov 1850	James Carney b 27 Oct 1850 s/o And^W & Mary Carney; Sps: John Timms & Margaret Carney. -BLO (p91)
10 Nov 1850	Mary Jane Henrick b 08 Oct 1850 d/o Mintha & Marg^t Henrick; Sps: Maurice English & Alice Maden. -BLO (p91)
17 Nov 1850	Mary Ann Arkins b 16 Oct 1850 d/o Jo^S & Ellen Arkins; Sps: Danl Donavan & Mary A.Hudson. -BLO (p91)
19 Nov 1850	Catherine Shane b 15 Nov 1850 d/o Jno & Margaret Shane; Sps: Isabella Ortner. -BLO (p91)
24 Nov 1850	Sarah Ann Cage b 13 Nov 1849 d/o And^W & Elisb^h Cage; Sps: Ann Holton. -BLO (p91)
01 Dec 1850	Teresa Quinn b 05 Oct 1850 d/o Jno F. & Cath Quinn; Sps: F. Martin & Ann M.Gavin. -BLO (p92)
02 Dec 1850	Anastasia Margaret Fahey b 15 Nov 1850 d/o David & Anastasis Fahey; Sps: Geo Mattingly & Cath Ryan. -BLO (p92)
03 Dec 1850	Joseph Francis Holme b 22 Nov 1850 s/o Jno M. & Elisabeth Holme; Sps: Jno & Mary Daily. -BLO (p92)
08 Dec 1850	Mary Ryan b 11 Nov 1850 d/o John & Anastasia Ryan; Sps: Timothy Doyle & Miss Purcell. -BLO (p92)
08 Dec 1850	Thomas Griffin b 02 Dec 1850 s/o Mich^l & Honor Griffin; Sps: Law Flannery & Marg^t Welsh. -BLO (p92)
12 Dec 1850	Margaret Cathern Bein b 14 Oct 1850 Va d/o Cath Bein; Sps: Mrs. Maher & Sarah Welsh. -BLO (p92)
14 Dec 1850	Mary Connor b 22 Nov 1850 d/o Bryan & Mary Connor; Sps: Maria Coffey. -BLO (p92)
25 Dec 1850	Margaret Callahan b 19 Dec 1850 d/o Tho^S & Mary Callahan; Sps: Jno Kelley & Sarah Welsh. -BLO (p92)
29 Dec 1850	Margaret Jenette Mulcahey b 26 Nov 1850 d/o Jno & Brdg^t Mulcahey; Sps: Mary Buckley. -BLO (p93)

121 baptisms in 1850

03 Jan 1851	Rose Ann Silk b 25 Oct 1850 d/o Ed^d & Mary A. Silk; Sps: Mary A. McMullin -BLO (p94)
13 Jan 1851	James McHenry b 07 Jan 1851 s/o J. J. & Martha McHenry; Sps: Wm McHenry & Ann Masters. -BLO (p94)
13 Jan 1851	Ann Brown b 04 Sep 1850 d/o Denton D. & Ann A. Brown; Sps: Pat^k Healey & widow Byrne. -BLO (p94)
13 Jan 1851	Michael Maguire b 05 Jan 1851 s/o Mat^w & Brdg^t Maguire; Sps: Wm & Elish^t Maguire. -BLO (p94)
13 Jan 1851	Ellen Kelley b 24 Oct 1850 d/o Pat^k & Brdg^t Kelley; Sps: Wm Flanagan & Mary Buckley. -BLO (p94)
17 Jan 1851	Nicholas McKenzie b Aug 1850 s/o Geo & Susan McKenzie; Sps: Art McGir & Mary E. Cahill. -BLO (p94)
21 Jan 1851	Thomas Tuey b 10 Dec 1850 s/o Mich^l & Brdg^t Tuey; Sps: Arthur McGir & widow Hanson. -BLO (p94)
__ Jan 1851	Mathias Lynch b 13 Dec 1850 s/o Ja^s & Marg^t Lynch; Sps: L. Obermyer & Cath Cus___. -BLO (p94)
26 Jan 1851	Samuel Aloysius (negro) b 26 Jan 1851 s/o Thos & Celestia, slaves of S. M. Semmes; Sps: Danl Nevis & Jno B. Byrne. -BLO (p95)
31 Jan 1851	Margaret Downey b 15 Jan 1851 d/o Thos & Mary Downey; Sps: Wm Kenney & Ellen Arkens. -BLO (p95)
01 Feb 1851	Mary McDonald b 20 Jan 1851 d/o Jno & Mary McDonald; Sps: Marg^t Hughes. -BLO (p95)
02 Feb 1851	Michael Birmingham b 12 Jan 1851 s/o Ja^s & Brdg^t Birmingham; Sps: Murtogh Kane. -BLO (p95)
02 Feb 1851	Cecilia Ann (negro) b Mar 1851 [1850?] d/o negroes Henry & Cecilia; Sps: Belinda. -BLO (p95)
07 Feb 1851	Mary McNeir, adult & convert, was conditionally baptised; Sps: widow Ways. -BLO (p95)
13 Feb 1851	Elizabeth Mattingly b 04 Jan 1851 d/o Henry & Christina Mattingly; Sps: Cecilia Mattingly. -BLO (p95)
16 Feb 1851	Ann Rohan b 07 Feb 1851 d/o Mich^l & Ann Rohan; Sps: Mich^l Tormey & Mary Dorsey. -BLO (p95)
16 Feb 1851	Peter McAtee b 21 Jan 1851 s/o Mich^l & Martha McAtee; Sps: Peter & Elisb^h Murphy. -BLO (p96)
16 Feb 1851	James Kenney b 25 Jan 1851 s/o Wm & Ann Kenney; Sps: Wm Arkins & Ellen Stapleton. -BLO (p96)

BAPTISMS

16 Feb 1851	Mary Burke b 15 Feb 1851 d/o Mich[l] & Cath Burke; Sps: Pat[k] & Mary Daly. -BLO (p96)
20 Feb 1851	Mary M[c]Candriss b 11 Feb 1851 d/o Pat[k] & Mary M[c]Candriss; Sps: Mich[l] & Mary Moran. -BLO (p96)
23 Feb 1851	Catherin Maguire b 21 Feb 1851 d/o Tho[s] & Marg[t] Maguire; Sps: Mich[l] Caton & Ann Ward. -BLO (p96)
02 Mar 1851	Isabella Ways b 22 Feb 1851 d/o Jno & Victoria Ways; Sps: Cecilia Ways. -BLO (p96)
03 Mar 1851	John Timms b 02 Mar 1851 s/o Jno & Rose Tims; Sps: Cath Carney & Ja[s] M[c]Girk. -BLO (p96)
06 Mar 1851	Catherin Lanin b 21 Feb 1851 d/o Peter & Ellen Lanin; Sps: Ed M[c]Dermot & Ellen Keing. -BLO (p96)
09 Mar 1851	Thomas Doyle b 01 Mar 1851 s/o Tho[s] & Mary Doyle; Sps: Bartley Daily & Mary Mathers. -BLO (p97)
11 Mar 1851	James Daily b 09 Mar 1851 s/o Ja[s] & Mary Daily; Sps: Jno Greenwood & Maria Grady. -BLO (p97)
13 Mar 1851	Patrick Lynch b 15 Feb 1851 s/o And & Brdg[t] Lynch; Sps: Tho[s] Kelley & Mary Lynch. -BLO (p97)
13 Mar 1851	James Malone b 08 Jan 1851 s/o Terrence & Mary Malone; Sps: Mary Thompson & A. Hager. -BLO (p97)
16 Mar 1851	John Edward Cassidy b 13 Feb 1851 s/o Ed[d] & Mary Cassidy; Sps: Jno Cassidy & Ellen Colvin. -BLO (p97)
16 Mar 1851	Michael Crowley b 28 Feb 1851 s/o Jer[h] & Mary Crowley; Sps: Pat Crawford & Ann Kindly. -BLO (p97)
23 Mar 1851	Mary Elizabeth Daily b 30 Jan 1851 d/o Pat[k] & Mary Daily; Sps: Bartley Daily & Mary Hodel. -BLO (p97)
30 Mar 1851	Peter Riley b 06 Mar 1851 s/o Francis & Cath Reiley; Sps: Ja[s] Calahan & Rose Duffey. -BLO (p97)
30 Mar 1851	Francis Thomas Kean b 13 Mar 1851 s/o An[t] & Maria Kean; Sps: Pat[k] & Mary Kean. -BLO (98)
30 Mar 1851	Ann Elizabeth Snoufer b 23 Mar 1851 d/o Joshua & Ann J Snoufer; Sps: Elisb[h] Hager & A. M[c]Gir. -BLO (p98)
30 Mar 1851	Thomas Hildreth M[c]Nair b 12 Mar 1851 s/o Ja[s] & Mary M[c]Nair; Sps: A. Hager & R. A. M[c]Cusker. -BLO (p98)
05 Apr 1851	Elisabeth Cage age abt. 30, adult & convert. -BLO (p98)
06 Apr 1851	Walter Daniel Keech b 05 Mar 1851 s/o Step G. & Susanna Keech; Sps: Nancy Donavan & L. Obermyer. -BLO (p98)

211

13 Apr 1851   Bridget Malone b 31 Mar 1851 d/o Tho^S & Brdg^t Malone;
Sps: Mat Guynon & Brdg^t Coffey. -BLO (p98)

13 Apr 1851   Susan Jane Carney b 29 Mar 1851 d/o Jno & Mary Carney;
Sps: Th Coulehan & Jane Carney. -BLO (p98)

20 Apr 1851   Patrick Purcell b 09 Mar 1851 s/o Robt & Mary Purcell;
Sps: Jno & Brdg^t Fogerty. -BLO (p98)

21 Apr 1851   Juliana Fait b 04 Mar 1851 d/o Jos & Cath Fait;
Sps: Tho^S B & Juliana Allen. -BLO (p99)

27 Apr 1851   Bridget Welsh b 24 Apr 1851 d/o Ja^S & Cath Welsh;
Sps: Wm & Susan Murphy. -BLO (p99)

28 Apr 1851   Daniel Kean b 22 Apr 1851 s/o Danl & Nancy Kean;
Sps: Mich^l Kean & Brdg^t Dooley. -BLO (p99)

07 May 1851   Martha Ann (negro) b 25 Apr 1851 d/o Alexus & Harriet,
slaves of H. Jamison; Sps: Elizabeth. -BLO (p99)

11 May 1851   Joseph Gonder b 24 Apr 1851 s/o And^W & Cath Gonder;
Sps: Jno & Mary Mullen. -BLO (p99)

11 May 1851   Mary Fedalis White b 24 Apr 1851 d/o Eze^l & Charlotte
White; Sps: Jo^S & Mary A. Cook. -BLO (p99)

11 May 1851   Mary Jane Cage b 31 Mar 1844 d/o Elis^h & And^W Cage,
conditionally baptised; Sps: Petronilla Byrne. -BLO (p99)

11 May 1851   John William Cage b 15 Sep 1848 s/o Eli^h & And^W Cage;
Sps: Jno Myers. -BLO (p99)

11 May 1851   Joseph Arnold b 26 Nov 1850 s/o Jos & Matilda Arnold;
Sps: Cec Mattingly. -BLO (p100)

11 May 1851   Lawrence Speelman b 22 Sep 1850 s/o Law^e & Marg^t
Speelman; Sps: Eze^l White. -BLO (p100)

13 May 1851   Mary Roach b abt. 01 May 1851 d/o Tho^S & Mary Roach;
Sps: Mary Curley. -BLO (p100)

13 May 1851   Thomas Andrew McAleer b 20 Apr 1851 s/o Geo & Mary
A. McAleer; Sps: Jno Colvins & Alice McGir. -BLO
(p100)

15 May 1851   Thomas Melia b 04 May 1851 s/o Jno & Elisb^h Melia;
Sps: Peter & Margaret Mulholland. -BLO (p100)

26 May 1851   James O'Ragen b 07 May 1851 s/o Mich^l & Sarah O'Ragen;
Sps: Ch McCarty & Mary Clarke. -BLO (p100)

29 May 1851   Ellen O'Neill b 07 May 1851 d/o Jno & Mary O'Neill;
Sps: Jno Daly & Silv O'Neill. -BLO (p100)

BAPTISMS

14 Jun 1851	Mary Sophis Hoffner b 25 May 1851 d/o Jos & Maria Hoffner; Sps: Cath Masters. -BLO (p100)
17 Jun 1851	Catherin Fallon b 09 May 1851 d/o Pat & Brdg^t Fallon; Sps: Ja^S & Jane Welsh. -BLO (p101)
19 Jun 1851	John Kean b 16 Jun 1851 s/o Pat^k & Mary M. Kean; Sps: Jno Kean & Cath Ryan. -BLO (p101)
22 Jun 1851	Margaret Cahill b 27 May 1851 d/o Jno & Mary Cahill; Sps: Pat^k McCauley & Cath Welsh. -BLO (p101)
29 Jun 1851	Edward Rogers b May 1851 s/o Ed & Mary Rogers; Sps: Mich^l Dolen & Jane Healey. -BLO (p101)
02 Jul 1851	James Keegan b 25 Jun 1851 s/o Mich^l & Brdg^t Keegan; Sps: Dom^k Kane & Ann Flatery. -BLO (p101)
20 Jul 1851	Bridget O'Grady b [blank] d/o [blank] & Bridget O'Grady; Sps: Mat^W Coffy & Brid Ryan. -JBB (p101)
20 Jul 1851	Margaret Gallagher b [blank] d/o John & Ann Gallagher; Sps: Nicholas Curley & Mary Kelly. -JBB (p101)
23 Jul 1851	William [Dolan] b 20 Jul 1851 s/o Miss Dolan, conditionally & privately baptised. -BLO (p101)
03 Aug 1851	Margaret Carter b 30 Jul 1851 d/o Hen & Cath Carter; Sps: Wm Carter & Marg^t Clarke. -JBB (p102)
10 Aug 1851	John Harrison Carter b 31 Mar 1851 s/o Jno & Rose Carter; Sps: Enoch McKinzie & Sarah A McKenzie. -BLO (p102)
10 Aug 1851	Mary Coleman b 08 Aug 1851 d/o Mich^l & Johana Coleman; Sps: Jno McDonald & Ann Pole. -BLO (p102)
14 Aug 1851	Bridget Tierny b 09 Aug 1851 d/o Mich^l & Ellen Tierny; Sps: Pat^k _____ & Marg^t Hughs. -JBB (p102)
18 Aug 1851	Owen Mathews b 13 Aug 1851 s/o Peter & Mary Mathews; Sps: Catherine Corrigan. -JBB (p102)
24 Aug 1851	Catherine Elizabeth McLaughlin b 16 Jul 1851 d/o Hen & Harriet McLaughlin; Sps: John Myers & Mary Shane. -JBB (p102)
25 Aug 1851	John Thomas Ryland age abt. 15 mo, s/o And Jackson & Mary J. Ryland. -BLO (p102)
26 Aug 1851	Clara Regina Snoffner b 26 Jun 1851 d/o Joshua & Anne Snouffer; Sps: Ja^S McHenry & Rosanna McCusker. -JBB (p102)
27 Aug 1851	Catherin Farrell b 14 Aug 1851 d/o Pat^k & Mary Farrell; Sps: Alex^r McDonald & Betsy Carlos. -BLO (p103)

31 Aug 1851 Mary Elizabeth Morris b 06 Jan 1851 d/o Cransh[W] & Rod Morris; Sps: Sarah Ann M[c]Kinzie. -JBB (p103)

31 Aug 1851 Thomas Garvey b 08 Aug 1851 s/o Mich[l] & Marg[t] Garvey; Sps: Tho[s] & Brdg[t] Garvey. -JBB (p103)

31 Aug 1851 Michael Gill b (blank) s/o Pat[k] & Ellen Gill; Sps: Bryan Shehy & Ann Shehy. -JBB (p103)

07 Sep 1851 Ann Mary Lutman b 11 Mar 1851 d/o Gerard & Frederica Lutman; Sps: Mariana Melman. -JBB (p103)

11 Sep 1851 Martha Ann Donaho b 18 Jan 1851 d/o Pat[k] & Ann Donaho; Sps: Pierce Byrne & Reb Donahoe. -BLO (p103)

12 Sep 1851 Thomas O'Day b 10 Aug 1851 s/o Tho[s] & Marg[t] O'Day; Sps: Tho[s] Glen & Brdg[t] Coen. -BLO (p103)

14 Sep 1851 John Conelly b 09 Aug 1851 s/o And[W] & Cath Conelly; Sps: Tho[s] & Mary Kane. -BLO (p103)

05 Oct 1851 Mary Warthon b 30 Sep 1851 d/o Joseph & Mary Warthon; Sps: Mary Myers. -JBB (p104)

10 Oct 1851 Michael Sullivan b 25 Nov 1850 s/o Jere & Catherin Sullivan; Sps: Mich[l] Garity & Nancy Donavan. -JBB (p104)

18 Oct 1851 Isias Werd b 06 Jan 1851 s/o Isias Werd & Susanna Werd; Sps: Jno M[c]Kenzie & Sarah A.M[c]Kenzie. -JBB (p104)

26 Oct 1851 Alice Eliz Clark b 20 Oct 1851 d/o Walter & Ann Clark; Sps: Ed Rule & Julia Collins. -JBB (p104)

28 Oct 1851 Agnes Dowling b 08 May 1851 d/o George & Mary Dowling; Sps: Ja[s] Murtagh & Mary Lynch. -JBB (p104)

03 Nov 1851 Bridget Conley b 09 Oct 1851 d/o Pat[k] & Cath Conley; Sps: Th O'Neill & Brdg[t] Ruan. -BLO (p104)

09 Nov 1851 Edwd M[c]Keon b 31 Oct 1851 [twin] s/o Edwd & Elln M[c]Keon; Sps: Jno Hughes & Susan M[c]Glowan. -JBB (p104)

09 Nov 1851 Francis M[c]Keon b 31 Oct 1851 [twin] s/o Edwd & Ellen M[c]Keon; Sps: Michael Kelly. -JBB (p104)

09 Nov 1851 Thos James Campbell b 15 Oct 1851 s/o Jas & Ell(en) Campbell; Sps: Alex Hager & Cath Quinn. -JBB (p105)

10 Nov 1851 Margaret Emma Clabaugh b 13 Oct 1851 d/o Jas & Cath Clabaugh; Sps: Arth M[c]Girr & Marg[t] McCosker. -JBB (p105)

16 Nov 1851 Ellen Costello b 08 Nov 1851 d/o Peter & Cath Costello; Sps: Tho[s] O'Neil & Ell Noland. -JBB (p105)

18 Nov 1851	Mary Larkin b 01 Jul 1851 d/o Tho[S] & Brdg[t] Larkin; Sps: Chas Murray & Mary Healy. -JBB (p105)
20 Nov 1851	Michael O'Neal b 16 Nov 1851 s/o James & Margaret O'Neal; Sps: H O'Brien & Mary Daily. -JBB (p105)
23 Nov 1851	John Welsh b 13 Nov 1851 s/o John & Sar Welsh; Sps: Ber[d] Mahoney & Mary Hopkins. -JBB (p105)
24 Nov 1851	Sophia L. W. Gilpin b 15 Apr 1851 d/o Charles & Julia Gilpin; Sps: Ber[d] A. Dougherty. -John McCaffrey (p105)
29 Nov 1851	Mary Ellen Faulkner b 24 Nov 1851 d/o Tho[S] & Marg[t] Faulkner; Sps: Jno O'Roark & Marg[t] Reynolds. -BLO (p105)
02 Dec 1851	Mary Williamson b 07 Nov 1851 d/o Tho[S] & Honor Williamson; Sps: Martin Werd & Ellen Conway. -JBB (p106)
02 Dec 1851	Mary Ann Shriver b 22 Nov 1851 d/o Hen & Eliz Shriver; Sps: Mary Ann Williamson. -JBB (p106)
04 Dec 1851	Ann Clark b 13 Oct 1851 d/o Charles & Margaret Clark; Sps: James Noonan & Ann Garvey. -JBB (p106)
07 Dec 1851	John Henry Kelly b 26 Nov 1851 s/o John & Bridget Kelly; Sps: Jos Mattingly & Rose A. Fitzpatrick. -JBB (p106)
09 Dec 1851	Margaret M[c]Caffrey b 30 Nov 1851 d/o Ja[S] & Ell M[c]Caffrey; Sps: Mary Sullivan. -JBB (p106)
09 Dec 1851	Denis Kelley b 27 Nov 1851 s/o Jno & Honora Kelley; Sps: Dan[l] Harrigan. -BLO (p106)
11 Dec 1851	John M[c]Donald b Dec 1851 s/o Jno & Mary M[c]Donald; Sps: Mich[l] Coleman & Ann Sheehey. -BLO (p106)
14 Dec 1851	Edward Horan b 07 Nov 1851 s/o Mart & Mary Horan; Sps: Pat[K] & Alice M[c]Cahan. -JBB (p106)
21 Dec 1851	Margaret Ann Ennis b 12 Nov 1851 d/o Jno & Cath Ennis; Sps: Pat[K] Brady & Cath Caughlin. -JBB (p106)
25 Dec 1851	James Baldwin b 12 Oct 1851 s/o Sam[l] & Ellen Baldwin; Sps: Jno Dirkin & Ann Durkin. -JBB (p106)
30 Dec 1851	Elizabeth Byrne b 08 Nov 1851 d/o John & Ellen Byrne; Sps: Jas Thompson & Honor Ambrose. -JBB (p106)
30 Dec 1851	John Alloes b 25 Oct 1851 s/o Mich[l] & Nancy Alloes Sps: John Durkin & Julia Brown. -JBB (p106)
30 Dec 1851	Robert Maddy b 02 Oct 1851 s/o Edw[d] & Brdg[t] Maddy; Sps: Mart Fitzgerald & Brdg[t] Hesen. -JBB (p106)

109 baptized in 1851

This concludes the records of baptisms we chose to include, certainly not all that are available. For those needing records of a later time, some are available for viewing on microfilm at the Maryland State Archives in Annapolis. Copies of these microfilm can be purchased at a nominal fee ($10). Recognize that the Roman Catholics were prolific, and that both the C&O Canal & railroad brought a mass influx of new people into the area and new churches were being built. The Internet allows one to see what is available at:

<html//www.mdarchives.state.md.us>
Look under Special Collections.

In summary Western Maryland Catholic Churches include: St. Patrick (Cumberland) 1819-1988, [includes St. Ignatius, Mt. Savage & St. Mary, Cumberland], St. Michael (Frostburg) 1852-1984, St. Mary (Lonaconing) 1858-1984, St. Ann (Grantsville) 1909-1986. Baptisms after 1920 are restricted. HAPPY HUNTING.

DEATHS & BURIALS

The records of deaths that have been found are very meager in the early years, and come from two different lists. Those italicized are believed to be from St. Ignatius, from a single page listing. These lists have been combined for date continuity. We refer you to "Tombstone Readings From St. Ignatius, now St. Patrick's Cemetery 1825-1994 Mt. Savage, MD", compiled by Thomas E. Lancaster, for additional information.

10 Dec	1829	*Old Mr. Carter*
22 Mar	1830	*Ann Mattingly, wife of Henry Mattingly*
24 Jul	1830	*Sebastian Murphy age 18*
30 Jul	1830	*Elizabeth Frost age 17 years, 3 mos. 8 days*
20 May	1831	*John Logsdon died age 62 years*
01 Sep	1831	*Grandmother Logue died in her ninety ninth year of age*

[Missing records]

	1837	*Moses McKenzie*
	1837	*Old Samuel McKenzie died about 86 years old*
Nov	1837	D. T. Hoane age 18
Nov	1837	P^t P. X̱onelan
Nov	1837	Mrs. Margaret McAleer
Nov	1837	Alexius Null age 7 weeks
11 Mar	1838	Joanna Null age 2 weeks
20 Mar	1838	Mrs. S̲. K̲erney died in Frostburg
25 Mar	1838	B. McGarity
25 Mar	1838	Pat Kelly
17 Apr	1838	Pvt Morne
29 Apr	1838	Barney Collins
21 May	1838	*Ambrose Magers*
14 Jul	1838	James McCormick
29 Jul	1838	George McGauglin
Jul	1838	James Francis Mattingly
02 Aug	1838	Catherine Sarah Ann Brown
29 Aug	1838	John Cowan
31 Aug	1838	Elizabeth Whalen, infant, a year old
Aug	1838	Mary Ann Mattingly w/o Geo Mattingly
Sep	1838	child of Henry Coolman
Sep	1838	new born infant
25 Sep	1838	Mary Catherine Messer, one year old
25 Sep	1838	*William McKenzie aged about 42*
29 Sep	1838	James Boyle

30 Sep	1838	_____ Diamond
01 Oct	1838	_____ Jackson, infant d/o William Jackson
01 Oct	1838	Dutch child 3 years old
03 Oct	1838	infant of George Mattingly
05 Oct	1838	Patrick Barnett about 40 years old
06 Oct	1838	Ellen Kelly 13 years old
06 Oct	1838	David McAvory abt. 55 years old
07 Oct	1838	Mary Remfrey abt. 22 years old
13 Oct	1838	*Honora Moore died about 3 yrs. old*
14 Oct	1838	Catharine Mosey one day old
17 Oct	1838	infant d/o Mr. Morgan five months old
23 Oct	1838	Mr. Asken died near Old Town
23 Oct	1838	Sylvester s/o _____
	1838	David Kelly age 9 years
01 Nov	1838	child of Mrs. Duffy age 3 years
01 Nov	1838	child of Mrs. O'Brian
01 Nov	1838	Mr. Lines age 58 years
03 Nov	1838	Daughter of Mrs. Halfins age 5 years
05 Nov	1838	child of John Shannon age 6 months
07 Nov	1838	Mr. L. Hussey
29 Nov	1838	*Richard Carter at the age of about 50*
25 Mar	1839	*Mrs. Logsdon, wife of Raphael about 60 years old*
15 Dec	1838	Thomas McNamara, died suddenly
16 Dec	1838	Philip Manaher, died suddenly
31 Dec	1838	Cornelius Cox
02 Jan	1839	Michael Cahoun
17 Jan	1839	Sarah Ann Catharine, infant d/o H. Messman
22 Jan	1839	Dutch Brown's daughter, age 2 years
24 Jan	1839	John Kelly
29 Jan	1839	Mrs. Browning died @ Sandyround
	1839	Charles Leo, infant d/o Thomas Leo
08 Feb	1839	Sarah Leo (childbirth?)
14 Feb	1839	Mrs. Jane McMahon
16 Feb	1839	Sebastian Gramlick
25 Feb	1839	Nancy w/o Christopher McDonald died in Old Town
03 Mar	1839	daughter of David Kelly age 7 years
04 Mar	1839	Paul Folient
07 Mar	1839	Mrs. McCormick
08 Mar	1839	Patrick Clarke, laborer on the canal, died at Town Creek
24 Mar	1839	Miss Elizabeth Young died near Old Town
26 Mar	1839	Owen McIntyre died suddenly
27 Mar	1839	Robert Caton
07 Apr	1839	Dominick Henly
08 Apr	1839	Patrick Conway died suddenly by a bank falling on him
08 Apr	1839	infant d/o James Rooney

DEATHS

15 Apr	1839	John Glenman died on Mr. Lockwood's works
19 Apr	1839	Thos Shay died on Gorman's section, age abt. 55 years
20 Apr	1839	Dennis Wilan died on Sweeney's section, age abt. 50
30 Apr	1839	John, infant s/o Joseph Atkins
01 May	1839	Mr. Quin died in Cumberland age abt. 45 years
01 Jun	1839	Mr. Cross's son, abt. 14 years old, was killed on the works
12 May	1839	John Seival (Ger)
17 May	1839	Michael Philbin abt. 40 years old
23 May	1839	*Raphael Logsdon, Sr.*
24 May	1839	Patrick Kelly on Crawley's section
29 May	1839	*Anthony Arnold, Jr. about 20 years old*
11 Jun	1839	Thomas Fannon died on Mr. Crawley's section, abt. 38 years
14 Jun	1839	*Mr. Dean's son 11 years old* (maybe Leonidas Dean b 19 Jul 1829 s/o Francis & Mary Dean)
15 Jun	1839	Barbara Baltus, infant d/o John Baltus
16 Jun	1839	infant of Richard Connolly, a few hours old
21 Jun	1839	F. Slaver at Old Town
24 Jun	1839	Callagan's child
27 Jun	1839	Isabella d/o James Brady, 4 months old
30 Jun	1839	Patrick McGarrity killed himself, was buried on the towpath
01 Jul	1839	Monehan's child, six months old
03 Jul	1839	Joseph Thier (Ger), abt. 40 years old
07 Jul	1839	James Hopkins s/o Patrick Hopkins
09 Jul	1839	Edward Ryan 11 months old
09 Jul	1839	John Mulcakey 3 months old
15 Aug	1839	William Hashbyer, infant s/o William
15 Aug	1839	Mrs. Baltis died on Thurmlasts section
25 Aug	1839	Michael Leonard died in Cumberland age 30 years
30 Aug	1839	John Henry Brown s/o Henry, 1 day old
07 Sep	1839	Abner Ravenscraft, convert, abt. 20 years old
18 Sep	1839	___ Coughfman
21 Sep	1839	Michael Larkins
08 Oct	1839	Charles Echart infant s/o C. Echart
10 Oct	1839	James Brady, laborer, abt. 40 years old
15 Oct	1839	orphan boy abt. 13 years old
04 Nov	1839	Englelast Snider abt. 4 years old
06 Nov	1839	D. Goffney
10 Nov	1839	W. Rabberson, from Buffalo NY
24 Nov	1839	Bridget McLandra abt. 58 years old
03 Jan	1840	Philip McCann
27 Jan	1840	Mary Frotz died at Lonacony
06 Mar	1840	Mark O'Rourke
18 Mar	1840	Seth Clancy (convert)

219

20 Mar	1840	Mr. Mealey
15 Apr	1840	Hugh Conigan
18 Apr	1840	Paul Collier
02 May	1840	Peter Hussey
06 May	1840	John Dougherty
16 May	1840	John, infant s/o John Maginnis
21 Jun	1840	John Donelly was drowned
23 Jun	1840	*Eli Winters about 18 years old*
16 Jul	1840	infant s/o John Recker
17 Jul	1840	Teresa Gallagher, 15 months old
18 Jul	1840	Margaret d/o Henry & Elizabeth Keeman, 13 months
28 Jul	1840	Charles & Edward, twin s/o Hugh & Mary O'Neil
07 Aug	1840	Michael Porter, Sheriff
10 Aug	1840	J. Cox
21 Aug	1840	Old Henry Porter abt. 65 years old
22 Aug	1840	Elizabeth Schram age 10 months
04 Sep	1840	Teresa Vildecampage 16 years
07 Sep	1840	Hanna, infant d/o Charles & Rosa Cavenaugh
17 Sep	1840	N. Baltis age abt. 58
Oct	1840	Mary Devine
Oct	1840	Pat Getney was killed falling from _ores
05 Oct	1840	Pat Culcanon was killed on the day of the election
24 Oct	1840	a German soldier
12 Nov	1840	Martin Doyle died in Cumberland
26 Nov	1840	John Dowling was killed by a machine on the Public Works
22 Dec	1840	Margaret d/o James Kelly blacksmith, 21 years old
02 Jan	1841	Mathew Murphy, a labourer, abt. 56 years old
10 Jan	1841	Miss Polly Mattingly age abt. 56 years
10 Jan	1841	John Mullen
15 Jan	1841	Winefred Gillan w/o Patrick abt. 42 years
31 Jan	1841	James McAcbin
01 Feb	1841	John infant s/o Patrick & Mary Kenney
26 Feb	1841	_____McManis near Old Town
01 Mar	1841	John Harma
01 Mar	1841	infant s/o George Capollo
02 Mar	1841	Henry, infant s/o Henry & Elizabeth Brown
03 Mar	1841	Tobias F____, (convert) colored man of Dr Harley
10 Mar	1841	Anna Snow age 6 years
26 Mar	1841	John Maginnus had drowned
24 Apr	1841	James Malone, no relation in this country, died on Savage Mountain
22 May	1841	William Herd converted on his deathbed
29 May	1841	a child 1/2 hour old, privately baptized
10 Jun	1841	mother of above child, on Swelling's section

DEATHS

05 Jul	1841	Mrs. Arnold w/o Anthony Arnold at Mt. Savage
10 Jul	1841	Mrs. Bishop in <u>Fairborn</u> Mt. Church
11 Jul	1841	Edward Brown near Cumberland
Jul	1841	Martin McDornus drowned about this time
02 Aug	1841	Saml Healy infant s/o Dr. Healy
Aug	1841	Joseph Heips about this time, married
05 Aug	1841	infant child of Hanna
11 Aug	1841	Catharine Lintz, married
31 Aug	1841	infant child (<u>Dutch</u>)
19 Sep	1841	Mrs. Sarah Brown
	1841	John Malony died near Old Town, some days before
19 Sep	1841	Dutch woman below Old Town
07 Oct	1841	James Jennings died Monday
Oct	1841	two small children at Narrows
13 Oct	1841	Jno (I believe) Banit at Savage Furnace
06 Nov	1841	child from near Narrows
18 Dec	1841	child of McCan
19 Jan	1842	Mrs. Esther Herd (widow) after a long illness
	1842	Washington, a wagoner at Kizer [Keyser, now WV]
	1842	Ann Brown after a long sickness
	1842	D. a soldier at the <u>Kudanty</u>?
Jun	1842	Mary Guess Scissin child of W. Scissin
	1842	Several small children of Mrs. Head
02 Aug	1842	Dutch woman-Weigert
25 Aug	1842	Mary C. Black, child
Sep	1842	Mr. McGuire near Old Town without a priest
Sep	1842	Mr. Donelly at Old Town unexpectedly
Sep	1842	woman near Old Town, convert
20 Sep	1842	Barney Guders (furnacer) suddenly
20 Sep	1842	Mrs. Finsey (present__ D. O.)
29 Sep	1842	German child at Cumberland
18 Oct	1842	Mrs. Leo (convert) at Frostburg
21 Oct	1842	Arthur Rodgers, Flintstone, single
27 Oct	1842	John Moore, Frostburg, single
22 Dec	1842	Nichols D. Kearney, Cumberland, single
24 Dec	1842	Mr. Fitzpatrick, Cumberland, married
16 Jan	1843	Mary infant of Jno Hershberger
30 Jan	1843	German child, Cumberland
03 Feb	1843	child of widow Devcovan, Cumberland
04 Feb	1843	Mathias Murray, married, at Narrows
04 Feb	1843	Gilea Costillo, old maid at _____
15 Feb	1843	James Green,laborer, near Cumberland, married
07 Mar	1843	John Sanks Casio infant s/o Arthur Casio, Cumberland
14 Mar	1843	infant girl (3 years) Murray from Narrows

221

21 Mar	1843	child of Mrs. Masters, aged 2 yrs, in Old Town
06 Apr	1843	Patrick Hussey, Blooming Rose, age abt. 60
08 Apr	1843	Thos Brogan, Arnold's Settlement, age abt. 35
10 Apr	1843	Ellen McGir age 13 years at Cumberland
13 Apr	1843	George Marks (convert) at Cumberland age abt. 20
04 May	1843	Robert Mahony (col'd man of Geo Mattingly) age 25, Cumberland, single
06 May	1843	George Joseph Keoller, age abt. 65 near Cumberland
07 May	1843	John McMahan, Cumberland, age abt. 35
15 May	1843	Patrick Connor, Cumberland age abt. 55
23 May	1843	Elizabeth Dueker, Ger girl (____), age abt. 20
24 May	1843	Nancy Young, old maid at Old Town, age abt. 73
09 Jun	1843	Ms. Mahoney in Almhouse, age abt. 50
19 Jun	1843	George Brown, child of Benj. Brown, age 8 years
07 Jul	1843	Hipp child of Widow Hipp & Joe Hipp dec'd, age 2 years
09 Jul	1843	child of Slocase age abt. 3 years, Cumberland
28 Jul	1843	Thos McGovern's child age 17 months
29 Jul	1843	child
30 Jul	1843	Marcellus Brown age 20, Cumberland
31 Jul	1843	Catharine Collins infant of John Collins, age 19 mo.
02 Aug	1843	Philip Cronin, married, was drowned in the river at the Narrows
10 Aug	1843	Dutch Henry near Old Town, age abt. 30
11 Aug	1843	Widow Moor at Cumberland
13 Aug	1843	Susan Myer's child age 1 1/2 years at Cumberland
15 Aug	1843	James Warren's son age 17 months at Cumberland
17 Aug	1843	Widow Cronnin's child, age not many months at Cumberland
19 Aug	1843	John s/o Darby Clerk age 5 months
01 Sep	1843	Elizabeth w/o Mat^{as} Coffey age 29 years at Cumberland
04 Sep	1843	Joseph Gonder at Cumberland age 15 years
04 Sep	1843	Mary Hughes w/o Henry Hughes, Narrows, childbirth
11 Sep	1843	Jos Arnold's infant child, near Dr Smiths
13 Sep	1843	Kolber's child age 1 year, Cumberland
14 Sep	1843	John Ambrose's daughter age 6 years, killed at the falling of a chimney
22 Sep	1843	Mrs. Barrot at Mt. Savage furnace
04 Oct	1843	son of Herman Duckman age 2 years at Cumberland
10 Oct	1843	child
11 Oct	1843	Widow McCan at Old Town
14 Oct	1843	Thos Murtaugh age abt. 53 at Cumberland
28 Oct	1843	child of Mary & Henry Hughes age 7 weeks
31 Oct	1843	John Hanna age abt. 50 near Cumberland

[Missing Sept thru Dec 1843]

DEATHS

13 Jan	1844	Nicholas P. Ryan age abt. 55, married, at Old Town
17 Jan	1844	Mary infant of Widow Hipp age 4 years
Jan	1844	Ann McGuire's infant at Mt. Savage
01 Feb	1844	Anthony Kelfe age 21, killed by wagon wheel running over him
03 Feb	1844	Thomas Dixon age abt. 55 at Mt. Savage Furnace
20 Feb	1844	Alexander A. Stambaugh age abt. 3 years at Cumberland
22 Feb	1844	Owen Foley age abt. 30 at alms house
25 Mar	1844	Mary w/o And Conlon, age abt. 40, childbirth, at Cumberland
30 Mar	1844	Joseph Breting, child of Joe Breting age 18 months at Cumb.
31 Mar	1844	Eliza Reynolds w/o Michael at Mt. Savage furnace
31 Mar	1844	Mary Foley w/o William age abt. 35, childbirth, at Mt. Savage furnace
05 Apr	1844	Daniel Folard age 55 at Mt. Savage
08 Apr	1844	Widow Ryan's child at Old Town
16 Apr	1844	Patrick Crow age abt. 55 at Old Town
29 Apr	1844	Andrew O'Neill age abt. 60 at Cumberland
May	1844	Hugh Donelly age 65 years at Old Town
20 May	1844	Kennedy on Public Works
06 Jun	1844	child of Hugh O'Neill, Evit's Creek
07 Jun	1844	John infant child of Peter Dillon age 9 months at Cumberland
18 Jun	1844	Mary Dillon w/o Pat Dillon age abt. 28
22 Jun	1844	Mary Ann Sharp infant 2 months old
28 Jun	1844	Bernard McGee age abt. 50 at Old Town
Jun	1844	child of John Gormon age abt. 1 year
09 Jul	1844	Julia Miraldy, married, age abt. 40 at Cumberland
Jul	1844	Sarah Beatty w/o Thomas, age abt. 25, childbirth at Cumberland
22 Jul	1844	Brady's child age abt. 2 years at Cumberland
22 Aug	1844	child at the furnace
23 Aug	1844	child at Mt. Savage Furnace
01 Sep	1844	Jno Rarig age 9 months, s/o of Peter & Mary Rarig, drowned
21 Sep	1844	child at Mt. Savage Furnace
30 Sep	1844	Mary Tims, married, at Old Town
14 Oct	1844	son of Jno Fitzpatrick age 6 years near Cumberland
16 Oct	1844	Elizabeth age abt. 20, slave of Widow Byrnes at Frostburg
22 Oct	1844	William Ryan abt. 60, crushed in the ore mines at Cumb.
Nov	1844	Lally's infant at Mt. Savage
03 Dec	1844	Christopher Tobin age 72 years at Mt. Savage

11 Dec	1844	Mrs. Follard age abt. 35, childbirth, at Mt. Savage
Dec	1844	child at Mt. Savage furnace
20 Dec	1844	Barbara Meter age 16 years, near Frostburg
07 Jan	1845	Thomas s/o Darby Clarke age 1 month
13 Feb	1845	James Birmingham age abt. 37 at Mt. Savage
16 Feb	1845	Patrick Brady age abt. 40, married, at Cumberland
17 Feb	1845	Mary d/o James Brown at Mt. Savage
23 Feb	1845	Carlif's child age 4 years at Mt. Savage furnace
28 Feb	1845	John Whelan age 6 years near Cumberland
03 Mar	1845	another child of Carlif age 3 years at Mt. Savage
04 Mar	1845	Bernhard Clair (German), married, at Cumberland
10 Mar	1845	Michael Hopkins age abt. 20, single, at Cumberland
13 Mar	1845	Maginnis's child age 4 years, at Mt. Savage
14 Mar	1845	Jno s/o David McDonald, age 3 years, at Mt. Savage
15 Mar	1845	William s/o Mrs. Hughes, age 7 years, at Mt. Savage
16 Mar	1845	Mrs. M____ Kelly aged woman at Mt. Savage
27 Mar	1845	Mary child of Calvin's at Mt. Savage
31 Mar	1845	Thomas Clarke age 9 years at Mt. Savage
01 Apr	1845	Michael Lynch age 3 1/2 years at Mt. Savage
08 Apr	1845	William Gallahan age 6 months at Mt. Savage
12 Apr	1845	Valentine Schrimp age 1 year at Cumberland
20 Apr	1845	Dan[l] Brosnahan age 44, suddenly at Cumberland
21 Apr	1845	Maurice Condon age 14 months, near Mt. Savage
22 Apr	1845	William J. Hayden, married, at Cumberland
22 Apr	1845	Elizabetha Garahan age abt. 40, in childbirth
12 May	1845	Jno Condon age 7 years, near Frostburg
15 May	1845	Francis _____, a German, almshouse
18 May	1845	Mrs. Elizabeth Casey, married, at Mt. Savage
21 May	1845	Mrs. Madgey Twigg, age 36, at Mt. Savage
27 May	1845	Ann Farley age abt 40, at Mt. Savage
01 Jun	1845	James McKenna age abt. 40, near Frostburg
06 Jul	1845	Mary Mulchaey d/o Jno age 2 weeks
11 Jul	1845	Ellen child of ____ Byrnes, age 15 months, at Braddock's Run
Jul	1845	Richard Barrot, age 19, at Mt. Savage
Jul	1845	a pole, Mt. Savage, suddenly
13 Jul	1845	Joshua McKinzie age 60, near Cresap Town
14 Jul	1845	a daughter of McDonald, age 6 years, at Mt. Savage
16 Jul	1845	Belie Hoffman age 25 years
19 Jul	1845	child of Myers, at Cumberland
24 Jul	1845	Stephen, a negro at Jon[a] Arnolds
28 Jul	1845	Mary Ellen Ficklin, age abt. 55, at Cumberland
29 Jul	1845	Mary Martha Kelley, age 8 years, near Old Town
13 Aug	1845	Joseph Schribly, age abt. 17 years, at Cumberland
17 Aug	1845	a child age 7 months, 6 miles from Cumberland

21 Aug	1845	a daughter of Eckington, age 1 year, at Cumberland
23 Aug	1845	boy of Dressman's, age 8 years, at Cumberland
30 Aug	1845	William Gainer age abt. 60, at Evit's Creek
02 Sep	1845	James Garner age abt. 55, at Cumberland
Sep	1845	daughter of Henry Ferle age abt. 16 months, at Cumberland
24 Sep	1845	Ellen E. Campbell age 18 months

[Missing thru Apr 1846]

18 Apr	1846	infant d/o Peter Hein, Cumberland
29 Apr	1846	infant child of Jno R. Brook
23 May	1846	infant child of J. Cahill age 18 months
02 Jun	1846	infant child of Pat^K Coffey age 2 years
04 Jun	1846	boy of Mrs. Healy, age 6 years, Cumberland
07 Jun	1846	Mrs. Wheeler (convert), Cumberland
10 Jun	1846	Cath Kenny age 7 years
12 Jun	1846	boy of Mrs. Healy, age 3 years
23 Jun	1846	Mary Ellen child of R. Martens, age 3 years
26 Jun	1846	child of Jno Ennis, Cumberland
28 Jun	1846	child of widow Heydon
17 Jul	1846	child of Ja^S Hughes age 3 months
22 Jul	1846	child of Tho^S Leo, Cumberland
23 Jul	1846	child of Jno Delough, age 3 1/2 years
28 Jul	1846	child of Jno Delough, age 10 years
29 Jul	1846	child of Den Lynch, age 13 months
04 Aug	1846	d/o Geo Viroller, age abt. 2 years
12 Aug	1846	Alexander Low age 71, Patterson Creek
12 Aug	1846	child of Jno McMahan, age 15 months, Cumberland
12 Aug	1846	d/o Mrs. Roberts, age 2 years, Cumberland
14 Aug	1846	child of Mr. Zaub age 6 weeks
15 Aug	1846	Cath Collins age 6 years, Cumberland
15 Aug	1846	Henry Schriber age 63, Cumberland
16 Aug	1846	s/o Jno Delough age 7 years
17 Aug	1846	boy of James Hughes age 2 years
23 Aug	1846	girl, German, age 2 years, Cumberland
24 Aug	1846	d/o Jno Eckart age 2 years, Cumberland
01 Sep	1846	a German child age 10 years, Cumberland
04 Sep	1846	Ber^d Brady, mashed in the coal mines, married
07 Sep	1846	Mary Kering, ch^{d}birth, age 20, Cumberland
08 Sep	1846	Jno Connor age abt. 50, married, Cumberland
08 Sep	1846	Tho^S Murphy age abt. 50, broken leg near Frostburg
13 Sep	1846	child of Mrs. Carey, Cumberland
19 Sep	1846	s/o Titus, a German, age 9 years
20 Sep	1846	another child of Mrs. Carey
24 Sep	1846	Mary Smith age 13, near Cumberland

225

24 Sep	1846	Thomas McDermot age abt. 50, Cumberland
24 Sep	1846	Child of Draper age 1 year
25 Sep	1846	Tho^S Condon's child, age 1 month, near Frostburg
26 Sep	1846	Jno Eckart's child, Cumberland
26 Sep	1846	child of a German, Cumberland
28 Sep	1846	infant of Pat^K Kelley, Shantytown
30 Sep	1846	Mrs. Tims age abt. 20, Old Town
30 Sep	1846	Gertrude Shriver, widow, age 52
30 Sep	1846	Pat^K Coffey, age abt. 38, Cumberland
01 Oct	1846	Gerret Dressman age 64, Cumberland
01 Oct	1846	Mrs. Moher age abt. 30
02 Oct	1846	Widow Gainer's daughter age 5 years
11 Oct	1846	infant s/o Pat^K Mathews, Cumberland
16 Oct	1846	Lawrence Furstenberger age abt. 55
17 Oct	1846	Granny McKenzie age abt. 83, near Cresaptown
21 Oct	1846	Mich^l McNulty's child, Shantytown
28 Oct	1846	a young child in Cumberland
02 Nov	1846	James s/o P. J. Cahill age 4 years
02 Nov	1846	Mary C. Gordon age 3 months
09 Nov	1846	Widow Garner's child age 2 years
10 Nov	1846	Mrs. Thos Larkins age abt. 25, Narrows
10 Nov	1846	child of Jno Theil, age a few ____
11 Nov	1846	Mr. Gavan, stranger, age abt. 50
12 Nov	1846	d/o Maher age 2 years
21 Nov	1846	Mrs. Jno Gormon age abt. 35
21 Nov	1846	d/o Fr Hoyes age 2 months
25 Nov	1846	Widow Collins age abt. 30
__ Dec	1846	Granny Pickens (convert) age abt. 65
13 Dec	1846	s/o David Kenny age 18 months
17 Dec	1846	infant of Egmyers
		83 within this year
20 Jan	1847	Mary A. Gorman age 5 years
24 Jan	1847	Danl Smith age abt. 80
25 Jan	1847	James Kelley age 40, killed in Maryland Mine Co. railroad tunnel by fall
27 Jan	1847	infant of Ja^S Murphy age 8 years
21 Feb	1847	Tho^S Watkins age 8 years
24 Feb	1847	Owen, negro of Dr. O'Donnel, 5 years
25 Feb	1847	s/o Henry Dressman age 5 years, near Cresaptown
03 Mar	1847	Mrs. And. McMohan age abt. 30, Cumberland
10 Mar	1847	child of Ja^S McQue age 2 years
14 Mar	1847	Heaney's child age 18 months
16 Mar	1847	s/o Robt Johnson age 15 months
20 Mar	1847	Thomas Smith age 9 years

DEATHS

21 Mar	1847	child of Mrs. Healy age 9 months
23 Mar	1847	Richard Lastly age abt. 40, Cumberland
24 Mar	1847	Catherine w/o Richd Roe, age abt. 30 (prob childbirth)
01 Apr	1847	Mrs. Smith widow of Danl Smith age abt. 60
01 Apr	1847	infant of Richard Roe
11 Apr	1847	Aunt Kitty age 90, negress of H. A. Jamison
14 Apr	1847	d/o Robt Hales age 4 years
15 Apr	1847	s/o Brady age 3 years
20 Apr	1847	boy of Jno Block age 4 years
20 Apr	1847	s/o Jno McCall age 2 years
27 Apr	1847	Robt Hale age abt. 70?
04 May	1847	d/o late Danl Smith age 8 years
11 May	1847	Margaret w/o Mat^W Coffey age abt. 22
18 May	1847	d/o Ja^S Murphy age 7 years
13 Jun	1847	s/o Mr. Kelley 6 years
18 Jun	1847	child of a German age 3 months
23 Jun	1847	d/o Brady age 10 years
24 Jun	1847	child of Ed Mullen age 6 years
25 Jun	1847	s/o Ben^J Vicor age 3 years
01 Jul	1847	child of Henry Dressman age 1½ years
04 Aug	1847	Wm Davey, married, age __
12 Aug	1847	child of Tho^S McGovern age 14 months
16 Aug	1847	child of Jno Holtzman
28 Aug	1847	Regin's child, Cumberland
01 Sep	1847	Geo Metzger, married, Cumberland
02 Sep	1847	Sophia Goda, single, Cumberland
08 Sep	1847	Peter Connor age 20, Narrows
10 Sep	1847	Josephus Berry age 10 years
22 Sep	1847	s/o a German age 1½ years
03 Oct	1847	John Brunner, married, age abt. 45
28 Oct	1847	Priscilla Johnson age abt. 60 near Cresaptown
28 Oct	1847	John Delay age abt 55, married, Cumberland
02 Nov	1847	James C. O'Brien age 7 years accidently killed
04 Nov	1847	s/o May age 4 years accidently killed
16 Nov	1847	child of James Moore age 7 years, Narrows
17 Nov	1847	James Moore's child age 2 years_____
08 Dec	1847	child of Jno Skully age 1 year, Cumberland
		50 died in 1847

05 Jan	1848	child of Lainy age 6 weeks
28 Mar	1848	Tho^S McGovern age abt. 55, Cumberland
05 Apr	1848	Tho^S Murry age 15 years
02 May	1848	d/o Hughes age 7 years, Narrows
24 May	1848	child of Mr. & Mrs. Knotts age 15 months, Cumberland
25 May	1848	child of Vol Rerig age 4 years

30 May	1848	Andrew Hartman, violent death, Cumberland
06 Jun	1848	Henry Brokeman _____
05 Jul	1848	William Petechof, German, age 24 years
12 Jul	1848	Mary Kennedy, married, Public works
21 Jul	1848	Thomas Mullacly age 45, Cumberland
21 Jul	1848	s/o Ja^S Fate age 2 years, Cumberland
26 Jul	1848	Samuel Fisher, negro, Cumberland
31 Jul	1848	Rose, d/o Ja^S & Ev Bevens, abt. 1 year
01 Aug	1848	w/o Telly Gavner, age abt. __, canal
04 Aug	1848	James Gaughe age abt. 20, canal
04 Aug	1848	Pat^k Murray age abt. 14, canal
06 Aug	1848	_____ Shirkey, Old Town, canal
12 Aug	1848	Mary w/o Mat^W Coffey age abt. 18 years
12 Aug	1848	Thomas Flanagan age 13 years, canal
18 Aug	1848	daughter of a German age 5 years
20 Aug	1848	Sarah Brown age abt. 17 years, Cumberland
22 Aug	1848	Teddy Gardner, age abt. 55, Old Town
28 Aug	1848	Henry Wiser, age 22, Cresaptown
29 Aug	1848	Dina Gregor, age 20, canal
05 Sep	1848	James Bind age 40 years, single, Cumberland
06 Sep	1848	d/o Pat^k Hopkins age 9
07 Sep	1848	David Kenny age abt. 56, Cumberland
11 Sep	1848	s/o Ja^S Bohan age 7 years
28 Sep	1848	Toby Butter, canaller, near Old Town
29 Sep	1848	Hugh Donahue age abt. 35, Cumberland
04 Oct	1848	John Kearny age 35, Cumberland
09 Oct	1848	Ellen Kelley age abt. 20, Cumberland
16 Oct	1848	s/o Hildefer age 1 month
19 Oct	1848	Margaret Handel age 10 years, Cumberland
09 Nov	1848	Old Mr. Gillmartin age 65, Vulcan Furnace
19 Nov	1848	Pat^k O'Connor age abt. 40, Cumberland
20 Nov	1848	child of Hornhost age 1 month
17 Dec	1848	Widow Murry age abt. 55, Cumberland

39 deaths in 1848

16 Jan	1849	Ann w/o Pat^k Riley, age abt. __, Cumberland
17 Jan	1849	w/o Jon Timmis, age 23 drowned, Old Town
21 Jan	1849	d/o B. An___ age 11, Cumberland
22 Jan	1849	Granny Moelman age abt. 73, Cumberland
26 Feb	1849	Francis Bradley, ranch accident, age abt. 35?
26 Feb	1849	Foy _____ age abt. 25
18 Mar	1849	Peter Garrahanm age abt. 55, canal
24 Mar	1849	Jno Dunn (Thompson) age abt. 40, Cumberland
24 Mar	1849	Mrs. Saml McKenzie age abt. 70, Cumberland
03 Jun	1849	Keim White age 24, Cumberland
04 Jun	1849	John Kenney, Railroad, suddenly

DEATHS

22 Jun	1849	James McNamara, Public Works,___
25 Jun	1849	Ara Kishman, age 50, suddenly Public Works
25 Jun	1849	an Irishman recently from Ireland
29 Jul	1849	Pat^K Donahoe, miner abt. 35
01 Aug	1849	Jos Cahill Sr., age abt. 77, Cumberland
06 Aug	1849	infant child age 13 months
06 Aug	1849	a man at Town Creek
06 Aug	1849	another at the same place
10 Aug	1849	Pat^K Beatty Old Town (July 25 ?)
10 Aug	1849	child of Gilespy age 9 months
12 Aug	1849	infant of Galvin
13 Aug	1849	W. Sherlick Public Works
15 Aug	1849	Martin Nolin, canal
15 Aug	1849	another Irishman from the canal
16 Aug	1849	Fred^K of Fred^K Gramlick, age 16 months
16 Aug	1849	Patrick Coonan, canal
17 Aug	1849	infant of Smith, a German, age 2 weeks
18 Aug	1849	Lewis, a Frenchman age abt. 25, Public works
19 Aug	1849	Francis Harris, canal hand, Town Creek
22 Aug	1849	child age 2 years, Cumberland
28 Aug	1849	Tho^S Crahan age 15 years, Cumberland
28 Aug	1849	Richard Dunn age 55, Cumberland
29 Aug	1849	Cha^S McHenry age 56, from the canal
31 Aug	1849	Danl Tiernry age abt. 55, Cumberland
02 Sep	1849	Pat^K Caughlin age abt. 55, Cumberland
07 Sep	1849	a child age 16 months
10 Sep	1849	child of Peter Reilley age 3 years
12 Sep	1849	Patrick Conell age abt. 45, Cumberland
15 Sep	1849	Jno Dougherty, age abt. 40, Old Town
15 Sep	1849	infant child of Verpul's, Cumberland
15 Sep	1849	Mrs. Moran, abt. 25, married
16 Sep	1849	Michael Gannon, age abt. 30, married
16 Sep	1849	Pat^K Gallaher, age abt. 40, Old Town
21 Sep	1849	Mrs. Ellen Mulligan, age __, Cumberland
22 Sep	1849	Pat^K Cunningham, age abt. 45, Cumberland
23 Sep	1849	Ja^S McDermot age abt. 50, Cumberland
25 Sep	1849	____ Dunn, Public works
26 Sep	1849	Pat^K Yuchegan age abt. 60, Cumberland
26 Sep	1849	Miss Cariss, age abt. 25, Cumberland
29 Sep	1849	Michael Richards age 20
30 Sep	1849	Jno Clair, age 30, Old Town
01 Oct	1849	infant of Peter Wise
04 Oct	1849	Danl Harley, age ___, Cumberland
12 Oct	1849	child of Mulligan age 18 months
13 Oct	1849	Manning age abt. 21, a canal hand

14 Oct	1849	Anthony Merrick, canal hand
14 Oct	1849	a canal man age abt. 50
16 Oct	1849	Hughes child, abt. 15 months old
16 Oct	1849	another child age 4 years
20 Oct	1849	child of Thomas Digmor age 3½
20 Oct	1849	Laurence Conley age abt. 40, Cumberland
22 Oct	1849	Dennis Dugan, age ___,Cumberland
23 Oct	1849	a railroad man near Westernport
25 Oct	1849	s/o Jno Carney, age abt. 2 years
30 Oct	1849	a boy on the railroad, age abt. 10
03 Nov	1849	Quigley's child age 2 years, fell into a well, Old Town
04 Nov	1849	Patrick Hanson, age abt. 52, thrown from his horse
06 Nov	1849	Patrick Foley, age abt. 50, Public Works
07 Nov	1849	child of Ed O'Brien, fractured skull
10 Nov	1849	a boy on the railroad near Cresaptown
13 Nov	1849	laboring man crushed at Town Creek
16 Nov	1849	widow Mulhern, age abt. 70, Cumberland
16 Nov	1849	Hugh Maguire, canal hand age abt. ___
18 Nov	1849	James Cunningham, age abt. ___, Cumberland
20 Nov	1849	Peter Fitzsimmons, age abt. ___
23 Nov	1849	James _____, canal hand, fell into _____
28 Nov	1849	s/o Jno Eghart age 18 months
30 Nov	1849	Patrick Conelly age 16 years, Cumberland
04 Dec	1849	infant child age 3 days
12 Dec	1849	Julia Murphy age abt. 25, married
19 Dec	1849	Mrs. Fraser age abt. 70, Publis Works, Cumberland
19 Dec	1849	Arthur McNully, Old Town
23 Dec	1849	Mrs. Brown age abt. 30, Old Town
23 Dec	1849	her [Mrs. Brown's] infant child
27 Dec	1849	_____O'Brien, a stranger from _____
28 Dec	1849	James Fraser, stranger, age abt. 35
31 Dec	1849	Jno McAnally_____

91 died in 1849

03 Jan	1850	Fitzmorris, Cumberland
10 Jan	1850	Indy Frirney, married, on the canal
11 Jan	1850	Michael Kelley, near Cumberland
12 Jan	1850	Ellen, w/o Hez White age abt. 20, Cumberland
15 Jan	1850	infant child age 8 months
16 Jan	1850	Patrick Naughtin, Public Works
16 Jan	1850	Patrick O'Neill, age abt. 50
17 Jan	1850	David McMalian, Public works, age abt. ____
27 Jan	1850	infant child, Cumberland
28 Jan	1850	another infant
31 Jan	1850	And Ward, from railroad, shot

10 Feb	1850	Patrick Carey, drowned in Potomac
10 Feb	1850	Jno Dooley, drowned in Potomac
15 Feb	1850	John Mootey, married, Cumberland
20 Feb	1850	child of Farroll, Cumberland
23 Feb	1850	Darby Clerk's child
07 Mar	1850	Patrick Hanlon age abt. 35
13 Mar	1850	Pet^r Moran, drowned, Cresaptown
13 Mar	1850	Pat^k Cusick, near Cumberland
16 Mar	1850	child of Kenna, Cumberland
17 Mar	1850	an infant child
18 Mar	1850	Patrick Shaughney, drowned in Wills creek
24 Mar	1850	Leo Mill, age abt. 40, married
27 Mar	1850	Marcellus, infant s/o And Gondor
06 Apr	1850	infant child of Ja^S Hughes
07 Apr	1850	Tho^S Malone, married man
12 Apr	1850	John Fitzpatrick's child age 6 years
13 Apr	1850	negro boy of Tho^S Perry's
16 Apr	1850	w/o _____, Cumberland
21 Apr	1850	infant of Law Byrne, Old Town
22 Apr	1850	Thomas Leo, killed accidently by fall____
01 May	1850	McCue, Cumberland
03 May	1850	another man suddenly, Cumberland
16 May	1850	infant of Jno Collain
18 May	1850	Margaret w/o Denis Murphy, age abt. ____
24 May	1850	John Langon, age abt. 40
31 May	1850	Moran, age abt. 60
27 Jun	1850	a non resident Irishman at Hugh Carr's ____
31 Jul	1850	Mrs. Marrion, Cumberland
09 Aug	1850	child of Garvan age 10 months
20 Aug	1850	Mary Ann, w/o Peter Wise, Cumberland
21 Aug	1850	child of Luke Fitzmorris, age 2 years
25 Aug	1850	_____ Clarke from Pub works, age abt. 55
28 Aug	1850	child of Jno Gormon age 6 years
__ Sep	1850	Ja^S Ford killed by blast on railroad, age abt. 40
03 Sep	1850	Jno McEnally, railroad, age 45
09 Sep	1850	infant of Mrs. Ryan's
12 Sep	1850	wife of Noon on 20th sec. railroad
15 Sep	1850	Eli R. Plowman-fell from 5 story age abt. 45
16 Sep	1850	infant child, Cumberland
24 Sep	1850	Tho^S Cavauagh from Pub Works age abt. 34
26 Sep	1850	Bryan Sweetman, age 85, Cumberland
05 Oct	1850	Mrs. Timely age abt. 35
18 Oct	1850	Mary Melia age abt. 20, lockjaw
28 Oct	1850	child of Mich^l O'Neal
02 Nov	1850	John Day age abt. 60

06 Nov	1850	infant child of Day
11 Nov	1850	Patrick Kilduff, Cumberland
14 Nov	1850	Mrs. Beers, old woman
15 Nov	1850	infant of Melia-Pub works
15 Nov	1850	boy of Tho^S Donelly, drowning, age 6 years
03 Dec	1850	Mrs. Ben^d Smith age abt. 40
06 Dec	1850	Robt Welsh killed by railraod cars
07 Dec	1850	Thomas Adelsberger, drowned, age abt. 23
16 Dec	1850	d/o Con Brofey age 8 years
17 Dec	1850	w/o Curley age abt. 35
26 Dec	1850	Patrick McGar age abt. 60
30 Dec	1850	Thomas Purcell age abt. 60

68 in all (1850)

17 Jan	1851	Wm Kane, railroad hand age abt. 37
17 Jan	1851	an infant child
02 Feb	1851	Jno Griffis age abt. 60
03 Feb	1851	child of Fr Donelly
05 Feb	1851	Collins - stranger
08 Feb	1851	d/o T. Degnon age 12
08 Feb	1851	Mary w/o Lohen age abt. 40
12 Feb	1851	Tho^S Dolon, single, age abt. 25
13 Feb	1851	widow Day, Cumberland
16 Feb	1851	Widow McCusker
22 Feb	1851	Eulick Burke age abt. 60
05 Mar	1851	Pat^k Reilley age abt. 60
06 Mar	1851	Pat^k Reilley's child age 3 years
07 Mar	1851	Thomas McLaughlin, hung, age abt. 25
07 Mar	1851	infant of Spadeage 2 years
11 Mar	1851	Ed^d Reilley age abt. 55
19 Mar	1851	child of Ryan Sheehey
18 Apr	1851	Thomas Downey age abt. 55, Cumberland
20 Apr	1851	John Fulton age 68
04 May	1851	child of widow Mooty
06 May	1851	John Ryan, Cumberland
10 May	1851	child of John Geelio
11 May	1851	Mrs. Carney, Cumberland
11 May	1851	John Calahan's two children
28 May	1851	Anbrosia, child of Dr Healy, age 7 years
05 Jun	1851	Michael Merrick age abt. 60
16 Jun	1851	Frances Ways age 4 years
23 Jun	1851	Elisabeth Holme age 24
25 Jun	1851	Terry Caughlin, Cumberland
09 Jul	1851	child of Daniel Kane
19 Jul	1851	Larkin's child age 5 years

04 Aug	1851	child of Mrs. Gallahan
07 Aug	1851	Tho^S McKenna age 20 years
15 Aug	1851	infant of M. Tierney
16 Aug	1851	son of Jno Healy, drowned, age 5 years
06 Sep	1851	Margaret, child of D Healy age 3 years
07 Sep	1851	child of Snouffer age 3 years
10 Sep	1851	Basil, child of Jos Actin
02 Oct	1851	child of Peter Mathews
03 Oct	1851	Pat^K McNamara's child
04 Oct	1851	widow Kennedy age abt. 50
09 Nov	1851	James Graham, Cumberland, age abt. 25
16 Nov	1851	stranger
18 Nov	1851	infant child of Ja^S McCue
23 Nov	1851	John Sheridan age 37
02 Dec	1851	widow Ryan in Old Town age abt. 50
07 Dec	1851	Martin Hamburg
08 Dec	1851	Sweeney, Cumberland

48 [deaths in 1851]

This completes the list of deaths, and the material about Western Maryland Catholics.

EVERY NAME INDEX

This every name index lists the spellings that exist in the hand-written records, therefore check all conceivable variations. Contractions of given names are grouped with the full spelling, if the latter exists on one or more pages. Name contractions use an apostrophe ('), in lieu of the superscript notation of the text, to make them more readable in the smaller font. Given names with illegible surnames and those without a surname (Negroes, both free and slaves,) are included on pages 293 and 294.

ACKERS
  Jos 35
ACKTIN
  Maria 45
ACRE
  Victoria 176
ACTIN
  Basil 233
  Jos 233
ADAM
  Muth 48
ADELSBERGER
  Ann 35, 36, 203
  Martha 35
  Mary 34, 36, 69, 73, 192, 203
  Math 36
  Thomas 198, 203, 232
ADERLHET
  Mary 124
AIKEN
  Ellen 125
AINSWORTH
  Ann M. 73
ALBRIGHT
  Matilda 60
  Susan 42, 43
  Susanna 43
ALLBRIGHT
  Catharine 96
  Daniel 96
  Jacob 96
ALLEN
  Cecilia 200
  Juliana 212
  Margaret Ann 200
  Mary 55
  Thos B. 72, 212
  William 67, 200

ALLOES
  John 215
  Mich'l 215
  Nancy 215
AMBROSE
  Cath 201
  daughter 222
  Honor(a) 170, 187, 193, 208, 215
  John 155, 163, 183, 208, 222
  Mich'l 201
ANAKAL
  Francis 76
ANDERSON
  ___ 51
ANGEN
  Mich'l 140
ARES
  Catherine 57
ARKINS
  Ellen 112, 181, 209
  Joseph 112, 181, 209
  Mary Ann 209
  Maurice 181
  Thomas 112
  Wm 34, 210
ARKLIE
  Andrew 58, 150
ARMSTRONG
  Mary A. 59, 62
ARNOLD
  Agnes 19
  Alley 9
  Anastasia 172
  Ann 8, 17, 29
  Ann, Mrs. 5
  Ann Teresa 147
  Anna 79

Anthony 11, 21, 24, 30, 43, 54, 80, 84, 87, 103, 147, 221
Anthony Jr. 28, 219
Anthony, Mrs. 221
Anthony Sr. 28
Antony 6, 10, 15, 19
Antony, Mrs. 10
Archibald 2 ,5, 7, 17, 21, 23, 28, 30
Betsy, Mrs. 11
Cecilia 18, 93, 167
Denis 121
Domonic 108
Elizabeth 7, 14, 79, 87, 147
Elizabeth, Mrs. 6, 10
Ellen 126, 152, 169
Esther 79
Fanny 7, 10, 12, 20, 43, 88, 93
Francis Thomas 139
G. 95
Grandfather 20
Hanna(h) 23, 161, 167
Harriet 22
Henrietta 14, 16, 17, 20, 28, 117, 142
infant 222
J. 51
James Henry 152
Jeremiah 16, 20, 29, 55, 92, 154, 161
Jerime 28
Jerimy 10
Jermy 22
John 1, 9, 167
John L. 30
John of Ant'y 30

Johnzee 5, 8, 10, 17, 19, 81, 87, 95
Johnzee, Mrs. 10
Johnzy 79
Jonathan 6, 12, 14, 16, 19, 21, 24, 27, 28, 29, 30, 41, 81, 93, 224
Jonathan, Mrs. 81
Jonsey 14
Jonsey, Mrs. 12
Joseph 9, 18, 31, 44, 103, 108, 121, 139, 150, 171, 186, 200, 212, 222
Leonidas 90
Lydia 20
Margaret 1, 7, 10, 11, 14, 28, 80, 81, 86, 87, 103, 186, 200, 212
Maria 5, 8, 80, 81, 90
Mary 7, 9, 10, 16, 17, 20, 43, 83, 84, 85, 86, 87, 88, 152, 154, 167
Mary Elizabeth 126
Mary Luisa 150
Matila 95
Matilda 108, 121, 139, 150, 172, 186, 200, 212
Matilda May 31
Mr. 11, 13, 42, 51
Mrs. 28
Nancy 16, 19, 44, 51, 96
Nathan 10, 14, 18, 28, 47, 126, 169
Nathaniel 152
Onea (Honora) 1
Patience 1, 80
Paul 9
Polly 8
Polly, Mrs. 8

235

BATTIS
Helena 98, 119
John 98

BATTLE
Ann 203
Bridget 203
Roger 203

BAUGHMAN
Carolina 107
Elizabeth 107
Nicholas 107

BEACON
Jesse 111
Mary 111

BEAL(E)
Charles 30, 45, 57,
96, 114
John 96
Margaret 114, 169
Marg't Durbin 96
Mary 114
Sarah J. 74

BEALL
Charles 131, 167
Lucinda 61
Margaret 131, 167
Susan 167

BEAN
Almedy 115
George 97, 115
James 115
Jermius Mich'l 97
John 97
Joshua 115
Margaret 115
Mary 97
Mary Elizabeth 115
Rebecca 45
Robert 115

BEAR
Peter, Mrs. 14

BEATLY
Cath 122

BEAT(T)Y
Catherine 53, 136,
143
James 66
Jesse 57
John 65, 176, 200
Mary 200
Mrs. 55
Pat'k 200, 229
Sarah 223
Thomas 57, 61, 62,
63, 136, 162, 223

BECKENBORN
Geo 185

BECKER
Francis 188, 196
Francis Wm 196
Helena 196

BECKERBAUM
Geo 193

BEDLER
Christina 195

BEERS
John James 207
Mary A. 207
Mrs. 232
Rich'd 207

BEGOLD
Clifton 89

BEHENY
Mich'l 168

BEIN
Cath 209
Margaret Cath'n
209

BEISEL
Ann 169
Demetrius Leo 145
Jno 169
Mary Frances 169

BEKENHAUS
Geo 122

BELION
Christina 195
Math's 195

BENFORCE
Melvina 38, 39

BENFRID
Jno 183
John Thomas 183
Melvina 183

BENS
Adam 110
Elizabeth 110
Joseph 110

BENSON
Cath 77

BENZ
Adam 97
Elizabeth 97
Eva 97

BEREAT
Nicholas 108

BERG
Herman 68
Mary 68

BERGAN
Francis 111, 134

BERGOIN
Cath 37

BERIGA
Ann 189
Jos 189
Waldburga 189

BERKART
Nicholas 54

BERKEY
And'w 178
Caroline 178
Geo 178
Mary 178

BERKHARD
Henry 173
Nicholas 173

BERKH(E)ART
Elizabeth 138, 139,
173
Nicholas 138, 139

BERKMAN
Elizabeth 33, 60,
64
Geo 60
Mary 60, 163
Mary E. 188

BERNARD
Susan I. 70

BERRY
Catherine 60
Josephus 227
Mich'l 61
Mr. 63

BERSEL
Jno Henry 37

BERTRAND
Christ'r 185
Mathias 185

BETTER
Agnes 185
Catherine 127, 140,
165, 185
Francis Romauld
165
Marcellus 127,
140, 165, 185
Marcellus H. 127
Mary Magdalen
140

BETZ
Barbara 121
Jno 121
Joseph 130

BEVANS
Eveline 166, 175,
188
Henry 175
James 175
James H. 188
Jos H. 194, 195
John G. 57
Rose 188

BEVENS
Ev 228
Jas 228
Rose 228

BI(E)SEL
Ann 111, 145
Anna 105
Henry John 105
James Francis 105
Jno 145

BIND
James 228

BIRD
Kesia 77

BIRMINGHAM
James 224

BISELY
Ann 123
John 123
Martha Ann 123

BISHOP
Mrs. 221

BLACK
Augustine 190
Charles 138
Francis John 108
John 25, 47, 48, 49,
50, 59, 70, 98,
108, 110, 122,
138, 156, 177, 190
John, Mrs. 47, 49,
50
Joseph Chrys'm 156
Lydia 110, 122,
156, 177, 190
Lydia Ann 108,
138
Mary 94, 156, 195
Mary Catharine
122, 221
Patrick 177

BLOCHER
Andrew 56
Anna 43
BLOCK
boy 227
Jno 227
BLOCKER
Mrs. 95
BLUBACH
Susana 154
BLUBAUGH
___ 82
Angima J., Mrs. 11
Ann 17
Ann Jememiah 5, 8,
79
Ben, Mrs. 10
Benjamin 7, 10, 14,
83, 86, 88, 89
Catherine 80, 82,
85, 88, 91
Cecilia 88
Dominic 79
George 10, 16, 17,
19, 27, 28, 29,
30,92
George Wash'n 88
Henry 87
Honor 6, 7, 8, 9,
18, 81, 82, 83, 85,
86, 87, 88, 89, 92
Jacob 5, 8, 10, 12,
14, 18, 79, 81, 82,
87, 88
Jacob, Mrs. 10, 14
John 27, 28, 30, 82,
89
Margaret 86, 129
Mary 7, 8, 10, 13,
14, 43, 81, 82, 83,
88
Mary Anjamina 82
Mary Ann Eliz 31,
92
Mary, Mrs. 12
Mother 20
Mrs. 10, 14, 43
Peter 88
Rachel 5, 8, 42, 80,
81
Ralph 14, 82, 85,
88
Raphael 8, 20, 27,
80, 81, 91
Rebecca 82
Simeon 85
Simon 31

Stephen 5, 8, 9, 14,
17, 19, 41, 80, 82,
85, 92
Stephen, Mrs. 10,
14
Susanna 91
William 85
BLUME
Cath 169, 170, 194
Jno 124
Margaret 124
BODAM
Jacob 98
Margaret 98
Thomas 98
BOHAN
Anthony 75
Catherin 173, 187
Ellen 76, 187
James 173, 187,
228
son 228
BOLAN(D)
John 207
Margaret 70
Martin 116
Mary 199, 207
Mary Ann 199
Michael 67, 185,
199, 207
Thos 193
BOLDEN
Catherine 59
Mich'l 124
BOLEN(D)
Mary 36
Mich'l 36, 175
BOMPACHER
John 142
Petrus 142
BOOKHULSE
Mary 120
BORAN
Jno 124
BORDIN
Cath 143
BORGMAN
Henry 70
BOSSCI
Mary A. 198
BOTKE
And 147
Geo 147
Josephine 147

Mary 147
Mary 65
BOWFEE
Nick 149
BOWRY
Jno 138
BOXLEY
Mary A. 69
BOYD
Neoma 118
BOYER
Catharine Mary
102
Cunegunda 102
Francis 102
BOYLE
James 217
John 66
Margaret 67
Mary 202
Mary Alice 202
Peter 68, 188, 202
BRADDOCK
Pat'k 72
BRADFORD
Honora 187
Honora Frances
187
J. S. 187
Jon'n 192
Melvina 192
William Henry 192
BRADL(E)Y
Francis 228
Peter 74
BRADY
___ 109
Ann 155, 157, 176,
189
Bernard 155, 167,
189, 225
Brdg't 176
child 223
daughter 227
Edward 195
Eliza 164, 176
Hugh 143, 155,
176, 189
Isabella 102, 219
James 26, 102, 219
John 38, 105, 191
Margaret 102
Mary 38, 55, 71,
134, 137, 144,
177, 185, 195, 199

Mary Catharine
109
Michael 60, 153,
185
Orfine 195
Ortha 38
Patrick 38, 39, 58,
60, 136, 140, 161,
162, 177, 215, 224
Rose Ann 162
Roseanna 162
son 227
Thos 137, 181
BRAILER
Augustine 154,
157, 160
BRAMER
Mary 52
BRANT
Cha's 199
James Moses 199
Mary Ann 199
BRAZIL
Catharine 108, 136
BREAKER
Catolina 45
BRE(E)LER
Augustine 154,
157, 160
BREENE
Marg't 78
BREMER
Eliza 114
Ludolph 114
Mira 114
BRENAN
J'o 26
BRENDT
Mary J. 69
BRENEN
Mr. 173
BRENHAN
Eliz 98
BRENNAN
Bridget 74
Charles C., Rev. 3
Ellenora 168
James 77
Mary 168
Patrick 168
W., Rev. 3
BRENNEN
John 168
Peter 78

BRETING
Catherin 132, 136,
141, 152, 188, 193
Jno 151
Joseph 136, 193,
223
Mary 181
BREUDING
Catharine 113
Elizabeth 113
Joseph 113
BREULER
August'e 150
BREW
Mary 207
BRIAN
Judith Ann 31
BRIEN
Ann 35, 36, 150,
156
Bridget 56
Jno 34
BRIEVES
Sarah 17
BRINGER
Mathias 64
BRINHER
Mathias 69
BRINKER
Casper Henry 69
Geo 64
Luisa 194
BRISCO(E)
Catherine 99, 105,
117, 139
Dianna 81
James 99
John 137, 139, 146,
147
Mary 117
Michael 99, 117,
139
Sarah 146
Thomas 98
William 146
BRITT
James 105
John 105
Winefred 105
BRO_THIN
Joseph 47
BROD
Sar 142
BRODBURN
Henry 72

BRODRICK
Cath 150
John 150
Mary 38, 39, 62
Mich'l 150, 182,
197
BRODROCK
Catherine 127
Hannah 127
Michael 127
BROFEE
Patrick 162
Sarah 162
Thomas 162
BROFEY
Catherin 205
Cornelius 174, 205,
232
daughter 232
Elizabeth 174, 185,
205
James 204
Jared 195
John 39, 185
Kaun 185
Mary 38, 39, 192
Mrs. 176
Sarah 186, 204
Thomas 180, 186,
190, 204
BROFIELD
John 96
Mary 111
Sarah 96, 111
Thomas 96, 111
BROGAM
Harman 51
BROGAN
Catherin 138
Ellen 125
Francis 142
Maria 138
Mary 125, 152,
168
Thomas 125, 138,
222
BROGMAN
Mary 135
BROKAND
Elizabeth 128
Garity Henry 128
Herman 128
BROK(E)MAN
Ann Maria Eli'h
175
Anna Maria 107

Elizabeth 149, 157,
175
Gerard 113
Henry 37, 65, 157,
228
Herman 149, 175,
198
John Henry 66,
149, 196
Jos 36, 64, 65, 67,
188
Margaret 113
Mary 112, 188
Mary A. 66
Mary E. 64
Sarah 36
BROOK(E)
Cath 187
infant 25
Jno 187
John R. 58, 159,
166, 225
Mary Ellen 187
Mr. 183
Mrs. 183
Jno 192
BROOKS
Baptist 66
BROPHEE
Catherin 132
Sarah 132
Thomas 132
BROSIUS
Felix, Rev. 2
BROSNAHAN
Catharine 94
Daniel 25, 35, 94,
224
Franc's 34, 36
Mary 38
Saml 36
BROSNEHAN
Mary 39
BROWN
Andrew 48
Ann 33, 109, 146,
177, 210, 221
Ann A. 210
Ann Elizabeth 125
Ann Mary 132, 197
Anna 31, 104
Anna Maria 115
Barbara 26, 36, 46
Barbary A. 34
Benj Jr. 33
Benjamin 42, 222

Caspar 46, 47, 180,
184
Catharine 31, 56,
94, 103, 105 190
Catherin Sara A.
217
Charles 49, 107,
110, 125
Charles 49, 107,
child 230
Cornelius 126, 159
Dan'l 133
dau 218
Denton 190
Denton D. 197, 210
Dutch 218
Edward 221
Elizabeth 58, 59,
97, 100, 106, 109,
117, 119, 126,
33, 140, 151, 164,
165, 177, 183,
184, 187, 190
Elizabeth Ann 159
Eva 60
George 72, 176,
178, 222
Henry 45, 97, 106,
116, 117, 133,
149, 165, 190,
219, 220
Herman 35, 36,
132, 187
James 121, 150,
159, 224
John Bernard J. 165
John Henry 106,
116, 117, 219
John Thomas 107,
110, 190
Julia 215
Latitia 107, 110,
115, 125
Marcellus 31, 123,
222
Margaret 51, 61,
106, 120, 150
Margaret Cat'e 133
Mary 34, 36, 63,
65, 73, 116, 126,
148, 149, 159,
178, 180, 182,
189, 190, 201, 224
Mary Ann 159, 201
Mary Catherin 132
Mr. 48
Mrs. 230
Patrick 106, 150,
201
Petronella 31

239

CAHEL
Marg't 33
CAHILL
Ann 187
Dennis 1
infant 225
J. 225
James 226
John 187, 195, 200,
213
Jos A. 38
Jos Sr. 229
Leo 35, 36, 70
M. S. 189
Margaret 213
Mary 187, 195,
199, 200, 213
Mary C. 200
Mary Elisabeth 75,
196, 200, 210
P. J. 70, 180, 192,
208, 226
Philip T. 189
Rose 35, 36
Sophia 199
CAHOE
Margaret 110
CAHOUN
Michael 218
CAIN
Ann 116
Anthony 51, 100,
105, 173
Barth'w 77
Bridget 71, 108,
122
Daniel 203
Debra 98, 110
Elisa 203
James 116, 122
John 31, 71, 98,
110, 124
Marcella 132
Mary 77, 110, 116
Michael 77, 98,
108
Owen 110
Pat'k 203
Thomas 76, 108,
122
CALAHAN
Alexander 178
Ann 144, 178
children 232
John 178, 232
Margaret 129
Peter 144

CALLAGAN
child 219
CALLAHAN
Ann 101, 134, 148,
151, 206
Anna 111
Catherin 102, 126,
206
Elizabeth 62
George 151
James 168
John 101, 111, 126,
128, 134, 144,
151, 206
Margaret 209
Mary 126, 209
Mary Ann 134
Nancy 168
Peter 168
Thomas 111, 209
Wm 184
CALLAN
Ellen 103
Jno 70
Michael 112
CALLEN
Ellen 140
CALVIN(S)
Mary 65, 224
CAMMEL
Mary Joanna 135
Michael 135
Sali 135
CAMPBELL
Ann 62
Cath 65
Daniel 99
Ellen 76, 214
Ellen Elizabeth
153, 225
James 52, 153,
180, 214
John 129
Margaret Ann 180
Mary A. 37
May 139
Michael 99, 100
R. Byrne 52
Rebecca 99
Thomas 60
Thos James 214
CANE
Catherine 61
CANEY
John 113
Mary 113
Patrick 113

CANFIELD
Ph 171
CANNAY
John 102
CANNON
Mich'l 73
CAPELLER
George 119
John Harman 119
CAPHUS
Mary 195
CAPOLLO
George 220
infant 220
CARBINE
Mary 62
CAREY
Ann 68, 195
child 225
Dan'l 147, 169
James 63, 68, 195
Mary 63, 147, 169
Mrs. 225
Patrick 231
Rachel 169
Rose Ann 147
CARICUN
Rudolph 69
CARIGAN
Catherine 44
CARIN
Mr. 138
CARISS
Miss 229
CARLIF
child 224
CARLIN
Francis 62, 153
Patrick 55, 56, 59,
127
CARLIS
Ann 160
Betsey 167
Betty 160
Elizabeth 103
Michael 103
Patrick 98, 103,
160, 167
CARLOS
Betsy 213
Elisabeth 208
Patrick 46, 208
CARMINE
Ann 161

CARNAY
Elizabeth 95
Mary 95
Pat 95
CARNEY
Andrew 126, 209
Bridget 136, 149,
164
Catherin 62, 63,
143, 164, 203, 211
Daniel 149
Darby 73
George Patrick 208
James 73, 159,
170, 203, 209
Jane 201, 208, 212
John 63, 136, 143,
201, 212, 230
Lavina Jane 152
Lorinda 126, 127,
152
Margaret 209
Mary 143, 156,
168, 198, 201,
203, 209, 212
Mary Ellen 38, 39
Mary Margaret 203
Michael 73, 74,
126, 136, 149,
152, 164, 168
Mrs. 232
Patrick 164, 208
Peter 58, 63, 67,
68, 158, 172, 175,
201
Polly 58
Rose 72, 205
son 230
Susan Jane 212
Winifred 73
Wm 152, 203
CARNIAN
Ann 72
CARR
Hugh 203, 206,
231
James 104, 150
James, Mrs. 48
John 104
Mary 72, 104, 203,
206
Mary Ann 150
Sarah 150
CARROL(L)
Ann 151
Catharine 112
Ellen 102
John 112, 161

241

244

CUN(N)INGHAM
cont.
Miss 195
Patrick 155, 229
Peter 155
Thomas 57, 126,
155, 177, 186
CURLEY
Andrew 130, 151,
170
Catherin 74, 77
Mary 212
Mrs. 232
Nicholas 274, 13
CURNELEY
John 53
CURNOR
Rosanna 107
CURRAN
Eleanor 76
Ellen 76
CURREN
Brdg't 198
Mary 74
Mary Ann 198
Pat'k 198
Terrance 209
CURRY
Mary 124
CUSHMAN
Cath 35, 67
CUSHMAUGH
Cath 201
CUSHNAGH
Cath 73
CUSHWA
Cath 36
CUSICK
John 55, 149, 170,
192
Joseph'e Lenora
170
Mary 74, 113, 140,
149, 170, 192
Mary Adelia 192
Pat'k 177, 231
Rosanna 149
DAGNON
Bridgt 61
DAIL(E)Y
Bartley 211
Ellen 163
James 211
Jno 209

Mary 163, 209,
211, 215
Mary Elizabeth 211
Pat'k 77, 163, 211
Sarah 73, 77, 78
DAIRZ
Basil 183
DAL(E)Y
Anthony 95, 132,
141
Catharine 95, 132,
141
Hen 186
John 138, 212
Mary 122, 211,138
Mary Ann 141
Michael 95
Patrick 105, 131,
138, 212
DANCH
Jno 64
DANEN
Thos 154
DANER
Emma 164
Ann 34, 36, 186
Ann Maria 182
Cath 138
Jno 182
Lenah 54
Margaret 54
Mary Catherin 182
DARAKE
Jane 145
John 145
Mary 145
DARCY
Elizabeth 120
William 120
DARKEY
F___ J. 77
James 34, 167
DAUGHERTY
Ann 61
B. 76
Bern'd 76, 190,
198
Brdg't 199
Cath 133
Cecilia 67
D. A. 60
Isabella 98
James 32
Jno 132, 152
Julia 124
Margaret 97, 152
Mary 135

Mary Ann 97, 152
Michael 135
Owen 171, 176
Patrick 61, 95, 97,
119, 136
DAVEY
Elizabeth 162, 189,
208
John 162
Mr. 65
William 162, 227
DAVID
Nora 102
DAVIDSON
Phyllis i
DAVIS
Elizabeth 119
Jane 119
Mary Ellen 166
Michael 166
Sarah 158, 166,
172
William 119
DAVY
Elizabeth 168, 184
Michael 184
William 139, 184
DAY
child 232
John 231
widow 232
DAYLY
James 180
Jno 180
Mary 180
DEACON
Jerome 144
Jesse 144
John 105
Judith 105
Mary 105, 144
Nathan 105
Thomas 111
DEAH
Teresa 68
DEAL
Cath 56
DEAN
Ann E 64, 163
Catherin 142
Elizabeth 23, 59
Frances 12, 91
Francis 6, 8, 10, 14,
18, 21, 24, 27, 28,
29, 30, 43, 80, 85,
86, 87, 88, 89, 90,

Francis (cont.)
91, 92, 93, 96,
113, 142, 219
Francis, Mrs. 12,
13, 88, 89
Henry 113
Leonidas 90, 219
Margaret 96
Mary 90, 91,92,
93, 96, 142, 219
Mr. 88, 219
Mrs. 28, 88
Polly 18, 29
Polly Mary 113
Susanna 93
DEGMAN
Brdg't 194
DEGMON
Mich'l 59
DEGNAN
Mich'l 132
DEGNON
Bridget 71, 34
daughter 232
John 163
Margaret 163, 196,
201
Mary 142
Mich'l 55, 152
Sarah 142
Thomas 142, 163,
196, 232
DEHELISS
Mich'l 59
DEIRGER
Eliz'h 56
DEKON
Jesse 180
Mary 180
Sylvester 180
DELANY
Mary 38
DELAY
Ann 198
Denis 186
Dent 74
James 205
John 227
DELOUGH
child 225
Jno 225
son 225
DEMERIS
Ann 207
Ann Josephine 207
Jos 207

DEMERIS cont.
John Albert 207
DEMPSEY
Ann 143, 165
John 143
Margaret 165
Thomas 143, 165
DENMAN
Henry 31
Mary Cath 57
DENNER
Emily 33
DENN(E)Y
Mary 51
Cha's 143, 185
DENTZ
Catherin 160
John 160
Peter George 160
DERMEDY
Honora 154
DERMODY
Catherin 189
Honora 177, 189,
200
John 177, 189, 200
Mary Ann 177
DERMOTY
Honor 149
John 149
Pat'k 149
DERN
Wilemina 76
DERNON
Licetta 58
DESMON
Honor 182
Jeremiah 182
Jno 182
DEVCOVAN
child 221
widow 221
DEVENNY
Hugh 122
James 122
Margaret 122
DEVINE
Mary 220
DEVRON
Honor 132
John 132
Michael 132
DI(A)MOND
____ 218

Patrick 98
DICISAND
Wm   20
DICK
Mary 70
DICKEN
James 94
Jesse 94, 171
Jona 39
Judith 94
Mahala Catherin
171
Mary 94, 171
Nathan 94
Rebecca Ellen 94
DICKERSON
Geo W. 74
DIERKA
Margaret 118
DIERKE
Margaret 107
DIERKES
Catharine 105
DIGMOR
child 230
Thomas 230
DIGNON
David 180
Marg't 180
Thos 180
DILLAN
Edward 54
DILLON
Ann 118
Bridg't 69, 71, 197,
203
Daniel 145
Edward 110, 145,
160
James 193
John 148, 223
Julia 178
Louisa 160
Luisa 145
Mary 31, 118, 126,
139, 148, 223
Mrs. 56
Pat 223
Peter 31, 61, 99,
116, 118, 139,
148, 178, 193, 223
Sally 69, 180, 193
Sarah 178
Thomas 160
DINNERMAN
Cath 161

DINNEY
Ch 164
DIRK
Elizabeth 53
DIRKIN
Jno 215
DIXON
Mary 59
Thomas 223
DOHERTY
Allen 161
Brdg't 143
DOLAN
Ann 71
Bernard 71
Bridg't 124
Cath 39
Ellen 35
James 54
John 202, 205
Joseph Thomas 189
Mary 189, 202,
205
Mary A. 35, 36,
195
Mich'l 202, 205,
207
Miss 213
Pat'k 204
Rose 170
Susan 202
Thos 189
William 213
DOLEN
James 131
Mary A. 198
Mich'l 213
DOLON
Cath 209
Ellen 36
Mary Ann 209
Peter 209
Rose   180
Thos 36, 38, 232
DONAGHOE
Jane Emilia 31
Rebecca Ellen 31
DONAHO(E)
Ann 94, 105, 158,
181, 188, 201, 214
Anna 121
Edward 158
Elizabeth 158, 181,
195
Francis 195
George 201
Hugh 56

Jas 201
James Campbell
158
James Walter 94
Jane 94, 105
Jane Emilia 50
Margaret Am'a 121
Martha Ann 214
Mary 201
Mary Ellen 201
Patrick 94, 105,
121, 158, 173,
188, 201, 214, 229
Reb 146, 214
Rebecca 94, 111,
121
Rebecca Ellen 188
Sar A. 158
Thomas 52, 94,
111, 158, 181, 195
Thomas W. 94
William 105
DONAHU(E)
Hugh 228
Patrick 57, 201,
207
DONALLY
Mich'l 67
DONAN
John 63
DONAVAN
Brg't 186
Dan'l 209
Nancy 166, 182,
186, 201, 211, 214
DONAVON
Dan'l 35
Ellen 36
Nancy 36
DONCLAN
P. 26
DONELAN
Pat'k 201
Thos 172
DONELLY
Ann 168, 202
boy 232
Catharine 95
child 232
Francis 55, 174,
187, 203, 232
Francis Patrick 174
Henry 202
Hugh 95, 223
James 147
Jane 36, 203
John 167, 220

247

DONELLY cont.
John Hen Ambr'e
202
Leonadas 37
Margaret 75
Margaret Helen
203
Mary 95, 147, 168
Mary Elizabeth 187
Mary Jane 34, 181,
187
Mr. 221
Thomas 34, 232
William 147, 168
DONELON
Bridget 205
Mary Ann 205
Thos 205
DONELY
Margaret 191
DONLEN
Patrick 32
DONLON
Bridget 192
John 53, 56, 66,
192
Mary 54
Mrs. 47
Thos 192
DONLY
P. 149
DONOLLY
John 133
DONOVAN
Ellen 35
Nancy 35
DOOLEN
Julia Ann 72
DOOLEY
Brdg't 212
Jno 231
Mary 173
DOONAN
Brdg't 205
Elizabeth E. 189
Francis 205
Jno 168, 182, 205
DOONEN
Elisabeth 199
Eliz't C. 35
Jno 199
DORAN
Ellen 203
Honora 203
John 203

DORE
Jno 197
Ther 197
DORNER
Ann M. 146
George 146
Jno 146
DORSEY
James 206
Mary 206, 210
Pat'k 62
Sarah 50
DOUD
Rose 152
DOUGHERTY
B. 204
Ber'd A. 215
Bern'd 204
Bridget 72
Catharine 116, 194
Catharine El'a 102
Cecelia 191
Cecilia 180
Hugh 116
James 113, 116
Jane 51
John 102, 220, 229
Mary 102
Mary A. 74
Sarah 32, 38, 39,
113, 117
DOUGHERY
Ellen 158
John 158
Thomas 158
DOWD
Bridget 121
Catherine 104
Patrick 104, 121
Rosa 104, 121
DOWDEN
Geo 66
Marg't 66
DOWLING
Agnes 214
Dom 205
Edward 38, 110
George 214
John 110, 114, 220
Margaret 110
Mary 35, 36, 196,
214
Mary E. 75
Mich'l 38, 39
Sarah 38
William 38, 39

DOWN(E)Y
Catharine 65, 98,
109
Ellen 35, 36, 37
J. 25
Jane 137
Jno 130
Lucinda 190
Mary 99, 109, 137,
173, 190
Thomas 109, 137,
152, 173, 190, 232
DOWNS
Wm 78
DOYLE
Ann 66, 154, 168,
178
Bridget 159
Catherin 69, 73
Hugh 159
Marcus 75
Mark 206
Martin 220
Mary 211
Nancy 124
Pat 176
Sarah 35, 36, 195
Terry 154
Thomas 211
Timothy 209
Wm 195
DRAPER
child 226
George 176, 190
Mary 176, 190
Mary Ann 190
Michael 176
DRESSMAN
Ann Elisabeth 193
boy 225
Catherine 126, 146,
148, 165, 177,
193, 199
child 227
George 54, 64, 146,
185, 199
George Henry 126
Gerret 226
H. 26, 185
Hen Sr. 177
Henry 51, 97, 126,
148, 169, 177,
193, 226, 227
Hillary 199
John 95
John Garrot 148
John Henry 199
Mary 185, 195
Mary Catherin 185

Mary Elizabeth 177
Sally 95
son 226
DRISH
Genevia 196
John 196
William 196
DRIVER
Philomena Cath
175
DROPPEK
Harman Bernard
104
DROPPER
Barney 66
DUCKMAN
Herman 222
son 222
DUDSON
Cath 73
DUEKER
Elizabeth 222
DUFF(E)Y
Calahan 211
Bridget 72
child 218
Edward 209
Ellen 208
J. P. 57
John 156
Mary 31, 47, 100,
105, 151, 156,
Mary Jane 105
Mrs. 218
Oliver 65
Rose 211
Thomas 68, 72,
156, 199, 209
William 52, 105
DUGAN
Dennis 230
Thos 77
DUMFREY
Mary 151
DUMIRE
Catharine 101
DUMPHRY
Mary 73
DUNANT
Jno 151
DUNBAR
Thos 165, 195
DUNCAN
James 72

249

ERSKIN
Catherin 162, 179
John 162
Mary Ann 179
William 162, 179
EVANS
George 48
Martha 55
EVAS/EVISMAN
Mary 110
EVELINE
Barbara 121
Margaret 121
Mathias 121
EVERT
Mary 58
EVINSTINE
E., Mrs. 45
EVISMAN
Mary 111
F____
Tobias 220
FACK
Johan 181
FAHEY
Anastasia Mrg't
209
Anastasis 209
David 209
FAILAR
Elizabeth 46
FAIT
Cath 212
Jos 212
Juliana 212
FAITH
Cath 36, 196
Jos 194, 196
Lewis 196
FALEI
Jno 151
Teresa 151
FALKNER
James 187
Marg't 187, 205
Thos 187, 198
FALL
Francis 45, 156
Teresa 118, 156
FALLEN
Catharine 126
Mary 152, 158
Michael 126
Pat'k 126

Susan 126
Thomas 152
FALLON
Arthur 179
Betty 71
Brdg't 204, 213
Catherin 74, 213
John 71, 204
Margaret Ann 204
Michael 70, 79
Patrick 76, 179,
213
Susan 179
FALLS
Mary 147
FANNING
Mich'l 78
FANNON
Mary 48
Thomas 219
FARLEY
Ann 165, 224
Bridg't 163
Catherine 62
Ellen 63
Francis 71
Patrick 165
FARRALL
Ann 129
John 129
William 129
FARRAN
Nail 55
FARREL(L)
Ann 75, 109, 120,
145, 158, 199
Bernard 115
Bridget 55, 68,115,
116, 117, 210
Caron 55
Catharine 120, 171,
213
Elizabeth 74, 98,
120
Francis Thomas
149
James 120, 187,
199, 201
John 47, 109, 117,
145, 155, 156, 199
Kearn 170
Keern 139
Margaret 47, 112,
169
Mary 117, 122,
149, 173, 213
Mathew 145

Michael 120
Nancy 156
Neal 149
Norman 156
Patrick 56, 59, 75,
103, 112, 115,
118, 129, 174,
184, 213
Peter 38, 39, 109
Thomas 120, 130,
160, 206
FARROLL
child 231
FARTAY
Martin 71
FASIN
Maria Mag 147
FATE
Cath 175
Jas 175, 228
Jno 63
John Joseph 175
Jos 60
son 228
FAUGHTMAN
Fr 188
Frances Eliz'h 188
Henry 188
Mary 188
FAULETT
Sophy 107
FAULKNER
_ 208
Margaret 69, 193,
202, 215
Mary Ellen 215
Thos 74, 215
FAY
Ann 115, 142, 145,
174, 181
Bridg't 37
John 142
Mary Ann 115
Michael 174
Mrs. 49, 190
Patrick 48, 115,
130, 142, 174, 181
FEAL(E)Y
Ann 132, 141
Elizabeth 132
Ellen 94
J. 25
Jane 94
Mary 141
Patrick 132, 141,
170
Thomas 25, 94

FEAR
George Jr. 55
FECTIG
Matilda 65
FEENEY
Judith 202
Mary 202
Mich'l 202
FEIRLE
William 47
FELBY
Mary 63
FELE
Eliza 124
Valentine 124
FELLY
Eliz 147
FENAGAN
Biddy 55
FENEGAN
Cat 45
FERGUSON
Bridgt 78
Mary 201
FERLE(Y)
____dalen 119
Ben'd 133
Catharine 119, 138,
195
daughter 225
Douglas 138
Elizabeth 109, 119,
133, 138, 139,
149, 159, 192, 195
Henry 60, 64, 109,
119, 138, 195, 205
Joseph 37, 119
Margaret 119
Mr. 51
Nicholas 139
Valentine 109
Wendland 139,
159, 192
Wind 152, 155,
173
FERLI
Elizabeth 164
Francis Melc'e 164
Windly 164
FERLY
Vindelin 54
FICKLIN
Mary Ellen 224
FIECHEL
Christina 51

FINCK
Onder 46
FINEGAN
Martha 36
Nat'l 38, 39
FINK(E)
Anthony 174, 179,
194
Elizabeth 123, 174,
179, 194
Joseph 194
Mary Catherin 179
FINLEY
Ann 146
John 146
Mary Ann 146
Rosanna 54
FINNEGAN
Mary 171
Patrick 57, 171
Thomas 171
FINNEY
Mich'l 142
Thos 65
FINNEYERN
Bridget 133
FINNIGAN
Bridget 120
Martha 206
Michael 120
Patrick 120
FINNITY
Wm 154
FINSEY
Mrs. 221
FIRE
Mary 172
FIRLE(Y)
Cath 159
Elisb'h 173
Henry 159
Mary Elizabeth 159
FIRM
Cath 190
FIRSTENBERG
Elizabeth 64
FISHER
Ann 93
Brunigrunda 57
Catharine 105, 142,
194
Eleanor 107
George 142
Joseph 48, 105,
142, 194

Samuel 107, 228
Simon 46
William Henry 107
FITE
Maurice 163
FITZGERALD
Eliza 47
Ellen 175
James 58, 175
John 112
Julia 158, 175
Mart 215
FITZMAURICE
Bridget 146
Jane 146
Mary 146
Mich'l 146
FITZMORRIS
_____ 230
Bridget 173
child 231
Ellen 134
Jane 146, 173
John 66
Luke 231
Mary 134, 163
Mary Jane 146
Michael 53, 134,
146, 163, 173
Thomas 163
FITZPATRICK
Catherine 58, 143,
183
child 231
Ellen 97, 101, 133,
158, 183
James 26, 97
John 52, 97, 109,
133, 158, 162,
183, 223, 231
Margaret 129
Mary Ellen 158
Michael 133
Mr. 221
Pat'k 129
Rose A. 215
son 223
FITZSIMMONS
Peter 68, 230
FLACK
Herman 66
FLAHERTY
Andrew 175
Catharine 122, 168
Elizabeth 175
Ellen 163
John 122

Joseph 175
Michael 122, 175
Mrs. 131
Owen 163
FLALTY
Martin 131
Rose 131
FLANAGAN
Ann 124
Francis 124
John 72
Julia 124
Martin 75
Mary Ann 112, 124
Peter Francis 124
Thomas 228
William 124, 210
Mich'l 196
FLAN(N)IGAN
Anthony 118
Catherin 129
John 106
Marg'ret 36, 190
Mary 129
Mary Ann 117
Michael 129, 190
Peter 117
FLANNAGAN
Francis 157
James 157
Julia 157
Mary 122
Michael 117
Mr. 51
FLANNERY
Law 209
FLATERY
Ann 213
Dom'k Kane 213
FLATL(E)Y
Judith 200
Martin 52, 124,
153, 159, 172, 200
Mary 172
Michael 159
Peter 177
Rose 124, 159,
172, 200
FLEMMING
Martin 71
FLETCHER
John 118, 123, 126,
135
John Frederick 126
Teresa 126, 135
Teresa Roseann
135

FLICKINGER
Elizabeth 79
George 79
FLINN
Bridget 113
Catherine 61
John 47
FLOOD
Bridget 110
Catharine 120
Charles 134, 163
James 120
John 120, 134
Margaret 110, 134,
163
Patrick 110, 134,
135, 163
FLYN(N)
Bridget 119, 165
Catherin 137
Daniel 60, 140
Edward 73, 182
James 72, 78
Joanna 154
John 107, 117, 128
Margaret 107, 117
Mary 137
Mary Ann 165
Michael 117, 137
Patrick 107, 165
FOACHTMAN
Henry 60
FOG(H)ERTY
Brdg't 75, 212
Jno 212
FOGLEPOLE
Ber'd 97
Elizab'h 97
Henry 97
Mary Elizabeth 97
FOGMAN
Francis 68
FOLARD
Daniel 223
FOLAT
Jerome 115
Jushua 115
Sophia 115
FOLEY
Brian 203
Brien 202
Elizb'h 178
Ellen 154
Frances 154
Madga 202

FOLEY cont.
Mary 202, 203,
204, 223
Michael 154, 202,
204
Owen 223
Patrick 230
William 56, 110,
134, 223

FOLGER
Jno 64

FOLIART
Thomas 116

FOLIENT
Paul 218

FOLIET
Thomas 51

FOLK
Barbara 142
Peter 142
William 142

FOLKMAN
Thos 188

FOLLARD
Margaret Jane 125
Mrs. 224
Rose 125
Thomas 125

FOLLEN
Thos 161

FORD
Ann 140, 162
Anthony 140
Bart'w 206
Bridget 137, 163
Eleanor 75
Ellen 130, 206
James 206, 231
Jeremia 137, 144
John 119
Mary 100, 102,
119, 137, 140,
163, 165
Owen 100, 119,
140, 163
Patrick 100, 206

FOR(R)ESTER
James 38, 207
Mary 68
Rose 182

FORREST
Mary 134

FOWLER
Margaret 124

FOX
Ann 71, 205
Bridget 76, 118
Cath 76
Henry 51, 106,
118, 142, 157
John 142
Mary 118, 124,
142, 157
Mrs. 160
Rd. Rev. 169
Thomas 157
William 154

FOY
Elizabeth 69, 165
James 165
Mary 165

FOYLEN
John 122

FRADY
Bern 147
M. Cath 147

FRAEVER
Henry 61

FRASER
James 230
Mrs. 230

FRASS
Henry 196

FREIDHOF
Peter 153

FREITH
Caspar 180
Eva 180
Peter 180

FREITHOF
Peter 60, 63
Peter, Mrs. 63

FRE(I)VER
Mary 64
Henry 199

FREN_
Cath 185

FRENKE
Claymore 74

FRIEL
William 114

FRIRNEY
Indy 230

FRITHOF
Pet 159

FROST
Ambrose Mesh'k
88

Catherine 6, 8, 18,
27, 30, 82, 85, 88
Elizabeth 12, 217
Ellen 133
Josiah 1, 30, 80
Mary 80
Mary Ann 49
Mesech/Meshack
82, 85, 88
Meseck, Mrs. 15
Mrs. 20, 49
Rebecca 1
Sylvester Na'n 85
Thomas 82

FROTZ
D. 104
Daniel 47
Mary 219

FUKE
Anton 147
Elizabetha 147

FULL
Teresa 135

FULLENKAMP
Harman Bernard
104
Henry 104
Mary Catharine
104

FULLER
John 107
Michael 107
Susan 107

FULTESS
Ann 69

FULTON
John 232

FURSLENBERG
Eleanora 198

FURSTENBERGER
Lawrence 226

FYNAN
William 71

GADULTIG
Ellenor Ann 117
Esra 117
Nancy 117

GAFFNER
Jno 198

GAGLIGAN
Brdg't 200
Pat'k 200

GAHAN
Honor 140

GAIETY
Jane, Mrs. 11

GAINER
Bridg't 37
Cath 38
daughter 226
Elisa 38, 67, 148
Maria 35, 36, 66,
67, 128, 197, 208
Marie 64
Pat'k 35, 128
widow 184, 189,
226
William 225

GAINES
Elisa 204

GALA
Ant 148
M. 148

GALAGER
Pat'k 202

GALAHER
Mary 148
Thos 148

GALITIZEN
Demetrius Aug'e
1, 2
Prince, Rev. 1

GALLAGHER
Ann 115, 213
Charles Mich'l 115
Francis 115
John 213
Margaret 213
Teresa 220
Thomas 51, 98
William 119

GALLAHAN
child 233
Ed 158
Mrs. 149, 233
William 224

GALLAHER
Ann 72, 141
Bridget 148, 165
Edward 56, 141,
161
Elizabeth 141, 161
Ellen 194
Hugh 141, 172
Jane 141
John 69, 165, 207
Margaret 194
Mary 165, 166,
172
Mary Jane 74
Nancy 207

GALLAHER cont.
Patrick 62, 140, 165, 229
Thomas 166, 172
William 57, 138, 161, 172

GALLAHEY
Dan'l 67

GALLISE
Thos 73

GALLON
Jas 67

GALVIN
Catherin 64, 162, 200
Elizabeth 71, 201, 203, 204
infant 229
James 71, 200
Jane 162
Nancy 165
Pat'k 162

GANER
Mrs. 174

GAN(N)ON
Ann Maria 144
Bridget 144
Jas 171
Margaret 72
Michael 229
Patrick 144
James 142

GANT
Levi 133
Maria 133
Priscilla Ann 133

GANTER
Elizabeth 120

GANTY
Anthony 202
Ellen 202
Jno 202

GAR___
Cath 72

GARAHAN
Bridget 129, 159
Catherine 74, 99, 110, 136, 158
Elizabeth 113, 159
Elizabetha 224
James 99
Margaret 110
Miss 47
Peter 47, 110, 158, 173
Thomas 113, 170

GARDNER
Margaret 68
Mary 172
Teddy 228

GARIET(T)Y
Elisa 17
James, Mrs. 10

GARITY
Bernard Joseph 89
James 89
Jane 89
Mich'l 214
Sarah 200

GARLAN(D)
Alexina 199, 206
Alexona 35
Cath 174
James 137
Margaret 137
Mary Ann 137

GARLICK
Alexena 36
C., Mrs. 13

GARLITS
C. 27
Mary 145

GARLITZ
Catherine 112
Christian 20, 24, 83, 84, 85, 88
Christopher 79, 90, 114
Christy 48
Christy, Mrs. 59
Crosley 83
Dennis Lewis 136
Drusa Emily 166
Elinora 84
Elizabeth 83
Ellen 133, 166
Henry 23, 57, 85, 158, 166
Israel 54, 112, 114, 133
Isreal 53, 123, 156, 166, 173
Jane 145
Joh 28
Johanna 56
John 48, 96, 112, 114, 133, 156
John Thomas 79
Joseph Jere'h 93
Lucy 156, 158, 166
Mary 32, 104, 112, 114, 133, 156, 160
Mary A. 48
Mary Elizabeth 96

Moses 88
Mrs. 89
Nancy Elizabeth 166
Noah Sylvester 166
Patrick Theod'e 158
Reb 155
Rebecca 18, 19, 93, 94, 96, 102, 104, 123, 136, 166
Rebecca Jane 102
Sally 90
Samuel 94, 104, 112, 133, 166
Samuel Peter 112
Sarah 20, 83, 84, 85, 94, 112, 143, 166
Sarah Ann 123
Sarah [Sally] 88
Soloman 93, 94
Solomon 96, 102, 123, 136, 166
Susan 104, 166
William 90, 104

GARNER
child 226
James 116, 117, 225
Margaret 116, 170
Patrick Jno 37
Thomas 116
widow 226

GARNIER
James 165
Margrt 165
Michael 165

GARRAHAN
Elizabeth 140
Ellen 63
James 140
Mr. 34
Thomas 140

GARRAHANM
Peter 228

GARRATY
Mary 76

GARRET
Mary 131
Thos 72

GARRHITY
Sarah 139

GARRIGEN
Henry 75

GARRIGHTY
Mary 118

GARRITY
Ann 73
Pat'k 73, 205

GARRY
John 57

GARVAN
child 231

GARVEY
Ann 73, 77, 215
Brdg't 214
John 105
Marg't 214
Mary 177
Mich'l 214
Thomas 214

GARVIN
Catherine 115, 134
Henry 168
Hil 164
Mary 134
Michael 115
Philip 50, 115, 130, 134

GATELY
Catherine 154
Margaret 154
Patrick 154

GATEMAN
Ant 194

GATENARIN
Margaret 114

GATES
Rosanna 56

GAUGHAN
Pat 111

GAUGHE
James 37, 228

GAUGHEN
Ellen 70

GAUGHOUR
Honor 47

GAVAN
Marg't 74
Mr. 226

GAVIN
Ann M. 209
Catharine 109
Philip 109

GAVNER
Telly, Mrs. 228

GAYNER
Catharine Wina 105
Elizabeth 105

GAYNER cont.
William 105
GEATTY
Mrs. 57
GEELIO
child 232
John 232
GEGAN
Jos 69
GEGEHAN
Jno 204
GEIS
Adel 174
GENNEN
Bridget 127
Pat'k 127
GEPHARD
Sim L. 64
GERDEMAN
Henry 35
Honor 67
GERDENER
Anthony 37
GERDERMAN
Hen 36, 201
GERDIMAN
Ann 155
Ant 155
Windlin Erl'h 155
Honor 187
GERITY
Mary 117
GERKEN
Fred'k 69, 199
Henry 69, 199
Rebecca 199
GERMANN
Aloysius 157
GERNER
Eliza 124
GERRETY
Jas 128
Jno 128
Mary 68, 128
Michael 128
GERRITY
Hugh 165
Margrt 165
Patrick 165
GERS
Adelaid 169
Casper Henry 169
Catharine 121

Henry 169
GERTNER
Margaret 135
GESSMER
Wm 59
GES(S)NER
Ann Maria 141
Margaret 171, 189
Michael 171
Mrs. 142
Nicholas George
189
William 69, 171,
189
GETNEY
Pat 220
GETTUNE
Jane 133
GETTY
James 16, 18, 19,
155
Jane 18, 19, 102,
112, 155
Jos 23
GEVANS
Maria 199
GIBBONS
Bridget 76
J. 76
Rich'd 77
GIBE
Lydia 118
GIBSON
Mary 207
Mich'l 207
GILESPIE
Ann Gertrude 203
Ant 196
Elizabeth 203
William 203
GILESPY
child 229
GILGIN
Brdg't 75
GILL
Ellen 214
Michael 214
Patrick 73, 207,
214
GILLAN
Elizabeth 112
Patrick 112, 220
Winefred 112, 220

GILLESPY
Edward Anthony
176
Elizabeth 176, 188,
197
Ellen 197
Jno 197
John Baptist 188
Mary Ann 197
Pat 176
William 176, 188,
197
GILLISE
James 125
Michael 125
Sarah 125
GIL(L)MARTIN
Arthur 184
Catherin 135
Elizabeth 161
James 135, 161,
169, 184
Margaret 78
Mary 135, 161,
184
Mr. 228
Thomas 62, 184
GILNEY
Ed 109
GILPIN
Charles 215
Julia 215
Sophia L. W. 215
GINELLY
Jas 199
GINTER
Elizabeth 53
GIRK
Ger 32
GIVEN
Thomas 99
GLAP
John 133
GLASS
Caroline 173
John 55, 173
Mary 50, 173
GLEASON
Elisabeth 206
GLEN(N)
Ann 74
John 72
Thos 206, 214
GLENMAN
John 219

GLESTY
Ant 155
GLICK
Eliz 97
GLOB
Catherin 178
Geo 178
Margaret 178
GLOSSE
Ann 191
Caspar 191
Catherin 191
GLYNN
Ann 70
GOCHE
Honora 183
Honora Margaret
183
Jno 64, 183
Mrs. 189, 190
GOCHEY
Henry Herman 195
Jno 36, 195, 197
Mary C. 195
GODA
Sophia 227
GOFFNEY
D. 219
GOLDE
Margaret 123
John 146
Michael 46
GOLDSBAUGH
Eva 63
GOLEN
Honna 126
Michael 126
GONDER
And'w 212
Andrew 122, 212
Elizabeth 122, 132
Joseph 212, 222
GONDOR
Andrew 56, 149,
168, 182, 190,
192, 198, 204, 231
Ann 190
Catherin 149, 168,
182, 190, 192,
198, 204
Emma 198
Marcellus 204, 231
Mary 182
Mary Elizabeth 182
Mrs. 138, 182, 189

GONDOR cont.
Thomas Edward
149
Thos, Mrs. 61
GONNON
Jas 180
Mary 180
GORAMY
Thos 77
GORDON
Andrew 54
Ann 35
Bridget 155
Edward 155
Mary C. 226
Thomas 155
GORELL
Mary 68
GORMAN
___ 219
Ann 39
Catherine 55, 121,
140
Honora 137, 204,
208
John 51, 121, 140
Julia 152
Juliann 121, 140
Mary 189
Mary Ann 121,
208, 226
Mich'l 59, 183,
187
Mr. 51
Mrs. 51
Patrick 54, 119,
121, 204, 208
Teddy 149
GORMERLY
Thos 205
GORMON
Ann 38
child 223, 231
Eliza 164
Hanna 57
Jno, Mrs. 226
John 164, 223, 231
Julien 164
Marg't 34, 164
Mary 35
Mich'l 161, 200
Pat'k 70
GORNEY
James 105
GORRELL
Mary 68

GOULD
Mary 151
GOULDEN
Bridget 177
Ellen 146, 193
James 193
John 146, 193
Mary 31, 45, 102,
148, 177
Michael 51, 102,
111, 148, 177
Philip 148
Thomas 193
GOULDIN
Ann 139
Ellen 139, 207
John 139, 207
M. A. 206
Michael 207
GOULDON
Ann 36
Marg't 36
GOULIN
Ann 198
GR___
Mary 186
GRACE
Maria 36
GRADY
Jno 206
Maria 211
GRAESER
Herman 53
GRAHAM
Catharine 110
Den's 66
James 233
Mary 77
Mich'l 140
GRAMBER
Mrs. 145
GRAMKEY
Eliza 100
Henry 100
Susan Ann Cath 100
GRAMLICH
Eliz'h 143
Francis 143
GRAMLICK
Adam Sebastian 104
Ann Elizabeth 152
Cath 37
Catherin Barb'a
186

Elizabeth 50, 104,
109, 132, 138,
152, 161, 164,
171, 184, 185, 192
F. M. 68, 184
Frances 109, 138
Francis 50, 51, 64,
132, 152, 157,
164, 171, 185,
192, 195
Francis Martin 171
Fred'k 229
John Martin 171
Martin 58, 171,
182, 185, 186, 189
Mary 185
Mrs. 157
Rosetta 186
Sebastian 38, 104,
218
Wendelin Joe 192
GRANEY
Pat'k 76
GRASER
Hen 62
Herman 62
GRAY
Francis 68, 195
Herman 69, 195
Mary 68, 69, 195
GREASER
Hannah 53
GREBRUCH
John Henry 151
GREBUNCH
Catherin 151
Henry 151
GREEN
Augustus 5
Catherine 57
Cloey 13
Clotilda 16
James 221
Jane 38
Sally 14
Sarah 16
GREENWOOD
Jno 211
GREGOR
Dina 228
GREGORY
Francis 69
Jas 167
GRELLER
Catherin 152
George 152

Margaret 152
GRENKER
M. A. 36
GRESER
Henry 163
GRETER
Herman 190
GRIFFIN(S)
Honor 209
Hugh 53, 170
Mich'l 209
Thomas 209
Wm 65
Hugh 53
GRIFFIS
Jno 232
GRIFFITH
Geo 70
Harriet 70
GRIFFY
Elizabeth 59
GRISMAN
John 110
Mary Magdalena
110
Salome 110
GROSH___
Ann 202
GROSKINS
Jno 190
GROSKUP
Ann 191
Jno 191
GROSS
Nancy 69
GROSSKUPP
Honor 193
Jno 193
GROTTIE
Philomena 58
GRUBE
Bernard 130
Catherin 130
Elizabeth 130
GUDERS
Barney 221
GUNTER
Mary Ann 50
GUYNON
Mat 212
HABERKAMP
Cath 174
Jno 174

255

HABERKAMP cont.
Mary Sabrina 174
Xavier 174
HACK
Elisb'h 129, 176
John 54
Nicholas 60
HACKIN
Margaret 113
HADEL
Jos 73
HAE(C)K
Cath 185
Elizabeth 137, 191
John 137, 185, 191
Juliana 191
Nicholas 137, 185
HAFFNET
Ann 199
Jos 199
Willwmina Ele'a
199
HAGAN
Bridget 102, 122,
171, 201
Catharine 46, 171,
201
Francis Henry 122
Hugh 102, 122
Hugh D. 171
Pat'k 202
Thomas 63, 102,
201
HAGANMEYERS
Frederick 96
Mary Ann 96
HAGAR
Eva 177
HAGEN
Ann Jane 144
Bridg't 144
Hugh 144
HAGER
A. 211
Albert 183
Alex 214
Ann 73
Elisb'h 211
Eva 183
Joseph Peter 183
HAGERTY
Catherin 206
Daniel 190
Mary 190, 206
Pat'k 190, 206

HAICTLIN
Gilligan 68
HAJA
Mary 93
HAKIL
Elisb'h 165
HALBECK
Mary 135
HALE(S)
daughter 227
Rob't 227
Stewart 38
HALFINS
daughter 218
Mrs. 218
HALL
Peter 74
HALPIN
Thos 139
HAMBURG
Martin 233
HAMER
Cath 183
Maria Teresa 183
Simeon 183
HAMERMILK
Mary A. 189
HAMILTON
Lasres 35
Mich'l 66
HAMLIN
Maria C. 65
HAMMER
Adam 47, 108,
147, 160, 179
Ann Mary 147
Elizabeth 108, 160,
179
John 179
HAMMERSMITH
Geo 65
M. A. 66
HAMMOND
John 44
HANAGAN
Mary 73
HANDEL
Elisab'h 38
Margaret 228
Ann 153
Catherin 153, 196
Henry 153, 196
Mary 196

HANDLIN
Mich'l 164
HANDLY
Mary 61, 168
Pat'k 157
HANDY
Judy 170
HANEY
Edward 51, 146
Jane 146
John 46, 146
HANFORD
Owen 45
HANGERBERGER
Elizabeth 44
HANGLIN
Ellen 172
HANIGAN
Michael 108
HANIKAN
Francis 116
Mary 116
Thomas 116
HANKIN
George 31
HANLEN
Jno 68
Mich'l 178
HANLIN
Mich'l 57
HANLON
Bridget 204
Cath 204
Michael 69
Patrick 204, 23
HANN
Ann 193, 201
James William 201
John 193
Miles 193, 201
HANNA
Billy 82
James 144
John 61, 144, 222
Margrt 144
HANNEHAN
Anthony 150
Margaret 150
Mary 150
HANNEY
John 124
Margaret 124
Maria 124

HANNIGAN
Mary 71
HAN(N)ON
Bar 176
Mich'l 143
Thos 203
William 44
HANSON
Bridget 156
Elizabeth 38, 39
Margaret 122
Margaret A. 156
Mary A. 176
Patrick 122, 156,
230
widow 210
HAPS
Cath 198
Jon 198
William 198
HARD
Geo 60, 157
Julian 157
Peter 157
HARDING
Eleanor 80, 81
HARDT
Geo 178, 184, 191
John 184
Julia 178
Juliann 184
HARDY
Elizabeth 91, 144
Grafton 144
John Henry 144
Valet 144
HARETT
Cath 192
HARING
Mary 183
HARKIN(S)
Ed 102
John 101
Joseph 101
Nelly 101
HARLEY
Dan'l 229
Dr. 220
HARMA
John 220
HARMON
H. 26
HARMONY
Catharine 97
Elizabeth 95

HARMONY cont.
Henry 95
Jacob 95
HARPIN
Thos 148, 154
HARRIGAN
Dan'l 215
HARRIS
Francis 229
Martin 182
Mary 168
Mich'l 137
HARRISON
Catherin 164
Mary 153, 160,
164
Mich'l 164
Michael 56, 160
William 57, 160
HARSHBARGER
Mr. 51
HART
Donel 203
Elizabeth 138
George 54, 117,
138, 145
Juliana 145
Juliann 138
N____ 65
Oney 55
Teresa 51
Thomas 55
Winey 137
HARTLY
Caroline 62
HARTMAN
Andrew 228
John 116
HARTT
Adam 160
HARVEY
Mary 168
HASEN
Christina 194
Mary C. 179
HASHBERGER
John S. 109
HASHBYER
John 104
Mary 104
William 219
William Henry 104
HASHTON
Mary 172

HASLIN
Danl 145
HASSEN
John Henry 192
Jos 192
Martha M. 192
HAUFMAN
Catharine 51
HAUN
Caterine 46
HAUPT
Isabella 46
HAVERCAMP
John 102
HAVERCOMB
John 57
HAVESTRY
Pety 47
HAVRIN
Mary 75
HAW
Martin 47, 99
HAWN
John 116
HAYDEN
Ann 208
Harriet(t) 23, 157,
171, 174
Mary 205
Mich'l 202
William Henry 174
William J. 174, 224
Wilm 14, 157
HAY(E)S
Cath 60
Mary Catharine 32
Denis 118
HEACK
Eliz'h 138
HEAD
children 221
Mrs. 221
HEAGER
Albert 63
HEAL(E)Y
Anbrosia 232
Ann 195, 203, 207,
208
boy 225
Bridget 164, 170,
202
Catherin 208
child 227
D. 233

Dr. 46
Eliza 164
Emily 98, 113,
136. 159, 183, 198
Emily Ambrosia
159
Frederick Hof'n 183
James 203
James Francis 195
Jane 213
Jno 141, 195, 208,
233
Laughlin 202
Margaret 38, 198,
233
Maria 37, 203
Mary 197, 215
Mary Elisabeth 202
Mary Jane 203
Maurice 136
Mich'l 170, 202
Mrs. 225, 227
Patrick 98, 136,
159, 183, 208, 210
Sam'l 221
Sam Geo Baker 98
son 233
Teresa 34, 59, 60,
61, 66, 67, 111,
162, 170, 174
Th. MD 25
Thomas 74, 98,
113, 136, 142,
159, 183, 198
Thos, Dr. 144, 221,
232
Thos Jr. 198
Thomas Michael
113
William 157, 164
Wm Smith 197
HEANEY
Bridget 176
Cath 188
child 226
Edward 176
Jane 66, 176, 182
HEARD
Esther 126
Mary Ellen 126
William 126
HECK
Cath 191
Elizabeth 151, 160,
179
John 160
Mr. 51
HECKERT
Cath'n 66, 177

Henry 177
Henry Augustine
177
John 177
HEDRICK
John 106
HEDYAN
Ann 208
HEFFNER
Cha's 32, 33
HEFREN
Andrew 158
John 158
Nancy 158
Thos 151
HEGEN
Mary 152
Thos 138
HEILMAN
John 127
Lorinda 127
Mordica 127
HEILTIFFER
Jno 65
HEIME
Peter 160
HEIN
infant 225
Margaret Ann 178
Mary Louisa 16
Matilda 35, 36, 67,
178, 186, 194
Peter 60, 172, 178,
183, 186, 194, 225
HEINART
Catherin 156
Francis 156
Joseph 156
HEIP(S)
Henry 127
Joseph 127, 211
HELDEFER
Catherin 196, 198
Jno 196, 198
John Henry 196
Marg 36
Margaret 198
HELDIFER
Eva 173, 175
HELDINFER
John 175
HELFACH
Apl Catharine 123
John 123
Valentine 123

HELFING
Val 139
HELFREE
Catharine 102
Valentine 10
HELFREY
Eva 155
Valent 155
HELFRI
Juliana 145
Mary 145
Valentine 145
HELFRICH
Bernard Henry 108
Cath 188
Con 36
Eva 184
Eve Catharine 108
Valentine 108, 184, 191
HELLER
Thos 204
HELMET
Rebecca 56
HELMPRACT
Rev. 191, 193, 194
HELMSTEDER
Francis 107
Joseph 107
Thiela 107
Fran A. 177
HELMSTETER
George 177
Maria T. 177
HELMSTETLER
Francis A. 198
HELMSTETTER
Antony 154, 180
Mary 154
Teresa 154
HELSEN
Ant 58, 59
HELSHAUS
John 119
HELSON
Antony 136
HELWIG
And 188
Margr't 188
HEMBLING
Marg't 178
HEMER
Adam 106
Elizabeth 106

John Joseph 106
HEMP
John 95
HEMPEY
Joseph 48
HEMSTETTER
An't 55
HENAGAN
Bridget 151
HENAGEN
Francis 151
Marg't 151
Mary 151
Patrick 164
HENDLE
Catharine 102, 122, 179
Henry 102, 122, 179
Mathias 179
HENDRIXSON
Elizabeth 52
HENEY
Edward 127
Jane 127
Thomas 127
HENIGAN
Bartholomy 105
Margaret 105
Patrick 105
HENIGEN
Thomas 58
HENISY
R. N. 203
HENKEY
Eliza 114
Gerard 110
John 110
John Albert 110
Mary Elizabet 110
HENL(E)Y
Dominick 218
Francis 68
Jno 68
HENNAGAN
Anthony 58, 164
HENNAGEN
Mary 164, 170
HENNER
William J. 44, 45
HENNEY
Margaret 106
Michael 106
Pat 106

HENNIGAN
Thomas 170
HENNIGER
Rosanna 67
HENOG(H)EN
Francis 127
Mary 127, 162
Sarah 127
HENRICK
Marg't 209
Mary Jane 209
Mintha 209
HENRY
Ann 71
Dutch 222
James 97
HEORRN
And 147
HERD
Esther 221
William 50, 220
HERENDON
Caroline 150
HERMAN
Dorothea 123
John 123
HERN
Margaret 120
HERR
Catherin 67
HERRING
Charlotte 73
HERROGEN
Ant 137
HERS(C)HBERGER
Mary 33
Elizabeth 184
Francis 184
Johann Lebart 182
John 60, 64, 128, 138, 157, 184, 221
Joseph 157
Mary 221
Mary Ann 128, 157
Mary Elizabeth 138
Mary Magdalen 138
HERSHEBERGER
John 114
John Sebastian 114
Mary Ann 114
HESEN
Bernardina 123
Brdg't 215
Catherine 123

Christina 123, 196
Elis 147
Henry 123
Lewis 123, 196
HESKEL
Frances 123
HESM
Ludos 147
HESSE
Andrus 147
HEVARD
Marg't 77
HEVRIN
Andrew 98
Anna 98
John 50
Michael 98
Thomas 103, 118
HEVSEN
Andrew 131
Bridget 131
Nancy 131
HEYDEN
Ann 71
Harriet 65
Winifred 205
HEYDON
child 225
widow 225
HEYER
Ann Heyer 137
Hon 183
Mary Ann 141
HEYLER
Lidia 95
Teresa 45
HICKEY
Elisabeth 204
Ellen 72
John 72
Mich'l 204
HICKSENBAUGH
Aaron 125, 136
Adam 160
Cath E. 125
Elizabeth Cath 125
Henr'a Petr'a 136
Leo Sampson 160
Rachel 125, 136, 160
HIGGINS
Bridget 125
Dan'l 76
Francis 108
Honora 150

HIGGINS cont.
Margaret 167
Miles 56, 150, 167
Thomas John 167
William 150
HILDBERGER
Mr., Rev. 188
HILDEBRAN(D)
George 56, 59
HILDEFER
son 228
HILE
Margaret 82
Mary Jane 82
Rob 82
HILL
Catherin 69
Mrs. 12
HIMES
Marg't 126
HINDER
Margaret 98
HINDES
James 100
Marshall 100
HINE(S)
Ann 73
Cath 170
James 113
Margaret 113
Matilda 67, 75
Peter 67, 75
HINKLEBORN
Mary A. 121
HIPP
child 222
Ellen 193
Gertrude 111
Helen(a) 100, 111,
185
Jno Adam 37
Joseph 100, 111,
222
Mary 223
widow 222, 223
HIRONS
Hannah 58
HIX
Thomas 110
HIXENBAUGH
Aaron 8, 11, 16
Anastasia 16, 18
Anastatia 17
Catherine 17, 19
Elizabeth 16

Henry 19
Honora 11, 20
Honora Elisa 16
James 62
Mary 8
Mrs. 11
Sophia 19
William 62
HIXENBOX
Aaron 10
Anastatia 15
Elisa Honora 15
Mrs. 14
HIXONBAUGH
___ 44
Aaron 7, 9, 50
Adam James 85
Catherine 6, 7, 82,
85, 113
Henrietta 82
John W. 79
Mary 42
Mrs. 9, 104
William 79, 82, 85
HOAME
Marg't 127
HOANE
D. T. 217
Denis 93
HOARN(e)
Margaret 141
Mary 141
Pat'k 141
William 141
HOCKINS
George Lewis 195
Molly 195
HOCTON
John 80
HOCTOR
John 6
HOCTREN
Ant 178
HODEL
John 38, 78
Joseph 32, 136,
162, 188, 193
Mary 34, 36, 184,
188, 211
Sar 78
Thomas 35, 36
HODERBRECK
Rev. 185
HOELSTEN
Anthony 64, 184
Eliz'h 184

HOFFMAN
Belie 224
Cath Margaret 102
Desire 113
Ellen 70
Mrs. 159
widow 208
Zelei 136
Zelie 113
HOF(F)NER
Jos 193, 213
Ann Maria 190
Catherin Lavina
190
Jos 190
Mary Sophis 213
HOGAN
Catherine 127, 141
Ellen 61, 64, 168,
171
Garret 127
Michael 127
Thomas 67
HOGEN
Cath 137
HOGLAN
Jno 68
HOGMIRE
H. 28
HOL___
Nancy 181
HOLEAN
Mary 36
HOLLAND
Humphy 34, 36
Julia (Murphy) 58
Mary 35
Thos 71
HOLME(S)
Elisabeth 209, 232
Jno M. 68, 209
Joseph Francis 209
Sarah Jane 77
HOLOMS
Mat'h 198
HOLT
Barbara 101
HOLTAMAN
Mrs. 132
HOLTON
Ann 200, 209
HOLTZ
Barbara 125
HOLTZER
Jacob 194

Rebecca 194
HOLTZMAN
Anselm Hughes
155
Augustine 107,
110, 131, 173
Augustus 94, 95
Cath 155
child 227
Isaac Augustine
173
John 49, 155, 180,
227
John Thomas 94
Louisa 94, 131
Louisa Frances 131
Mar't Louisa 110
Mary 94, 173
Mary Elizabeth 110
Mary Louisa 95
Mr. 50
Mrs. 50
Sam'l Ecclas'n 95
Sarah 33
Sarah Ann 94
Thomas Gibson
180
HONADT
Jos 187
HONE
Ann 74
John 156
HONIST
Dina 197
Jos 197
Mary Dina 197
HONSOLY
Pat'k 200
HOOK
Elizabeth 46
HOOP
Catherin 191
Con 66
Jno 66
HOPE
Cath 192
Conrad 192
John 192
Maria 192
HOPKINS
___ 12
Ann 164
daughter 228
Ellen 126
James 99, 219
Martin 205

HOPKINS cont.
Mary 99, 112, 113,
115, 126, 129,
164, 195, 215
Michael 141, 224
Mr. 47
Mrs. 148
Patrick 57, 99, 112,
126, 129, 164,
191, 195, 219, 228
Thomas 34, 36
Wm 51
Wm Mrs. 51

HORAN
Edward 215
James Francis 201
Martin 201, 215
Mary 201, 207,
215
Pat'k 76
Rich'd 72

HORNBAUGH
Josephine 68
Maria Anna 32
Maria Joseph'e 32
Mary 36
Mary A. 68

HORNE
John 103
Margaret 162
Martin 162
Mary 103, 143, 162
Michael 103
Patrick 53, 103

HORNEY
Maria 114

HORNHOST
child 228
Joseph 67

HORTON
John 114

HOSNEU
Geo 142

HOUSE
Ann 51

HOWARD
Catherine 163, 184
Ellen 184
Fanny 156, 191,
198, 202
Frances 128
Henry 191
James 37
Jno 38
Marg't 202
Thomas 163, 184
Wash 187

HOWE
Andrew Thomas
122
Barbara 205
Elizabeth Ann 189
James 50, 122,
138, 166, 189
Joseph Wash'n 166
Julia 205
Mary 138, 142,
166, 189
Mary Ann 122
Pat'k 205
William Henry 138

HOWELL
Louise H. 54
Maria Louisa 136

HOYE(S)
daughter 226
Ellen 169
Fr 226
Patrick 134
Peter 169
Rose 161, 169

HOYLE
Elizabeth 46
Mary 46

HUDDLESON
Mr. 48, 50, 99

HUDELSON
J. 141

HUDSON
Jacob 148, 188
Margaret Eli'h 148
Mary A. 209
Mary Jane 188
Rebecca 148, 188

HUFMAN
Henry 133

HUFT
Charles 123
Dorothea 123
Lewis 123

HUGH(E)S
boy 225
Brdg't 71
Cath 163
child 222, 225,
230, 231
daughter 227
Elizabeth 153
Elizabeth Ann 147
Ellen 71
Geo 66
Henry 63, 112,
122, 147, 222
Isabella 200

James 151, 180,
200, 225, 231
John 60, 155, 169,
180, 214
John James 200
Lawrence 201
Margaret 71, 112,
115, 156, 213
Margaret Ann 193
Mary 36, 56, 112,
115, 122, 146,
147, 153, 156,
169, 180, 222
Michael 156
Mrs. 224
Nicholas 112, 118,
151, 193, 201
Omah 201
Omey 151
Pat'k 163
Terence 153
Terry 169
Thomas 115
William 115, 156,
224

HUMEL
Geo 66, 181
Magdal 181
Mary Catherin 181

HUMIL
Geo 187
Magdl'a 187

HUNT
Robert 67, 165

HUNTER
Ann 43

HURD
Mrs. 51

HURLEY
Jno 68
Nancy 104, 115

HUSAN
Cath 97

HUSSEN
Wm 74

HUSSEY
Ann 125
Bridget 116
John 113
L., Mr. 218
Mary 53, 57, 113
Patrick 222
Peter 49, 113, 220
Philip 107
Rosa 51, 113

HUTSON
Elizabeth 75
Rebecca 39

HYER
Ann 163
Francis 53, 163,
168
Henry 163

IRESSLEIN
Elizab 147

IRONS
Mary 56

IRWIN
Marg't 201

JACKSON
And 213
Elizabeth 64,
138, 139
Henry 56, 183, 186
infant 218
Michael 138
Thos 125
William 218
William Henry 183

JACOBS
Sarah 43

JAMES
Ben 71

JAMESTON
Jane Frances 86
Priscilla 86
Samuel 86

JAMISON
Adel 175
Adolphus 191
Ann 20
Byran, Mrs. 136
Cath 129, 136
Catherine M. 58
Cecilia 167, 169,
187
Cecilia Jos' 133
Elenora 189
Eliza Ann 128,
167, 189, 205
F. 50
Fran B. 129
Francis 48, 128,
162, 167, 186, 189
Francis A. 50, 205
Francis Henry 167
Francis Samuel 166
H. 212
H. A. 178, 202,
227
Henrietta 166, 191
Henry 128

JAMISON cont.
Henry Adolphus 58, 128
Jeremiah 12, 100, 110
John O'Neill 128
Louisa 110
Mary 100, 144
Mary Josephine 205
Mr. 48, 63
Mrs. 12
Priscilla 12
Richard 12, 110, 166
Richard B. 133
Rosa 110
Rosella 166
Rosila Ann 133
Sam'l 12, 167
Thos 167, 189, 202

JASSNER
M. Magd 147

JEFFERYS
John 86
Margaret 86
Priscilla 86

JENDER
Alled 53

JENKINS
Charles 99
Louisa Teresa 55, 125, 133, 134

JENNINGS
James 221

JERRET
Elizabeth 35, 36, 192

JESSE
183

JOERGEN
Anna Mary 140

JOHNSON
Amos 194
Elisabeth 197, 180
John 176, 197
Mary 176, 184
Mary Elizabeth 180
Mimi 194
Pracilla 148
Priscilla 86, 227
Rachel 81
Robert 176, 184, 226
son 226
William 180, 197

JOHOE
Ann 60

JONES
Clotila 18
Fanny 201
Grace 153
Maria 65
Mary 150, 167

JORDAN
Harmon 51
Jno 203

JOYCE
Bartley 77

JURDON
Laurence 119
Michael 119
Rose 119

K_IVE
William 72

KAIN
Bart'w 207
Catharine 119, 133
Daniel 107
Debora 133
John 133
Marcella 55
Maria 33

KALLALA
Ann 203

KANAGH
Pat 139

KANE
Ann 155, 202, 205, 207
Ann Maria 154
Anthony 154
child 232
Dahlia 207
Daniel 232
Deborah 155
Debra 178
Ed 70
Geo William 185
John 155, 178, 191, 207
John Daniel 128
Maria 128, 154
Mary 185, 214
Mary Ann 39
Mary Eliza 178
Thos 214
William 72, 232

KANNAGH
Cath 189
Pat'k 189

KANNAW
Pat'k 65

KANNY
Mary 126

KARMAN
Henry 44
Margaret 106

KARMEN
Elizabeth 106
Henry 106

KARNEY
Bridget 123
Catherine 61
Jas 141
John 123, 172
M. 48
Margaret 172
Mary 122
Michael 123

KART
Barbara 101
Jacob 101
Margaret 101

KASSON
Caspar 70

KAUFMANN
Cath 147

KAVANAGH
Ch 159

KAVANUGH
James 61

KEACH
Mich'l 64

KEALTY
Cath 127

KEAN
Ant 160, 211
Bart'w 73
Daniel 212
Francis Thomas 211
John 213
Maria 211
Mary 73, 160, 211
Mary Ann 38
Mary M. 213
Mich'l 212
Nancy 212
Pat'k 73, 211, 213

KEANEY
Jane 74

KEARN(E)Y
Ann 54
Bridget 98 120
Ellen 100

Esther 47
Frances 109
Hester 50
J. 51
James 126
Jane 52
John 46, 64, 107, 109, 120, 135, 228
Margaret 54, 64, 68, 126, 135, 144, 149, 177, 182, 199
Mary 102, 107, 120
Mary Ellen 102
Michael 144, 196
Mr. 48
Nichols D. 221
Pat 111, 120
Rose 120

KEBEL
Margaret 32

KEBLE
Regina 118
Teresa 31, 154

KEBLER
Ardoy 68

KEECH
Elisb'h 206
Step G. 211
Susanna 211
Walter Daniel 211

KEEGAN
Ann 167, 173
Brdg't 213
Catherin 173
Ed 189
James 213
Jno 151
Mich'l 213
Patrick 55, 143, 173

KEELEY
Elisa 207
Jno 207
Mary 207

KEEMAN
Elizabeth 220
Henry 220
Margaret 220

KEENAN
Betty 121
Bridget 162, 185
Catharine 140, 157
Edward 185
Elizabeth 140, 155, 162, 204
Francis 204

KEENAN cont.
Margaret 171, 204
Maria 171
Mary 121
Mary Ann 204
Michael 157
Peter 162, 185
Thomas 121, 140,
171
KEENE
Cath 124
KEENEN
Mrs. 56
Peter 56
KEHNFUL
Karl 157
KEING
Ellen 211
KELER
Adam 103
Catharine 103
Peter 103
Rosina 103
KELFE
Anthony 223
KELLE
Mrs. 119
KELLER
Geo 197
Margaret 124
Mary 168
Peter 124
Rosina 124
KELL(E)Y
Andrew 122
Ann 111, 128, 134,
159
B. M. 145
Bridget 53, 59,
167, 170, 180,
189, 191, 193,
210, 215
Camilla 99
Catharine 119, 120.
136, 137, 145,
159, 165, 176,
197, 204, 208
Christopher 172
Cornel 163, 182
daughter 218
David 99, 111, 218
Denis 215
E. 94
Edward 165, 170
Elenora 186
Eliza 99

Ellen 66, 112, 119,
176, 210, 218, 228
Ellen Catherin 197
Fanny 208
G., Mr. 49
G., Mrs. 49
Honor(a) 141, 151,
163, 169, 178,
186, 215
Hugh 99
infant 226
James 43, 94, 100,
118, 119, 124,
137, 139, 145,
155, 159, 167,
172, 220, 226
Jane 36, 94, 128,
175, 196
John 61, 62, 117,
119, 137, 141,
150, 154, 163,
165, 167, 169,
170, 175, 186,
209, 215, 218
John Henry 208,
215
John William 189
Joseph Aloys's 108
Julia 206
Lawrence 159
M.____, Mrs. 224
Margaret 174, 220
Margaret Ellen 196
Martin 175
Mary 35, 36, 72,
76, 100, 116, 128,
139, 143, 155,
172, 176, 180,
182, 191, 208, 213
Mary Ann 70, 71,
141,176
Mary Jane 108
Mary Martha 94,
224
Michael 54, 101,
105, 111, 119,
128, 134, 159,
172, 197, 214, 230
Michael, Mrs. 101
Miss 138
Mr. 46, 52, 227
Mrs. 52, 61, 110
Patrick 61, 69, 72,
75, 198, 176, 180,
182, 189, 191,
197, 204, 206,
208, 210, 217,
219, 226
Regina 115
Rose 72, 199

Rose Ann 159
Sarah 165
son 227
Susan 99
Sylvandus 99
Thomas 55, 64, 70,
75, 128, 139, 158,
175, 189, 196,
197, 211
widow 60, 61, 65,
172
William 100, 128,
161, 163, 176, 206
KEMP
Harietta 89
Harriet 203
Henry 89
Mary 192
Mary Ann 55
William 89
KEN(N)EDY
____ 213
Bridget 131, 153,
165
Catherin 170, 173
John 131, 153
Mary 32, 34, 52,
53, 55, 56, 59, 111
154, 159, 170,
173, 180, 189, 228
Mrs. 172
Owen 65
Patrick 32, 33, 163,
186, 194
Sabrina 34, 36,
171, 174, 184
Sibrina 70
Rose 131
widow 233
William 170, 189
KENNA
Chas 66, 174
child 231
KENNAGH
John 189
KENNAN
Elizabeth 167
John 167
Thomas 167
KENN(E)Y
Ann 71, 186,201,
210
Cath 225
David 226, 228
James 182
John 97, 220, 228
Margaret 70, 186

Mary 54, 170, 201,
220
Mathew 70, 71
Mr. 54
Nancy 97
Nicholas 198
Patrick 36, 46, 170,
220
Peter 71, 205
Rose 159, 182, 198
Sarah Ann 159
son 226
William 159, 182,
186, 198, 201, 210
KENOP
____ 101
Christian 101
KEOLLER
George Joseph 222
KEON
Maria 33
KERBY
Jno 169
Margrt 182
Mary 182
KERCHBURG
William 52
KERCHER
Adelaid 137
Henry 137
KERDMAN
Anna 109
Bernard Anth'y
109
John 109
KERFIEL
Phebe Ann 37
KERFUL
Charles 175, 191
Charles Lewis 175
Phebe 175
Phebe Ann 191,
202
Rachel 191
KERING
Mary 225
KERMAN
Elisb'h 198
KERNE
Mary 204
KERNEY
B. 149
Cath 202
Frances 167
Jno 140, 186

262

KERNEY cont
  Marg't 140, 203
  Martha 186
  Mich'l 137, 196, 203
  S., Mrs. 217
KERVICH
  Keim 37
KERVICK
  K. 36
KERWICK
  John Patrick 207
  Keirn 207
  Mary A. 207
KETTER
  Henry 56
KEVLAGHAN
  Thomas 47
KEVRIN
  Nelly 107
KEYHO
  Ann 140
  Francis 140
  Thomas 140
KIENTZBERG
  Caroline 179
  Mary 179
  Wilhelm 179
KIGNEY
  Mich'l 205
KILBORN
  Maria 118
  Pat 146
KILDUF(F)
  Mary 205
  Thomas 205
  John 111
  Patrick 111, 143, 201, 232
  Peter 113
  Rosa 111
KILGARLAND
  Jno 74
KILLBANE
  Maria 49
KILLDUFF
  Ellen 158
  Pat'k 158
  Rose 158
KILLEN
  Margart 136
KILMARTIN
  Jos 194
  Mary 194

Mary Ann 194
KILROY
  Marg't 205, 207
  Michael 205
  Pat'k 205
KIMMEL
  Susan 63
KINDLY
  Ann 211
KINE
  Catharine 61, 111
  Dan'l 140
KING
  Ann 73, 208
  Bridget 137, 154
  Cath 187
  Catherine Ann 31
  Daniel 137
  Dominick 77
  Edward 56, 137, 154
  Elizabeth 144, 180
  Ellen Kink 154
  Hugh 208
  Julia 76
  Margaret 144, 162, 181, 186, 204
  Mary 46, 143, 169
  Mary A. 184
  Mary Elizabeth 169
  Michael 151, 169, 208
  Pat'k 208
KINK
  Ellen 154
KINNEY
  Mary 57
KIRB(E)Y
  George 117, 139, 163
  James August'e 117
  Keern 139
  Margaret 117, 139, 163
  Margaret Ann 163
  Mary 157
KIRKER
  Anna Maria 159
  Henry 159
  Mary 159
KISHMAN
  Ara 229
KITSON
  John 104

KITTY
  Aunt 227
KITZMILLER
  Marg't 129
KIVEEHAN
  Thomas 95
KIVLAHAN
  James 108
  Mary 108
  Thomas 108
KLINK
  Cecilia 160
  George Peter 190
  John Francis 106
  Joseph Anthony 131
  Mary 106
  Mary 131, 160, 190
  Valentine 116, Vandeline 131
  Windel 160
  Windlein 106
  Windlen 190
KLOSTERMAN(N)
  Dina 67
  Heinrich 157
  Johanis Bernh'd 157
KNABB
  Hen 149
KNAP(P)
  Barbara 150, 176
  Casper 176
  Catharine 140
  Jno 176
  Joan Bern 140
  Henry 140
  Susan 142
KNEELAN
  Martin 202
KNEISS
  Jno 65
KNETZ
  Adam 112
  Elizabeth 112
  Lawrence 112
KNIGHT
  Catherin 170
  Elizabeth 169, 170
  Laurence 169, 170
KNIGHTHALT
  Gertrude 189
  Nich's 189

KNIGHTHAR(D)T
  George 187
  Gertrude 139, 193, 195
  N. T. 187
  Titus 139, 195
  Valentine 139
KNIVIS
  Barb 175
  Jno 175
Knoble
  Bernard 194
  Cath 194
  Henry 194
KNOIS
  Barbara 193
  John 193
KNOST
  Mrs. 60
KNOTT(S)
  child 227
  Leo 67
  Mr. 227
  Mrs. 227
KNYTELHARDT
  Gertrude 181
KOCH
  Richard i
KOCKERAN
  Ann 167
KODA
  Sophia 66
KOHLER
  Mary Fackler 198
KOHLMAN
  Alet 169
  Ann 126
  Ber'd 33, 175
  Christina 187
  Elenora 160
  Elizabeth 160
  Henry 198
  Mary 186, 187
  William 160
KOIN
  Cath 103
  John 103
  Pat 103
KOLB
  Elizabeth 171
KOLBER
  child 222
KOLEMAN
  Ann Maria D. 146
  Henry 146

KOLEMAN cont.
Mary A. 146
KOL(L)MAN
Ann 187
Hen 148
Wm H. 187
KOON
Mary Anna 43
KORHNOFF
Frederika 188
KORNHOF(F)
Frederica 198
Jno 188, 196
William Aug's 188
KOUB
Jno 155
KRAIG
Martha 32, 33
KRAMER
John Frederic 140
Jos 140
KRAUS
C. N. 198
Regina 31
KREG
Sara Ann R. 158
KREIG(H)BAUM
Ann M. 34, 169
Demet 32, 33
Elisabeth 15, 145
Fanny 158
Frances 105, 145,
Giles Dyer A. 158
Henry 105, 145,
158
Jona 34
Pet 149
Stanislaus K. 145
KRELLER
Catharina 181
George 130, 181
Margaret 130
Nicholas 130
Q. Pappert 181
KREMER
Fred'k 190
John Henry 190
Mary A. 190
KREMLICH
Francis 140
KRI(E)GBAUM
Ann 18
Anna 9, 10, 84
Anna Marie 92
C. 21

Conrad 84, 85, 87
Conrad, Mrs. 12
Demetrius L. 90
Elisa 12
Elizabeth 9, 12, 17,
19, 98
F., Mrs. 104
Fanny 17, 90, 92,
132, 134
Frances 93, 96
Henry 15, 18, 21,
24, 28, 30, 90, 92,
93, 96, 132
Henry, Mrs. 10
James 87
Maria 7, 9
Mary 18, 82, 92
Mary Caroline 85
Mary Louise 96
Mrs. 21, 28, 49, 84,
85, 87, 90
Peter 21, 22
Priscilla 18, 84, 85,
87, 92
Stephen M. 132
Susan 9, 18, 29,
Susanna 10, 12
William Conrad 23,
93
KRIGHBAUM
Henry 43
J. P. 36
KRINCH
Mary A. 54
KRUKIN
Mary 56
KRUSE
Arthur 150
Elenora 150
Ellen 150
KRUTCH
Mr., Rev. 68
KUHLMAN
Adelaid 178
Jno G. 178
John Stephen 178
KUHN
John 121
Joseph 97, 121
Mary 97, 121
KULKER
Henry 181, 185
Jno Henry 37
Mary 185
Mary Ann 185
KULMAN
Adelaid 135

Henry 97
Henry Dierich 97
Mary Adelile 97
KULULY
Mary 103
KUSLAN
George 118
KYLE
Elizabeth 62
LA___
Geo 69
LACUS
Joseph 118
LAHEY
F. 194
Philip 44
LAHING
Fred 191
LAIN
Fanny 17, 19
LAING
Bernard Francis
190
Fr 184
Fr Steffler 184
Francis 66, 150,
190
Fred'k 66, 187
Jos 66, 184
Mary 66, 184, 190,
197
LAINY
child 227
LALL(E)Y
Bridget 130, 162
Ellen 130
infant 223
James 76, 162
Michael 130, 162
Patrick 130
LAMPEY
Frantz 48
LANAHAN
Sarah 207
LANAN
Michael 110
LANCASTER
Jno 57
Mary 57
Mary Ann 63
Thomas E. iv, 94
LANCE
Aladdin 94

LAND
Julia 144
Michael 144
William 144
LANDBECK
Mary L. 64
LANDERS
Ellen 158
Joanna 146, 158
Maurice 146, 158
Thomas 146
LANDFIST
Mary 66
LANDRAGAN
Thomas 31
LANDRIGAN
Pat 105
LANDWIES
Louisa 64
LANE
D. 182
LANEHOFF
Catharine 100
Fred 100
Margaret 100
LANENDORFER
John 118
LANEY
John 47
LANGEN
Ann 136, 151
Bridget 151
Catherin 136
John 136
Mary 136
Michael 136, 151
LANGENDORF
John 51
LANGER
Mar Cass 147
Maria 147
LANGHAN
Mary 118
Michael 118
Patrick 118
LANGMAN
Anna 105
Mary 105
Michael 105
LANGON
John 231
LANGSDON
Jane 52

264

LANIGAN
Nancy 67
LANIN
Catherin 211
Ellen 211
Peter 211
LANNON
Michael 61
LAREL
Jno 194
LARKEY
Eliz'h 143
Leop 143
LARKIN(S)
Barny 96
Brdg't 215
Catharine 111, 197
child 232
Christina 176
James 128, 162
John 131, 194
Margaret 96, 105,
  114, 131
Mary 37, 68, 105,
  111, 128, 142,
  162, 194, 205, 215
Mary Ann 205
Michael 58, 162,
  219
Mrs. 143
Peter 197
Rose Ann 142
Thomas 49, 55, 66,
  96, 99, 105, 111,
  124, 127, 128,
  131, 142, 148,
  159, 194, 197,
  205, 215
Thos, Mrs. 226
William 131
LARRISON
Henrietta 183
LASALLEY
Cath 66
LASLEY
Cath 142
Rich'd 142
Thomas William
  142
LASTFRED
Mary 180
LASTL(E)Y
Catherine 120, 170
Mary Jane 170
Richard 170, 176,
  227

LAUAMES
Gertrude 52
LAUGHEY
Mary 57
LAUGHLIN
Bridg't 125, 164
Jane 121
Jos 150
Mary 34
Mich'l 150, 154
Stephen 60
LAUGHNAY
Maria 133
LAUGHNEY
Anthony 100
Catherine 100
Mary 149
LAUGHRAN
Mich'l 169
LAURENCE
Ellen 208
LAUTLER
Mich'l 175
LAVALE
Mary 75
LAVELL(A)
Ellen 108, 115
Mary 72
LAVELLE
Bridget 76
Ellen 59
Ellenora 162
Mary 149, 165
Mich'l 61, 126
Pat'k 61
Sophia 76
LAVIL
Mary 51
LAVIN
Betty 188
Cath 75
Elizabeth 188
Mich'l 188, 207
Peter 191
LAVINSKI
Agnes 138
Augustine 138
Mary Jane 138
LAWLER
Catherin 204
Mary 204
Thos 204
LEAHY
Ellen 76
Mary 77

Thos 76
LEATNER
Catharine 48
LEE
Cornelius 141
Ellen 141
James 153
LEGERMEISTER
Frederick Wm 140
Henri Arimini 140
LEGLAND
Eliz'h 54
LEGUS
Joseph 126
LEHEY
Bridget 168
Cornelius 168
Ellen 168
LEHMAN
Eva 182
LEHMEIER
Jno Mich'l 66
LEIBFRED
Maria 183
LEIBFRID
Francis 185
Geo 185
Teresa 185
LEIBZ
Bridget 206
LEIDEMEN
Anna 102
Barbara 102
Nicholas 102
LEIDIGER
Barbara 173
John 173
Nicholas 173
LEIDINGNER
Anna 106
Barbara 106
Nicholas 106
LEIFRED
Geo 60
LEING
Fred'k 64
Joseph 64
LEININGER
Christina 195
Mich'l 195
Weldbinga 195
LEIPFREID
George 64

LEITI(N)GER
Barbara 142
Mary 34
Mich'l 142
Susanna 142
LEITUNG
Barbara 125
Nicholas 125
LEMAR
Elizabeth 63
LEMER
Geo 131
Mary 131
LEMON
Henry 57
LENDEN
Cath 159
Charles 181
James 159
James Henry 159
LENDER
Cath 181
Jas 181
LENTZ
Francis George 184
Joseph 52, 184
Lucinda 165, 178,
  184
LEO
Cath 171, 186, 200
Charles 100, 218
child 225
Elisabeth Ann 71
John 129
Mrs. 221
Patrick 186
Richard 109
Sarah 31, 100, 109,
  129, 218
Thomas 31, 60,
  100, 109, 129,
  171,186, 200, 218,
  225,231
William 200
LEONARD
Brid't 78
James 131
Jno 180
Lawrence 78
Mary 131
Michael 167, 189,
  219
Rose Gonnon 180
Sarah 71

265

266

267

MAGERS cont.
Elizabeth 7, 10, 42, 85, 91
Jane 9
Jane, Mrs. 5
Lydia 80
Margaret 79
Mary 5, 7, 10, 17, 19, 28, 29, 81
Mrs. 30, 82
Nancy 29
Nathan 6, 7, 10, 81
Nathan, Mrs. 10
William 6, 9

MAGINNIS
child 224
Ellen 119
John 119, 220
Mary 53, 119, 204

MAGUIRE
Ann 36, 57, 124, 128, 151, 159
Anna 60
Bernard 76, 158
Brdg't 68, 207, 210
Catherin 136, 173, 211
Elizabeth 158, 210
Hugh 49, 69, 124, 182, 230
James 151
James Forrest 155
Jeffries 70
Jos 206
Marg't 211
Mary 75, 151, 155
Mary Ann 136
Mathew 71, 177, 210
Michael 136, 155, 210
Mrs. 193
Nancy 98, 121
Pat'k 204
Peter 98
Thos 158, 211
William 98, 201, 210

MAHAN
Ann 72, 148
Brdg't 75
Catherin 148
James 132, 148
Mary 123, 174, 200
Thos 174

MAHANY
widow 150

MAHAWN(E)Y
John 80
Milly 6, 8, 10
Milley A. 12
Molly 81
Nathan 80

MAHER
Ann 101
Catherin 75
daughter 226
James 97
John 101
Margaret 101
Martha 97
Mrs. 209
Patrick 46, 97

MAHON
Brdg't 207
Jno 207
Thomas 65, 207

MAHON(E)Y
Ber'd 215
Cath 203
Charles 117
Ellen 203
Esther 117
Hannah 203
John 166
John Henry 141
Margaret 189
Mary 152, 166, 183, 189, 208
Mich'l 203
Ms. 222
Owen 204
Robert 222
Thomas 128, 166, 178, 189, 208
Thomas 166
Wm 35, 36

MAIER
Ann 121

MAJORS
Ambrose 14
Mary 11, 13
Mrs. 11, 13
Nathan 83

MALLEN
Ann 146, 175
Elizabeth 146
Jno 146
Rosanna 146

MALLERIN
Ann 163

MALLIN
Alice 206
Mich'l 206

Patrick 206

MALLON
Ann 191
Henry 191
John 180, 191
Margrt 63
Mich'l 200

MALLOY
And 72
Mary 76

MALON(E)
Bridget 37, 180, 198, 212
Christ'r 192
James 192, 211, 220
John 76, 187, 198
Margaret 124
Mary 37, 124, 192, 198, 211
Mary Ann 192
Michael 198
Patrick 180
Rose 187
Ter(r)ence 114, 124, 211
Thos 180, 198, 212, 231
William 124

MALONEY
Bridget 154
Catherin 154
Jas 209
Thomas 154

MALONY
John 221
Mary 77

MALOWNY
Brdg't 171

MALOY
Geo 72
Jno 121
Patrick 61
Rob't 59, 158
Thomas 133

MANAHAN
Pat 137

MANAHER
Philip 218

MANDY
Ellen 208

MANGION
Mary 204

MANGUN
Ant 202

MANION
Edward 205
Ellen 128
Mary Susan 128
Patrick 128, 129
Tim 189

MANL(E)Y
Ann 169
Bridget 140
Catharine 52, 119
Edward 77
Ellen 158
James 140
John 102
Mariah 69
Mary 122
Patrick 140

MANN
Jno 167

MANNING
_____ 229
Betsy 158
Elizabeth 133
Ellen 73
Hugh 74
Michael 133
Richard 133, 134, 158

MARBURG
Bern 140

MARCH
Ennis 59

MARKS
George 141, 222

MARR
Cath 200

MARRION
Mrs. 231

MARSHALL
Francis Xavier vi, 2, 21, 23, 24, 25, 90
Hanson 98
Letty 97
Liehtia 49
Mary 98, 125
Mary Jane 98
Nancy 95, 107, 110, 115
Polly 97, 98, 115
Samuel 95
Th 94

MARTEN
Mary Ellen 225
R. 225

269

MATTINGLY cont.
Rose Ellen 34
Roseanna 149
Sam'l 6, 8, 13, 15,
18, 21, 23, 24, 27,
28, 29, 33, 37, 67,
79, 204
Samuel Laur'e 94
Samuel, Mrs. 10,
11, 13
Sicila 11
Silvester 16, 19, 22,
29, 121
Simeon 34
Susan 7, 10, 23, 33,
166, 177
Susanna 5, 11, 18,
43, 84, 88, 89, 91
Susannah 16
Sylvester 16, 64
Vincent 168
William 30, 32, 33,
56, 89, 143

MATTINLY
Jas T. 38

MAURAY
Catherine 61

MAY
Eva 152
George B. Casius
152
Matilda 44
Peter Philip 152
son 227

Mc___
Mary 37

McACBIN
James 220

McALEAR
Hugh 45

McALEE
Jas 200

McALEER
Agnes 153
Daniel 153
Geo 67, 201, 212
Hugh 100, 131,
182
Jane 153
Margaret 217
Mary 100, 131
Mary Ann 70, 201
212
Mary Ellen 201
Thomas Andrew
212

McAL(E)USE
Agnes 128
Dan'l 128, 129

McALICE
Danl 145

McANALLY
Jno 230
Marg't 77

McANARRY
Catherin 72
Mich'l 72

McANDRASS
Bridget 130
Mark 130
Thomas 130

McATEE
Catherin 159
John 191
Jonathan 50
Martha 136, 159,
191, 210
Matilda 136
Michael 54, 136,
159, 191, 210
Mr. 51
Peter 210

McAULEY
Ann 35, 36
Cath 35, 36, 186,
202
Elizabeth 35, 193,
200
Ellen 35, 36, 155
Pat'k 188
Thos 174

McAULLY
Daniel 62

McAULTY
Margaret 110
Pat'k 159

McAVORY
David 218

McAVOY
Betsy 56
John D. 77
Miss 127

McBRIDE
Catherin 154
Mary 154
Patrick 154
Screpta 61

McCABE
James 53, 139, 168
John 139
Margaret 129, 139,
168

Rose 168

McCAFFERTY
Rose Ann 53

McCAFFEY
Roseann 53

McCAF(F)REY
Ell 215
Frank 77
James 137, 215
John 141, 155, 163,
215
Margaret 137, 163,
215
Mrs. 116
Rosanna 115

McCAGHAN
Jane 39

McCAHAN
Alice 215
Cath 77
Pat'k 215

McCALL
John 144, 148, 162,
227
Mary 144, 162
son 227
Thomas 162
Ann 157

McCAN(N)
Barney 109
Bridget 109
Charles 128, 137,
138
child 221
Elizabeth 157
Ellen 60, 109,138
Georgesee 157
Margaret 128, 138
Mary 120, 146
Mary Brown 60
Philip 219
Sarah 128
widow 222

McCANA
Ann 106
Bridget Helena 106
Eugena 31
Hugh 106

McCANDRISS
Mary 205, 211
Pat'k 211

McCARR
Bridg't 151

McCARTEY
Margaret 116
Martin 109

McCARTHY
Jno 153
Mich'l 151

McCARTY
Ch 212
John 77
Mary 34, 66

McCARVY
Mary 51

McCAUL(E)Y
Ann 119,127, 153,
186
Bridget 153
Cath 177
Frances 99
Margaret 186
Mary Ann 127
Pat'k 67, 106, 147,
153, 213
Philip 117
Thomas 52, 119,
127, 153, 186

McCAVOY
Mary 108

McCAWLEY
Philip 52

McCLAIER
Peter 96

McCLARY
Peter 43

McCLAY
Anna 83
Hanna 82
John 83
Mrs. 83
Nancy 89
Peter 82, 83, 89
Rebecca 82
Thomas 89

McCLEAREY
John 45
Nancy 49, 117
Peter 12, 49

McCLE(E)RY
Ann 173
Ellen 141
Elizabeth Ellen 156
John 58, 129, 156,
167
Margaret 167
Margaret Ann 129
Maria 129, 156,
160
Nancy 129, 144,
148, 156, 167

270

McCLE(E)RY cont.
Peter 53, 104, 129, 144, 148, 156, 167, 173
Thomas 33

McCLOSKEY
Catharine 122
Ellen 122
Peter 122

McCOFFEY
John 60

McCOFREY
Jno 186
Margrt 33

McCOLLOUGH
Pat'k 193

McCONNELL
Ann 98

McCORKERY
Ellen 32

McCORMAC(K)
Bridget 31, 32, 130, 145
Catharine 100, 169, 203
Edward 68
Ellen 155
Francis 55, 145
Honor 205
Jas 203
John 58, 150, 153, 155, 199, 203
Margaret 199
Mary 55, 68, 100, 124, 153, 155, 157
Mich'l 172
Mrs. 57
Patrick 32, 127, 153, 156
Richard 169
Sarah 203
Thomas 169
Wm 199

McCORMICK
Bridget 134
Catherine 50, 99
Ed 36
Francis 51, 127
James 217
Johanna 47
John 116, 137
Lucy 31, 112
Mary 31, 109, 119
Matthew 51, 102
Mrs. 218

McCORTEY
Margaret 31

McCOSKER
Marg't 214

McCOULEY
Ann 207

MCCOY
Alex 155
Margaret 34, 181

McCREARY
Martha 157
Matilda C. 59

McCUE
_____ 231
Ann 73
Catherin 205
child 233
James 143, 161, 205, 233
Mary 143, 161, 205
Mary Ann 161
William 143

McCUEN
Mary 59
Rosana 45

McCULLOUGH
James 205
Jno 205
Mary 205

McCUNE
James 130
Mary 158

McCUSKER
Ber'd 73
Catherine 60, 70, 129, 157
Ellen 60, 129, 138, 154
Francis 139
John 139
Margaret 139
Mary 70
Mary A. 149
R. A. 211
Rosanna 213
widow 232

McD_____
M. A. 64

McDAY
J. N. 69

McDERMIT
Edward 52

McDERMOT(T)
Ann 122, 199

Bridget 36, 130, 176, 204
Cha's 68, 194, 199
Edw 36, 71, 73, 122, 134, 176, 191, 211
James 162, 170, 229
John 72, 103
Maria 49, 122, 140
Martin 119
Mary 103, 119, 130, 140, 176
Mary Ann 199
Michael 131, 138, 148
Mrs. 131
Thomas 103, 122, 140, 226

McDicker
Lucy 121

McDONAL
Randal 73

McDONALD
Alex'r 213
Ann 59, 99, 107
Anses 153
Bridget 77, 101, 163
Cecilia 124
Christopher 46, 56, 99, 101, 125, 152, 218
daughter 224
David 169, 224
E. 26
Edward 98
Eliza Jane 152
Ell 78
Grace 152, 169
Honor(a) 159, 169
James 159
Jane 107, 124, 140
John 101, 152, 213, 215. 224
Martha 153
Mary 152, 161, 215
Mary Ann 161
Mary Marg't 77
Michael 52, 159, 162
Nancy 101, 218
Nelly 52
P. 25
Patrick 107, 124, 140, 161, 169
Phil 101
Rose 188

McDONEL(L)
Aneas 55
Ann 161
Dav 149
Elizabeth 124
Grace 124
Jas 64
Jno 124
Margaret 199
Michael 70, 72
Rannel 124

McDONNALD
David 133
Honor 133
John 133

McDONNEL(L)
Christ 129
Michael 63

McDONO(U)GH
James 77
Mary 77
Mich'l 77
Ted 74, 75

McDONUGH
Darly 207

McDORNUS
Martin 221

McDUNATH
Pa'k 78

McELROY
Mary 160

McENALLY
Bridget 206
Honora 76
John 157, 206, 231
Miles 75
Pat 149
Sarah 151
Susan 160

McENTIRE
James Patrick 163
Jane 163
Pat'k 163

McFERGUSON
Ellen 201
James 201

McGAN
Ellen 167
Jas 168
Jane 143
Marcella 143, 167
Richard 143, 167

McGAR
Mary 143
Patrick 143, 232

271

273

McKINZIE cont.
Rody E. 179
Sally 123
Samuel 123, 125,
133, 145, 166
Samuel F. 125,
136, 155, 158, 169
Samuel Sampson
178
Sarah 148, 175
Sarah Ann 143,
148, 158, 159, 214
Susan 148, 178
Susan Matilda 192
Susanna 65
William Enock 136

McKITRICK
Ellen 130
Jane McEntyee 130
Patrick 130

McKLENN
Bridget 101
James 100, 110
Jno 73
Margaret 100, 110
Peter 100
Thomas 110

McKONIGLE
Bridget 31, 99
Cornelius 99
Margaret 99

McKOVERN
Ann 109
Ellen 109
Mary 52
Thomas 109

McKOWAN
Catharine 101
James 101

McKRAN
Catharine 119
Mary Ann 119
Patrick 119

McKRAW
Ann 53
Thos 78

McKUIRE
Ann 59
Catherine 88
Elizabeth 88
James 56
Michael 53
Thomas 88

McKUREY
Margaret 118

McKUSKER
Lucy, Mrs. 11

McLAIN
Bridget 71

McLANDRA
Bridget 219

MCLANEY
James 111

McLAUGHLIN
___ 76
Ann 208
Bridg't 142
Catharine 34, 36,
66, 70, 76, 111,
175, 185, 199, 202
Catherine Eli'h 213
Ch 140, 151, 196
Ellen 162
Harriet 192, 204,
213
Harriet Marg't 204
Henry 65, 192,
204, 213
Honora 36, 111
James 39, 183
Jane M. 38
Jno 208
Julia 162, 183
Lewis Edwin 192
Mart 127
Mary 35, 36, 74,
75, 186
Michael 52, 53,
141, 162, 182, 183
Mrs. 59
Roger 183
Sarah 68, 70
Teresa 208
Thomas 38, 111,
207, 232
widow 68
William 60, 139,
161

McLEER
Leonidas 129

McLOORSHOCK
Ed 67

McLUCKY
Fr. 168

McMAHAN
Andrew 152, 185
Brd't 77
child 225
John 165, 222, 225
Joseph 207
Julia Ann 185

Margaret 74, 165,
168
Mary 63, 152,
165, 175, 180, 185
Pat'k 207
Pet 74
Philip 152
Sarah 207
Susan 34

McMAHON
Andrew 51
Jane 218

McMALIAN
David 230

McMANIS
___ 220

McMAN(N)US
Edward 63, 180
Eliza 205
Ellen 76, 97, 180
Hugh 123
Hugh L. 76
James 119, 124,
205
John 76, 97, 139,
205
J. P. 207
Margaret 205
Mary 119
Mary Ann 180
Michael 119
Nancy 119
Patrick 97, 139
Rosa 97, 112
Rose 127, 139
Rose Ann 63, 162
180

McMENAMEN
James 71

McMOHAN
And 146
And, Mrs. 226
John 144
Mary 144

McMULLEN
James Francis 98
Laurence 98
Marg't 98

McMULLIN
Mary A. 53, 210

McNAIR
Andrew 125
Catherine 125
James 203, 211
Jno 203
John James S. 203

Lavina 125
Mary 38, 203, 211
Thomas Hildreth
211

McNALLEN
Pat 131

McNALL(E)Y
Ann 125
Bridg't 143
Cath 139
Dan'l 139, 172
Elizabeth 172
Hugh 125
John 111, 141, 172
Jane 115
Mary 111, 130,
172
Patrick 125, 130
Rosa 111
Sarah 141, 168,
172
Susan 130, 141
Thomas 130

McNAMARA
child 233
Dan'l 77
James 229
John 103, 117, 206
Marg't 76, 77
Pat'k 233
Thomas 218

McNAULY
D. 193

McNEER
Andrew 107
Catherine 107
Elenor Jane 107

McNEFF
___ 193
Jno 52, 144

McNEIL
Pat'k 180
Thos 71

McNEIR
James G. 69

McNEVE
Rosvia 38

McNULLY
Arthur 230
Margart 134

McNULTY
Arthur 111
Bridget 105
child 226
Jane 105

McNULTY cont.
John 171
Margaret 55, 105,
  111, 128, 146,
  160, 171, 176
Mary 146
Michael 130, 146,
  171, 226
Mrs. 128
McQUADE
Edward 52
McQUAID
Arthur 179
McQUE
child 226
Jas 226
McQUICKER
Matilda 49, 109, 12
Mrs. 15
McQUILIAMS
Nancy 114
widow 114
McQUILLAN
Bridget 75
McTAG
Thos 75
McTAGUA
Mary 73, 208
McTEE
Honor 164
McVAY
Ann 144
Michael 144
McVEY
Anna 161
Pat'k 161
McVIC(K)ER
Matilda 30
Lucy 7
McVICOR
Lucy 28
McVIG(G)ER
Lucy 16, 19
Matilda 16, 17, 18
McVIGOR
Mat'a 139
McWILLIAMS
Bridg't 179
Catherine 129, 146,
  169
Daniel 129, 146,
  153, 169, 173
Denis 169
Hugh 146

MEAD
Adam 106
MEAL(E)Y
James 136
John 33, 146, 165
John A. 32
Mary 55, 146
Mr. 220
Mrs. 138
widow 165
MEALUE
Peter 141
MECHLER
Ant Ber 177
MEDLER
Joanna 70
MEDLEY
Peter 164
MEHENNY
Honora 154
Mich'l 154
MEIBERG
Ber'd 179
John Joseph 179
Mary 179
MEIMON
Frederick 100
MELARKEY
Mary 140
MELCHER
Johanna 70
MELEBERGER
Casper 118
John Adam 118
Susan 118
MELIA
Bridget 35, 36
Elizabeth 35, 36,
  206, 212
infant 232
James 120
Jno 212
Mary 34, 36, 63,
  231
Rose Ann 34, 36
Thomas 212
MELMAN
Gerard William 107
Henry/Harry 107
Mariana 214
Mary 100, 197
MELMON
Mary 105
MELON
Jno 205

Rose A. 205
Patrick 104
MENAGH
Mich'l 199
MENKING
Isabella 98
John 98
Mary 98
MENNE
John 179
MENNER
John 65
MENNERT
Jno 160
MERKEL
Elizabeth 147
La'd 147
Leopald 147
Leopold 126
Mary Ann 147
Wilhelmina C. 126
MERKLE
Bernard 99
Catherine 99
Elizabeth 103, 121,
  126
Leopold 103, 121
Samuel 103
William 99
MERLMAN
A. N. 194
MERRICK
Anthony 200, 230
Michael 232
MERTZ
Ambrose 118
Ann Mary 146
Anna 185
Anna M. 120
Catharine 118
Geo 146
George H. 185
John George 146
Mary Dorothea 185
Yorick 118
MESSER
Mary Catherine
  217
MESSMAN
Ann 36
Arnold Henry 145
Catherine 96, 145
Elizabeth 68
H. 26, 218
Henericy 54
Henry 64, 145

Sarah Ann Cath
  218
Ann 35
METER
Barbara 224
METZGER
Anne Magdalen
  188
Geo 184, 188, 227
Margrt 184, 188
MEY
Johannan Petrim
  182
Petris Phil. 182
MEYER(S)
Adeline 195, 197
Antony 136
Catherine 134
Christina Mary 161
Elizabeth 136, 161,
  193
Fred'k 194
George William
  193
Henry 60, 136,
  161, 193, 201
John 34, 197
John Henry 201
Lickna 38
Martin 75
Peter 134
Susan 134
Thomas 197
MIBERG
Ber'd 187
Mary 187
Mary Ann Eliz'h
  187
MIBRICK
Ann 148
Barney 54
Bernard 148, 165
John Henry 148
MIDDLETON
Matilda 54
MILBORN
Harriet 44
MILL
Leo 231
MILLER
Augustine 134
Caspar 184
Catherine 132, 134
Elizabeth 96, 123,
  140, 149, 181
Jno 36, 123, 181

MILLER cont.
Juliann 140
Lydia 141
Mary 132, 184
Michael 35, 36,
132, 184
Peggy 144
Peter 96, 140
William 134

MILLIER
Michael 46

MILLISON
Harriet 18

MILLMAN
Mary Ann 96

MILLS
Arthur 112
Nancy 112

MILVAY
Ann 73

MINNOGUE
Ann 208
Mary 208
Mich'l 208

MINNON
Jos 189
Joseph William 189
Mary 189

MINTRUP
Cath 194
Jno 194
John Joseph 194

MINTRUSS
Cath 172
Henry 172
William 172

MIRALDY
Julia 223

MISAL
Barbara 108, 118
John 47, 108, 118
John George 118
Joseph 108

MISSEL
Fred'k 197

MITCHEL(L)
Catherine 130
Eliza 130
Marg't 154
Patrick 60, 146
Thomas 130

MIX
B. 207
Mary 207
William Henry 207

MOELMAN
Arle 181
Granny 228
Mary 188

MOHAN
Mary 138

MOHER
Mrs. 226

MOHLMAN
Hen 174
John Henry 174
Mary 121, 174
Mary Eliz'h 121

MONAHAN
And 59
Ant 164
Barny 96
Brian 131, 172,
193
Bridget 172
Brien 137
Darb(e)y 34, 59,
149, 174, 194
Ellen 172
James 127, 174,
193
John Thomas 194
Margaret 127, 182
Mary 36, 70, 78,
128, 137, 172,
174, 178, 193, 194
Mary Catherine 193
Michael 127, 172,
182
Pat'k 67, 74, 106
Rose 150, 171
Rosina 172
Sarah 137
Sibey 199
William 182

MONAHEN
Anna 114
Brian 114
Margaret 114

MONAUGHAN
Anthony 49

MONEHAN
child 219

MONIGAN
Anthony 107

MONIHAN
Ant 129
Rose 129

MONNELLY
Michael 99

MOODY
Bridget 138
John 138
Joseph 138
Mary 74

MOONEY
Mary 171
Patrick 105, 171

MOOR
widow 222

MOORE
___ 19
Catherine 13
child 227
Honora 218
James 227
Jane, Mrs. 12
John 192, 221
L. 26
Levi 61, 178, 192
Lucinda 178, 192
Mary 178
Sarah 44
William 75

MOOT(E)Y
Bridget 120, 167,
202
child 232
John 120, 167, 202,
231
John Francis 167
Mary Jane 202
Pat 120
widow 232

MORAN
___ 231
Ant 74
Cath 200
Dan'l 77
Ed 76
Ellen 204
John 65, 200
Margaret 69, 144
Martin 201
Mary 154, 294,
207, 211
Mich'l 211
Mrs. 229
Pat'k 74, 200
Pet'r 231
Thomas 53
William 204

MORATHEY
Timothy 58

MORE
Jane 16, 17
John 19, 31
Rachel 16

Sally 19
Sarah 16, 17

MORGAN
Ann 112, 148, 180
Catherin 180
Dan'l 141
Elizabeth 112
Ellen 112
infant 218
James 112, 148,
153, 180
John 157
Mary 148, 157,
160
William 8, 157,
160

MORLMAN
Catherine Eli'h 193
Henry 193
Maria 193

MORNE
Pvt. 217

MORRIS
Cransh'w 214
George 196
Granshaw 196
Mary 64, 73
Mary Elizabeth 214
Pat'k 64
Rod 214
Roda A. 192
Rody 196

MORRISON
Catherine 52
Charles 132
Edmond 123, 134
Elizabeth 123, 134
Emily Frances 198
John 67, 198
M. 77
Mary 77, 132, 202
Mary Jane 188
Redmond 51
Sophia 132
Teresa 198
William 134

MORRISSY
John 168
widow 168

MOSER
Maria 109

MOSEY
Catharine 218

MOUD
Adam 104
Teresa 104

276

MOUREL
Hannah 57
MOUREY
Thos 72
MUDD
Athanasius 101
Athanasius 100
Henry Edgar 100
Priscilla 100
MUELLER
Jno 150
MULANY
Mary 76
MULASKY
Thos 149
MULCAHA
Biddy 135
MULCAHAEY
Patrick 119
MULCAHEY
Bridget 142, 170, 183, 196, 209
Honor 183
John 108, 119, 142, 170, 183, 196, 209
John Bapt 31
Margaret 60, 63, 142
Margaret Jenet' 209
Mary 119, 170
Michael 183
Patrick 61, 142, 183
Thomas 196
William 142
MULCAHI
Margrt 150
MULCAHIL
Bridget 102
John 102
MULCAHY
Jno 178, 186
MULCAKEY
John 219
MULCHAEY
Jno 224
Mary 224
MULCRONE
Michael 75
MULDRONY
Catherine 99
Cecilia 99
James 99

MULEHIE
Marg't 58
MULHANEY
Ann 188
MULHAVIN
M. 76
MULHERN
widow 230
MULHOL(L)AND
Catharine 94
H. 26, 95, 141
Margaret 212
Michael 55, 94, 133
Peter 49, 96, 98, 212
MULIGAN
Bridget 108
MULLACLY
Thomas 228
MULLADY
Denis 137, 154
MULLAN
Ann 94
Anna 104
Anna Nancy 104
Edward 47, 94, 103, 104, 109
J. 26
John George 94
MULLANY
Den 126
MULLAR
E. 108
MULLARK(E)Y
Thomas 59, 169
MULLEDY
Elizabeth 110
MULLEN
Ann 123, 142, 178
Ber'd 208
child 227
Dan Marcellus 123
Edward 25, 43, 123, 127, 142, 178
Emily Cecilia 178
John 68, 179, 212, 220
Marga't 122
Mary 32, 33, 123, 185, 212
Mrs. 127
Patrick 67
Rosanna 179
Sarah 35, 178

William Thomas 142
MULLER
Ann 190
Ed'd 190
Elizabeth 163
John 34, 165, 173, 184
Laura Joseph'e 190
Margaret 37, 103, 165
Mary 190
Mary Margaret 163
Peter 163, 197
MULLHOLLAND
Charles Henry 166
Helen Jenkins 156
Louisa Teresa 156
Michael 156, 166
Teresa 166
MULLIGAN
child 229
Christina 206
Ellen 229
James 78, 206
Jane 206
Marcus 122
Mark 66, 164
Mary 78
MULLIGARD
Mark 173
MULLIN
John 175
Mary 197
Rosanna 175
MULREAL
Bridget 49
MULVAN(E)Y
Ann 154
Francis 154
Owen 71
Thos 154
MULVAY
Martin 70
Michael 70
Thos 75
MULVEEL
Bridget 99
MULVEY
Margaret 206
Mich'l 206
Owen 206
MUNY
Cath 191
MURATHY
Ellen 146

Timothy 46
MURPH(E)Y
Aaron Seb'n 90
Ann 65, 71
Anna Elizabeth 89
Barney 143
Bernard 146
Bridget 143, 146, 169
Caroline 137
Catherine 38, 65, 76, 125, 180, 197, 206, 207
Catherine El'h 85
Daniel 200
daughter 227
Denis 173, 175, 207, 231
Elizabeth 31, 62, 74, 117, 210
Ellen 148, 171, 180
Francis 56, 75
infant 226
J's 103
James 9, 42, 84, 85, 89, 90, 92, 125, 167, 173, 180, 207, 226, 227
Jer 207
Joana 146
John 109, 172, 180
John William 92
Judy 141
Julia 230
Margaret 133, 166, 175, 181, 231
Marietta 66
Mary 75, 78, 85, 89, 90, 92, 171, 173
Mary Ann 109
Mathew 220
Maurice 58, 155
Mrs. 9, 69, 151, 164
Nic 145
P. 26
Patrick 35, 71, 146, 148, 169, 173, 181
Peter 148, 169, 210
Richard 47
Rosa 109
Rosan 163
Roseann 34
Sarah Jane 137
Sebastian 217
Susan 207, 212
Thomas 180, 191, 225

279

281

RAFETY
Mary 171
RAINEY
Mary 141
RAMIS
Christina 76
RAMUS
Christiana 38, 39
RANEY
Julia 161
Mary 132, 161
Patrick 132, 161
Sarah 132
RAPE
John 78
RARIG
Jno 223
Mary 223
Peter 223
RASMAN
Marg't 95
RAVENSCRAFT
Abner 106, 219
RAY
Martha 54, 127
READ
Alexus 134
Harriet 134
Mary Jane 134
READER
Alexius 99, 159
Harriet(t) 99, 159
James 159
Teresa 99
REBO
Cath 191
Henry 191
Sarah Catherin 191
REBROKE
Cath 187
RECKER
infant 220
John 220
REDMON(D)
Ann 34, 120, 137, 167
Catharine 48
Hanna 79
James vi
James, Rev. 2
Marg't 34, 67, 184
REED
James 103, 131, 146, 160

REGAN
Cath 207
Ellen 207
Pat'k 77, 207
Tim 36
REGEAR
Johanna 38
REGEN
Cath 58, 177, 193
Mary Ann 177
Mary Luisa 193
Pat'k 177, 193
Tim 193
REHY
Ann 201
REIFS
P. 26
REIL(L)EY
Ann 70
Anthony 199
Bridget 124
Cath 124, 174, 211
child 229, 232
David 164
Ellen 173
Ed'd 232
Francis 124, 174, 211
James 174
Jane 199
Jno 74
Judith 164
Mary 70
Mary Ann 199
Patrick 164, 199, 232
Peter 199, 229
Susan 153
Thos 71
REIL(L)Y
Ann 70
Ann Jane 38
Cath 200
Frances 209
J's 26
Jane 201, 209
Jno 37
Marg't 34
Pat'k 157
Peter 201
Thos 73
REIRIGH
Margaret 96
REMFREY
Mary 218
REMPHE
Gerard Henry 107

REN__GHAM
Ann 76
REREICH
Juliam 117
REREICK
Anna Margarita 108
Juliam 110
Julian 108
Margaret 108
Nicholas 108
Peter 26, 50, 96, 108
Peter Jr. 50
REREIGH
Mary 30
Mrs. 30
Peter 30
REREIK
Susan 116
Valentine 116
RERHIG
Peter 19
RERIC
Susan 123
Valentine 123
RERICK
Margaret 123
Peter 123
Valentine 50
RERIG
Alexander King 194
Barb 68, 197
child 227
Eliza 133
Elizabeth Ann 149
John 150
Julia Patricia 178
Juliann Ann 54
Margaret 36, 37, 127, 133, 140, 148, 151, 157, 158, 163, 166, 177, 194, 197
Mary 145, 150, 151, 157, 158, 179, 187
Mary Ann 177
Mary Barbara 197
Mary Catherin 145
Mary Marg't S. 127
Peter 54, 68, 133, 145, 148, 150, 151, 157, 158, 166, 177, 179, 187, 190, 197
Susan 127, 132, 178, 194

Susanna 149
Valentine 127, 149, 178, 194,
Vol 227
RERIK
Margaret 123
Peter 123
RETBROKE
Elizabeth 112
REY
John 111
Valp Carolina 111
REYNOLDS
Ber'd 61, 72, 73, 132, 151, 161, 162, 171, 200
Biddy 146
Bridget 158, 161, 171
Catherin 132, 153, 161, 171
Elizabeth 52, 153, 223
Ellen 154
Francis 132, 146, 161
Honor(a) 111, 128, 158
James 154, 171
John 47, 53, 111, 128, 146, 158, 171
Margaret 75, 161, 215
Mary 111, 154, 162
Mary Ann 161
Michael 71, 153, 223
Mrs. 33
O. 26
Peter 56
Thomas 128, 135, 146, 161
Timothy 71
RHEY
Oliver 70
RHINEHARD
Catherine 60
RHINEHAR(D)T
Andrew 69
Catherine 135
Joseph 135
Margaret 135
RHOAD
Elizabeth 54
RHONE
Ann 206

282

RHO(O)NEY
Ann 65
Devon 71
Jno 76
Mar 151
Mary 163, 165,
170
Patrick 163, 170
Sophia 59
Thos 151
William 170

RICE
Barbara 105
Elizabeth 45
Levi 66
Lord Ervin F. 105
Margrt 189
William 105

RICHARD(S)
Ellen 203
Honora 204
James 65, 203
Jno 204
Joanna 203
Mary 204
Michael 61, 76,
171, 229
Thos 65

RICHART
John 30

RICHMOND
Elisb'h 65

RICHSTEIGER
Ann 184
George 184
Margaret 184

RICKAD
Mich'l 158

RICKELANAN
Mary 144

RICKELMAN
Henry 121, 183,
192
Jno 195
Lucy Margaret 121
Mary 62, 64, 159,
174
Mary 64
Mary Eliz'h 121

RICKER
John 103, 115, 116
Mary 103, 116

RICKERT
John 106

RICKMAN
Anthony 105

Elizabeth 105
Henry 105

RICKSTIGER
Geo 196

RIDGEL(E)Y
Ann Elizabeth 44
Ann Isabella 81
Elijah 80, 81, 82,
85, 87, 89
Eli(jah), Mrs. 12
Elinor (a) 82, 85,
87
Elinora Maria 82
Elisa 89
Ellen 16, 158
Ellen M. 57
Jacob 89
Martha Emilia 85
Mary Ann 45, 80
Nelly [Elinor] 89
Rebecca 35, 87
Wil(l)iam 24

RIGNEY
Cath 175

RILEY
Ann 65, 109, 141,
151, 162, 165, 228
Anthony 129
Barney 55
Bernard 129, 167,
207
Catharine 109, 182,
195
Catherine Ann 139
David 103, 118,
129, 145, 161
Ed 112, 125
Elizabeth Ann 167
Elten 207
Francis 180, 187,
195
Hugh 173
James 101, 107,
116, 139, 173
Jane 182, 187
Jane Ann 31
John 109, 198, 199
Judah 103, 118
Judy 172
Julia 105, 129, 145
Lulia 199
Margaret 103, 122,
125, 129, 167,
174, 180
Mary 57, 116, 130,
151, 195, 207
Michael 70, 109,
128, 145, 182
Miles 151

Mr. 49
Mrs. 49
Patrick 118, 128,
162, 228
Peter 182, 211
Susan 116, 118,
139, 173
Terrance 125
William 48, 49

RINEBERG
Lewis 57

RINEHART
Catharine 118
Charles Henry 166
Eliza 166
John 118
Joseph 114, 118
Sam'l 166

RIVELL
Catherine 98
Mary 98
Michael 98

ROACH
Jane 141, 173
Jessie 173
John 72, 141
Mary 212
Michael 141
Pat'k 126
Thos 212
Wm 183

ROAN
John 77

ROBERTS
Agnes 125
daughter 225
Mary 94, 166
Mrs. 225
Rebecca Ellen 94
Sarah Jane 166
William 94, 166

ROBINETT(E)
Cassandra 48
Eliza A. 50

ROBINSON
Ann 77
Charles 159
Ellen 54, 101, 122,
143, 179
Ellender 159
George Wash'n 112
Joshua 159
Mary A. Rebecca
122
Priscilla 112
Rody Ellen 179

Solomon 101, 122,
143, 179
Solomon Jacob 143
William 112
William Henry 101

ROBISON
Eli 65
Ellenora 53
Jno 73
Rody Resella 143
William 143
William Andrew
143

ROCK
Andrew 200
Martin 200
Mary 200
Michael 200
Mrs. 134
Patrick 54
Peter 200
Sibilian 200

RODDY
Cath 96
Elleonora 12
James 12
Wm 12

RODE
Elizabeth 107

RODENER
Ann 153

RODGERS
Arthur 221
Mary Catharine
100
Patrick 100, 121
Rose Ellen 121
Sally 121
Sarah 100

RODY
Catherine 126
John 126
Mary 126

ROE
Catherine 175, 185,
227
Edward Mathew
175
infant 227
Margaret 52, 53
Richard 185, 175,
227
Rose Ann 185

ROGERS
Bridget 138
Cath 170
Edward 213

ROGERS cont
Mary 56, 213
Patrick 170
Sarah 135, 170
ROH
Casper 187
Elizabeth 187
Joseph 187
ROHAN
Ann 210
Brid't 77
Mich'l 210
ROHE
Caspar 67
Casper H. 63
ROLL
John 109
Mary 109
Matthew 109
ROLLIN
Christine 175
ROLLMAN
Henry 63
ROLOFF
Francis, Rev. 2
ROMAN
Adam 103, 112
Ann 159
Ann Maria 159
Catharine 103, 127
George 112, 148
John A. 159
Martin 127, 179
ROMNEY
Sophia 52, 97
ROONEY
Anna 111
Brian 113
Edward 113
infant 218
James 111, 137,
218
Mary 113
Mich'l 136
Sabina 111
Sabrina 137
Sophia 31, 107,
151
Thomas 56, 62,
111, 139
ROONY
Sophia 134
ROSE
Anthony 59
Barbara 169
Catherin 169

Michael 169
ROSEN
Ant 189
Elizabeth Ann 189
Martha 189
ROSENBERGER
Baldesa 137
Ball's 185
Balthason 54
Belthafier 163
Elizabeth 137, 139,
163, 185
Henry Joseph 163
Jno B. 179
John 101
John Charles A. 101
John Martin 137
Magdalen 101
Mary Margaret 185
ROSEY
Ant 167
John Francis 167
Margaret 167
ROSS
Honora 46
ROTH
Margaret 67, 186,
194
Mary 185
ROUARD
John 76
ROURKE
Christ 32
Mary 139
ROW
Margaret 32, 110
Mary 112
ROWAN
Michael 76
ROWE
Caroline 47
ROWLEY
Thos 76
RUAN
Brdg't 214
RUCKER
Adelaid 135
Anthony Aug's 135
Francis Anthony
174
Helena 174
John 45, 135, 174
RUDDY
Anthony 142, 159,
168

Catherin 136, 142,
168
Edward 138
Ellen 168
John 72, 118, 133,
144
Martin 144, 170
Mary 103, 144
Michael 57, 71,
142, 160, 169, 205
Thos 173
RUEBELIN
Margaret 181
RUF
Mart 54
RULE
Ed 214
RULOF
Mathew 96
RUMBLER
Mr., Rev. 54
RUMPLER
Mr., Rev. 130, 198
RUPERT
Frederick 187
Mary 187
Mary Catherin 187
RUPTWEGT
Barbara 179
Frederick 179
Mary Margaret 179
RUSH
Mr. 47, 49
Mrs. 49
Patrick 99
RUSLEIN
George 57
RUSSEL
Ellen 203
Mr. 209
RUTH
And 73
RUTT
Nancy 56
RYAM
child 223
widow 223
RYAN
Alice 152
Anastasia 209
Ann 118, 125, 139,
208
Bridget 38, 149,
202, 213

Cath 34, 69, 120,
122, 135, 152,
162, 171, 176,
192, 203, 207,
209, 213
Edward 97, 219
Elizabeth 23, 65,
126, 154, 169,
190, 192
Eliza Joseph'e 118
Ellen 77
Frances 139, 176
Frances Ann 32
infant 231
James William 97
John 31, 33, 163,
209, 232
Margaret 107, 111,
125, 149, 152
Maria 47, 96
Mary 31, 35, 36,
77, 97, 104, 107,
108, 114, 120,
130, 132, 142,
149, 152, 155,
164, 209
Mary Adelia 155
Mary Ann 114, 201
Mathew 108
Matthew, Rev. 2
Michael 66, 107,
125, 135, 149
Mrs. 61, 126, 128,
133, 231
Nathan 97
Nicholas G. 118
Nicholas P. 139,
223
Patrick 130, 202,
209
Peter 126
Philip 120, 124,
126, 135, 152,
176, 192, 203, 206
Rebecca 97
Sarah 32, 33, 59,
62, 108
SAMMES
Ab'r 49
SAMMON
John 75
SAMON(S)
Cecilia 128, 138,
184
Celilia 155
Daniel 127
Jno 75
Margaret 127
Mary 138

284

SHANE cont.
Jeremiah 73
Jno 179, 197, 209
Margaret 36, 179, 197, 209
Mary 213
Mary Ann 35, 36
SHANEN
Brdg't 194
SHAN(N)OHAN
Bridget 173
Christopher 173
Joseph 173
SHANNON
child 218
Dan'l 174
James 104
John 104, 218
Mary 98, 104
SHARP
Catherine 62
Geo Henry 157
Mary 157
Mary Ann 157, 223
SHAUGHNEY
Patrick 231
SHAY
Thos 219
SHAYER
Zach'a 68
SHEA
Fer 190
Jer 181
John 133, 145, 165, 177
John Patrick 165
Mary 35, 133, 145, 165
Mich'l 166
Nicholas 145
Philip 133
SHEEHAN
Pat'k 206
SHEEHEY
Ann 215
child 232
Ryan 232
SHEEHIN
Cath 74
SHEEHY
John 160
Rachel 160
William Edmond 160

SHEHAN
Cath 73
Kale 208
Pat'k 73
SHEH(E)Y
Ann 205, 214
Bern'd 205
Bryan 214
Edward 205
John 169
Mary 168
Mary J. 168
SHELLHAUS
John Peter 142
SHEL(L)HOUSE
Barbara 190
Catherin 190
Elizabeth 37, 176
John 50, 100, 151
J. P. 158, 160, 190
Mrs. 176
P. 176
SHELLY
Peter 170
SHELVIN
Anthony 76
SHENOFF
Adelaide 120
Joseph L. 120
Mary Elizabeth 120
SHEPLER
Henry 115
James Solomon 115
Letitia 115
SHERIDAN
Ann 119, 169, 206
Anna 111
Cath 72
Cornelius 72
Dennis 191
John 161, 169, 174, 208, 233
Julia 52, 162
Margaret 71
Mary 59, 75, 116, 126, 161, 164, 183, 191, 208
Mrs. 138
Nancy 161
Thomas 178, 191, 208
Thomas Edward 208
SHERIDEN
Jno 56
Mary 142, 144
Thos 34

SHERIN
Edward 69
SHERLICK
W. 229
SHERRY
James 145
Michael 25, 115
SHERWOOD
Elisabeth 75
SHETHEN
Christ'na 136
Jno 136
SHIELDS
John 204
Margaret 204
Mary 196
SHINDLER
Mary 182
SHINGLE
Ellen 193
George 185
Jno 185, 193
Mary 185, 193, 196, 170
SHINICK
Michael 170
Mrs. 164
SHINOCK
Catherin 155
Mary 155
Michael 155
SHIRCLIFF
Leonard 42
William 42
SHIRKEY
_____ 228
SHRIBER
Elizabeth 141
Henry 141
Mary Ann 141
SHRIMP
Casp 176
SHRIVER
Catherin Eli'h 116
Elizbh 190, 215
Ellen 189
Gertrude 226
Henry 35, 36, 116, 175, 215
Jacob Anthony 116
John 38, 39
Mary Ann 215
Philomena Cat'n 175

SHUE
Nicholas 130
Susan 130
SHUELRICK
Cath 142
SHULDA
Christian 186
Julian 186
Mary Julian 186
SHULDT
Francis 137
SHULS
Christ'n 58
SHULTE
Christian 144
Julia 144
Mary 144
SHULTEN
Christian 161
Julia 161
William 161
SHULTZ
Bernard 174
Elizabeth 174
Garret 145
Margaret Cat'e 145
Mary 145, 174
Pat 174
SHUMMEN
Anna 98
Gertrude 98
John 98
SHURA
Cornelius 145
Jos 145
Luisa 145
Mathias 145
SHUTMILLER
Cath M. 67
SHUTMULLER
Hen 146
SIBLE
Catharine 102
Gertrude 102
John 102
SICK
Edward 142
SICKEL
Mary Ann Han'h 92
SIGERON
Wm 156

SIGERSON
Mary 182
Mary Elizabeth 182
Susan 34, 180
William 63, 182
SILK
Edward 34, 172, 210
Mary 49, 97
Mary A. 210
Rose Ann 210
SIMMES
Mr. 49
SIMPKINS
Margaret 43
SIMPSON
Catherine El'h 93
David 93, 104, 123, 136
John 104
Nancy 93, 104, 123, 136
Rebecca 136
Sarah Jane 93
SINNET
Mich'l Thomas 143
SINOD
Thos 137
SIPE
Rebecca 71
SKALLY
James 73
SKELLY
Catherin 182
Jno 182
Mary 182
SKULLY
child 227
Jno 227
SLATER
Rose Ann 53, 55
SLATTERY
Cath 67, 68, 188
SLAVER
F. 219
SLAVIN
Rosann 104
SLAVINSKI
Agnes 161
Ann 161
Augustus 161
SLICER
Mr. 58

SLIEGER
Catha'n 147
SLOAN
Ann 173
David 173
John 49
Mathew 173
SLOCASE
child 222
SLOHAN
Elizabeth 155
John 155
Mary 155
SLOKASE
Bridget 131
John 131
Margaret 131
SLOVINISKEY
Agnes 114
Augustus 114
Joseph 114
SLOWN
John 117
Margaret 117
Mary Ann 117
SMESING
Jno 182
SMESY
Jno B. 121
SMIDTH
Catharine 99
SMISING
Catharine 99
John 99
Mary 99
SMITH
_____ 88, 92
Ann 33, 121, 143, 150, 181, 189, 197
Ann M. 191
Barney 115, 150
Bernard 128, 166, 201
Ben(nar)d, Mrs. 232
Betsey, Mrs. 12
Cath Lorella 38
Catharine 49, 55, 58, 99, 107, 112, 115, 150, 156, 187
Cha's Augustine 136
Charles 125
Christina 193
Dan'l 226, 227
Dan'l, Mrs. 227

daughter 227
Elizabeth 18, 68, 99, 121, 148, 156, 160
Ellen 181
Felicita 84
Francis 156
George 68, 112
Harriet 34, 69
Hart E. 36
Henrietta 81
infant 229
Isaac 87, 88
Isaac John 90
Isaac, Mrs. 10
Issack 171
Jacob 112, 135, 187
James 121, 180
Jane 74
John 92, 121, 125, 144, 154, 160, 176, 180
John G. 30
Jno L. 180
John Peter 171
Leonard 12, 99, 101, 104, 134, 156, 166, 197
Leo(nard) Jr. 129
Leo(nard) Mrs. 12
Loretta Cath'n 132
Lydia Ann 47, 98
Margaret 56, 180
Margaret Ann 148
Maria 18
Maria, Mrs. 12
Mary 49, 87, 88, 90, 92, 115, 122, 143, 225
Mary Ann 32, 103, 149, 171
Mary Catherin 135
Mary Eliza V. 99
Mary G. 135
Mary Jane 55, 87, 136
Mary Martha 110
Mary Mrs. 108
Michael 59, 160, 193
Mr. 101
Mrs. 30, 176, 197
P. 25
Pat'k 25, 56, 120, 135, 143, 181, 197
Peter 103
Rachel 84
Robert 81, 84
S., Dr. 51, 222

Samuel 84
Sarah Jane 197
Susan 52, 103, 128, 166
Susan Catherin 187
Thomas 103, 148, 161, 226
William 90
SMITHIN
Francis 32
SMITHING
Mary 109
SMITTING
Anamelia 48
John Jr. 48
SMUCKS
Jacob 95
SNAIR
Ann 137
SNEIDER
Catharine 100
SNEIVE
Barbara 50
SNIBELY
Hen 182
SNIDER
Englelast 219
SNOFFNER
Clara Regina 213
Joshua 213
SNOUF(F)ER
Anne 213
Ann Elizabeth 211
Ann J. 211
child 233
Joshua 211
SNOW
Anna 220
SNOWEN
Anna 48
SNUEUN
Anna 102
Barbara 102
SNURE
Catharina 111, 176
Elizabeth 118
SNYDER
Betsy 101
Catherin 160
Charles Edward 101
Elizabeth 160
Jacob 160

288

SUMER
  Anna Maria 108
  Bernard Henry 108
SUMMA
  Anna Maria 111
SUMNER
  Francis 187
SUNTABEN
  Ann M. 188
  Cha's 188
SWALLENHAUS
  Ch 131
SWANIGAN
  Jas 64
SWANN
  Louisa 96
SWEENEY
  ___ 219, 233
  Catharine 101, 102,
    113
  Ed 101, 113, 208
  John Denis 113
  Mary Alice 101
  N. 25
SWEETMAN
  Bryan 231
SWELLING
  220
SWIFT
  Ant 174, 182
  Bridget 182
  Cath 174, 182
  Pat'k 133
TAFE
  Bridget 150
  Edward 150
  Peter 150
TAVELLESS
  Julia 52
TAYLOR
  Elizabeth 124
TECKEL
  Eliz 177
THAY
  Margareta 46
THAYER
  Abraham 148
  John Thomas 167
  Rebecca 148, 167
  Stephen 148, 167
THEIL
  child 226
  Jno 226

THIER
  Joseph 219
THILDE
  John 165
  Maria Eva 165
  Wilhelmina 165
THISTLE
  Margaret Ann 60
  Rebecca E. 60
THOMAS
  Henry 191
THOMPSON
  Betsy 134
  Charlotte 38, 39
  Francis 191
  James 61, 62, 116,
    142, 178, 180,
    191, 203, 215
  Jno Dunn 228
  John 37
  Mary 178, 191,
    211
  Mary Ann 203
  Patrick 178
THOMSON
  Catherine 125
  Eliza Jane 125
  Sarah 125
  William 125
THURMAN
  Peter 202
TIERN(E)Y
  Ann 134
  Bridget 213
  Catherin 196
  Daniel 46, 229
  Elisab'h 196
  Ellen 213
  infant 233
  Jas 196
  John 134
  Mich'l 71, 176,
    233
  Peter 74
  Winfred 74
TIERNRY
  Dan'l 229
TIGHE
  Mary 67
  Michael 67
TIMELY
  Mrs. 231
TIMMIS
  Jon, Mrs. 228
TIMMON(D)S
  Ann 17, 134

Anna 42
  James 45
  Jerome 17
  John 56, 146
  Julia 90
  Mary 146
  Nancy 5, 8
  Nancy, Mrs. 6, 8
  O. Filia 17
  T. 25
TIM(M)S
  Ann 205
  Catherin 129, 156,
    185, 199
  Ellen 72
  James 199
  John 64, 72, 209,
    211
  Mary 223
  Mary Ellen 185
  Michael 129
  Mrs. 226
  Rose 211
  Thomas 129, 135,
    156, 185, 199
TIPPET(T)
  George 36, 192
  Susan 36
  Susan C. 34, 69,
    197, 203, 207
  Susan E. 65
  Susan G. 71
TIPPETTS
  Geo 35
TIRNAN
  James 62
TITUS
  son 225
TOBE
  Elizabeth 63
TOBIN
  Christopher 223
  John 10
  Mr. 13
TOKENBACK
  Elizabeth 116
TOKENBERGER
  Elizabeth 51, 117
TOLBECK
  Barny 135
TOLIN
  Christopher 111
TOME
  Susan 59

TOMLINSON
  ___ 113
  Ann 97, 113
  Jesse 44, 97, 113
  Sebastian 97
TOOLE
  John 73
  Mary 73
TOPPER
  Julia Ann 152
  Mary Louisa 152
  Samuel L. 58, 152
TORMEY
  Mich'l 210
TOUGHEY
  Austin 151
  John 151
  Mary 151
TOULE
  John 113
  Mary 113
  Winefred 113
TOY
  Mary 159
TRAC(E)Y
  Ann 67
  Felix 65
  Hugh 208
  John 208
  Malachy 208
  Mary 208
  Pat'k 164
TRAINER
  John 124, 143
  Mary 143
  Roseanna 143
TRANER
  John 111
TRECHLER
  Jno 53
TRESTLER
  Mary 46
TRIMBLE
  Anna 86
  Elisa, Mrs. 12
  Elizabeth 86
  John 46, 79, 86
  Joseph 79
  Margaret 86
TRIMBLESON
  Ann 93
  Jesse 93
  W. John 93

290

WAGNER cont.
M. Magd 147
WAGONER
Catharine 102
Francis 102
John Henry 102
WALKER
Clara 76, 200
Rosilia 204
Sam'l A. 200
WALL
Martin 78
WALLACE
____ 47
Ann 208
Ann E. 74
Daniel 139
Elizabeth 139
Jane 32, 33, 59
John 139
WALSH
Jas 150
WAMPE
Mary 126
WANCILER
Marcus 47
WANDEL
Geo B. 152
Josephine 152
WANIDIASS
Cath 140
WANKEL
Josephine 97
WANKLE
Anna Josephine 101
Cath 101
Josephine 101
Peter 101
WARD
And 230
Ann 211
James 156
John 133, 156
Margaret 49, 72, 74
Mary 133, 156,
176, 183, 192
Mrs. 137
Patrick 105
Thos 138, 176
WARE
Cecilia 179
WARREN
Charles 151
Henry 100
James 151, 222

John Allegany 100
Margaret 151
Martin 76
Rebecca 100
son 222
WARTHON
Joseph 214
Mary 214
WASSEN
Maria 51
WATERS
Greenbury 48
WATKINS
Thos 226
WATMYER
Jno 175
Lewis Edward 175
Maryann 175
WATSON
Martha Ellen 141
WATTS
Joab 38
WAUGHHAN
Anthony 130
WAVER
Christian 101
WAYS
Cecilia 206, 207,
211
Charles Henry 206
Elisb'h 206
Frances 232
Geo Ed 77
Isabella 211
Jno 211
Jos H. 206
S. D. 207
Victoria 211
WEAVER
Christian 107
Mary 38
Mary A. 70
WEBER
Car M. 179
Eliza 139
Francis 139
Mary 139
WEGAMAN
Caroline Mary 179
WEGAS
Ann 145
Herman 145
Mary 145
WEGER
Mary 131

WEGES
Herman 195
John 195
Mary 195
WEGET
Mary 145
WEGMAN
Dominick 67
Dut 198
Frances 198
Jno 58, 64
Jno I. 161
Jon 63
Joseph 67, 161,
175, 190, 194, 198
Mary Ann Fr's 198
WEGNON
Jos 179
WEGUS
Harman 120
Henry William 120
Mary 120
WEIGER
Barney 137
Catherin 137
Hen 144
John Barney 137
WEIGERT
221
WEIGES
Ber'd 181
WEIMER
Cath 174
WEINER
Henry 174
Mary Elizabeth 174
WEINSTEN
Mary 172
WEISEL
Epha 54
Eva 172, 194
Eve 130, 137, 163
John 194
Joseph Peter 172
M. 172, 185
Margaret 194
Mary Eliza 130
Michael 54, 57,
130, 154, 163, 194
Mr. 60, 137
WEISLING
Cath 33
Gar 57
WEITSEL
Elias 143

Fanny 143
Sarah Ann 143
Susan 143
WELAN
Mary 146
WELCH
Capt 50
Mr. 51, 52
William 97
WELDS
Susan 195
WELMAN
Bernadine 74
WELSH
Ann 202
Bridget 76, 168,
203, 212
Cap W. 26
Catharin 66, 71,
128, 129, 178,
208, 212, 213
Edward 183
Ellen 132, 153, 168
James 120, 165,
212, 213
Jane 213
John 68, 70, 108,
115, 153, 165,
174, 179, 215
Julia 202
Margaret 72, 75,
209
Martin 195
Mary 106, 113,
120, 183, 195, 203
Michael 153, 168
Mrs. 125, 126
Patrick 120, 129
Richard 183
Robt 232
Sarah 73, 77, 201,
209, 215
Thomas 78, 129
Timothy 202
William 109, 121,
155
William Capt'n
100
WEMPE
Catherin Eliz'h 178
Francis 150, 178,
191
John Frederick 191
Maria 191
Mary 150, 178
WEMPI
Francis 121
Mary 121

The following given names appear in the text with illegible surnames.

293

This final page presents the given names for Negroes, both free and slaves, who had no surname. The text identifies servants and slaves by their employer or owner if this information was presented in the records. A number of others had surnames and are identified in the every name index. The microfilm text denotes these in many cases with various abbreviations such as "bl, c, col'd, etc." The authors have included these notations in the text.

www.ingramcontent.com/pod-product-compliance
Lightning Source LLC
Chambersburg PA
CBHW060150280326
41932CB00012B/1709